Michelin has been back in Formula One for just three years. Our tyres have improved, our victories have multiplied. The tenacity of our partner teams and our people challenged the balance of power this season. We race for tyre perfection. For the track or for you, every Michelin tyre shares this passion for performance. Now you know why Michelin races ahead.

Share the Spirit

MICHELIN

© November 2003, Chronosports S.A.

Lausanne: Jordils Park, Chemin des Jordils 40, CH-1025 St-Sulpice, Switzerland. Tel. : (+41 21) 694 24 44. Fax : (+41 21) 694 24 46.
Paris: Chronosports France, 9 rue de Normandie, F-75003 Paris, France. Tel. : (+33) (0)1 47 20 46 22. Fax : (+33) (0)1 48 04 06 80.
Milan: Chronsports Italia, Via Razori 4, I-20145 Milan, Italy. Tel. : (+39) 02 4810 2477. Fax : (+39) 02 4853 1805.

This is a Parragon book
Copyright © Parragon

This edition published in 2003

Parragon
Queen Street House
4 Queen Street
Bath BA1 1HE, UK

ISBN 1-40542-089-8

Printed and bound in France

FORMULA 1 YEARBOOK
2003-04

Pictures
LAT Photographic, Thierry Gromik, Steve Domenjoz, Mario Renzi

(LAT Photographic: Steven Tee, Lorenzo Bellanca, Charles Coates,Michael Cooper, Peter Spinney, Steve Etherington, Jack Atley, Glenn Dunbar, PICME, Chris Dixon)

Conception and Grands Prix reports
Luc Domenjoz

Page layout
Cyril Davillerd, Solange Amara, Sabrina Favre

Results and statistics
Tino Cortese, Cyril Davillerd, André Vinet

Drawings 2003
Pierre Ménard

Gaps charts
Michele Merlino

Technical summary
Giorgio Piola

Thierry Gromik uses Nikon material for all his pictures.

Contents

Foreword

"As you can well imagine, the 2003 season is one which I will never forget. In July 2002, when Flavio told me I would be racing for the team, I would never have dared hope for such an incredible year. Of course, I knew I would be trying my best. I knew I had the ability to succeed, but above all, I knew that in Formula 1, there is a huge gulf between hope and reality.

Before embarking on this season, it would have seemed too optimistic to think about winning a Grand Prix. However, come the end of the year, it seems that my craziest hopes have been more than met. It's incredible to think I took two pole positions and actually won a race. I finished sixth in the world championship and I became the youngest ever driver in history to take pole position and then to win a Grand Prix!

There were other great moments too, like demonstrating my Renault in the streets of Madrid in front of a passionate crowd and finishing second in "my" Grand Prix in Barcelona.

Of course, a season like that is down to the efforts of an entire team. It is the result of the work carried out by hundreds of men and women who have given their all throughout the year. It is this work, much of it out of the limelight back in the factory as well as at the race tracks, and the thousands of hours of dedication from our engineers, technicians and mechanics which have allowed us to finish fourth in the Constructors' Championship. I cannot find the words to describe such strong emotions. It all happened so quickly. And now, just eight months after competing in my first grand prix with Renault, I find myself writing this preface to The Formula One Yearbook.

We are not planning to stop there, now that we are going so well. For 2004, obviously, we will be aiming higher. We are working even harder to do better still and achieve our objectives which, one day, will lead us to the world title. And I think that once again, the reality will match our hopes."

Fernando Alonso,
November 2003

SEASON'S ANALYSIS

The 2002 season was one of the most boring years in the sport, but 2003 was closely contested, with both the Drivers' and Constructors' championships going down to the wire. Although the Michael Schumacher-Ferrari partnership won again, it was no longer crushingly dominant. This entertaining championship also featured maiden victories for two future "greats," Fernando Alonso and Kimi Raikkonen. Tyres played a key role, as did race strategy, now that the qualifying procedure rules have been changed completely. Formula 1 was reborn this year.

A tough fight

by Didier Braillon «L'Equipe»

Didier Braillon
49 years old, he first got involved in F1 working for French weekly, Autohebdo, before running Grand Prix International magazine. When the publication folded in 1984, he worked as press officer for the RAM team. In 1987, he worked for Le Sport newspaper before looking after media relations for the Larrousse team. In 1989, he joined France Soir, switching to the weekly Course Auto and joined the motoring pages of L'Equipe in 1992 where he works to this day.

By the time he crossed the line at the end of the final grand prix of the season on 12th October at Suzuka, Michael Schumacher was already world champion....by exactly 59.487 seconds! Having won the race with a handy lead, Rubens Barrichello had just deprived Kimi Räikkönen of the ten points he absolutely had to score if he hoped to be in with a shot at the title. However, even if some strange quirk of fate had seen the number one driver in the McLaren-Mercedes camp take the chequered flag in first place, Michael Schumacher, eighth after a rather scrappy race would have had the satisfaction of making his own way to the title as the single point for eighth place meant he did not have to rely on the bravura performance of his team-mate.

"I really cannot comment on this event," admitted the man who had just beaten the record of five titles, which he held jointly with the legendary Juan Manuel Fangio. *"I can't find the right emotions, but I can feel them for the team although not for me. I feel empty and exhausted and only proud of what we have achieved all of us together."* Usually, he finished his races as fresh as a daisy, often in stark contrast to the condition of his rivals – his hair dry and a fresh face – but this time, it seemed the athlete had been made to work. His eighty five minutes of racing were punctuated by a collision with Takuma Sato which forced him to make an unscheduled pit stop to change the nose on his F2003-GA, then he had a coming together with his brother's Williams-BMW during a late braking move which flat-spotted his tyres to such an extent that the vibrations seriously affected his vision going down the straight. Added to all this was seven months of tension which had in one instant finally slipped away. From the 9th March in Melbourne's Albert Park to this breathtaking final, the fight over sixteen rounds had been

tough and quite the opposite of the 2001 and 2002 seasons. He had an unusually erratic start to his campaign, breaking his barge boards running over the kerbs in Australia, then he collided with Jarno Trulli in Malaysia and crashed in the downpour in Brazil. Schumacher got back on course in Imola where he gave the Ferrari F2002 the final win of its glorious career, despite the agonising death of his mother only a few hours earlier. At the next grand prix in Spain, he switched to the new F2003-GA, taking its maiden win. However, it took until the Canadian Grand Prix on 15th June for him to finally move into the lead of the championship. But a long run of poor performances from Ferrari, combined with Bridgestone struggling to perform, saw his lead whittled away to virtually nothing. As the teams rumbled into the Monza paddock, Juan Pablo Montoya was just one point behind and Kimi Räikkönen two. Schumacher won at Monza, but the new points system introduced in 2003 meant that he only just extended his advantage. By winning the United States Grand Prix, he definitively shook off Montoya, who had a scrappy, ill-considered race, compounded by a penalty which was not really fair. That left Räikkönen and although the Ferrari team leader arrived in Japan with a nine point lead, he was still vulnerable to attack.

"The end of the season has been very hard and this race was particularly difficult, probably one of the most difficult I have ever faced," he admitted, finally free of his doubts and demons. *"At Hockenheim and Budapest, some people had written us off in the title fight, but now we have done it! That is our strength, the fact that we never give up the fight."* At the end of the Japanese GP, a race that got underway under the ever present threat of a few drops of rain, the statistics also rained down.

A fifth consecutive constructors' title since 1999 for Ferrari; fourth consecutive drivers' crown since 2000 for Michael Schumacher, 70 wins, including 51 for the Scuderia; 1038 points scored; 18,453 racing kilometres in the lead since the start of his career and the rest. Success was even sweeter this year, coming as it did at the last moment. The previous year, with seventeen races on the calendar, Ferrari had won fifteen of them – eleven for Michael and four for Rubens Barrichello – leaving Ralf Schumcher's Williams-BMW and David Coulthard's McLaren-Mercedes to take just one apiece.

This time with eight wins – six for Michael Schumacher and two for Rubens Barrichello-Ferrari won just half the races, but there were more winners on the score card this year. BMW-Williams won four; two for each of its drivers; two for McLaren, one for Coulthard, one for Räikkönen; one for Renault courtesy of Fernando Alonso and one for Jordan-Ford and Giancarlo Fisichella. Of the twenty drivers who took part in the series on a regular basis, no less than eight of them were winners and that must have something to do with the new rules pushed through by the FIA president Max Mosley, shortly before the start of the season.

Friday qualifying over a single lap was run in championship order, handicapping the early runners as the track provides less grip, and thus theoretically reducing the performance gap throughout the field. Saturday qualifying, again over a single lap, this time with the slowest car from the previous day going first could also be affected by unforeseen circumstances. The weather could play its part, as was clearly proved in Japan, where Michael Schumacher was only 14th on the grid after making his run on a damp track. With Kimi Räikkönen running when it was dryer, the session could have played a big role in the outcome of the championship. The format also meant that the slightest error at the wheel would see a driver relegated to the back of the grid, while Saturday saw strategy come into play, as cars had to run with a fuel load which would seem them through to their first fuel stop in Sunday's race.

Different strategies and jumbled up grids meant that races could suddenly throw up some interesting surprises. On top of that was the move aimed at reducing the value of a race win and spreading the points out a bit more. The points gap between first and second place now came down to just two points, 10 to 8, as opposed to the old 10 to 6. Before the season, many of these changes were regarded as being "anti-Schumacher" and "anti-Ferrari" rules. But the fact that the Scuderia had to wait until the final round in Suzuka to claim both championships cannot simply be put down to these new regulations. Tyres played a big part, with Michelin showing a definite performance advantage in its third year of competition. Up against the Japanese Bridgestone tyres, in the heatwave conditions which swept through Europe this summer, the French product was incontestably superior. The Williams-BMWs, McLaren-Mercedes and Renaults all showed an astounding turn of speed, while Ferrari suddenly paid the price for its very exclusive partnership with Bridgestone.

There were some low blows in the tyre war with the Scuderia and its supplier questioning the width of the Michelin contact patch when the tyre was worn, just prior to the Italian Grand Prix. The problem stemmed from the fact that these measurements were only taken when the tyres were new. The rule was hastily "clarified" and tyre width was measured after the race. The French company insisted it had not been deliberately cheating, but was forced to make some last minute changes to its manufacturing process. There was much grinding of teeth over this matter, but the bare facts reveal that after this incident, Ferrari and Bridgestone won the remaining three rounds of the championship.

The fight between the Scuderia and its rivals was not all down to tyres. The fifty day testing

ban from 14th July to 2nd September slowed the development of the cars at the precise moment when Ferrari really needed to take a step forward. On top of that, the F2003-GA, evolved from the dominant F2002, did not adapt well to the new race weekend format.

It was exceptionally efficient in quick corners, where it could make the difference up against its rivals, but it was less convincing on more sinuous tracks and it appeared to have a very narrow operational range, requiring fine tuning of its mechanical and aerodynamic set-up to work well.

The restrictions in running time, with only one lap on Friday and Saturday afternoons and the restrictions of parc ferme preventing further fine tuning between the end of qualifying and the start of the race were all

factors which meant that Michael Schumacher and Rubens Barichello had to fight with a less than perfect armoury. At the end of the day, the best car – in theory- won the day, fitted with tyres which were often less than the best, but with the advantage of having an exceptional champion behind the wheel. Schumacher is the best driver of his era and why not maybe of all the fifty four years of the Formula 1 World Championship.

In taking his sixth title, Schumacher is now out on his own in the pantheon of champions and can take his place alongside the greatest in the history of the sport. It remains to be seen in 2004 if this admirable result was just another step on the road or whether, despite being contracted to Ferrari until the end of 2006, there will never be more than six stripes on his cap.

∧
A man in love with his car. It was a case of man and machine in perfect harmony and once again it was hard to beat.

<
Out on his own. Michael Schumacher can be proud of his sixth title, as it took some winning.

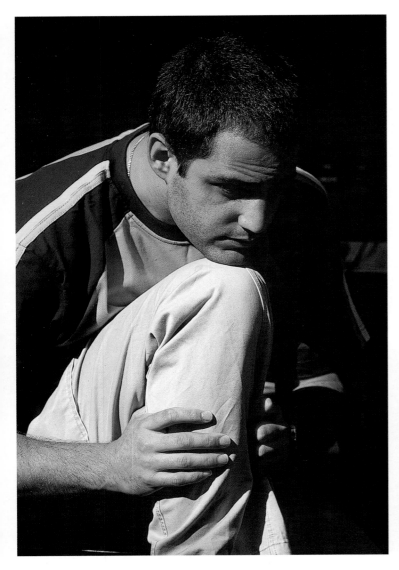

The two faces of Juan Pablo Montoya

Behind the wheel, he is a flamboyant hero. As Frank Williams says with admiration which one senses is occasionally tinged with disappointment: *"when he drives, it's nuclear war in the cockpit."* The car was not always perfectly set-up, sometimes he would go over the edge, with spins in Melbourne, Montreal and Budapest which BMW-Williams technical director, Patrick Head, admitted was *"not really necessary."* But he also knew how to rein himself in to finish on the podium eight times in a row from Monaco to Monza. It was thus thanks to this hitherto unknown steadiness that he managed to challenge Michael Schumacher for the title towards the end of the season. He was one point down after Hungary, three

after Italy, so that he had reason to be hopeful as the series headed for the United States. It was there, in front of thousands of Colombians chanting his name, that he drove his messiest race. He stupidly tried to win it on lap 3 in an ill considered move on Rubens Barrichello. *"Depending who I am up against, I might not try a move,"* he affirmed on arriving in Indy. *"If I have to tackle one or other of the two championship contenders, I won't do so in the same way. One will have everything to lose and the other has all to gain."* Barrichello was therefore one of those who had to be passed with care, but in pushing him off the track, Montoya was given a drive-through penalty, which ruined his chances. Hasta luego, muchacho...

^
After a rewarding summer, Juan Pablo Montoya and the Williams team were unable to turn their hopes into reality over the last two rounds.

Williams, short but sweet!

What's its wheelbase? BMW-Williams refused to divulge the wheelbase, the distance between the front and rear axles, on its FW25. Was it more or less than three metres? Sam Michael, in charge of engineering development admitted that *"this is the shortest Williams ever."* When it first ran in the winter, it had not been very convincing, to the extent that, briefly, the team considered starting the championship with the previous year's FW24. In the end, the new cars headed off for the Australian Grand Prix, but it was not until the San Marino race that, according to Patrick Head, the transformation was made. *"We came from a long way back,"* he admitted in July. *"This car is very different to its three predecessors since we joined forces with BMW in 2000 and we had a lot of trouble with it. We had to learn quite a bit about it before we could begin to exploit it properly."* Getting near the front of the grid and, starting in Monaco, winning races, required a further step forward. *"We had to keep improving the aerodynamic efficiency and make a few mechanical changes."* The team was waiting for a new wind tunnel to be brought into service to replace the rather old fashioned unit, which handicapped its performance when compared to Ferrari. The aerodynamic programme was led by a quartet made up of Antonio Terzi, Jason Somerville, Nick Alcock and John Davies, who worked very hard. Combined with Michelin's supremacy in the summer, the FW25 was turned into a high flying F1 car, capable of fighting for the title. The extension and strengthening of the partnership with BMW, extended to at least 2008, can only accelerate the momentum.

Jenson Button had a worthy first season despite the tense atmosphere which reigned in the BAR camp.
>

< Kimi Raikkonen, his brakes blazing, was the most tenacious pretender to the crown.

The rule changes saw Minardi make the most of what it had, even though it failed to trouble the scorer.
∨

Good points and bad points

Coming to Suzuka, Kimi Räikkönen trailed Michael Schumacher by nine points and thus had a mathematical chance of becoming world champion. He only had one win to his name, dating back to Sepang in March, but the top man at McLaren was still up against his opposite number at Ferrari, who had six victories on his score card! One could blame this strange state of affairs on the new points system in force in 2003, the same as used in the World Rally Championship by the FIA, as well as all major series. Points were now allocated to the top eight as follows: 10, 8, 6, 5, 4, 3, 2 and 1. It reduced the gap between first and second from four to just two points. From the start of the 1991 season to the end of 2002, points were allocated 10, 6, 4, 3, 2 and

1. Giving ten to the winner was supposed to give an extra reward for winning the race, compared with the scoring system used since 1961, which went as follows: 9, 6, 4, 3, 2, 1. There was also a rule which meant drivers could only retain a certain number of scores, which messed up the championship on two occasions. In 1964, Graham Hill would have won the title, beating John Surtees and in 1988, Alain Prost would have beaten his team-mate Ayrton Senna. Back to the 2003 season, with the old points system, Michael Schumacher would have been crowned champion one race earlier, in Indianapolis, to take a relatively straightforward sixth title. He would have had 77 points, against 62 for Juan Pablo Montoya and 61 for Kimi Räikkönen.

Drivers

1.	**M. Schumacher**	**93**
2.	K. Räikkönen	91
3.	J.P. Montoya	82
4.	R. Barrichello	65
5.	R. Schumacher	58
6.	F. Alonso	55
7.	D. Coulthard	51
8.	J. Trulli	33
9.	J. Button	17
10.	M. Webber	17
11.	H-H. Frentzen	13
12.	G. Fisichella	12
13.	C. Da Matta	10
14.	N. Heidfeld	6
15.	O. Panis	6
16.	J. Villeneuve	6
17.	M. Gene	4
18.	T. Sato	3
19.	R. Firman	1
20.	J. Wilson	1
21.	A. Pizzionia	0
22.	J. Verstappen	0
23.	N. Kiesa	0
23.	Z. Baumgartner	0

Constructors

1.	**Scuderia Ferrari Marlboro**	**158**
2.	BMW WilliamsF1 Team	144
3.	West McLaren Mercedes	142
4.	Mild Seven Renault F1 Team	88
5.	Lucky Strike BAR Honda	26
6.	Sauber Petronas	19
7.	Jaguar Racing	18
8.	Panasonic Toyota Racing	16
9.	Jordan Ford	13
10.	European Minardi Asiatech	0

Bridgestone plays solitaire

Bridgestone was accused of having been responsible for Ferrari's serious lack of form in the summer, from the European to the Hungarian grands prix, when Michael Schumacher only picked up eight points from five races. But they fought back starting with the Italian Grand Prix. At the end of the fifty day long testing ban, Ferrari arrived in force for the session at Monza, starting on 2nd September, testing no less than twenty five combinations of construction and tyre compound, using eight hundred tyres. The Japanese manufacturer opted to centre most of its test programme on its top team, to the detriment of its other partners – BAR, Jordan, Sauber and Minardi. French rival Michelin adopted the opposite policy. In order to develop its product as quickly as possible, it relied equally on Williams, McLaren, Renault, Toyota and Jaguar. *"We draw our strength from working in private testing with a maximum number of cars, working on the same programme,"* explained Pascal Vasselon, the man in charge of Michelin's F1 programme. *"Then, with each team, we look at the data but also that acquired by the others, which helps everyone make what tends to be the best choice."* Kees van de Grint, the Bridgestone engineer allocated to Ferrari, defended the option to go it alone. *"There are pluses and minuses,"* he maintained. *"Naturally, the more one tests with different top teams, the more one*

learns, but reaction time and the speed of producing the tyres is slowed as the time needed to analyse data is increased. It was our decision to work with just one top team, even if that deprived us of comparative data. With Ferrari, we win and lose together."

A big disappointment this season, despite a lucky win in Brazil, the Jordans really lacked reliability.
∨

Ferrari still on top

The 2003 opened with a radical overhaul of the Formula 1 sporting regulations that affected both qualifying and the races and had significant technical repercussions. The modifications were actually finalised on the eve of the World Championship, when to all intents and purposes, the teams (with the exception of McLaren) had already completed work on the designs of their new cars.

Draws: Giorgio Piola

Going into the 2003 season, the teams were all trying to bridge the yawing gap that divided them from the Ferrari F2002, the yardstick against which the entire field inevitably had to be measured. The Maranello-based team's principal rival, Williams BMW, presented its new FW25 ahead of the F2003-GA and it was immediately apparent that it was more of a development of the previous year's Ferrari rather than a logical progression from the FW24. For its part, the new Ferrari introduced more accentuated Williams-style fins, thanks to a masterpiece of miniaturisation of the entire mechanical and rear-end packages. The tapering of the body work in this area was stunning to say the least, deriving from another feature already seen on the Jordan at the 2000 edition of the German GP; that is to say, a drastic reduction of the section of the front part of the side-pods so as to better channel the flow of air around the rear of the car. The cast-titanium gearbox was lighter than ever and also particularly compact thanks to a design derived from a project that was actually aborted two years ago. This had featured a single cylinder block and gearbox casting and while the concept proved to be impractical, it did respond to the need to reduce the stress on the gearbox imposed by the suspension mounts. This idea had a deter minant influence on one of the F2003-GA's brand-new features: the front arm of the lower suspension wishbone is located directly on the engine, directing forces longitudinally through to the chassis, which also permits a further reduction in the dimensions of the gearbox. A further curious coincidence is also worth mentioning: Williams and Ferrari both modified the wheelbase of their cars, but while the FW25 is shorter than the FW24 by 5 cm, the F2003-GA took the opposite route, with the wheelbase being stretched by 5cm with respects to the F2002. Ferrari achieved this altering the distance between the driver and the front axle, with a significant benefit in terms of aerodynamics. McLaren chose to follow the successful strategy adopted by Ferrari in 2002 and start the season with a revised and improved 2002 car and prepare a revolutionary replacement for introduction at a later date.

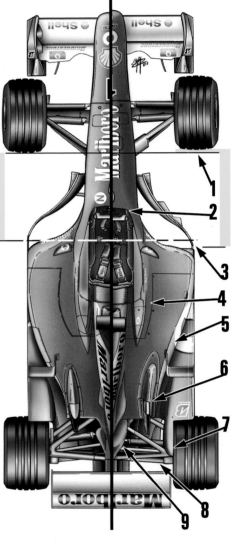

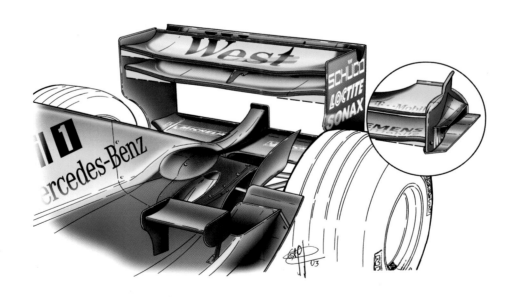

REAR WING

McLaren has introduced a new rear wing that recalls the front wing used last year at Monza. It has two principal planes that rise notably either side in proximity to the end-plates. This feature is intended to reduce the creation of vortices in this delicate area and thus improve the efficiency of the wing itself. A similar feature was introduced last season with the lower place attached to the deformable structure behind the gearbox.

TOP VIEW F2002 AND F2003-GA

In the comparison between the old F2002 on the left and the new F2003-GA one can seen how the front axle has been distanced from the sidepods (highlighted in yellow) that have in turn been set back (3) along with the cockpit. The coke-bottle shape of the rear section (5) is extremely accentuated and begins in an advanced position with a kind of horizontal lower lip. The position of the exhausts within the chimneys is also different. The chimneys themselves are larger (6) and asymmetric in shape so as to better channel the air in the central section of the car. (7). The fins in front of the rear wheels wrap around the tyre and extend as far as the rear axle line. (8) During the season the rear suspension is due to be fitted with aerodynamic suspension arm fairings. (9) The new gearbox and, above all, the new rear suspension has permitted improved extraction of the air from the lateral channels.

GUIDE VANES

The dual guide vanes within the front wheels are also from the Williams school, building on what Willis had already introduced from the 2002 Canadian GP. The most significant novelty is the aerodynamic profile linking the vanes to the chassis. Note the small knife-edge section in the upper part and the U-shaped link with the bulb acting as the central mount of the lower wishbone. The steering arm is incorporated within the upper wishbone rather than being mounted in the middle of the upright.

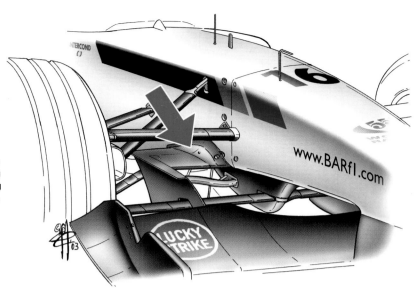

MCLAREN MP4-18

The moderately tapered nose develops from a high chassis that dips sharply (in a manner very similar to that of the March from 1988) and forms almost a single unit with the front wing to which it is anchored via two small, short support pylons. The nose is very slim and has a shorter overhang with respects to the front axle.

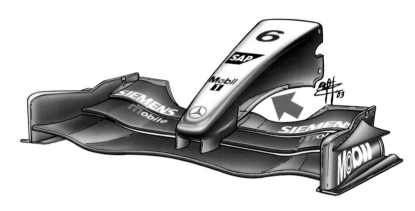

NOSE

The brand-new front wing reiterates the concept already seen on the McLaren and Renault at the rear. The main plane is strongly warped and rises sharply in the area adjacent to the end-plates. In the lower part there are two vertical intermediate vanes with the central part of the plane rising sligthly as highlighted in yellow.

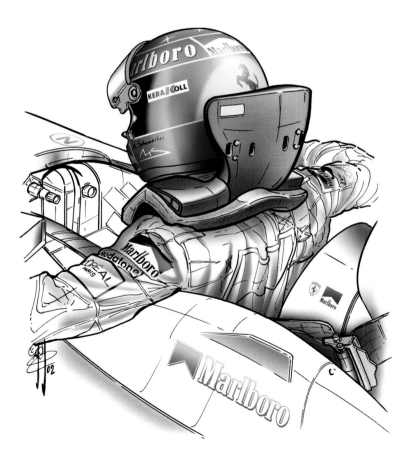

HANS COLLAR

During the 2002 season, the Federation gave the teams the job of testing a system for the protection of the driver's neck called the "Hans", ready for obligatory use in 2003. This "head and neck support" device, used with success in American racing, created a great deal of doubt and perplexity among the Formula One drivers who tested it last season - in particular the Sauber and Renault pilots. The harshest critics were Jacques Villeneuve and David Coulthard, who complained of a notable reduction in freedom of movement, difficulty in buckling on their helmets, which incorporate an antiblocking system actioned by pressure on the safety belts. Drivers also criticised Hans for diminished lateral visibility in the case of an accident.

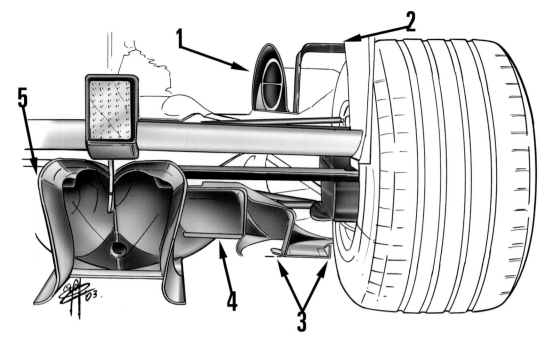

DIFFUSER

Great attention has been paid to the aerodynamics of the new Toyota with the large chimneys **(1)** for the oval-section exhausts. The small winglets **(2)** placed in front of the rear wheels are also from the Ferrari school, as is the step **(4)** in the lateral diffuser channels. The diffuser also features sophisticated details such as the vertical fins **(3)** inside the wheels and those slight inclined (highlighted in yellow) on the inboard section. The central channel with its omega shape **(5)** recalls that of the Jordan.

CHIMNEYS

During the 2003 season Renault has introduced these chimneys **(1)** sharply inclined outwards and placed almost alongside the small winglets over the sidepods. **(2)** The exhausts blow in the upper part. **(3)** On the launch of the car hot air was exhausted via these vents **(3)** (as highlighted in the drawing) that were eliminated from the definitive coachwork (left). The large Williams-style fin **(4)** instead remained while the exhaust terminals were faired with a small chimney (left).

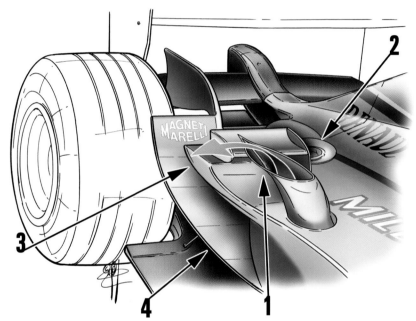

SIDEPODS

The front of the sidepods has been radically redesigned with the leading edge sharply cut away to create a kind of divergent knife-edge area with the stepped bottom. This feature was seen for a few races in embryonic form on the Jordan modified for the German GP 2000. In this case the divergence is much more pronounced. In practice, the sidepods skin the mechanical components to the millimetre given that the two small swellings reveal the layout and dimensions of the radiators. In the case of hot temperatures, two lateral vents can be opened much further forwards than those used on the F2002, in front of the fins.

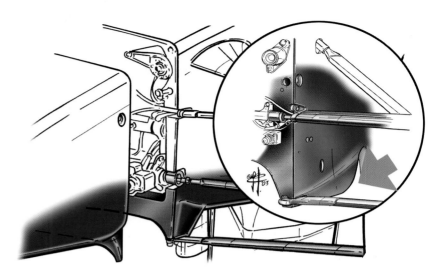

REAR SUSPENSION

Williams was the last of the top teams to abandon coil-over dampers in favour of torsion bars. The layout of the suspension is very compact with the torsion bars **(3)** inclined in place of the coaxial springs. The layout features two dampers **(1)** placed transversally, located above the gearbox like the third damper **(2)** The torsion bars **(4)** are inclined and are partially enclosed with the gearbox casting.

TWIN KEEL

The new C22 represents the logical evolution of the 2002 car that in turn developed the concepts expressed with the 2001 model. Obviously, the twin keel lower front wishbone mounts introduced by Sauber itself on the C19 in 2000 have been retained. The feature attracted a number of followers in the 2002 season as it allows the advantages offered by the dished-type front wing to be exploited fully. This year, only Jordan has followed Sauber's lead in this respect, albeit with a less extreme version.

JORDAN

Painstaking attention has been paid to the aerodynamics of the Jordan which has retained the sophisticated warped lower plane of the rear wing (highlighted in yellow in the drawing). This feature had already been seen in 2002 The upper wishbone has an aerodynamic fairing **(3)** together with the track rod.

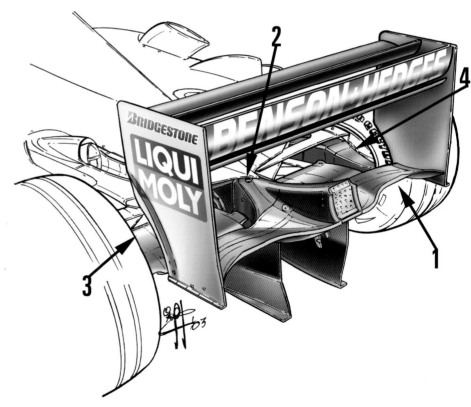

BARGE BOARD

The MP4/17D introduced at the start of the season is a car very different to the one that disputed the 2002 championship with new aerodynamics, engine, gearbox and rear suspension. The new barge boards behind the front wheels attracted a great deal of attention being lower than those used on last year's MP4/17 (circled) and integrated with new elements attached to the dual lower wishbone mounts. The sophisticated assembly features a horizontal section with a sinuous link to the lower part of the barge board. This last is cut away, as on the Ferrari and presents the horizontal section required by the regulations.

THE PLAYERS

Ten team bosses, twenty drivers, dozens of engineers and PR staff, hundreds of mechanics, marshals, journalists and photographers and thousands of spectators: they are all players in this 2003 world championship. In this book, we will settle for looking at the twenty drivers.

Ferrari

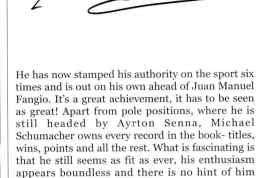

1. Michael SCHUMACHER

DRIVER PROFILE

- Name — SCHUMACHER
- First name — Michael
- Nationality — German
- Date of birth — January 3rd 1969
- Place of birth — Hürth-Hermühlheim (D)
- Lives in — Vufflens-le-Château (CH)
- Marital status — married to Corinna
- Kids — daugther (Gina-Maria) and son (Mick)
- Hobbies — karting, watches, movies, karaoke
- Favorite music — Anastasia, rock
- Favorite meal — italian food
- Favorite drinks — apple juice with mineral water
- Height — 174 cm
- Weight — 75 kg

- Web — www.michael-schumacher.de

STATISTICS

		PRIOR TO F1
• Nber of Grand Prix	195	1984-85 Karting
• Victories	70	Junior Champion (D)
• Pole positions	55	1986 Karting 3rd (D & EUR)
• Fastest lap	56	1987 Karting
• Podiums	121	Champion (D & EUR)
• Accidents/offs	23	1988 F. Koenig Champion,
• Not qualified	0	F. Ford 1600 (EUR) (2nd)/
• Laps in the lead	3959	F. Ford 1600 (D) (6th)
• Kms in the lead	18515	1989 F3 (D) (3rd)
• Points scored	1038	1990 F3 Champion (D)
		1990-91 Sport-prototypes
		Mercedes (5th & 9th)

F1 CAREER

1991	Jordan-Ford, Benetton-Ford. 4 pts. 12th of Championship.
1992	Benetton-Ford. 53 pts. 3rd of Championship.
1993	Benetton-Ford. 52 pts. 4th of Championship.
1994	Benetton-Ford. 92 pts. **World Champion.**
1995	Benetton-Renault. 102 pts. **World Champion.**
1996	Ferrari. 49 pts. 3rd of Championship.
1997	Ferrari. 78 pts. Exclude of Championship (2nd).
1998	Ferrari. 86 pts. 2nd of Championship.
1999	Ferrari. 44 pts. 5th of Championship.
2000	Ferrari. 108 pts. **World Champion.**
2001	Ferrari. 123 pts. **World Champion.**
2002	Ferrari. 144 pts. **World Champion.**
2003	Ferrari. 93 pts. **World Champion.**

2. Rubens BARRICHELLO

DRIVER PROFILE

- Name — BARRICHELLO
- First name — Rubens Gonçalves
- Nationality — Brazilian
- Date of birth — May 23rd 1972
- Place of birth — São Paulo (BR)
- Lives in — Monaco (MC)
- Marital status — married to Silvana
- Kids — one boy (Eduardo)
- Hobbies — jet-ski, golf
- Favorite music — Biaggo Antonacci, pop, rock
- Favorite meal — pasta
- Favorite drinks — Pepsi light
- Height — 172 cm
- Weight — 78 kg

- Web — www.barrichello.com.br

STATISTICS

		PRIOR TO F1
• Nber of Grand Prix	180	1981-88 Karting (5 times
• Victories	7	Brazilian Champion)
• Pole positions	9	1989 F. Ford 1600 (3rd)
• Fastest lap	11	1990 Opel Champion
• Podiums	43	Lotus Euroseries,
• Accidents/offs	27	F. Vauxhall (11th)
• Not qualified	0	1991 F3 Champion (GB)
• Laps in the lead	597	1992 F3000 (3rd)
• Kms in the lead	2853	
• Points scored	337	

F1 CAREER

1993	Jordan-Hart. 2 pts. 17th of Championship.
1994	Jordan-Hart. 19 pts. 6th of Championship.
1995	Jordan-Peugeot. 11 pts. 11th of Championship.
1996	Jordan-Peugeot. 14 pts. 8th of Championship.
1997	Stewart-Ford. 6 pts. 13th of Championship.
1998	Stewart-Ford. 4 pts. 12th of Championship.
1999	Stewart-Ford. 21 pts. 7th of Championship.
2000	Ferrari. 62 pts. 4th of Championship.
2001	Ferrari. 56 pts. 3rd of Championship.
2002	Ferrari. 77 pts. 2nd of Championship.
2003	Ferrari. 65 pts. 4th of Championship.

He has now stamped his authority on the sport six times and is out on his own ahead of Juan Manuel Fangio. It's a great achievement, it has to be seen as great! Apart from pole positions, where he is still headed by Ayrton Senna, Michael Schumacher owns every record in the book- titles, wins, points and all the rest. What is fascinating is that he still seems as fit as ever, his enthusiasm appears boundless and there is no hint of him getting jaded by it all; something which his less successful rivals would do well to try and emulate. As he gave his famous victory leap on the podiums at Monza and Indianapolis, where he could finally celebrate after a rotten summer, he was as excited as he had been when he did it for the first time at Spa, in 1992. Demonstrative, positive, full of boundless energy, the maestro was without equal yet again.

His credo consists of two words: "winning day." Every morning, God willing, he smiles his big smile and declares that this is definitely a winning day. We don't know whether in his daily life, Rubens is quickest at pushing his trolley down the supermarket aisles, but during a grand prix weekend, we do know what he can do. He was often quicker than his team-mate this season, especially in qualifying in the second half of the year and he pulled off two convincing and stylish wins at Silverstone and Suzuka. However, he rarely matched Schumacher in the races, especially this year when his car did not have a major advantage over his rivals. But every time it went wrong and for whatever reason, he always said it was a shame, because today he definitely had victory in his sights!

Jean Todt

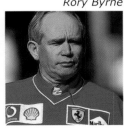

Nigel Stepney,
Ross Brawn

Rory Byrne

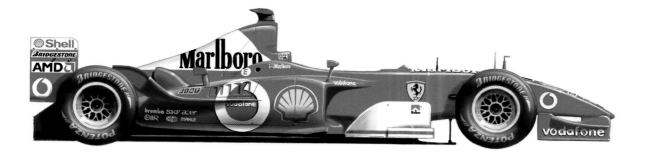

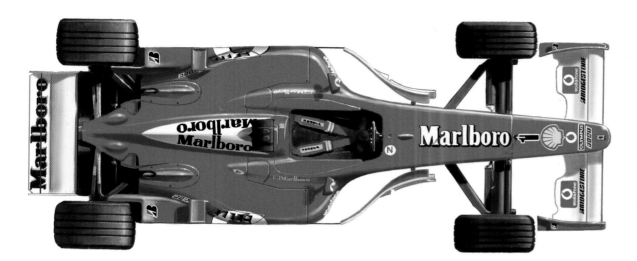

**FERRARI F2003-GA
MICHAEL SCHUMACHER
CANADIAN GRAND PRIX**

P. MÉNARD

Ferrari F2003-GA

SPECIFICATIONS

- Chassis — Ferrari F2003-GA (Spanish GP to Japanese GP)
- Type — Carbon fibre and honeycomb, composite structure
- Engine — 3000 Ferrari Type 052- V10 (92°)
- Displacement — 2997 cm³
- Valves — 40, pneumatic distribution
- Electronic ignition — Magneti Marelli
- Transmission — Ferrari 7 speed longitudinal gearbox, operated by semi-automatic sequential electronically controlled gearchange
- Clutch — Sachs - AP
- Radiators — Secan
- Fuel / oil — Shell
- Brakes (discs) — Brembo (ventilated carbon)
- Brakes (calipers) — Brembo
- Spark plugs — NGK
- Shock absorbers — not revealed
- Tyres — Bridgestone Potenza
- Wheels dimension — 13"
- Wheels — BBS
- Suspensions — independant roll bar / push rods (FR/RE)
- Weight — 600 kg, driver , on board camera , ballast
- Wheel base — 3050 mm
- Total length — 4545 mm
- Total width — 1796 mm
- Total height — 959 mm
- Front track — 1470 mm
- Rear track — 1405 mm

TEAM PROFILE

- Address — Ferrari SpA
  Via A. Ascari 55-57
  41053 Maranello (MO)
  Italy
- Phone number — + 39.536.949111
- Fax number — + 39.536.946488
- Web — www.ferrari.it
- Founded in — 1929
- First Grand Prix — Monaco 1950
- Official name — Scuderia Ferrari Marlboro
- General manager — Jean Todt
- Technical manager — Ross Brawn, Paolo Martinelli (engine)
- Racing activities manager — Stefano Domenicali
- Chief designer — Rory Byrne
- Chief engineer (race) — Ignazio Lunetta
- Technical manager (race) — Nigel Stepney
- Racing engineer (M.S.) — Chris Dyer
- Rcing engineer (R.B.) — Gabrielle Delli Colli
- Number of employees — 700
- Sponsors — Philip Morris (Marlboro), Shell, Vodafone, Fiat, Bridgestone, AMD, Olympus • Acer, Brembo, Magneti Marelli, Mahle, OIIR, SKF • Europcar, Facom, Finmeccanica, Fila, Infineon, Iveco, Momo, NGK, Sachs, Technogym • BBS, Cima, Mecanica, Mecel, Poggipolini, PTC, Sabelt, VeCa, TRW

TEST DRIVERS 2003

- Luca BADOER (I)
- Felipe MASSA (BR)

STATISTICS

- Number of Grand Prix — 686
- Number of victories — 167
- Number of pole positions — 166
- Number of fastest lap — 167
- Number of podiums — 525
- Number of drivers Championship — 13
- Number of constructors Championship — 13
- Total number of points scored — 3038,5 (3082,5)

POSITION IN WORLD CHAMPIONSHIP

1958	2ⁿᵈ – 40 ⁽⁵⁷⁾ pts	1970	2ⁿᵈ – 55 pts	1982	1ˢᵗ – 74 pts	1994	3ʳᵈ – 71 pts
1959	2ⁿᵈ – 32 ⁽³⁸⁾ pts	1971	4ᵗʰ – 33 pts	1983	1ˢᵗ – 89 pts	1995	3ʳᵈ – 73 pts
1960	3ʳᵈ – 24 ⁽²⁷⁾ pts	1972	4ᵗʰ – 33 pts	1984	2ⁿᵈ – 57,5 pts	1996	2ⁿᵈ – 70 pts
1961	1ˢᵗ – 40 ⁽⁵²⁾ pts	1973	6ᵗʰ – 12 pts	1985	2ⁿᵈ – 82 pts	1997	2ⁿᵈ – 102 pts
1962	5ᵗʰ – 18 pts	1974	2ⁿᵈ – 65 pts	1986	4ᵗʰ – 37 pts	1998	2ⁿᵈ – 133 pts
1963	4ᵗʰ – 26 pts	1975	1ˢᵗ – 72,5 pts	1987	4ᵗʰ – 53 pts	1999	1ˢᵗ – 128 pts
1964	1ˢᵗ – 45 ⁽⁴⁹⁾ pts	1976	1ˢᵗ – 83 pts	1988	2ⁿᵈ – 65 pts	2000	1ˢᵗ – 170 pts
1965	4ᵗʰ – 26 ⁽²⁷⁾ pts	1977	1ˢᵗ – 95 pts	1989	3ʳᵈ – 59 pts	2001	1ˢᵗ – 179 pts
1966	2ⁿᵈ – 31 ⁽³⁹⁾ pts	1978	2ⁿᵈ – 58 pts	1990	2ⁿᵈ – 110 pts	2002	1ˢᵗ - 221 pts
1967	4ᵗʰ – 20 pts	1979	1ˢᵗ – 113 pts	1991	3ʳᵈ – 55.5 pts	2003	1ˢᵗ – 158 pts
1968	4ᵗʰ – 32 pts	1980	10ᵗʰ – 8 pts	1992	4ᵗʰ – 21 pts		
1969	5ᵗʰ – 7 pts	1981	5ᵗʰ – 34 pts	1993	4ᵗʰ – 28 pts		

SUCCESSION OF DRIVERS 2003

- Michael SCHUMACHER — all 16 Grand Prix
- Rubens BARRICHELLO — all 16 Grand Prix

End of the line?

Last year, the F2002 car had crushed the opposition. Michael Schumacher took the title after just eleven of the seventeen races, with the constructors' crown coming home after race thirteen. This time, the Scuderia and its driver had to wait until the final round to take both titles. Eleven wins for Michael Schumacher, four for Rubens Barrichello in 2002, left the opposition with just a few crumbs from the table. This time, despite winning eight races, six with Schumacher and two with Barrichello, the job was much tougher. Descended from the almost perfect F2002, the F2003-GA did not produce a big step forward, while Bridgestone was in the doldrums for a long time. The new timetable for the weekend, with cars staying in parc ferme between qualifying and the race also prevented the team from perfecting the car's set-up, so that it could only show off its potential in a narrow area of operation. Jean Todt and his men now face the frightening question as to whether the 2004 car will follow this pattern.

Williams BMW

3. Juan Pablo MONTOYA

DRIVER PROFILE

- Name — MONTOYA ROLDAN
- First name — Juan Pablo
- Nationality — Colombian
- Date of birth — September 20th 1975
- Place of birth — Bogota (COL)
- Lives in — Monaco (MC), Oxford (GB), Miami (USA) and Madrid (E)
- Marital status — married to Connie
- Kids — -
- Hobbies — water ski, computers and video games
- Favorite music — rock
- Favorite meal — pasta
- Favorite drinks — orange juice
- Height — 168 cm
- Weight — 72 kg
- Web — www.jpmontoya.com

STATISTICS

- Nber of Grand Prix — 50
- Victories — 3
- Pole positions — 11
- Fastest lap — 9
- Podiums — 20
- Accidents/offs — 6
- Not qualified — 0
- Laps in the lead — 331
- Kms in the lead — 1565
- Points scored — 163

PRIOR TO F1

- 1981-91 Karting (2 times Jr World Champion)
- 1992 F. Renault (COL)
- 1993 Swift GTI (COL)
- 1994 Karting-Sudam 125 Champ. Barber Saab (3rd)
- 1995 F. Vauxhall (GB)
- 1996 F3 (GB)
- 1997 F3000 (2nd)
- 1998 F3000 Champion
- 1999 CART Champion
- 2000 CART (9th)

F1 CAREER

- 1997 Williams- Renault. Test driver
- 2001 Williams- BMW. 31 pts. 6th of Championship.
- 2002 Williams- BMW. 50 pts. 3rd of Championship.
- 2003 Williams- BMW. 82 pts. 3rd of Championship.

4. Ralf SCHUMACHER

DRIVER PROFILE

- Name — SCHUMACHER
- First name — Ralf
- Nationality — German
- Date of birth — June 30th 1975
- Place of birth — Hürth-Hermühlheim (D)
- Lives in — Hallwang (Salzburg) (A)
- Marital status — married to Cora
- Kids — one boy (David)
- Hobbies — karting, tennis, cycling, backgammon
- Favorite music — soft rock
- Favorite meal — pasta
- Favorite drinks — apple juice with mineral water
- Height — 178 cm
- Weight — 73 kg

- Web — www.ralf-schumacher.net

STATISTICS

- Nber of Grand Prix — 115
- Victories — 6
- Pole positions — 4
- Fastest lap — 7
- Podiums — 23
- Accidents/offs — 24
- Not qualified — 0
- Laps in the lead — 357
- Kms in the lead — 1725
- Points scored — 235

PRIOR TO F1

- 1978-92 Karting
- 1993 F3 ADAC Jr. (2nd)
- 1994 F3 (D) (3rd)
- 1995 F3 (D) (2nd), Winner F3 Macau
- 1996 F3000 Champion (J)

F1 CAREER

- 1997 Jordan-Peugeot. 13 pts. 11th of Championship.
- 1998 Jordan-Mugen-Honda. 14 pts. 10th of Championship.
- 1999 Williams-Supertec. 35 pts. 6th of Championship.
- 2000 Williams-BMW. 24 pts. 5th of Championship.
- 2001 Williams-BMW. 49 pts. 4th of Championship.
- 2002 Williams-BMW. 42 pts. 4th of Championship.
- 2003 Williams-BMW. 58 pts. 5th of Championship.

He could have had it all, but instead he lost it all at Indianapolis in a messy race which proved he still has a lot to learn in terms of keeping a cool head and not playing to the gallery. After his win in Monaco, it seemed that Montoya had changed, combining an ability to get the car home in a podium position with a more measured approach. His speed and aggression cannot be questioned, but his lack of professionalism and couldn't-care-less attitude even upsets the press who admire his talent behind the wheel. Apart from a few grunts and some shoulder shrugging, he has a limited vocabulary. His famous, "if you can't win, then at least try and finish second," seems to be the sum total of his analytical ability.

A hero at the start of the summer, he dropped to near enough zero by the end of the year. Back to back wins at the Nurburgring and Magny-Cours put him in the hunt for the title. Unfortunately, what followed did not match up to expectations. Then he sat out the Italian Grand Prix, still suffering the effects of a terrible testing accident at Monza ten days earlier, when his car suffered a mechanical failure and that definitively put him out of the running. He was guilty of several unforced errors which saw him end up in the gravel, but then in Budapest he proved capable of pulling off overtaking moves which no one had thought he had in him. He even disposed of his brother, whom it was thought he held in awe. Furthermore, on the human side, he has evolved into a nice guy with a canny ability for dealing with the media.

4. Marc GENÉ

DRIVER PROFILE

- Name — GENÉ
- First name — Marc
- Nationality — Spanish
- Date of birth — March 29th 1974
- Place of birth — Sabadell (E)
- Lives in — St Quirze del Valles (E)
- Lives in — single
- Kids — -
- Hobbies — books, movies and sports
- Favorite music — Dire Straits, rock and techno
- Favorite meal — pasta and paella
- Favorite drinks — milk
- Height — 173 cm
- Weight — 69 kg
- Web — www.marcgene.com

STATISTICS

- Nber of Grand Prix — 32
- Accidents/offs — 4
- Points scored — 5

PRIOR TO F1

- 1987 Karting (2nd)
- 1988 Kart Champion (E)
- 1989 Karting Jr. (EUR) (10th) Karting World Chpshp. (19th)
- 1990 Kart Sr. Champion (E)
- 1991 Kart Sr. Champion (CAT.) Karting World Chpshp. FA (13th)
- 1992 F. Ford (E) (5th)
- 1993 F. Ford Festival (2nd) F. Ford (EUR) (2nd)
- 1994 F3 (GB)
- 1995 F3 (GB) (10th)
- 1996 II Golden Cup Champion FISA Superformula
- 1997 F3000
- 1998 Open Fortuna Nissan Champion

F1 CAREER

- 1999 Minardi-Ford. 1 pt. 17th of Championship.
- 2000 Minardi-Fondmetal. 0 pt. 19th of Championship.
- 2001 Williams- BMW. Test driver
- 2002 Williams- BMW. Test driver
- 2003 Williams- BMW. 4 pts. 17th of Championship.

Sir Frank Williams

Patrick Head

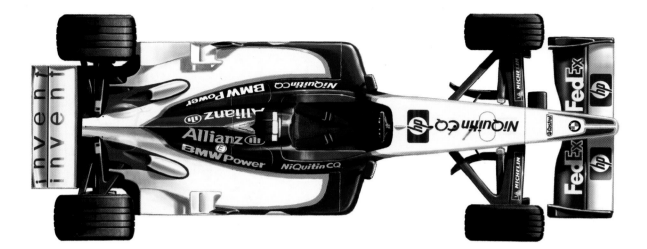

**WILLIAMS FW25-BMW
JUAN PABLO MONTOYA
GERMAN GRAND PRIX**

Williams FW25-BMW

SPECIFICATIONS

- Chassis — *Williams FW25*
- Type — *Carbon Aramid epoxy composite*
- Engine — *V10 BMW P83 (90°)*
- Displacement — *2998 cm³*
- Valves — *4 valves per cylinder*
- Electronic ignition — *BMW*
- Transmission — *WilliamsF1 semi-automatic 7 gears + reverse*
- Clutch — *Automotive Products*
- Radiators — *Secan / IMI Marston*
- Fuel / oil — *Petrobras / Castrol*
- Brakes (discs) — *Carbone Industrie*
- Brakes (calipers) — *AP Racing*
- Spark plugs — *Champion*
- Shock absorbers — *Williams / Penske*
- Tyres — *Michelin Pilot*
- Wheels dimension — *13 x 12 (FR) / 13 x 13,7 (RE)*
- Wheels — *O.Z. Racing*
- Suspensions — *WilliamsF1 independant roll bar / push rods (AV/AR)*
- Steering wheel — *WilliamsF1*
- Weight — *600 kg, driver, on board camera, ballast*
- Wheel base — *not revealed*
- Total length — *4540 mm*
- Total width — *not revealed*
- Total height — *not revealed*
- Front track — *not revealed*
- Rear track — *not revealed*

TEAM PROFILE

- Address — *Williams F1 Grove, Wantage, Oxfordshire, OX12 0DQ - Great Britain*
- Phone number — *+44 (0) 1235 7777 00*
- Fax number — *+44 (0) 1235 7777 39*
- Web — *www.bmw.williamsf1.com*
- Founded in — *1969*
- First Grand Prix — *Argentina 1975 (ARG 1973, under ISO)*
- Official name — *BMW WilliamsF1 Team*
- Team principal — *Sir Frank Williams*
- Technical director — *Patrick Head*
- Director BMW Motorsport — *Dr Mario Theissen, Gerhard Berger*
- Chief designer — *Gavin Fisher*
- Chief engineer — *Sam Michael*
- Chief of aerodynamics — *Antonia Terzi*
- Team manager — *Dickie Stanford*
- Chief mechanic — *Carl Gaden*
- Race engineer (J.P.M.) — *Tony Ross*
- Race engineer (R.S.) — *Gordon Day*
- Number employees — *420*
- Sponsors — *BMW • HP • Anheuser-Busch, Allianz, 7UP, Accenture, FedEx, Reuters, NiQuitin CQ • Western Union, ORIS, Nike, MAN Nutzfahrzeuge AG, O.Z. Racing, PPG, Bogner • Xilinx • Castrol, Michelin, Petrobras • CIBER • Spinal Injuries Association*

STATISTICS

- Number of Grand Prix — *478*
- Number of victories — *112*
- Number of pole positions — *123*
- Number of fastest lap — *125*
- Number of podiums — *286*
- Number of drivers Championship — *7*
- Number of constructors Championship — *9*
- Total number of points scored — *2341,5*

Gerhard Berger

POSITION IN WORLD CHAMPIONSHIP

Year	Result	Year	Result	Year	Result	Year	Result
1975	9th – 6 pts	1983	4th – 38 pts	1991	2nd – 125 pts	1999	5th – 35 pts
1976	not classified	1984	6th – 25,5 pts	1992	1st – 164 pts	2000	3rd – 36 pts
1977	not classified	1985	3rd – 71 pts	1993	1st – 168 pts	2001	3rd – 80 pts
1978	9th – 11 pts	1986	1st – 141 pts	1994	1st – 118 pts	2002	2nd – 92 pts
1979	2nd – 75 pts	1987	1st – 137 pts	1995	2nd – 112 pts	2003	2nd – 144 pts
1980	1st – 120 pts	1988	7th – 20 pts	1996	1st – 175 pts		
1981	1st – 95 pts	1989	2nd – 77 pts	1997	1st – 123 pts		
1982	4th – 58 pts	1990	4th – 57 pts	1998	3rd – 38 pts		

TEST DRIVERS 2003

- Marc GENÉ (E)
- Marko ASMER (EST)
- Ricardo SPERAFICO (BR)
- Olivier BERETTA (MC)

Marc Gené

SUCCESSION OF DRIVERS 2003

- Juan Pablo MONTOYA — *all 16 Grand Prix*
- Ralf SCHUMACHER — *all Grand Prix except Italy*
- Marc GENÉ — *1 Grand Prix (Italy)*

Beaten at the last

An erratic performance saw Juan Pablo Montoya's chances of taking the title evaporate at the penultimate race in Indianapolis. However, Frank Williams' teams was still in with a chance of taking the Constructors' title when the circus arrived in Suzuka, which would have suited him perfectly. Over the years, the team always preferred to see its engineers wear the victor's laurels, rather than one of its drivers. With no points scored in Japan, it was not to be. However, with four wins this year, against just one in 2002, the team is definitely on its way up again. A difficult beast during winter testing, the short FW25 continued to step up the pace throughout the year thanks to mechanical and aerodynamic improvements. With help from Michelin, it became the quickest car on the grid in terms of pure speed. But Juan Pablo Montoya and Ralf Schumacher need to polish up their act, having made several unforced errors during the year.

McLaren Mercedes

5. David COULTHARD

DRIVER PROFILE

- Name — COULTHARD
- First name — David
- Nationality — Scottish
- Date of birth — March 27th 1971
- Place of birth — Twynholm (Scotland)
- Lives in — Monaco (MC)
- Marital status — single
- Kids — -
- Hobbies — spending time with friends, movies
- Favorite music — Pop, Moby, Eminem, Robbie Williams
- Favorite meal — pasta
- Favorite drinks — tea and mineral water
- Height — 182 cm
- Weight — 72,5 kg

- Web — www.davidcoulthard-f1.com

STATISTICS

		PRIOR TO F1
Nber of Grand Prix	157	1983-88 Karting (3 times Jr.
Victories	13	Champion and Open Kart (Scot.), 2
Pole positions	12	times Champion Super Kart1 (GB))
Fastest lap	18	1989 Champion F. Ford 1600 (GB)
Podiums	60	1990 F. Vauxhall-Lotus (4th),
Accidents/offs	17	GM Lotus Euroseries (5th)
Not qualified	0	1991 F3 (GB) (2nd), Winner
Laps in the lead	894	F3 Macau and Marlboro Masters
Kms in the lead	4195	1992 F3000 (9th)
Points scored	451	1993 F3000 (3rd)
		1994 F3000 (9th)

F1 CAREER

1994   Williams-Renault. 14 pts. 8th of Championship.
1995   Williams-Renault. 49 pts. 3rd of Championship.
1996   McLaren-Mercedes. 18 pts. 7th of Championship.
1997   McLaren-Mercedes. 36 pts. 3rd of Championship.
1998   McLaren-Mercedes. 56 pts. 3rd of Championship.
1999   McLaren-Mercedes. 48 pts. 4th of Championship.
2000   McLaren-Mercedes. 73 pts. 3rd of Championship.
2001   McLaren-Mercedes. 65 pts. 2nd of Championship.
2002   McLaren-Mercedes. 41 pts. 5th of Championship.
2003   McLaren-Mercedes. 51 pts. 7th of Championship.

6. Kimi RÄIKKÖNEN

DRIVER PROFILE

- Name — RÄIKKÖNEN
- First name — Kimi Matias
- Nationality — Finnish
- Date of birth — October 17th 1979
- Place of birth — Espoo (SF)
- Lives in — Wollerau (CH), Espoo (SF), Chigwell (GB)
- Marital status — engaged with Jenni Dahlman
- Kids — -
- Hobbies — snowboard, skateboard, jogging
- Favorite music — U2, Darude, Bomfunk Mc, Eminem
- Favorite meal — pasta, chicken, finnish dish with reindeer
- Favorite drinks — ananas juice, water and milk
- Height — 175 cm
- Weight — 65 kg

- Web — www.kimiraikkonen.com

STATISTICS

		PRIOR TO F1
Nber of Grand Prix	50	1988-99 Karting
Victories	1	1998 Champion karting
Pole positions	2	Formule A (SF & Nordic)
Fastest lap	4	1999 Karting
Podiums	14	Formule A (SF) (2nd),
Accidents/offs	7	World championship
Not qualified	0	Formule Super A (10th)
Laps in the lead	159	2000 F. Renault
Kms in the lead	769	Champion (GB)
Points scored	124	

F1 CAREER

2001   Sauber-Petronas. 9 pts. 9th of Championship.
2002   McLaren-Mercedes. 24 pts. 6th of Championship.
2003   McLaren-Mercedes. 91 pts. 2nd of Championship.

Was he still racing in F1 this season? He certainly was when it started, as he ably picked up a win in Melbourne, which should have gone to others. But after that, he definitely struggled with the one lap qualifying format, according to his boss because "he intellectualises too much and asks himself too many questions," instead of locking his visor down and going for it. Coulthard always started too far back on the grid to play a part in the race, which was usually his forte. As the summer approached, it seemed his contract would not be renewed. But in the end, he has been kept on for a ninth straight year. Was it because there was no one better? Looking at the statistics, one has to say the answer is probably yes.

Through the magic of the new points allocation system, he was Michael Schumacher's only rival come the final race, even though he only had that one win in Sepang, back in March. It was the first of his career, followed by his first pole position at the Nurburgring, but none of this seemed to move him. His temperament meant that he was never really disappointed, nor was he ever ecstatic. In fact, the Ice Man made his compatriot and predecessor at McLaren, Mika Hakkinen seem like an over-emotional extrovert. Raikkonen still lacks a perfect understanding of the technical nuances of the sport and, although capable of beating him on the track, he still relies on David Coulthard, who helped him have a great season.

Ron Dennis

Martin Whitmarsh

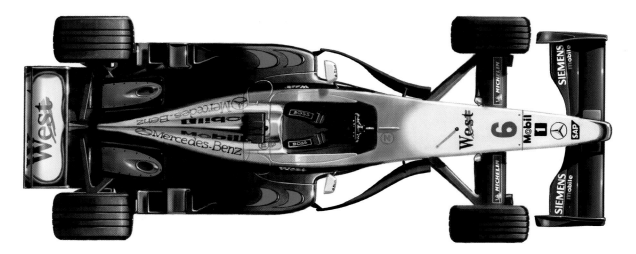

MCLAREN MP4/17D-MERCEDES
KIMI RÄIKKÖNEN
MALAYSIAN GRAND PRIX

McLaren MP4/17D-Mercedes

SPECIFICATIONS

- Chassis — McLaren MP4-17D
- Type — Moulded carbon fibre/aluminium composite
- Engine — V10 Mercedes-Benz F0110M (72°)
- Displacement — 2997 cm³
- Valves — 4 valves per cylinder
- Electronic ignition — TAG Electronic Systems
- Transmission — McLaren semi-automatic 7 gears + reverse
- Clutch — AP Racing
- Radiators — McLaren / Calsonic / Marston
- Fuel / oil — Mobil sans plomb / Mobil 1
- Brakes (discs) — Hitco
- Brakes (calipers) — AP Racing
- Spark plugs/battery — NGK / GS Battery
- Shock absorbers — Penske/McLaren
- Tyres — Michelin
- Wheels dimension — 13"
- Wheels — Enkei
- Suspensions — roll bars / push rods with double wishbone (FR/RE)
- Weight — 600 kg, driver, on bord camera,ballast
- Wheel base — not revealed
- Total length — not revealed
- Total width — not revealed
- Total height — not revealed
- Front track — not revealed
- Rear track — not revealed

TEAM PROFILE

- Address — McLaren International Ltd. Woking Business Park, Albert Drive, Woking, Surrey GU21 5JY Great Britain
- Phone number — +44 (0) 1483 728 211
- Fax number — +44 (0) 1483 720 157
- Web — www.mclaren.com
- Founded in — 1963
- First Grand Prix — Monaco 1966
- Official name — West McLaren Mercedes
- General director — Ron Dennis
- General manager — Martin Whitmarsh
- Vice President Mercedes-Benz Motorsport — Norbert Haug
- Technical Director — Adrian Newey / Mario Illien (Mercedes-Ilmor)
- Operations director — Jonathan Neale
- Executif director — Neil Oatley
- Chief designer — Mike Coughlan
- Chief engineer — Stephen Giles
- Race engineer (D.C.) — Phil Prew
- Race engineer (K.R.) — Mark Slade
- Number of employees — 520
- Sponsors — Reemtsma (West) • SAP, Warsteiner, Hugo Boss, Schüco • Advanced Composites Group, Canon, Charmilles, GS Battery, Yamazaki Mazak, TAGHeuer, Enkei, Sonax, Computer Associates, Sports Marketing Surveys, Kenwood • Mobil 1, Siemens mobile, Michelin, BAE SYSTEMS, Computer Associates, Sun, Loctite, 3D Systems • T-Mobile

STATISTICS

- Number of Grand Prix — 559
- Number of victories — 137
- Number of pole positions — 114
- Number of fastest lap — 112
- Number of podiums — 354
- Number of drivers Championship — 11
- Number of constructors Championship — 8
- Total number of points scored — 2790,5

Norbert Haug

POSITION IN WORLD CHAMPIONSHIP

Year		Year		Year		Year	
1966	7ᵗʰ – 3 pts	1976	2ⁿᵈ – 74 pts	1986	2ⁿᵈ – 96 pts	1996	4ᵗʰ – 49 pts
1967	8ᵗʰ – 1 pt	1977	3ʳᵈ – 60 pts	1987	2ⁿᵈ – 76 pts	1997	4ᵗʰ – 63 pts
1968	2ⁿᵈ – 51 pts	1978	8ᵗʰ – 15 pts	1988	1ˢᵗ – 199 pts	1998	1ˢᵗ – 156 pts
1969	4ᵗʰ – 40 pts	1979	7ᵗʰ – 15 pts	1989	1ˢᵗ – 141 pts	1999	2ⁿᵈ – 124 pts
1970	4ᵗʰ – 35 pts	1980	7ᵗʰ – 11 pts	1990	1ˢᵗ – 121 pts	2000	2ⁿᵈ – 152 pts
1971	6ᵗʰ – 10 pts	1981	6ᵗʰ – 28 pts	1991	1ˢᵗ – 139 pts	2001	2ⁿᵈ – 102 pts
1972	3ʳᵈ – 47 pts	1982	2ⁿᵈ – 69 pts	1992	2ⁿᵈ – 99 pts	2002	3ʳᵈ – 65 pts
1973	3ʳᵈ – 58 pts	1983	5ᵗʰ – 34 pts	1993	2ⁿᵈ – 84 pts	2003	3ʳᵈ – 142 pts
1974	1ˢᵗ – 73 pts	1984	1ˢᵗ – 143,5 pts	1994	4ᵗʰ – 42 pts		
1975	3ʳᵈ – 53 pts	1985	1ˢᵗ – 90 pts	1995	4ᵗʰ – 30 pts		

TEST DRIVERS 2003

- Alexander WURZ (A)
- Pedro DE LA ROSA (E)

SUCCESSION OF DRIVERS 2003

- David COULTHARD — all 16 Grand Prix
- Kimi RÄIKKÖNEN — all 16 Grand Prix

Old pots

After two wins to kick off the season, courtesy of David Coulthard in Melbourne and Kimi Raikkonen in Sepang, the FIA's spring cleaning of the sporting regulations seemed to have moved the goal posts! The MP4-17D, an evolution of the 2002 car, with some MP4-18 parts attached seemed to be facing a short future before put out to grass. But the new car, a masterpiece of minimalism was running late and first turned a wheel in May, with its race debut constantly put back, before being canned conclusively. Ron Dennis then announced that the 2004 car would definitely be an MP4-19 and that the current car was not actually that old, as it was in a constant state of evolution. It must have grated on the nerves of a man who always strives for perfection. He was right though, as the car featured new suspension, electronics and rear bodywork as part of a major evolution. But you don't always make the best soup in old pots.

7. Jarno TRULLI

DRIVER PROFILE

- Name — *TRULLI*
- First name — *Jarno*
- Nationality — *Italian*
- Date of birth — *July 13th 1974*
- Place of birth — *Pescara (I)*
- Lives in — *Monaco (MC) and Pescara (I)*
- Marital status — *single*
- Kids — *-*
- Hobbies — *music, cinema, karting, computers*
- Favorite music — *pop, rock, jazz, blues*
- Favorite meal — *pizza*
- Favorite drinks — *Coca-Cola*
- Height — *173 cm*
- Weight — *60 kg*

- Web — *www.jarnotrulli.com*

STATISTICS

		PRIOR TO F1
Nber of Grand Prix	113	1983-86 *Karting*
Victories	0	1988-90 *Champion Kart 100 (I)*
Pole positions	0	1991 *World Champion*
Fastest lap	0	*Kart 100 FK*
Podiums	2	1992 *Kart 125 FC (2nd)*
Accidents/offs	16	1993 *Kart 100 SA (2nd)*
Not qualified	0	1994 *World Champion*
Laps in the lead	52	*Kart 125 FC and*
Kms in the lead	234	*Champion Kart 100 FSA*
Points scored	71	*(EUR & Nord USA)*
		1995 *Kart 100 FA Champion (I)*
		1996 *F3 Champion (D)*

F1 CAREER

1997 *Minardi-Hart, Prost-Mugen Honda. 3 pts. 15th of Championship.*
1998 *Prost-Peugeot. 1 pt. 15th of Championship.*
1999 *Prost-Peugeot. 7 pts. 11th of Championship.*
2000 *Jordan-Mugen-Honda. 6 pts. 10th of Championship.*
2001 *Jordan-Honda. 12 pts. 9th of Championship.*
2002 *Renault. 9 pts. 8th of Championship.*
2003 *Renault. 33 pts. 8th of Championship.*

8. Fernando ALONSO

DRIVER PROFILE

- NAME — *ALONSO DÍAZ*
- First name — *Fernando*
- Nationality — *Spanish*
- Date of birth — *July 29th 1981*
- Place of birth — *Oviedo (E)*
- Lives in — *Oviedo (E) and Oxford (GB)*
- Marital status — *single*
- Kids — *-*
- Hobbies — *sports on TV, movies, computers*
- Favorite music — *spanish groups*
- Favorite meal — *pasta*
- Favorite drinks — *mineral water*
- Height — *171 cm*
- Weight — *68 kg*

- Web — *www.fernandoalonso.com*

STATISTICS

		PRIOR TO F1
Nber of Grand Prix	33	1984-98 *Karting,*
Victories	1	*Champion Jr. (E) (93-94-95-96)*
Pole positions	2	*World Champion Jr. (96)*
Fastest lap	1	*Inter-A Champion (E & I) (97)*
Podiums	4	*Inter-A Champion (E) (98)*
Accidents/offs	3	1999 *Euro-Open Champion*
Not qualified	0	*Movistar Nissan*
Laps in the lead	97	2000 *F3000 (4th)*
Kms in the lead	441	
Points scored	55	

F1 CAREER

2001 *Minardi-European. 0 pt. 23rd of Championship.*
2002 *Renault. Test driver*
2003 *Renault. 55 pts. 6th of Championship.*

A painful year! Ironically his only podium finish came at Hockenheim, where the team had strung up some garlic in the garage to stave off bad luck and deal with a bad case of flu which saw the driver collapse, physically exhausted at the end of the race. Up against the immense talent of Fernando Alonso, with whom he gets on famously, Jarno Trulli experienced an odd two sided season. In practice and qualifying, he was quick to set up his car and he shone when it came to being super quick over a single lap. In the races, he rarely made the most of the equipment at his disposal. He was not consistent enough and was prone to deep depression when he felt things were not going his way. Sometimes, he was the architect of his own downfall.

Within the team, he has a nickname which sums him up perfectly: "little bull." He gets two mentions in the record books: in Sepang, he became the youngest ever driver to take pole position in F1 and he followed that up in Budapest, by becoming the youngest ever Grand Prix winner. These successes are just the first step on what is bound to be a long and rewarding career. Fernando Alonso has been well schooled by Renault since he became the team test driver in 2002, after a year in a Minardi and his greatest strength is total self-confidence. He has nerves of steel and in qualifying and especially in the race, he drives beautifully. It is tempting to compare him to Michael Schumacher, even though he refuses to consider that option.

Flavio Briatore, Pat Symonds

Mike Gascoyne

Patrick Faure

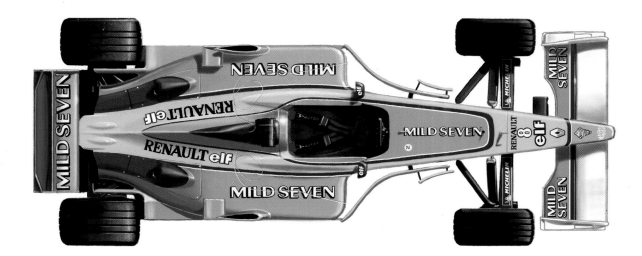

**RENAULT R23
FERNANDO ALONSO
HUNGARIAN GRAND PRIX**

Renault R23

SPECIFICATIONS

- Chassis — Renault R23
- Type — Carbon fibre composite manufactured by Renault
- Engine — V10 Renault RS23 (110°)
- Displacement — 3000 cm³
- Valves — 4 valves per cylinder
- Electronic ignition — Magneti Marelli
- Transmission — Renault F1 automatic 6 gears + reverse
- Clutch — Not revealed
- Radiators — Secan / Marston
- Fuel / oil — Elf
- Brakes (discs) — Hitco (carbon fibre)
- Brakes (calipers) — AP Racing
- Spark plugs/battery — Champion
- Shock absorbers — Dynamics
- Tyres — Michelin
- Wheels dimension — 13"
- Wheels — BBS
- Suspensions — Double wishbone, push rod/roll bar (FR/RE)
- Weight — 600 kg, driver, on board camera, ballast
- Wheel base — 3100 mm
- Total length — 4600 mm
- Total width — 1800 mm
- Total height — 950 mm
- Front track — 1450 mm
- Rear track — 1400 mm

TEAM PROFILE

- Address —
  Renault F1 UK
  Whiteways Technical
  Centre, Enstone,
  Chipping Norton,
  Oxon OX7 4EE
  Great Britain

  Renault F1 France
  1-15, avenue du
  Président Kennedy
  91177 Viry-Châtillon
  France
- Phone N° — +44 (0) 1608 678 000 — +33 (0) 1 69 12 58 00
- Fax N° — +44 (0) 1608 678 609 — +33 (0) 1 69 12 58 17
- Web — www.renaultf1.com
- Founded in — 1973
- First Grand Prix — British 1977
- Official name — Mild Seven Renault F1 Team
- Executif Vice president of Renault and President / General Director of Renault F1 Team — Patrick Faure
- General director — Flavio Briatore
- Technical director — Mike Gascoyne
- Engineering director — Pat Symonds
- Chief designer — Tim Densham, Mark Smith
- Engine departement dir. — Denis Chevrier
- Race engineer (7) — Alan Permane, Nicholas Chester
- Race engineer (8) — Paul Monaghan, Rod Nelson
- Number of employees — 670
- Sponsors — Mild Seven, Elf, Michelin, Hanjin Group, 3D Systems (ADM), Alpinestars, Altran, Catia, Charmilles Technologies, Elysium, Clearswift, Fluent, Lancel, Lectra, Magneti Marelli, Network Appliance, Schroth, Star CD, Stonesoft, Tetco Technologies, Tridion, Veritas, Vistagy

STATISTICS

- Number of Grand Prix — 156
- Number of victories — 16
- Number of pole positions — 33
- Number of fastest lap — 19
- Number of podiums — 41
- Number of drivers Championship — 0
- Number of constructors Championship — 0
- Total number of points scored — 423

POSITION IN WORLD CHAMPIONSHIP

1977	not class.	1983	2ᵗʰ – 79 pts
1978	12ᵗʰ – 3 pts	1984	5ᵗʰ – 34 pts
1979	6ᵗʰ – 26 pts	1985	7ᵗʰ – 16 pts
1980	4ᵗʰ – 38 pts	2002	4ᵗʰ – 23 pts
1981	3ᵗʰ – 54 pts	2003	4ᵗʰ – 88 pts
1982	3ᵗʰ – 62 pts		

TEST DRIVERS 2003

- Allan McNISH (GB)
- Franck MONTAGNY (F)

SUCCESSION OF DRIVERS 2003

- Jarno TRULLI — all 16 Grand Prix
- Fernando ALONSO — all 16 Grand Prix

Denis Chevrier

Franck Montagny

Back to winning ways

It was twenty years almost to the day since it had last won as a team, before becoming an engine supplier. Now, Renault was winning again. There was little in common between Alain Prost's win in Austria in 1983 and Fernando Alonso's victory in Hungary. The Frenchman won at the wheel of a turbo, built entirely at Viry, but now only the normally aspirated wide-angle V10 comes from the suburbs of Paris, while the rest of the team is run from the former Benetton factory at Enstone in England. The RE23, built by the "createur d'automobiles" under the lucid management of Flavio Briatore, proved to be the surprise of the season. All the more so, as it survived a difficult winter, peppered with failures and blow-ups, which delayed its development. Now, it is time to move up a gear, fighting for wins on a regular basis. With that in mind, was it a wise decision to abandon the revolutionary engine?

Sauber Petronas

9. Nick HEIDFELD

DRIVER PROFILE

- Name — HEIDFELD
- First name — Nick
- Nationality — German
- Date of birth — May 10th 1977
- Place of birth — Mönchengladbach (D)
- Lives in — Stäfa (CH)
- Marital status — engaged to Patricia
- Kids — -
- Hobbies — tennis, golf, motorcycle, music, movies
- Favorite music — big hits, Outkast, Zucchero
- Favorite meal — pasta, appetizers
- Favorite drinks — orange juice with mineral water
- Height — 164 cm
- Weight — 59 kg

- Web — http://nick-heidfeld.rtl.de/

STATISTICS

		PRIOR TO F1	
Nber of Grand Prix	66	1986-92	Karting
Victories	0	1993	Formule A Laval (F)
Pole positions	0	1994	F. Ford 1600
Fastest lap	0		Champion (D)
Podiums	1	1995	F. Ford Champion
Accidents/offs	9		1800 (D), F. Ford (D) (2nd)
Not qualified	0	1996	F3 (D) (3rd)
Laps in the lead	0	1997	F3 Champion (D)
Kms in the lead	0	1998	F3000 (2nd)
Points scored	25	1999	F3000 Champion

F1 CAREER

1997	McLaren-Mercedes. Test driver
1998	McLaren-Mercedes. Test driver
1999	McLaren-Mercedes. Test driver
2000	Prost-Peugeot. 0 pt. 20th of Championship.
2001	Sauber-Petronas. 12 pts. 8th of Championship.
2002	Sauber-Petronas. 7 pts. 10th of Championship.
2003	Sauber-Petronas. 6 pts. 14th of Championship.

10. Heinz-Harald FRENTZEN

DRIVER PROFILE

- Name — FRENTZEN
- First name — Heinz-Harald
- Nationality — German
- Date of birth — May 18th 1967
- Place of birth — Mönchengladbach (D)
- Lives in — Monaco (MC)
- Marital status — married to Tanja
- Kids — one daughter (Léa)
- Hobbies — aviation, VTT
- Favorite music — U2, Rolling Stones, Simple Minds, Elvis
- Favorite meal — paella, fish and pasta
- Favorite drinks — apple juice, mineral water
- Height — 178 cm
- Weight — 63 kg

- Web — www.frentzen.de

STATISTICS

		PRIOR TO F1	
Nber of Grand Prix	157	1980-85	Karting
Victories	3	1986-87	F. Ford 2000
Pole positions	2	1988	F. Opel Lotus
Fastest lap	6		Champion (D), 6th Euroseries
Podiums	18	1989	F3 (D) (2nd)
Accidents/offs	27	1990	F3000 (7th)
Not qualified	0		Sport-prototypes (16th)
Laps in the lead	150	1991	F3000 (14th)
Kms in the lead	750	1992	F3000 (J) (14th)
Points scored	174		Sport-prototypes (13th)
		1993	F3000 (J) (9th)

F1 CAREER

1994	Sauber-Mercedes. 7 pts. 13th of Championship.
1995	Sauber-Ford. 15 points. 9th of Championship.
1996	Sauber-Ford. 7 points. 12th of Championship.
1997	Williams-Renault. 42 pts. 2nd of Championship.
1998	Williams-Mécachrome. 17 pts. 7th of Championship.
1999	Jordan-Mugen Honda. 54 pts. 3rd of Championship.
2000	Jordan-Mugen Honda. 11 pts. 9th of Championship.
2001	Jordan-Honda, Prost-Acer. 6 pts. 13th of Championship.
2002	Arrows-Cosworth, Sauber-Petronas. 2 pts. 18th of Champ.
2003	Sauber-Petronas. 13 points. 11th of Championship.

Anonymous! He hardly left a trace, after those far off promising days in the F3000 Junior Mercedes Team. Working alongside Heinz-Harald Frentzen, they were the odd couple from Monchengladbach, separated by a big age gap. Heidfeld runs the risk of becoming the forgotten man, when it was not so long ago that he dreamt of a great future with McLaren. A consistent performer, who goes about his work in a diligent manner, his image is waning. If he picks up a few points, the result is attributed to his car rather than to his talent. Maybe he lacks ambition, after being so mollycoddled in his youth.

When the weather is unpredictable, his brain cells come to life! As the end of his career approached, he was unable to put together a string of consistent performances. But in Indianapolis, he made it to the podium, making the right tyre choices at the right time, reviving his reputation as a great strategist. It was all a bit too late. Having made his F1 debut with Peter Sauber, after driving for him in Sports Cars, Frentzen returned to his alma mater, like a prodigal son. But history rarely repeats itself. Faced with a car which lacked any sparkle, apart from his American exploit, Heinz-Harald was out of the limelight. After Prost, Arrows and Sauber, maybe taking part is no longer enough.

SAUBER C22-PETRONAS
HEINZ-HARALD FRENTZEN
AUTRALIAN GRAND PRIX

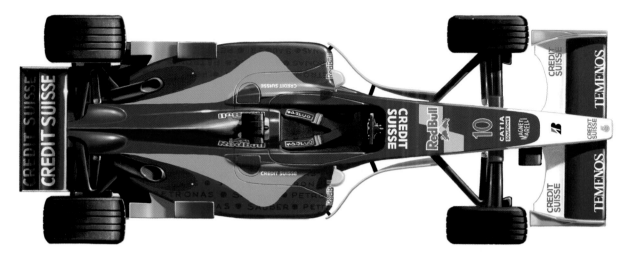

Sauber C22-Petronas

SPECIFICATIONS

- Chassis — Sauber C22
- Type — Carbone fibre
- Engine — V10 Petronas 03A (90°) (Ferrari 051 version 2002)
- Displacement — 2997 cm³
- Valves — 40 valves
- Electronic ignition — Magneti Marelli
- Transmission — Sauber longitudinal semi-automatic 7 gears + reverse
- Clutch — Sachs Race Engineering
- Radiators — Calsonic
- Fuel / oil — Shell / Petronas
- Brakes (discs) — Brembo
- Brakes (calipers) — Brembo
- Spark plugs/battery — Champion / SPE
- Shock absorbers — Sachs Race Engineering
- Tyres — Bridgestone Potenza
- Wheels dimension — 265/55R13 (AV) - 325/45R13 (AR)
- Wheels — O.Z. Racing > 12"-13 (AV) / 13.7"-13 (AR)
- Suspensions — Double wishbone, push rods / roll bar (FR/RE)
- Weight — 600 kg, driver, on board camera, ballast
- Wheel base — 3100 mm
- Total length — 4470 mm
- Total width — 1800 mm
- Total height — 1000 mm
- Front track — 1470 mm
- Rear track — 1410 mm

TEAM PROFILE

- Address — Sauber Motorsport AG
  Wildbachstrasse 9
  CH - 8340 Hinwil
  Switzerland
- Phone number — + 41 1-937 90 00
- Fax number — + 41 1-937 90 01
- Web — www.sauber-petronas.com
- Founded in — 1970
- First Grand Prix — South Africa 1993
- Official name — Sauber Petronas
- General director — Peter Sauber
- Technical director — Willy Rampf
- Engine department dir. — Osamu Goto
- Team manager — Beat Zehnder
- Chief engineer (track) and race engineer (H.H.F.) — Jacky Eeckelaert
- Race engineer (N.H.) — Rémi Decorzent
- Chief mechanic — Urs Kuratle
- Number of employees — 270
- Principal sponsors — Petronas, Credit Suisse, Red Bull
- Sponsors — 2ii.net, Adelholzener Alpenquellen, Albert Stoll Giroflex, AS Elevators, Astarte New Media, Balzers, Bridgestone, Brütsch/Rüegger, Catia, Cisco Systems, DaimlerChrysler, Elektro Frauchiger, Emil Frey, Ericsson, Fluent Deutschland, Hermann Bubeck, Italdesign / Giugiaro, Kaeser Kompressoren, Klauke Industries, Lista Group, Magneti Marelli, Microsoft, Mobile TeleSystems, MSC.Software, MTS, Ozalid, Paninfo, Pilatus, Plenexis, Puma, Sachs Race Engineering, Silicon Graphics, Sun World, Swisscom Mobile, Temenos, TLT, Vescal, Walter Meier, Winkler Veranstaltungstechnik

STATISTICS

- Number of Grand Prix — 179
- Number of victories — 0
- Number of pole positions — 0
- Number of Fastest lap — 0
- Number of podiums — 6
- Number of drivers Championship — 0
- Number of constructors Championship — 0
- Total number of points scored — 141

POSITION IN WORLD CHAMPIONSHIP

1993	6ᵗʰ – 12 pts	1999	8ᵗʰ – 5 pts
1994	8ᵗʰ – 12 pts	2000	8ᵗʰ – 6 pts
1995	7ᵗʰ – 18 pts	2001	4ᵗʰ – 21 pts
1996	7ᵗʰ – 11 pts	2002	5ᵗʰ – 11 pts
1997	7ᵗʰ – 16 pts	2003	6ᵗʰ – 19 pts
1998	6ᵗʰ – 10 pts		

Peter Sauber

Jacky Eeckelaert

TEST DRIVERS 2003

- Neel JANI (CH)

SUCCESSION OF DRIVERS 2003

- Nick HEIDFELD — all 16 Grand Prix
- Heinz-Harald FRENTZEN — all 16 Grand Prix

A late charge

Independence is a costly luxury. While relying on Petronas to finance the purchase of a late 2002 specification Ferrari engine, Peter Sauber still suffers from the lack of support from a major manufacturer. This is felt in the difficulty of raising a good development budget. A straightforward design, the C22 showed several weaknesses in terms of pure speed and reliability, as it suffered several surprising mechanical failures after the early season races saw the team score points on three consecutive occasions. Then, because of a rather basic aerodynamic package, the team had to wait for the arrival of new bodywork to make it into the points once again. The highlight of the year came at Indianapolis where the two cars picked up ten points between them; more than they had accumulated over the rest of the year The Swiss team is pinning its hopes on a new wind tunnel, which has taken up much of its time and energy. It is due to come into service very soon and will be one of the most advanced in the world. Will it be enough to finally attract a major partner?

Jordan Ford

Poor old Giancarlo took his first grand prix win, but was deprived of celebrating on the podium. Because of a cock-up by FIA when it came to studying the timing screens, he was first awarded second place, before taking his rightful place as winner four days later. It was a lucky win in a mad grand prix, but it was a worthy reward for all his hard work, given that, in the opinion of many, he is one of the best drivers on the grid. But he flattered only to deceive. Fed up with driving a car which lacked speed through lack of funding, he soon became half hearted about his job, showing no fire in his belly. In similar circumstances, someone like Olivier Panis would not have thrown in the towel.

11. Giancarlo FISICHELLA

DRIVER PROFILE

- Name — FISICHELLA
- First name — Giancarlo
- Nationality — Italian
- Date of birth — January 14th 1973
- Place of birth — Rome (I)
- Lives in — Rome (I) and Monaco (MC)
- Marital status — married to Luna
- Kids — daughter (Carlotta) and son (Christopher)
- Hobbies — football, tennis, stream fishing, pool
- Favorite music — Elton John, Madonna, Robbie Williams
- Favorite meal — "bucatini alla matriciana" (pasta)
- Favorite drinks — Coca-Cola and orange juice
- Height — 172 cm
- Weight — 64 kg
- Web — www.giancarlofisichella.com

STATISTICS

		PRIOR TO F1
Nber of Grand Prix	123	1984-88 Karting
Victories	1	1989 World Karting
Pole positions	1	Championship cat. 100 (4th)
Fastest lap	1	1990 Intercontinental Karting
Podiums	10	Championship (3rd)
Accidents/offs	18	1991 Karting (EUR) (2nd),
Not qualified	0	F. Alfa Boxer
Laps in the lead	36	1992 F3 (I) (8th)
Kms in the lead	176	1993 F3 (I) (2nd)
Points scored	94	1994 F3 Champion (I)
		1995 DTM/ITC Alfa Romeo

F1 CAREER

1995 Minardi-Ford. Test driver.
1996 Minardi-Ford. 0 pt. 19th of Championship.
1997 Jordan-Peugeot. 20 pts. 8th of Championship.
1998 Benetton-Playlife. 16 pts. 9th of Championship.
1999 Benetton-Playlife. 13 pts. 9th of Championship.
2000 Benetton-Playlife. 18 pts. 6th of Championship.
2001 Benetton-Renault. 8 pts. 11th of Championship.
2002 Jordan-Honda. 7 pts. 11th of Championship.
2003 Jordan-Ford. 12 pts. 12th of Championship.

12. Ralph FIRMAN

DRIVER PROFILE

- Name — FIRMAN (Jr.)
- First name — Ralph
- Nationality — British / Irish
- Date of birth — May 20th 1975
- Place of birth — Norfolk (GB)
- Lives in — London (GB)
- Marital status — single
- Kids — -
- Hobbies — golf, cycling, jogging
- Favorite music — pop musique, Madonna, Elton John
- Favorite meal — pasta
- Favorite drinks — water and EJ10
- Height — 185 cm
- Weight — 78 kg
- Web — www.ralphfirman.com

STATISTICS

		PRIOR TO F1
Nber of Grand Prix	14	1986-92 Karting,
Victories	0	Champion Jr. (GB) (90),
Pole positions	0	Champion Sr. (GB) (92)
Fastest lap	0	1993 F. Vauxhall Jr.
Podiums	0	Champion (GB)
Accidents/offs	3	1994 F. Vauxhall Jr. (GB)
Not qualified	0	(4th), F3 (International)
Laps in the lead	0	1995 F3 (GB) (2nd)
Kms in the lead	0	1996 F3 Champion (GB),
Points scored	1	Winner GP Macau
		1997 F. Nippon (J)
		1998 F. Nippon (J) (7th)
		1999 F. Nippon (J) (4th)
		2000 F. Nippon (J) (9th)
		2001 F. Nippon (J) (4th)
		2002 F. Nippon Champion (J),
		GT (J) (2nd)

F1 CAREER

2003 Jordan-Ford. 1 pt. 19th of Championship.

If Ralf Firman had been an actor he could have been a stand-in for Pierce Brosnan. But the man who had a double was often in double trouble on the track. When he was given the job, Eddie Jordan said he could be "the surprise of the season." It was not to be. He is the son of a mechanic who worked for Emerson Fittipaldi, before going on to set up the Van Diemen racing car company. He came to Formula 1 with the previous year's Formula Nippon title in his back pocket. In terms of driving style, he was erratic, never using the same line twice and generally he was out of his depth. On top of that, he was unlucky enough to be injured in practice in Hungary and had to sit out two races.

12. Zsolt BAUMGARTNER

DRIVER PROFILE

- Name — BAUMGARTNER
- First name — Zsolt
- Nationality — Hungarian
- Date of birth — January 1st 1981
- Place of birth — Budapest (H)
- Lives in — Budapest (H)
- Lives in — single
- Kids — -
- Hobbies — jet-ski, ski
- Favorite music — pop, rock
- Favorite meal — pasta
- Favorite drinks — Coca-Cola
- Height — 178 cm
- Weight — 71 kg
- Web — www.zsolt.baumgartner.hu

STATISTICS

		1997 F. Renault (D) (2nd)	
		1998 F. Renault	
Nber of Grand Prix	2	(School La Filière)	
Accidents/offs	0	1999 F. Renault 2000	
Points scored	0	(D & EUR) (3rd)	
		2000 F3 (D) (9th)	
PRIOR TO F1		2001 F3 (D)(17th), F3000	
1994-95 Karting Jr. A (H) (2nd)		2002 F3000 (15th)	
1996 Go-kart		2003 F3000 (14th)	

F1 CAREER

2003 Jordan-Ford. 0 pt. 24th of Championship.

He stood in for Ralf Firman in Budapest and Monza and soon confirmed what was obvious from his performances in F3000: the Hungarian had plenty of funding but very little talent and should not have even made it to the F1 grid!

Eddie Jordan

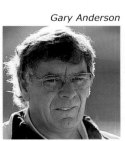

Gary Anderson

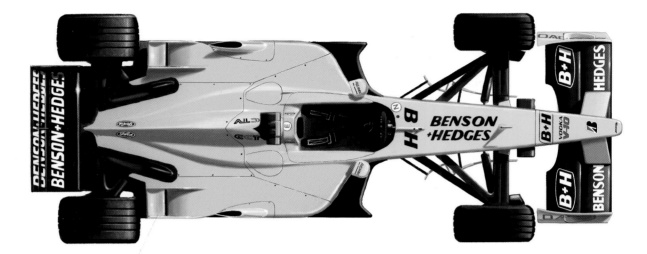

**JORDAN EJ13-FORD
GIANCARLO FISICHELLA
BRAZILIAN GRAND PRIX**

Jordan EJ13-Ford

SPECIFICATIONS

- Chassis — Jordan EJ13
- Type — Carbone fibre
- Engine — V10 Ford Cosworth CR-3 (72°)
- Displacement — 2998 cm³
- Valves — 4 valves per cylinder
- Electronic ignition — not revealed
- Transmission — Jordan longitudinal with sequential electrohydraulic gear changes , 7 gears + reverse
- Clutch — Jordan / Sachs
- Radiators — Secan / IMI Marston
- Fuel / oil — Elf / Elf
- Brakes (discs) — Carbone Industrie
- Brakes (calipers) — Brembo
- Spark plugs/battery — not revealed /not revealed
- Shock absorbers — Jordan/Penske
- Tyres — Bridgestone Potenza
- Wheels dimension — 13"
- Wheels — O.Z. Racing
- Suspensions — Double wishbone, push rods / roll bar (FR/RE)
- Weight — 600 kg, driver, on bord camera, ballast
- Wheel base — + 3000 mm
- Total length — 4650 mm
- Total width — 1800 mm
- Total height — 950 mm
- Front track — 1500 mm
- Rear track — 1418 mm

TEAM PROFILE

- Address — Jordan Grand Prix Limited Dadford Road, Silverstone, Northamptonshire, NN12 8TJ Great Britain
- Phone number — +44 (0) 1327 850 800
- Fax number — +44 (0) 1327 857 993
- Web — www.f1jordan.com
- Founded in — 1981
- First Grand Prix — USA 1991
- Official name — Jordan Ford
- General director — Eddie Jordan
- Engineering director — Gary Anderson
- Design and development director — Henri Durand
- Operations manager — David Williams
- Team manager — Tim Edwards
- Assistant Team manager — Gerrard O'Reilly
- Chief mechanic — Andrew Stevenson
- Race engineer (G.F.) — Rob Smedley
- Race engineer (R.F.) — Dominic Harlow
- Number of employees — 200
- Sponsors — Benson and Hedges, Damovo, Bridgestone, Brother, Liqui Moly, RE/MAX Europe, Imation Corp., Ford Cosworth RS • Puma, Vielife, Celerant Consulting, Power Marque, Sparco, Laurent-Perrier, Schroth, Touchpaper, Extreme networks, Piaggio, Gametrac, Tiger Telematics

STATISTICS

- Number of Grand Prix — 213
- Number of victories — 4
- Number of pole positions — 2
- Number of fastest lap — 2
- Number of podiums — 18
- Number of drivers Championship — 0
- Number of constructors Championship — 0
- Total number of points scored — 274

POSITION IN WORLD CHAMPIONSHIP

1991	5th – 13 pts		1998	4th – 34 pts
1992	11th – 1 pt		1999	3rd – 61 pts
1993	10th – 3 pts		2000	6th – 17 pts
1994	5th – 28 pts		2001	5th – 19 pts
1995	6th – 21 pts		2002	6th – 9 pts
1996	5th – 22 pts		2003	9th – 16 pts
1997	5th – 33 pts			

TEST DRIVER 2003

- Zsolt BAUMGARTNER (H)

SUCCESSION OF DRIVERS 2003

- Giancarlo FISICHELLA — all 16 Grand Prix
- Ralph FIRMAN — 14 Grand Prix (all except Hun. & Ita.)
- Zsolt BAUMGARTNER — 2 Grand Prix (Hungary & Italy)

Zsolt Baumgartner

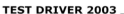

Financial crash

The team switched from Honda to Ford, who sold the team at a "discount" price the narrow V10 which had powered the Jaguars in 2002. Eddie Jordan was thus able to place the famous blue oval on his EJ13 and the engine supplier would have us believe it was an indication that this was an official partnership. A very unexpected win came its way in the chaos of Sao Paulo, early in the year. It was a welcome result, but owed a lot to circumstance. Scrabbling around to piece together a budget, the team went backwards after that. It suffered from a lack of testing, a driver in the shape of Giancarlo Fisichella, who soon lost motivation, while team-mate Ralf Firman was new to the sport and never showed much aptitude for it. Serious handicaps were made even worse by the arrival of the lamentable Zsolt Baumgartner for a couple of races and the endless engine failures during the summer. Maybe there just weren't enough greenbacks flowing through their bores.

Jaguar

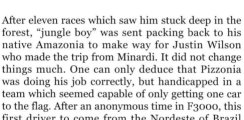

14. Mark WEBBER

DRIVER PROFILE

- Name — WEBBER
- First name — Mark Alan
- Nationality — Australian
- Date of birth — August 27th 1976
- Place of birth — Queanbeyan, NSW, (AUS)
- Lives in — Buckinghamshire (GB)
- Marital status — single
- Enfant — -
- Hobbies — VTT, guided planes, Playstation2
- Favorite music — INXS, U2, relaxing music
- Favorite meal — pasta, pizza, chocolate, ice cream and desserts
- Favorite drinks — apple juice, lemonade and mineral water
- Height — 184 cm
- Weight — 74 kg

- Web — www.markwebber.com

STATISTICS | PRIOR TO F1

STATISTICS		PRIOR TO F1
Nber of Grand Prix	32	1991-93 Karting,
Victories	0	Champion NSW and ACT (92)
Pole positions	0	1994 F. Ford (AUS) (14th)
Fastest lap	0	1995 F. Ford (AUS) (4th)
Podiums	0	1996 F. Ford (GB) (2nd),
Accidents/offs	4	F. Ford Festival Winner
Not qualified	0	1997 F3 (GB) (4th)
Laps in the lead	2	1998 FIA-GT Series (2nd)
Kms in the lead	8	2000 F3000 (3rd)
Points scored	19	2001 F3000 (2nd)

F1 CAREER

1999	Arrows-Supertec. Test driver.
2000	Benetton-Playlife. Test driver.
2001	Benetton-Renault. Test driver.
2002	Minardi-Asiatech. 2 pts. 16th of Championship.
2003	Jaguar. 17 pts. 10th of Championship.

15. Antonio PIZZONIA

DRIVER PROFILE

- Name — PIZZONIA
- First name — Antonio
- Nationality — Brazilian
- Date of birth — September 11th 1980
- Place of birth — Manaus (BR)
- Lives in — Monaco (MC) and Manaus (BR)
- Marital status — single
- Kids — -
- Hobbies — football, tennis, surf, protection of nature
- Favorite music — everything, from opera to rock
- Favorite meal — barbecue, churrascaria, chicken, pasta
- Favorite drinks — tropical fruit juice
- Height — 173 cm
- Weight — 68 kg

- Web — www.antoniopizzonia.net

STATISTICS | PRIOR TO F1

STATISTICS		PRIOR TO F1
Nbre de Grand Prix	11	1991-96 Karting,
Victories	0	Champion (BR)
Pole positions	0	1996 F. Barber Dodge (USA) (2nd)
Fastest lap	0	1997 F. Vauxhall (GB) (2nd)
Podiums	0	1998 F. Vauxhall Champion (GB)
Accidents/offs	3	1999 F. Renault Champion
Not qualified	0	(GB), F. Renault (EUR) (2nd)
Laps in the lead	0	2000 F3 Champion (GB)
Kms in the lead	0	2001 F3000 (6th)
Points scored	0	2002 F3000 (8th)

F1 CAREER

2001	Williams-BMW. Test driver.
2002	Williams-BMW. Test driver.
2003	Jaguar. 0 pt. 21st of Championship.

He is a PR man's dream in the David Coulthard mode, with plenty to say and a warm manner about him. He was helped in his career by the Australian rugby player, David Campese and is a cycling fanatic with two wheels making up much of his training programme. He led Jaguar towards the summit, when no one thought it possible. The big question remains: is Mark Webber a star of the future? Out of the cockpit, he holds all the aces. In the cockpit, he has got out of his F3000 habit of crashing on a regular basis and is now a consistent finisher. His driving style flows, so that it does not look so quick. His future might well lie with Flavio Briatore, who has his contract locked in his office drawer.

After eleven races which saw him stuck deep in the forest, "jungle boy" was sent packing back to his native Amazonia to make way for Justin Wilson who made the trip from Minardi. It did not change things much. One can only deduce that Pizzonia was doing his job correctly, but handicapped in a team which seemed capable of only getting one car to the flag. After an anonymous time in F3000, this first driver to come from the Nordeste of Brazil made it to F1 having earned his spurs as a Williams test driver, where he was praised for his work. Quick, analytical, on the pace immediately, his former employer admitted being baffled by his failure at Jaguar. He might have paid the price for being selected by Niki Lauda who also got the boot.

Tony Purnell

Malcolm Oastler

JAGUAR R4
MARK WEBBER
FRENCH GRAND PRIX

Jaguar R4

SPECIFICATIONS

- Chassis — *Jaguar R4*
- Type — *Carbon fibre*
- Engine — *V10 Cosworth Racing CR-5 (90°)*
- Displacement — *2998 cm³*
- Valves — *40 valves*
- Gestion électronique — *Pi 'VCS' System*
- Transmission — *Jaguar longitudinal with hydraulic high pressure system, 7 gears + reverse*
- Clutch — *AP Racing*
- Radiators — *IMI*
- Fuel / oil — *Castrol Racing / Castrol Fluid Technology*
- Brakes (discs) — *Carbone Industrie ou Brembo*
- Brakes (calipers) — *AP Racing*
- Spark plugs/battery — *Champion / JRL*
- Shock absorbers — *Jaguar/Penske*
- Tyres — *Michelin*
- Wheels dimension — *12.7"-13 (AV) / 13.4"-13 (AR)*
- Wheels — *O.Z. Racing*
- Suspensions — *Double wishbone, push rods / roll bar (FR/RE)*
- Weight — *600 kg, driver, on board camera, ballast*
- Wheel base — *not revealed*
- Total length — *not revealed*
- Total width — *not revealed*
- Total height — *not revealed*
- Front track — *not revealed*
- Rear track — *not revealed*

TEAM PROFILE

- Address — *Jaguar Racing Ltd*
  Bradbourne Drive, Tilbrook,
  Milton Keynes, MK7 8BJ
  Great Britain
- Phone number — *+44 (0) 1908 27 97 00*
- Fax number — *+44 (0) 1908 27 97 11*
- Web — *www.jaguar-racing.com*
- Founded in — *2000*
- First Grand Prix — *Australia 2000*
- Official name — *Jaguar Racing*
- General director — *Tony Purnell*
- General manager — *David Pitchforth*
  Nick Hayes (Cosworth Racing)
- Technical director, Ford — *Richard Parry-Jones*
- Engineering director — *Dr. Ian Pocock*
- Chief aerodynamics — *Ben Agathangelou*
- Performance director — *Dr. Mark Gillan*
- Chief engineer — *Malcolm Oastler*
- Chief designer — *Robert Taylor*
- Race engineer (M.W.) — *Peter Harrison*
- Chief engineer (A.P.) — *Stefano Sordo*
- Number of employees — *270*
- Principal sponsors — *HSBC, AT&T, EDS, DuPont, HP, Beck's*
- Suppliers — *Castrol, Michelin, Lear • Jaguar Shoes, Pioneer, Puma, Mumm, Japhiro, Rolex, Volvo Trucks, 3D Systems, MSC Software*

STATISTICS

- Number of Grand Prix — 67
- Number of victories — 0
- Number of pole positions — 0
- Number of fastest lap — 0
- Number of podiums — 2
- Number of drivers Championship — 0
- Number of constructors Championship — 0
- Total number of points scored — 39

John Hogan

POSITION IN WORLD CHAMPIONSHIP

2000	*9ᵗʰ – 4 pts*	2002	*7ᵗʰ – 8 pts*
2001	*8ᵗʰ – 9 pts*	2003	*7ᵗʰ – 18 pts*

TEST DRIVERS 2003

- None

Justin Wilson

SUCCESSION OF DRIVERS 2003

- Mark WEBBER — *all 16 Grand Prix*
- Antonio PIZZONIA — *11 Grand Prix (AUS, MAL, BR, RSM, E, A, MC, CDN, EUR, F, GB)*
- Justin WILSON — *5 Grand Prix (D, H, I, USA, J)*

Moving up a notch

Since it was born in 2000, the team only had a couple of brief moments of glory to show for itself, in Monaco and Monza. The bosses came and went in rapid succession and engineers were shown the door. The team's future seemed far from certain as it failed to achieve the results worthy of its famous name. The paradox was that, this year it started to make progress just when things looked bleaker still. David Pitchforth knew little about F1, the Ford budget was reduced and the R4 was very traditional both in terms of its aero package and its mechanicals. While the team never picked up the big points, it was nearly always there at every race; in testing, qualifying and even more so in the race. In with all these positive aspects was a negative: it seemed incapable of running more than one car. While Mark Webber shone, the other car, whether in the hands of Antonio Pizzonia or Justin Wilson was always crippled by appalling reliability problems.

B·A·R Honda

David Richards

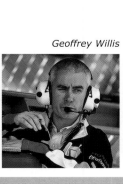

Jock Clear

Geoffrey Willis

16. Jacques VILLENEUVE

DRIVER PROFILE

- Name — *VILLENEUVE*
- First name — *Jacques*
- Nationality — *Canadian*
- Date of birth — *April 9th 1971*
- Place of birth — *St-Jean-sur-Richelieu, Québec, (CDN)*
- Lives in — *Monaco (MC)*
- Marital status — *engaged to Ellen*
- Kids — *-*
- Hobbies — *ski, playing guitar, music, electronics*
- Favorite music — *acoustic pop/rock, Semisonic, Lilac Time*
- Favorite meal — *pasta*
- Favorite drinks — *milk and "Root beer"*
- Height — *171 cm*
- Weight — *63 kg*
- Web — *www.jv-world.com*

STATISTICS

		PRIOR TO F1
• Nber of Grand Prix	131	1986 *Jim Russel School*
• Victories	11	1987 *Spenard-David driving*
• Pole positions	13	*school*
• Fastest lap	9	1988 *F. Alfa (I)*
• Podiums	23	1989-91 *F3 (I) (-, 14th, 6th)*
• Accidents/offs	14	1992 *F3 (J) (2nd)*
• Not qualified	0	1993 *Atlantic Formula (3rd)*
• Laps in the lead	633	1994 *IndyCar (6th)*
• Kms in the lead	2964	1995 *IndyCar Champion*
• Points scored	219	

F1 CAREER

1996	*Williams-Renault. 78 pts. 2nd of Championship.*
1997	*Williams-Renault. 81 pts.* **World Champion***.*
1998	*Williams-Mecachrome. 21 pts. 5th of Championship.*
1999	*B.A.R-Supertec. 0 point. 21st of Championship.*
2000	*B.A.R-Honda. 17 pts. 7th of Championship.*
2001	*B.A.R-Honda. 12 pts. 7th of Championship.*
2002	*B.A.R-Honda. 4 pts. 12th of Championship.*
2003	*B.A.R-Honda. 6 pts. 16th of Championship.*

17. Jenson BUTTON

DRIVER PROFILE

- Name — *BUTTON*
- First name — *Jenson*
- Nationality — *British*
- Date of birth — *January 19th 1980*
- Place of birth — *Frome, Somerset (GB)*
- Lives in — *Monaco (MC)*
- Marital status — *engaged to Louise*
- Kids — *-*
- Hobbies — *web surfing, video game, shopping*
- Favorite music — *Jamiroquaï, Kool And The Gang, the 70'*
- Favorite meal — *curry, fish and pasta*
- Favorite drinks — *orange juice*
- Height — *181 cm*
- Weight — *72 kg*
- Web — *www.racecar.co.uk/jensonbutton/*

STATISTICS

		PRIOR TO F1
• Nber of Grand Prix	66	1989-95 *Karting, Champion*
• Victories	0	*Cadet (GB) (90-91) / Open (GB)*
• Pole positions	0	*(91-92-93) / Jr. TKM (GB)*
• Fastest lap	0	*(91-92) / Senior ICA (I) (95)*
• Podiums	0	1996 *Karting (3rd in World Cup*
• Accidents/offs	14	*and championship) (USA)*
• Not qualified	0	1997 *Karting Super A*
• Laps in the lead	18	*Champion (EUR) and*
• Kms in the lead	80	*A. Senna Cup Winner*
• Points scored	45	1998 *F. Ford Champion and*
		F. Ford Festival (GB)
		1999 *F3 (GB) (3rd)*

F1 CAREER

2000	*Williams-BMW. 12 pts. 8th of Championship.*
2001	*Benetton-Renault. 2 pts. 17th of Championship.*
2002	*Renault. 14 pts. 7th of Championship.*
2002	*B.A.R-Honda. 17 pts. 9th of Championship.*

Five years after deciding he would rather win the lottery than go after more world titles, he has almost reached the end of the line and is no longer in control of his own destiny. For those who sensed a welcome breath of fresh air when he first walked into the paddock in 1996, this reversal of fortune seems like a terrible waste. Others think it's a case of him reaping what he has sown in 1999, when he embarked on the BAR adventure with Craig Pollock, friend turned team boss, to have fun without too many obligations and to put plenty of money in his pockets. "It's the law of supply and demand," was Villeneuve's justification. "If I am expensive, it's because someone has decided to pay me that amount." The only thing wrong with that argument was that the man paying the money was his manager and therefore in for a percentage!

Convincing on track and a lucky lad out of the car. He often got the better of team-mate Villeneuve and he also has a girlfriend who made the headlines, taking part in Fame Academy. "Louise's girlfriend" was even written on the side of his cockpit as a joke by his mechanics. His day job seems to be going pretty well too. He got off to a fantastic start with Williams, moved to Renault where he was kicked out to make way for Alonso and then found a berth at BAR. It might not seem like a great career move, but at Indianapolis and Suzuka, Jenson Button actually led a Grand Prix.

16. Takuma SATO

DRIVER PROFILE

- Name — *SATO*
- First name — *Takuma*
- Nationality — *Japanese*
- Date of birth — *January 28th 1977*
- Place of birth — *Tokyo (J)*
- Lives in — *Marlow (GB)*
- Marital status — *single*
- Kids — *-*
- Hobbies — *walks, being with friends*
- Favorite music — *pop, some japanese groups*
- Favorite meal — *Japanese cuisine*
- Favorite drinks — *fresh fruit juice, beer from time to time*
- Height — *163 cm*
- Weight — *60 kg*
- Web — *www.takumasato.com*

STATISTICS

• Nber of Grand Prix	18	1997 *Karting Champion (J),*
• Accidents/offs	4	*Honda driving school*
• Points scored	5	1998 *F. Vauxhall Jr. (GB)*
		1999 *F. Opel Euroseries (GB)*

PRIOR TO F1

1996 *Karting Champion (J)*		*(6th), F3 (GB)*
		2000 *F3 (GB) (3rd)*
		2001 *F3 Champion (GB)*

F1 CAREER

2001	*B.A.R-Honda. Test driver.*
2002	*Jordan-Honda. 2 pts. 15th of Championship.*
2003	*B.A.R-Honda. 3 pts. 18th of Championship.*

BAR's test driver and Jacques Villeneuve's replacement for 2004, he made an early debut, as he replaced the Canadian in Suzuka, finishing sixth. Honda is playing the chauvinism card, but it is taking a risk.

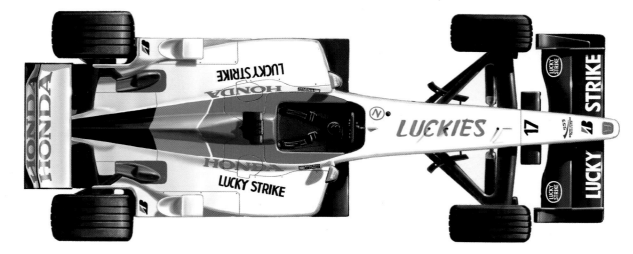

B·A·R 005-HONDA
JENSON BUTTON
AUSTRIAN GRAND PRIX

B·A·R 005-Honda

SPECIFICATIONS

- Chassis — *B.A.R 005*
- Type — *Carbone fibre, with honeycomb structure*
- Engine — *V10 Honda RA003E (90°)*
- Displacement — *3000 cm³*
- Distribution — *4 valves per cylinder*
- Gestion électronique — *Honda PGM-IG*
- Transmission — *B.A.R Xtrac longitudinal semi-automatic hydraulic 7 gears + reverse*
- Clutch — *AP Racing*
- Radiators — *Calsonic*
- Fuel / oil — *Elf / Nisseki*
- Brakes (discs) — *in carbon*
- Brakes (calipers) — *AP Racing*
- Spark plugs/battery — *NGK / 12v 5Ah*
- Shock absorbers — *Koni*
- Tyres — *Bridgestone Potenza*
- Wheels dimension — *Width 325 mm (FR) / 360 mm (RE)*
- Wheels — *BBS*
- Suspensions — *Double wishbone, push rods / roll bar (FR/RE)*
- Weight — *600 kg, driver, on board camera, ballast*
- Wheel base — *3140 mm*
- Total length — *4465 mm*
- Total width — *1800 mm*
- Total height — *950 mm*
- Front track — *1460 mm*
- Rear track — *1420 mm*

TEAM PROFILE

- Address — *British American Racing Operations Centre, Brackley, Northants NN13 7BD Great Britain*
- Phone number — *+44 (0) 1280 84 40 00*
- Fax number — *+44 (0) 1280 84 40 01*
- Web — *www.barf1.com*
- Founded in — *1997*
- First Grand Prix — *Australia 1999*
- Official name — *Lucky Strike B.A.R Honda*
- Director — *David Richards*
- Technical director — *Geoffrey Willis*
- Marketing director — *Hugh Chambers*
- General manager — *Nick Fry*
- Aerodynamics — *Willem Toet, Mariano Alperin-Bruvera, Simon Lacey*
- Team manager — *Ron Meadows*
- Chief mechanics — *Alistair Gibson*
- Race engineer (J.V.) — *Jock Clear*
- Race engineer (J.B.) — *Craig Wilson*
- Number of employees — *300*
- Principal sponsors — *British American Tabacco, Honda, Bridgestone, Intercond, Brunotti Europe BV, SINA, Amik Spa*
- Suppliers — *AlpineStars, BBS, BlueArc, Cablefree Solutions Ltd, Cartwright Group, CYTEC, De Vilbiss, EDS, Endless Advance Ltd, Glasurit Automotive Refinish, Koni, Lincoln Electric, Mac Tools, Matrix Network Solutions, NTT DoCoMo, PerkinElmer Instruments, Sandvik Coromant, Systar*

STATISTICS

- Number of Grand Prix — 83
- Number of victories — 0
- Number of pole positions — 0
- Number of Fastest lap — 0
- Number of podiums — 2
- Number of drivers Championship — 0
- Number of constructors Championship — 0
- Total number of points scored — 70

POSITION IN WORLD CHAMPIONSHIP

1999	*not class.*	2002	*8ᵗʰ – 7 pts*
2000	*5ᵗʰ – 20 pts*	2003	*5ᵗʰ – 26 pts*
2001	*6ᵗʰ – 17 pts*		

TEST DRIVERS 2003

- Anthony DAVIDSON (GB)
- Takuma SATO (J)

SUCCESSION OF DRIVERS 2003

Jacques VILLENEUVE	*15 Grand Prix (all except Japan)*
Takuma SATO	*1 Grand Prix (Japan)*
Jenson BUTTON	*15 Grand Prix (all except Monaco)*

Takuma Sato

Anthony Davidson

Mid-grid

A not-bad engine from Japan and a reasonable chassis: with its 005 car, British American Racing managed to figure honourably in the middle of the grid, but its future is far from clear. How long will Honda put up with results which do not match its glorious past in F1, when up against the might of Toyota, with whom it slugs it out toe to toe in Japan. It is no longer in charge of its own destiny as it shares its future with a team which is somewhat lightweight. There are also question marks about the team boss. David Richards is only a simple employee, not a shareholder, even though he is the owner of ISC, which controls the rights to the World Rally Championship and runs Prodrive, which amongst other projects, also runs the Subaru WRC cars. He claims to have put the right people in place at BAR, but it does not ring true. The team was riven with internal politics such as the arguments over Jacques Villeneuve's future.

Minardi Cosworth

18. Justin WILSON

DRIVER PROFILE

- Name — *WILSON*
- First name — *Justin*
- Nationality — *British*
- Date of birth — *July 31st 1978*
- Place of birth — *Sheffield (GB)*
- Lives in — *Northampton (GB)*
- Marital status — *single*
- Kids — *-*
- Hobbies — *video games, guided helicopters*
- Favorite music — *Coldplay, Travis*
- Favorite meal — *chicken*
- Favorite drinks — *orange juice, water*
- Height — *192 cm*
- Weight — *80 kg*
- Web — *www.justinwilson.co.uk*

STATISTICS

		PRIOR TO F1
Nber of Grand Prix	16	1987-90 *Karting, Champion*
Victories	0	*Wombell & Langbauch et*
Pole positions	0	*Fulbeck Club (GB) (90)*
Fastest lap	0	1991-92 *RACMSA Jr. (GB)*
Podiums	0	1994 *Formule A (GB) (5th),*
Accidents/offs	1	*F. Vauxhall Jr.*
Not qualified	0	1995 *F. Vauxhall Champion*
Laps in the lead	0	*Jr. (GB)*
Kms in the lead	0	1996 *F. Vauxhall (GB) (2nd)*
Points scored	1	1997 *F. Vauxhall (GB) (4th)*
		1998 *F. Palmer Audi (GB)*
		Champion
		1999 *F3000 (18th)*
		2000 *F3000 (5th)*
		2001 *F3000 Champion*
		2002 *World Series Nissan (4th)*

F1 CAREER

2003   *Minardi-Cosworth, Jaguar. 1 pt. 20th of Championship*

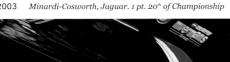

Paul Stoddart

19. Jos VERSTAPPEN

DRIVER PROFILE

- Name — *VERSTAPPEN*
- First name — *Joshannes Franciscus*
- Nationality — *Dutch*
- Date of birth — *March 4th 1972*
- Place of birth — *Montford (NL)*
- Lives in — *Monaco (MC), Montford (NL)*
- Marital status — *married to Sophie*
- Enfant — *daugther (Victoria), son (Max Emilian)*
- Hobbies — *karting, motorcycles, playing with his kids*
- Favorite music — *UB40, 70's rock*
- Favorite meal — *pasta and Dutch cuisine*
- Favorite drinks — *Coca-Cola*
- Height — *175 cm*
- Weight — *73 kg*
- Web — *www.verstappen.nl*

STATISTICS

		PRIOR TO F1
Nber of Grand Prix	107	1982-91 *Karting, Champion*
Victories	0	*(NL & Bénélux) (84 & 86),*
Pole positions	0	*Intercontinental A (EUR)*
Fastest lap	0	*(89), (B) (91)*
Podiums	2	1992 *F. Opel Champion*
Accidents/offs	21	*Lotus (NL)*
Not qualified	0	1993 *Champion F3 (D),*
Laps in the lead	0	*F. Atlantic (NZ) (4th),*
Kms in the lead	0	*Winner Masters F3*
Points scored	17	*(Zandvoort)*

F1 CAREER

1994	*Benetton-Ford. 10 pts. 10th of Championship.*
1995	*Simtek-Ford. (5 GP). 0 pts. not class.*
1996	*Arrows-Hart. 1 pt. 16th of Championship.*
1997	*Tyrrell-Ford. 0 pt. not classified.*
1998	*Stewart-Ford. (9 GP). 0 pt. not classified.*
2000	*Arrows-Supertec. 5 pts. 12th of Championship.*
2001	*Arrows-Asiatech. 1 pt. 18th of Championship.*
2003	*Minardi-Cosworth. 0 pt. 22th of Championship.*

It was certainly a dramatic arrival on the F1 scene for the young lad with a worrying similarity to a Transylvanian vampire. He financed his drive with Minardi by selling shares in himself on the Stock Market, promising untold riches to investors if his career took off. Only time will tell if it was a good investment. He started the year with Minardi, where he displayed an aggressive racing nature, characterised by some demon starts. He made the move to Jaguar in time for the German Grand Prix. He was under no pressure in the Italian squad and could calmly get on with learning his trade, once he had paid his bill. Once with Jaguar, he was expected to deliver and unfortunately that never really happened.

His career seems never ending; a strange product of Holland's obsession with Formula 1. Once again this year, Jos the Boss was back. However, in many ways his career ended ten years ago, when he was thrown like a Christian to the lions, when at a tender age, he was teamed up with Michael Schumacher at Benetton. Since then, armed with backing from a variety of often unusual Dutch sponsors, he has bought his way into a variety of teams. There was Simtek, Tyrell, Stewart, two stints at Arrows and even a drive with the Honda experimental team which came before the Japanese company aborted plans to enter its own team. Now he is with Minardi. Can he go any lower? Currently he is looking to move elsewhere.

18. Nicolas KIESA

DRIVER PROFILE

- Name — *KIESA*
- First name — *Nicolas*
- Nationality — *Danish*
- Date of birth — *March 3rd 1978*
- Place of birth — *Copenhague (DK)*
- Lives in — *Copenhague (DK)*
- Marital status — *single*
- Kids — *-*
- Hobbies — *engine development and road cars*
- Favorite meal — *T-bone steak with spicy butter*
- Favorite drinks — *freshly squeezed orange juice*
- Height — *178 cm*
- Weight — *72 kg*
- Web — *www.kiesa.com*

STATISTICS

		World Vice-Champion
Nber of Grand Prix	5	*(92 & 96), Chpt. (EUR) (3rd)*
Accidents/offs	0	1998 *F. Ford (GB) (4th),*
Points scored	0	*F. Ford Festival (GB) (3rd)*
		1999 *F. Ford Champion (GB),*

PRIOR TO F1

1990-97 *Karting: Champion*	*F. Ford (EUR) (3rd), F. Ford*
(DK) (Jr.90), (91 & 96),	*Festival (GB) (4th)*
(Scandinavia) (96), FIA Viking	2000 *F3 (GB) (6th)*
Trophy Winner (94 & 95),	2001 *F3 (GB) (14th) & (D)*
	2002 *F3000 (12th)*
	2003 *F3000 (7th)*

F1 CAREER

2003   *Minardi-Cosworth. 0 pt. 23rd du championnat.*

He won at Monaco in the F3000 race, but it was more by luck than judgement. So how come he replaced Justin Wilson at Minardi? It was because Nicolas Kiesa is as quick as Croesus.

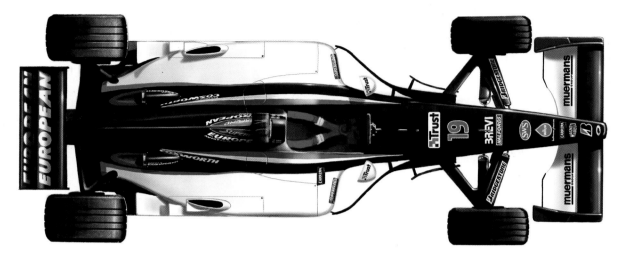

**MINARDI PS03-COSWORTH
JOS VERSTAPPEN
FRENCH GRAND PRIX**

Minardi PS03-Cosworth

SPECIFICATIONS

- Chassis — Minardi PS03
- Type — Carbon fibre, with honeycomb structure
- Engine — V10 Cosworth Racing CR-3 (72°)
- Displacement — 2998 cm³
- Distribution — 4 valves per cylinder
- Gestion électronique — Magneti Marelli Step 10
- Transmission — Minardi longitudinal, sequential, semi-automatic, hydraulic, 6 gears + reverse
- Clutch — AP Racing
- Radiators — Minardi
- Fuel / oil — Elf / Elf
- Brakes (discs) — Hitco / Brembo
- Brakes (calipers) — Hitco / Brembo
- Spark plugs/battery — Champion / not revealed
- Shock absorbers — Sachs
- Tyres — Bridgestone Potenza
- Wheels dimension — 13" x 12" (AV) / 13" x 13.7" (AR)
- Wheels — O.Z. Racing
- Suspensions — Double wishbone, push rods / roll bar (FR/RE)
- Weight — 600 kg, driver, on bord camera, ballast
- Wheel base — 3097 mm
- Total length — 4548 mm
- Total width — 1800 mm
- Total height — 950 mm
- Front track — 1480 mm
- Rear track — 1410 mm

TEAM PROFILE

- Address — Minardi Team SpA
  Via Spallanzani, 21
  48018 Faenza (RA) - Italy
- Phone number — +39 0 546 696 111
- Fax number — +39 0 546 620 998
- Web — www.minardi.it
- Founded in — 1974
- First Grand Prix — Brazil 1985
- Official name — European Minardi Cosworth
- Pres. General director — Paul Stoddart
- General director — Gian Carlo Minardi
- Technical director — Gabriele Tredozi
- Chief aerodynamics — Loïc Bigois
- Sports director — John Walton
- Team manager — Nigel Steer
- Chief mechanics — Sandro Parrini
- Race engineer (J.W.) — Alex Varnava
- Race engineer (J.V.) — Greg Wheeler
- Number of employees — 160
- Principal sponsors — European Aviation, Trust, Halfords, Muermans, Quadriga (Superfund), Wilux, Allegrini
- Suppliers — LeasePlan, Poderi Morini, Rustichella d'Abruzzo S.p.A., Ursini, Parmalat, Torrefazione ReKico Caffè • Magneti Marelli, Brevi, Carrera Jeans, Puma, 3D Systems, Cimatron, Beta, Netscalibur

STATISTICS

- Number of Grand Prix — 303
- Number of victories — 0
- Number of pole positions lap — 0
- Number of fastest lap — 0
- Number of podiums — 0
- Number of drivers Championship — 0
- Number of constructors Championship — 0
- Total number of points scored — 30

POSITION IN WORLD CHAMPIONSHIP

1985	not class.	1992	11ᵗʰ – 1 pt	1999	10ᵗʰ – 1 pt
1986	not class.	1993	8ᵗʰ – 7 pts	2000	not class.
1987	not class.	1994	10ᵗʰ – 5 pts	2001	11ᵗʰ – 0 pt
1988	10ᵗʰ – 1 pt	1995	10ᵗʰ – 1 pt	2002	9ᵗʰ – 2 pts
1989	10ᵗʰ – 6 pts	1996	not class.	2003	10ᵗʰ – 0 pt
1990	not class.	1997	not class.		
1991	7ᵗʰ – 6 pts	1998	not class.		

TEST DRIVER 2003

- Sergey ZLOBIN (RUS)
- Matteo BOBBI (I)
- Gianmaria BRUNI (I)

SUCCESSION OF DRIVERS 2003

- Justin WILSON — 11 Grand Prix (AUS, MAL, BR, RSM, E, A, MC, CDN, EUR, F, GB)
- Nicolas KIESA — 5 Grand Prix (D, H, I, USA, J)
- Jos VERSTAPPEN — all 16 Grand Prix

Nicolas Kiesa

Tail End Charlie

Bottom of the class, sitting near the radiator, as indeed it does every year. But Paul Stoddart has reasons to rub his hands other than feeling the heat. Because although his PS03 cars dragged their heels at the back of the pack, he proved he had a talent for finding money. A past master at the art of finding cash, he was always threatening to give away secrets about the Concorde Agreement, or to blow away the paddock if he was not given the money he reckoned he was owed from the bigger teams. Bernie Ecclestone ended up putting his hand in his pocket and from then on all was quiet, as it was on the track as well. The team's Tom Thumb status did not change. Jos Verstappen started the year partnered by Justin Wilson, who was replaced by Nicolas Kiesa once Wilson switched to Jaguar. Once again, the driver choice was all down to money. But at the end of the day, if the car can do no better than make up the numbers, it does not really matter who sits in the cockpit.

Toyota

20. Olivier PANIS

DRIVER PROFILE

- Name — *PANIS*
- First name — *Olivier Denis*
- Nationality — *French*
- Date of birth — *September 2nd 1966*
- Place of birth — *Lyon (F)*
- Lives in — *Varses near Grenoble (F)*
- Marital status — *married to Anne*
- Kids — *2 daugthers (Caroline, Lauren), 1 son (Aurélien)*
- Hobbies — *family, ski, cycling, tennis, boating, karting*
- Favorite music — *Florent Pagny, Barry White, Garou*
- Favorite meal — *Olive oil pasta, parmesan*
- Favorite drinks — *water and Coca-Cola*
- Height — *173 cm*
- Weight — *72 kg*

- Web — *www.olivier-panis.com*

STATISTICS

		PRIOR TO F1
Nber of Grand Prix	141	1981-87 *Karting*
Victories	1	1987 *Volant Elf Winfield*
Pole-positions	0	*Paul Ricard Winner*
Fastest lap	0	1988 *F. Renault (F) (4th)*
Podiums	4	1989 *F. Renault Champion (F)*
Accidents/offs	19	1990 *F3 (F) (4th)*
Not qualified	0	1991 *F3 (F) (2nd)*
Laps in the lead	16	1992 *F3000 (10th)*
Kms in the lead	53	1993 *F3000 Champion*
Points scored	70	

F1 CAREER

1994	*Ligier-Renault. 9 points. 11th of Championship.*
1995	*Ligier-Mugen-Honda. 16 pts. 8th of Championship.*
1996	*Ligier- Mugen-Honda. 13 pts. 9th of Championship.*
1997	*Prost-Mugen-Honda. 16 pts. 9th of Championship.*
1998	*Prost-Peugeot. 0 point. 18th of Championship.*
1999	*Prost-Peugeot. 2 pts. 15th of Championship.*
2000	*McLaren-Mercedes. Test driver.*
2001	*B.A.R-Honda. 5 pts. 14th of Championship.*
2002	*B.A.R-Honda. 3 pts. 14th of Championship.*
2003	*Toyota. 6 pts. 15th of Championship.*

21. Cristiano DA MATTA

DRIVER PROFILE

- Name — *DA MATTA*
- First name — *Cristiano Monteiro*
- Nationality — *Brazilian*
- Date of birth — *September 19th 1973*
- Place of birth — *Belo Horizonte (BR)*
- Lives in — *Monaco (MC)*
- Marital status — *single*
- Kids — *-*
- Hobbies — *play and listen to music, cycling*
- Favorite music — *rock, blues, jazz*
- Favorite meal — *Brazilian cuisine*
- Favorite drinks — *iced tea*
- Height — *165 cm*
- Weight — *59 kg*

- Web — *www.damatta.com*

STATISTICS

		PRIOR TO F1
Nber of Grand Prix	16	1990-92 *Karting, Champion*
Victories	0	*Minas (90-91), (BR) (91)*
Pole-positions	0	1993 *F. Ford Champion (BR)*
Fastest lap	0	1994 *F3 Champion (BR)*
Podiums	0	1995 *F3 (GB) (8th)*
Accidents/offs	1	1996 *F3000 (8th)*
Not qualified	0	1997 *Indy Lights (3rd)*
Laps in the lead	17	1998 *Indy Lights Champion*
Kms in the lead	87	1999 *CART (18th)*
Points scored	10	2000 *CART (10th)*
		2001 *CART (5th)*
		2002 *CART Champion*

F1 CAREER

2003	*Toyota. 10 pts. 13th of Championship.*

The gods of ill fortune have still not finished with him and the black cat still hovers in the back of his garage. "Yes, he's doing fine," Panis was quick to admit, although he never threw in the towel. He left BAR-Honda for Toyota but he still has not been able to leave his mark on Formula 1. Nevertheless, at the age at which Eddie Irvine bade farewell to the sport, he manages to maintain a youthful enthusiasm and an impressive turn of speed. He was plagued with endless mechanical woes or hobbled by his team's strategy. The great champions make their own luck, so they say and Michael Schumacher proves their point. Is it still the case? While he admits to having no regrets, Olivier Panis might have missed out on the chance of a great career.

The CART ace did not figure much on the score sheet, but he impressed nevertheless. As the reigning American champ, the likeable little chap with the stubbled chin likes to play the guitar and proved he had several cards up his sleeve. Cristiano Monteiro da Matta, who like Ayrton Senna da Silva goes by a longer name than he reveals to the public was chosen mainly for his publicity value in both the Americas and he pretty much repaid Toyota's faith in him. He had to get the hang of F1, after driving the heavier old-fashioned American cars and most of the circuits were new to him but he often matched his more experienced team-mate's pace.

Ove Andersson

Gustav Brunner

Ange Pasquali

**TOYOTA TF103
OLIVIER PANIS
GERMAN GRAND PRIX**

Toyota TF103

SPECIFICATIONS

- Chassis — *Toyota TF103*
- Type — *Carbon fibre, honeycomb structure*
- Engine — *V10 Toyota RVX-03 (90°)*
- Displacement — *2998 cm³*
- Distribution — *4 valves per cylinder*
- Electronic ignition — *Magneti Marelli*
- Transmission — *Toyota sequential, longitudinal hydraulic semi-automatic 7 gears + reverse*
- Clutch — *Sachs*
- Radiators — *Denzo*
- Fuel / oil — *Esso / Esso*
- Brakes (discs) — *Brembo*
- Brakes (calipers) — *Brembo*
- Spark plugs/battery — *not revealed / not revealed*
- Shock absorbers — *FFT/Sachs*
- Tyres — *Michelin Pilot*
- Wheels dimension — *13" x 12" (AV) / 13" x 13.5" (AR)*
- Wheels — *BBS*
- Suspensions — *Double wishbone, push rods / roll bar (FR/RE)*
- Weight — *600 kg, driver, on bord camera, ballast*
- Wheel base — *3090 mm*
- Total length — *4547 mm*
- Total width — *not revealed*
- Total height — *not revealed*
- Front track — *1424 mm*
- Rear track — *1411 mm*

TEAM PROFILE

- Address — *Toyota Motorsport GmbH Toyota-Allee 7 50858 Köln Germany*
- Phone number — *+49 (0) 223 418 23 444*
- Fax number — *+49 (0) 223 418 23 37*
- Web — *www.toyota-f1.com*
- Founded in — *1999*
- First Grand Prix — *Australia 2002*
- Official name — *Panasonic Toyota Racing*
- President — *Tsutomu Tomita*
- Vice president — *Ove Andersson*
- Director — *John Howett*
- Vice director — *Toshiro Kurusu*
- Team manager — *Ange Pasquali*
- Chief designer — *Gustav Brunner*
- General manager (race and engineer) — *Norbert Kreyer*
- General manager (design & developmt.) — *Keizo Takahashi*
- General manager (engine) — *Luca Marmorini*
- Number of employees — *580*
- Sponsors — *Panasonic • AOL Time Warner, AVEX Inc., Ebbon-Dacs, Kärcher, KDDI, Travelex • CATIA Solutions, EMC, EOS, ExxonMobil Corporation (Esso), KTC, Magneti Marelli, MAN, Météo-France, Michelin • BBS, DEA, Future Sports, M.B.A. Production + design, Nolan (X-lite), Puma, Sika, Sparco, St. Georges, Technogym, Vuarnet, Wella, Yamaha, ZF Sachs AG*

STATISTICS

- Number of Grand Prix — 33
- Number of victories — 0
- Number of pole positions — 0
- Number of fastest lap — 0
- Number of podiums — 0
- Number of drivers Championship — 0
- Number of constructors Championship — 0
- Total number of points scored — 18

POSITION IN WORLD CHAMPIONSHIP

2002   *10ᵗʰ – 2 pts*
2003   *8ᵗʰ – 16 pts*

TEST DRIVERS 2003

- Ricardo ZONTA (BR)

SUCCESSION OF DRIVERS 2003

- Olivier PANIS — *all 16 Grand Prix*
- Cristiano DA MATTA — *all 16 Grand Prix*

Tsutomu Tomita

Ricardo Zonta

Feet of clay

The colossus is still in its infancy and some of its bones have yet to join up. The team started with a clean sheet of paper, headed up by Ove Andersson, but it is clear that it is not yet organised enough to grab any passing chances. Overall, its car lacked reliability, especially in the first half of the season and it also tried some risky race strategies. The TF103s would often run light in qualifying, going for one more pit stop than the opposition. In Indianapolis it managed to shoot itself in both feet. Panis and Da Matta both pitted early in the race, when the first drops of rain arrived in order to quickly fit rain tyres to get the upper hand on the rest of the field. But they did it too son and they had to go back to dry tyres before the rain finally started for real! Why did not they mix their strategies in order to reduce the odds of failure? You cannot buy experience, but common sense is available to all.

SPOTLIGHT

It's a tradition in "The Formula 1 Yearbook:" to get a better grasp on the comings and goings of the championship just gone, we have asked journalists from five countries to describe "their" F1 season. Yet another way to go behind the scenes of 16 Sunday afternoon races.

Ferrari hold off Williams and McLaren

No question about it, this was the closest World Championship in years, and a welcome antidote to 2002, perhaps the dreariest Formula 1 season of all time.

Nigel Roebuck - Autosport, London

2003: a British point of view

In '02 Michael Schumacher clinched the title by late July, andeventually accumulated 67 more points than his nearest rival. In '03 hewon it, for a record sixth time, at the last race, in October, and only by a couple of points.

The FIA may claim that its rule changes, concerning qualifying andthe points system, contributed to this, but the fundamental reasons for this infinitely more combative season lay, as ever, with cars and drivers -and tyres. In 2003 Williams-BMW and McLaren-Mercedes signifcantly raised their game in the battle with Ferrari, and in this were aided very considerably by Michelin, who had much the better of the tyre war.

By the time the teams left the Hungaroring, in mid-August, Schumacher led the championship, but by now Montoya was only one point behind, and Raikkonen two. And so abysmal had Ferrari's showing been at this race - Michael was eighth, and lapped - that the smart money was on Juan Pablo or Kimi for the title.

The tide had certainly turned - but then it had frequently through the year. Logically, the initial advantage should have lain with Williams-BMW, for only they - of the top three teams - had their new car ready for the first race. Reliability problems delayed the debut of Ferrari's F2003-GA until Barcelona, race five, and McLaren began with an interim car, the MP4-17D, pending the arrival of the radical MP4-18 - which never happened...

The short-wheelbase Williams FW25 was way more adventurous in concept than its predecessor, and BMW had found yet more power, to the tune of 900bhp. Again the drivers were Montoya and Ralf Schumacher, and everything seemed to be in place.

Problem was, at first the car revealed nothing like its true potential. It may have been fundamentally superior to the previous one, but not until the Austrian Grand Prix, race six, was the expected leap in performance finally realised.

In those early races, the Williams-BMW results were scrappy, and when Ralf and JPM arrived at the A1-Ring, they were only sixth and seventh in the points. In terms of results, the weekend was again disappointing, but Montoya would have won if his engine had lasted, and the team at least came knew that real progress was being made on the aero front.

Then, at Monaco, Juan won brilliantly, making no mistakes under intense pressure from Raikkonen, and that made some amends for Melbourne, where he had spun out of the lead in the closing laps. Later, at Hockenheim, Montoya scored the most dominant victory of the season.

If there were no more wins, he continued to score well, and went to Indianapolis as most people's favourite for the championship. But an altercation with Barrichello led to a harsh 'drive through' penalty, which meant a sixth place finish, and the end of his title challenge.

On occasions Montoya drove untypically in 2003, reining in his natural instincts. "If you make a mistake in qualifying, and start from the back, you're history in the race," he said, "and if you don't finish, you're history in the championship."

After taking seven poles in 2002, JPM had only one this time, and was out-qualified 10-6 by his team mate. That said, his average grid position was better than his team mate's, so perhaps he had been right to change his approach. With nothing to lose at Suzuka, he was gone until slowing with hydraulics failure - just the kind of failure they don't have at Maranello.

Nigel Roebuck
55 years old, decided to quit his industrial job and enter journalism at the age of 24. In 1971, he starts writing for the American magazine «Car & Driver», before joining the British weekly motor racing magazine «Autosport» in 1976. He is covering Formula One since 1977, while workingfor the «Sunday Tmes», for the «Auto Week» and the Japanese magazine «Racing On».

Against all expectation, Montoya was the more consistent of the Williams-BMW drivers, R. Schumacher swerving between pathetic and scintillating through the season. In the early races, before the FW25's aero problems had been resolved, his team mate put his natural flair to work, and got more out of the car, but once it had become mannerly, Ralf's greater experience and set-up expertise allowed him to get, as Patrick Head put it, 'closer to the perfection of the car'. At midseason he won two races in seven days, and each time Montoya was second.

A mixed season for Michael's brother, then. You watched him win at the Nurburgring and Magny-Cours - and you remembered his letter from the management after Sepang, advising that if no improvement were forthcoming, neither would be a renewal of his contract.

You could say, with some justification, that if Williams and, to a lesser extent, McLaren, appeared to snatch defeat from the jaws of victory in the 2003 championship, their efforts were not aided by a row which erupted before the Italian Grand Prix. Someone at Bridgestone had studied Michelin's front tyres in post-race condition, and suspected the contact patch was too wide. Ferrari drew this to the attention of the FIA, who duly issued what they called 'a clarification', but which most people saw as 'a rule change'.

Henceforth, the governing body said, tyres would be checked and measured not only before a race, but also afterwards. The fact that Michelin had been manufacturing the tyres in the same mould for three years, but only now - after Ferrari/Bridgestone had had a quite lamentable race in Hungary - caused offence inevitably prompted cynicism in the paddock. Subsequent 'playing safe' changes to Michelin front tyres made little difference to their performance, but the episode certainly served to destabilise Williams and McLaren at a crucial point in the championship.

At the end of the day, though, you could say that the championship was won and lost during the first part of the European season. While Williams worked on honing their car, and McLaren did their best with what they had, Schumacher and his Ferrari put three consecutive wins on the board. Michael may

have started the year badly, but a solid run of good finishes - and another superb win, in Canada, with a brakeless car - took him into a midseason points lead he never lost.

For a time he seemed to go off the boil, frustrated by Bridgestone's lagging behind Michelin, and in these circumstances it was increasingly to Barrichello that Ferrari looked, particularly in qualifying. Rubens, in fact, had by far the best average grid position of any driver, and at Silverstone converted his pole position into the best victory of the season. He also won at Suzuka, and should have done at Interlagos.

It took Barrichello a little longer than Schumacher to get on terms with the F2003-GA. "It's definitely superior to the old car," he said at Monaco, "but also harder to drive and to set up."

Whatever, it was good enough to win both titles in the end. Raikkonen went to Suzuka with the flimsiest of chances of winning the championship, but in reality McLaren's MP4-17D - while occasionally the fastest car of all - lacked the consistent pace to take on Ferrari and Williams, not least because Mercedes are still some way off in the horsepower stakes.

Sometimes Kimi's flair and speed were dazzling, but, like Montoya, he was a man in only his third season of F1, and occasionally that showed. At both Barcelona and Montreal, for example, he went off on his qualifying lap, and thus started from the back, which is not how you score well on race day.

Raikkonen and David Coulthard won a race apiece, but the younger man soon asserted his authority in the team, for DC, after a fine start to the year, completely lost his confidence in 'one lap' qualifying, and began routinely to line up in mid-grid. Invariably, he raced well, but there were always too many cars to be passed - cars which should not have been ahead of him. Not Coulthard's best season, this.

Not Adrian Newey's, either. The MP4-18 was originally due to race early in the European season, but its debut was endlessly postponed. The car was quick, its drivers said after testing it, but never reliable enough to risk racing. You don't beat Ferrari that way.

Staying calm in
the face of adversity?

Mario Theissen was giving nothing away. He was quietly totting up the scores on Sunday evening at Suzuka, a mere hour after the end of the final race of the season. *"Of course we are disappointed,"* said BMW's sporting director. *"But overall, this was our best season since our comeback in 2000."* Theissen is not the excitable type, but the best season since 2000?

Anno Hecker – Frankfurter Allgemeine Zeitung

Up until the penultimate grand prix in the United States, BMW-Williams was in with a chance of winning both the Drivers' and Constructors' championships. What a triumph that would have been. Doing the double in the fourth year of the Anglo-German alliance, Ferrari knocked off its perch and its main rival on the home market also beaten. But forget all that. As the sun set in Japan, Theissen stood empty handed in the pits with the only consolation that, "at least the engine was not at fault." Indeed, it had worked without fail like a Swiss watch. But what good is a powerful engine if the rest of the car is not up to it? *"We will discuss this season in depth,"* explained an irritated Ralf Schumacher a few moments after the final race, before debriefing with his engineers. *"It's been a long time since it could have been so easy to beat Ferrari and become world champion."*

What are the causes? They are many and various. Theissen certainly spares no one in his analysis. *"We made technical, strategic and driving errors. We were simply not geared up to take the title."* Not ready? A car which is quick at the mid-point of the season can be better prepared for the next one. But can one expect two drivers, in the space of a few months, to improve at the wheel, when they are already 28 years old and are therefore part of the old boys club on the grid.

On top of that, Gerhard Berger, who was highly rated by the drivers, has left his role as sporting director. Rumours that Montoya is heading for McLaren-Mercedes in 2005 will have done nothing to help the young Schumacher's cause. It has been suggested that Montoya's planned switch had nothing to do with money, but stemmed from the fact he felt he was not getting the support he needs from the team and that Ralf Schumacher was highly regarded for his technical aptitude when it came to setting up the car. Of course, it is quite possible that it is just the Schumacher camp spreading these stories.

Whatever the truth of the matter, Montoya's departure would not suit BMW at all. It is all down to the political game of transfers and in this case, the hidden force is to be found in Stuttgart, in the shape of DaimlerChrysler. It has already attracted several engine specialists away from BMW's Bavarian lair, a subject Berger commented on at length during the course of the year: *"They need BMW's expertise and apparently not just on the engine side."*

It seemed that McLaren-Mercedes had created its own problems. When would that new car appear? It was delayed from the spring to the summer, then finally canned for good. It gave BMW-Williams some breathing space. *"If the new McLaren had really been as quick as they say, we would probably have been in trouble,"* explained Berger. Just as Mercedes was trying to smooth-talk people into believing that the MP4-18 was a technological marvel which had now been transformed into a laboratory for next year's car, BMW-Williams began to surround the enemy with old fashioned methods. It was only at the height of the crisis, at Silverstone, that DaimlerChrysler board member Jurgen Hubbert and McLaren boss Ron Dennis decided to concentrate all its efforts on the older car. It was good enough to get past the BMW-Williams and to chase Michael Schumacher right down to the wire.

Conclusions about this change of direction were denied by Mercedes motor sport boss Norbert Haug. *"Should we have concentrated earlier on the MP4-18? It is all hypothetical. What is certain is that we have learnt a great deal from the project."* At least McLaren will not have to waste time on this next year, when it plans to have the MP4-19 ready.

Anno Hecker
38 years old, worked first as a physical education instructor befor turning to journalism in 1986. After working as a political correspondent for a Bonn news agency, he joined "Frankfurter Allgemeine Zeitung" in 1991 to cover motor sports. He specialised in stories combinig politics and sport.

Fortunately, some great performances from Kimi Raikkonen allowed McLaren and Mercedes to come out of this season in reasonable shape. The confidence boost the Finn's skills have given the team might even lead to greater things in 2004. Norbert Haug could not help himself from looking at a few "what ifs" come the end of the season. What if Raikkonen's engine had not blown up when he was comfortably in the lead at the Nurburgring?

And there one has the heart of the problem, which Mercedes had tried to hide. Without Ilmor's development work, Raikkonen would not have done so well. The engine was definitely more powerful than in 2002. But behind the scenes, strife was brewing and the atmosphere was far from the relaxed one which existed in the days when the team was winning. For a long time now, Mario Illien has not felt comfortable in the McLaren-Mercedes family. This has been the case since the spring of 2002 when McLaren accused the engine of being down on power. *"It's typical of Ron to blame others,"* said Mario. In the summer of 2003, the Swiss engine designer felt that Mercedes was distancing itself from him.

There were rumours that he was about to leave and he had not wanted to make the trip to the French Grand Prix. But he turned up on race morning. *"Apparently, I've got to check that everything is working. Those I could rely on are not doing the job,"* said Illien.

Hardly the basis for a fruitful collaboration. Maybe the problems with the new engine for the MP4-18 were behind this tension.

After ten years together, divorce now looks on the cards. Illien wants to continue building F1 engines and Renault made him an offer this summer. Of course, it is not in DaimlerChrysler's interests to let him go and join the opposition. Especially as Illien would certainly not leave on his own, so this particular battle for the 2004 title had started well before the end of 2003.

The FIA is insisting on teams running one engine per race weekend starting in 2004. Some engine builders have been asking for this to be stretched to two engines; one for Friday and another for the last two days. The new BMW engine has already been track tested. *"We are very satisfied, both with its strength and its performance,"* said Theissen. Maybe that is why the competition is trying to have the one engine rule changed? *"I don't think so,"* said Theissen with a smile. As usual, he was staying calm in the face of adversity.

Ferrari wins, Italy loses

That is the paradox of the 2003 season which saw the Maranello team and Michael Schumacher march through the doors of F1 history.

Paolo Ciccarone - Radio Monte Carlo

Paolo Ciccarone, was born in Lucera, in the Italian province of Foggia on 29th May 1958. His Formula 1 career began as a freelance photographer for Autosprint, before he switched to journalism, working for motor sport magazine Rombo. Since April 2000 he has headed up Radio Monte Carlo's racing coverage. He follows the grands prix, digging out all the secrets Formula 1 has to hide. He has also worked for the digital TV station, Tele+. Over the past few seasons, he has written for daily papers like Avvenire and Gazzetta de Mezzogiorno, writing profiles of the heroes of Formula 1.

Ferrari dominates the racing, but the Italian flag flutters in crisis. Despite a first Formula 1 win for Giancarlo Fisichella and the strong showing from Jarno Trulli, nothing has really changed. The Italian motor industry has hit one of the lowest points in its history. Championships are deserted, drivers have an uncertain future, promotional championships have lost their identity and above all there is an acute shortage of money and investment.

These days, a Ferrari victory only warms the heart of the fan sitting at home, comfortably ensconced in an armchair in front of his television, or listening to the radio reports on the Monday after the races. There is certainly no sign of him in the grandstands.

The grands prix at Imola and Monza drew the smallest crowds on record, even with Ferrari fighting for the titles. It is a desperate situation when compared with years when the Scuderia from Maranello won nothing at all, but the grandstands were filled with fans. The high price of tickets can be held to blame, but it is also down to a lack of interest, despite the thrilling events of the 2003 season.

The new rules have made the sport less interesting, with just one qualifying lap in a format which is hard to follow, even for the specialists. Imagine how the casual observer with no real interest in the sport feels about it.

These are the key elements which influence the size of the crowd and the investment in Italian motor sport. As for Ferrari's triumph, it has had little influence on the Italian fans who are basically lazy. They do not watch F3 or touring cars, because they do not know there is a circuit near their home and they don't know the difference between a single seater and a sports car. But settled in front of their TV screens, they know everything about Schumacher, about Todt's strategies and Barrichello's wins.

When Ferrari wins, everything is fine, but when it loses, there is no one more dangerous than an Italian "tifoso." Fiercely critical, insults are hurled at the management – Jean Todt has not forgotten the letters demanding his resignation during the difficult periods in his management of Ferrari, whereas today they would happily erect a monument to him in every town square. The fans complain but it all ends there. They lack the passion they are credited with possessing. A Ferrari win does not attract investors in motor sport. If a company is interested, nothing less than a sticker on a Ferrari will do.

Unfortunately, given the costs of running a Formula 1 programme, very few companies can afford this luxury and most potential sponsors never get past the initial discussion. For those who really want to get involved,

Minardi does not really suit their needs. Sure, the Faenza-based squad is proud to keep going no matter what. It never knows what will happen from one race to the next, if it will be lining up on the grid or how it will do on the technical front, with no works engine and not much in the way of a chassis and no financial security. Nevertheless, the engineers and mechanics never complain and show a level of devotion to the team which deserves better.

Year after year, the "crisis" has become the main concern of not only the team, but also the sport in general. Can you remember the days when Minardi was not at the back of the grid?

Minardi is the "nice" team by definition, but in F1 a smile does not get you very far. Especially

as in Italy, when one talks about F1, the only topic is Ferrari. Therefore, for any investor considering coming into the sport, there is a major obstacle to surmount. Should I spend my budget with Ferrari or should I opt for a more reasonable deal with Minardi? Sometimes, there can only be one answer: it's better to do something else.

Instead of providing a stimulus, Ferrari's wins become an embarrassing comparison with what is the oldest team in the history of the championship.

The importance of the Maranello team stretches out to Faenza with investors dropping by the wayside. Here is an example: Minardi had a contract with Gazprom, the

Soviet gas giant. It is a large company with the vast potential of the Russian market and a development programme for the future. It had barely found the time to put its stickers on the side of the Minardis that McLaren, Williams and Jordan all rushed to Moscow to see if there was any room for negotiation in the deal.

They were all out to steal the deal off Minardi by talking about the prestige and winning record of Williams and McLaren or the image of Jordan. This resulted in Minardi losing its sponsor, while the management of Gazprom got into all sorts of bother.

If there are currently two Italian drivers in F1 it is down to Giancarlo Minardi, who gave Giancarlo Fisichella and Jarno Trulli their first drives. His team did not have any major sponsors, but Mr. Minardi preferred to be in debt in order to give these youngsters a chance to drive in F1.

Then along came Flavio Briatore with his flair, his savoir-faire and his communication skills. Today, Fisichella and Trulli are stars, guaranteed their place in the championship thanks to Briatore's decisions as head of Renault, formerly Benetton. He has become the real saviour of Italy's presence in the sport. It is also thanks to him that the Italian

language is still heard in the paddock and he should be remembered for that more than any dalliance with supermodels Naomi Campbell and Heidi Klum. All this is good for the press, who are thus forced to pay lip service to Formula 1. It is a good example of Briatore's ability to move the sport outside the pages of the specialist press.

We have spoken of Fisichella and Trulli and apart from them there is nothing. Do you know why? Ever since Paul Stoddart took control of Minardi, the chance to drive in F1 has been offered to drivers such as Mark Webber, Justin Wilson and Nicholas Kiesa, while the Italian drivers only get the chance to test, such as Gimmy Bruni who ran on Friday mornings.

Minardi's role as a racing school continues, but not with Italian drivers. So we come back to the original point. Ferrari could have put aside some of the interest and money to create a junior team at Minardi. Then maybe the situation would have been different.

Instead, the Maranello V10 engine went to the Sauber team in Switzerland and before that to Prost in France. When this team went bankrupt, the engines, gearboxes and the bills which Prost had to pay to Ferrari all stayed in Maranello.

The final Italian angle this season was Fisichella's win in Brazil. An Italian had not won a grand prix since the Japanese event in 1992, when Riccardo Patrese was first past the flag in a Williams-Renault.

A win for Fisichella and a front row start for Trulli increased the level of interest from the casual observer, but he would always want to know what happened to Schumacher and Ferrari.

The performance of these two drivers and their fame has created the idea amongst the tifosi that it would be nice to see an Italian driver in a Ferrari. Now, Schumacher is paired with Rubens Barrichello. He is a nice guy, a good driver and his family even has Italian roots.

With Schumacher having taken six world championship titles and the team boasting five consecutive constructors' titles from 1999 to 2003, the fans are happy, even if the Ferrari is driven by a German, with a Frenchman running the team, an Englishman heading up the technical department and a chief engineer who is South African.

The fans would like to be given the chance to cheer on a Ferrari driven by an Italian. Indeed, when Ferrari wins, it is also a victory for Italian prestige in general and the "made in Italy" brand. It would be good to see that philosophy widened to include the drivers.

A dark Thursday

The 11th September 2003 will now and forever be remembered as a black day for Canadian Formula 1 fans.

Stéphanie Morin – La Presse, Montréal

2003 vu du Canada

In the space of 24 hours, everything changed: in London, the FIA unveiled its proposed calendar for 2004, a calendar which did not feature the Canadian Grand Prix, pushed aside because of new anti-tobacco legislation. At the same time in Monza, Jacques Villeneuve told a small group of Canadian journalists that his days in the paddock were numbered. Here is the autopsy of a black Thursday.

Enthusiasts fiddled, tradition swept aside

2003 should have been a year of celebration. It marked the twenty fifth anniversary of the first ever grand prix staged in Montreal at the Ile Notre Dame circuit. In this country with a passion for ice hockey, few sporting events had captured our imagination as much as the grand prix back in October 1978. In freezing cold weather, Gilles Villeneuve took his maiden grand prix victory in front of an ecstatic crowd. It left an indelible impression: the driver from Berthier on the podium, laurel leaves around his neck and in his hand, no champagne, but a huge bottle of beer!

It provokes other memories too, such as Jean Alesi's only F1 win in 1995, Olivier Panis' accident in 1997 (he was a Montreal favourite,) the tragic death of Riccardo Paletti in 1982, the end of the amazing race lost by Nigel Mansell in 1991, when his Williams spluttered to a halt within sight of the flag. Based on a rich tradition, the Canadians were looking forward to another twenty five years of happiness and drama.

The news that the race had been scrubbed therefore hit Montreal like a bomb going off. Fans never thought that the introduction of tobacco laws would signal the death knell of their race. But Bernie Ecclestone's message was clear: no tobacco advertising, no grand prix in Montreal.

The public felt betrayed and swindled. It had stayed loyal to the race even in the bad times, even after the death of Gilles Villeneuve. How to explain that F1 had turned up its nose at the thousands of fans who pack the grandstands year after year? This year the crowds had been there from the start of Friday morning, despite the rain, just to see the four teams testing. At other tracks, Friday's activities take place in a mood of almost total indifference; not in Montreal. By crossing Canada off the list, Bernie Ecclestone proved he cared as much for the fans as he did for an old pair of socks. The calls of protest came in thick and fast. The Canadian and Quebec governments refused to crack under pressure from Ecclestone. Unlike their opposite numbers in Belgium, they decided to stand firm and to apply the law as it stood, without amendment or exemption, even if it meant losing the 80 million Canadian dollars that the race generated in terms of local income. Why so stubborn? For reasons of public health, they said, but also because the law was so complicated that working out an exemption was impossible.

Race promoter, Normand Legault decided to counter-attack. He went to plead Canada's cause, not to Ecclestone, but to the only ones who could change his mind, the major motor manufacturers in the sport. Legault knocked on the door at Toyota, Ford and BMW. His aim was to sell them the idea of an eighteenth race in Montreal, without tobacco advertising.

The move bore fruit. In mid-October, the World Motor Sport Council approved a second calendar with eighteen races this time, a first in the history of the sport. The Canadian Grand Prix was back on the programme, "subject to a satisfactory financial agreement with competing teams." All that was needed now was to reach agreement with all parties concerned and to find the money to compensate the teams...

The downward spiral of a champion

The last shreds of the dream which Jacques Villeneuve could cling to finally gave way during this season which was longer and tougher than a Canadian winter. The man from Quebec was living out his last season with BAR and hoped to set out his stall in the paddock to land another drive worthy of his talent for 2004.

To mark his determination, the 1997 world champion began the season with all guns

Stéphanie Morin quit a career in teaching to switch to journalism five years ago. A journalist with "La Presse" a Montreal daily, she covers several sports, including tennis, hockey and boxing, as well as Formula 1. Aged 31, this is her second year in the paddock.

blazing. Ever since David Richards took hold of the reins at BAR, the two men had been at loggerheads. From the very first day of winter testing in December at Jerez, hostilities resumed and Jenson Button got caught in the crossfire, having just landed from Renault.

Unhappy to see Richards praising the young Brit to the heavens, Villeneuve let fly some poisoned arrows in Button's direction. *"He's been beaten by all his team-mates. Up until now he has not had a very impressive career in F1. I will respect him when he is quicker."*

In mid-January at the Catalunya circuit near Barcelona, the Canadian put his head on the chopping block. *"If I finish the season behind Jenson, I will have to question my ability as a driver."* Villeneuve had just condemned himself to a season of beating Button come what may, but history would not work in his favour.

In Australia, relations between the two drivers took a turn for the worse. Apparently having problems with his radio, Villeneuve pitted one lap too late and the two drivers arrived in the garage at the same time. In the British press, Button accused Villeneuve of having deliberately sabotaged his race. The Canadian replied by saying he was a *"weak driver lacking in intelligence."* And David Richards? He smiled as he watched his drivers tear themselves apart in the media.

After this incident, Villeneuve's season was nothing more than a string of mechanical failures. He was forced to retire eight times before getting to the flag. Sometimes his steering wheel played up, sometimes his Honda engine gave up the ghost. Each time, Villeneuve came up with the same comment: After five years with BAR, I'm getting used to it."

While things were not going well in the cockpit, it was even worse outside the car. It seems that Richards had no intention of extending Villeneuve's contract and Honda was pushing hard to get Japanese driver Takuma Sato into the Canadian's car. Villeneuve tried hard to find a seat elsewhere before being dumped, but to no avail. There was very little movement in the top end of the driver market this year. One of only two world champions currently racing, he found himself knocking on closed doors.

To add further to his humiliation, Richards came up with an idea which really rubbed Villeneuve up the wrong way. He suggested holding a Fame Academy style shoot-out matching Villeneuve against a group of younger drivers, to see who would partner Button in 2004. This moment illustrated exactly what the BAR boss felt for his driver.

After the mechanical failures, the quarrels and the political games, the Canadian's season ended in dramatic fashion. He decided to pull out of the Japanese Grand Prix, the final race of the season, his last with BAR and quite possibly the last of his career. The news was put out in a press release from Villeneuve's manager Craig Pollock, indicating that the Canadian no longer had the motivation to race.

In Canada it was all consternation as Villeneuve had taken his final curtain call like a thief in the night and without any explanation. Later, we learnt that the team had demanded the driver remained silent to be allowed to get out of his contract. No matter; between Villeneuve and his supporters something had been broken for ever.

«The Show must go on...»

We are living through uncertain times. Take the case of Ferrari and Michael Schumacher. Before the start of the season everyone believed in their total superiority. And, although they did indeed become world champions yet again this year, we saw that they are not eternally invincible. That also applies to the tyre supplier Bridgestone. Michelin is now capable of winning everywhere and the Japanese company no longer has the undisputed upper hand. Another case in point is the Honda F1 situation.

Kunio Shibata – GP Xpress, Tokyo

2003 wo hurikaeru

For the Japanese, this name was synonymous with success, originality and incomparable dynamism. Sadly, that is no longer the case. A few years ago, who could have imagined that the Japanese giant would suffer so much? Compared to Toyota which has just finished its second season in F1 and is making gradual progress, Honda is treading water, rudderless and without any obvious planned structure.

Sato replaces Villeneuve. But at what cost?

Just before the final race of the season in Japan, BAR Honda officially announced that Takuma Sato would be Jenson Button's team mate next year. Villeneuve would no longer be part of the team he had created with his friend Craig Pollock five years earlier. It was (almost) as planned. Jacques had been in the bad books for a while and David Richards openly admitted that Jacques was costing too much for what he was delivering.

But the real surprise came on the eve of the grand prix. According to the team press release, Pollock called Richards to tell him: *"Jacques is not up to driving and I am asking you to release*

him from his obligations to drive in the Japanese GP." So the third driver, Takuma Sato, was brought in to fill the breach.

Being Japanese, I should be delighted that such an incredible opportunity was given to a future Japanese star and that he totally lived up to or

Kunio Shibata
45 years old, he left Japan, giving up his jov in journalism in 1982 to move to Paris and study Politocal Science. He became a freelance producer for Japanese television and havinf always been interested in motor racing, he began covering the Grand Prix for a press agency in 1987 when Satoru Nakajima arrived on the scene. He has written for the specialist Japanese magazine «Grand Prix Xpress» since 1991.

exceeded expectations. Even though this was his first race of the year and despite being under great psychological pressure as the team was fighting for fifth place in the championship, Takuma delivered the perfect result, finishing sixth. But there are still some unanswered questions as to how he landed the drive.

First off, did the Canadian really decide not to drive? He had arrived in Japan on the Monday before the race and answering questions from journalists at the airport, he clearly replied that he had come to race. Jacques spent the next day in Tokyo with his former team-mate Olivier Panis. *"Jacques' retirement really surprised me,"* said the Frenchman. *"When he was with me, he seemed to be perfectly normal. He was talking about Suzuka and his motivation seemed to be all in place."*

Only two days later, Pollock asked for Villeneuve to be excused from the race. What had happened in the interim? Jacques left Japan on Saturday, the day of qualifying. Was he waiting to make sure there was absolutely no chance he would be driving? No one knows the truth. But what is almost certain is that the former world champion would not have a drive next year and he had left without saying farewell to his fans.

It is very frustrating for those who witnessed Villeneuve's first two seasons in F1 and experienced his open nature and outspoken opinions. But that page has now turned for good.

Toyota and Honda: the tortoise and the hare

As I have already mentioned, Honda endured yet another difficult year. However, the season appeared to get off to a good start. Designed by Geoff Willis, former Williams aerodynamicist, the new BAR-Honda 005 seemed to be a good car straight from the crate. And never before had

Villeneuve done so much winter testing, which meant the team's number 1 driver had high hopes for the car's potential. But neither Jacques nor Jenson managed to pull off something special during the course of the year. Two fourth places was the best result for the British driver. As for the Canadian, he only finished in the points twice, both times in sixth place. He described this year as *"the worst season of my career."*

There was plenty of bad luck, but also far too many mechanical bothers and human error. More than that, the development of the car did not progress very much. Sato who was tasked with this job bears witness to that fact: *"Even if we find something that works in testing, for example a new aero part, we had to wait at least two months before it was ready to race. Of course, you have to check its reliability, but the team sometimes insists on doing 600 kilometres before signing it off. I think this approach is too cautious. We are not yet in a position to fight for the title. We have nothing to lose, so why be so careful?"*

The relationship between Honda and BAR appears to get closer. It is both financial and technical. Apart from supplying engines, Honda also designed the suspension and gearbox for next year's car. Honda has also become one of the main sponsors of the team and is gradually getting more involved in its management.

But relationships are somewhat frosty, not only between BAR and Honda but also between the management and the race engineers. At Suzuka, Michelin announced that the Anglo-Japanese team had requested a switch from Bridgestone. Not all the engineers were aware of this and were somewhat stupefied by the news. *"We have done an enormous amount of testing with Bridgestone and in the end it seems like it was all for nothing, as the data we have acquired with them will be no use whatsoever with the Michelin tyres. We will have to start all over again for next year."*

"I don't really understand," said another engineer. *"We are currently the number 2 team at Bridgestone after Ferrari. With Michelin, there is already Williams, McLaren and Renault, so we will just be making up the numbers."*

Compared with the situation at BAR-Honda, the Toyota strategy is much clearer. They do not have the luxury of a star driver like Villeneuve, but are concentrating on building up their technical structure. The Cologne-based Japanese team announced after Suzuka that they have finally secured the services of former Renault technical director, Mike Gascoyne. Only eighth in the championship, Toyota's second season has not exactly been convincing. Nor have they made giant strides forward. They progress slowly but surely and at least they know what they are missing. Gascoyne's appointment will definitely not be a quick fix, as the development of next year's car already began a long time ago and he will settle for adding a few touches to it. But the English engineer is not only a great designer, he is also a very good man manager. It should be worth keeping an eye on the Japanese giant as, for the moment, it is still half asleep.

Bridgestone – Michelin: total war

"It is very difficult, in fact almost impossible to measure the exact performance of a tyre." This is a favourite refrain from Pierre Dupasquier of Michelin Motorsport. *"But when the car is quick, it means the tyres are good, as it is the total package – chassis, engine, tyres, driver – which makes the difference."*

This year, Pierre had many more chances to proudly trot out his favourite phrase. The French manufacturer finally failed to pick up either of the two championships, but the Michelin-shod cars were quick enough whatever the circuit characteristics. So the Michelin tyres were good.

Better than the Bridgestones? Sometimes yes. Especially in the middle of the season, from Monaco to Hungary, when Michelin's superiority was obvious. One should not forget the return to form of BMW-Williams at the same time. On top of that, apart from Ferrari, the Bridgestone runners were often grouped together towards the back of the grid. And sometimes even the Prancing Horse was struggling to get to the front.

It took until the Italian Grand Prix for the Ferrari-Bridgestone tandem to strike back. The previous week, at Monza again, they did four days of testing. And it was only on the last day that they were able to make a tyre choice for this grand prix. Yasuhide Hamashima, Bridgestone's director of development, immediately called the factory in Kodaira-city in Japan to have the tyres made. No less than 2000 tyres were sent from the land of the rising sun to Italy. Michelin did not sit on its laurels. Just after the Hungarian GP, the FIA revealed that the width of the contact patch on its tyres did not conform to the regulations. The manufacturer contested the allegation, but finally it decided to modify its moulds and managed to bring brand new tyres to Monza. It was total war in both camps. Ferrari won the last three races of the season. But to say that this demonstrated the superiority of the Japanese manufacturer would be a bit simplistic. Hamashima-san endlessly repeated that, "ever since we started in the European F2 series in 1981, Michelin has been our main and strongest rival. And that is still the case today. There is no way we feel we have definitively beaten them." The battle will continue unabated.

Three days with Pierre Dupasquier: 72 Hours of pure passion

Having the privilege of following Michelin's Director of Competition during a racing weekend means being able to measure the strength of Michelin's commitment to competition and discover the passion that drives Pierre Dupasquier. In addition, it involves keeping a constant watch the seconds as they tick away on the stopwatch...

> Years of motor sport have not dimmed Pierre Dupasquier's enthusiasm.

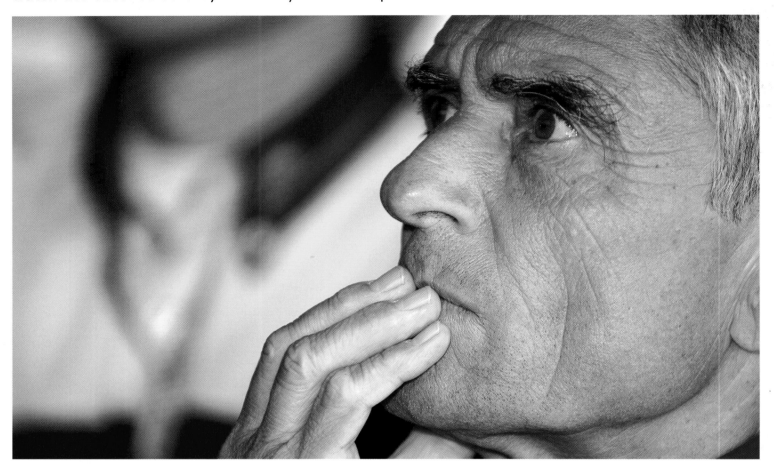

It also means preparing to live through some fairly testing moments. It started for us with a call from his assistant, Christine Chambon, after we had reserved our flight tickets and carefully organised our itinerary to match Pierre Dupasquier's proposed schedule. *"Pierre has been looking at the map and thinks it would be more interesting to travel from Assen to the Nürburgring by road rather than by air".* Back to square one! Just 24 hours before departure, we cancel our flight reservations and book a larger hire car to travel from the Dutch motorcycle Grand Prix to the European Formula 1 Grand Prix – just an ordinary working weekend for the man who has been in charge of the Competition Department for donkey's years. We arranged a new rendezvous for Thursday evening at Amsterdam airport and a smiling Pierre arrived, carrying only light luggage. We were ready to start our adventure.

> Trackside at Assen. Nothing can match the roar of a good four-stroke engine.

Heading for that 300th victory...

The programme starts with a drive of 185 km to Assen. The Dutch TT is one of the finest Grand prix events of the season. The course has a great reputation, the event always attracts huge crowds and the weather is often terrible. Pierre admits that he hasn't been to the event for quite some time *"It's the right time to go. Our competitors are trying to put on the pressure at the moment"* says Pierre with a hint of irritation. And the possibility of Michelin's 300th victory in the top category since 1973? *"It's just a way of putting our competitors in their place. An undeniable way of reminding them of Michelin's desire to be present in Grand Prix racing"*, he adds with a slight frown. *"Our everyday preoccupation is to prove to the teams that only Michelin is capable of offering such high quality service. In fact, some drivers and riders even stipulate in their contracts that they must drive on Michelin tyres!"*

With secrets of the paddock, racing anecdotes and tales of the exploits of his hockey-playing son, the miles simply fly by with Pierre Dupasquier. In the evening, we arrive at the hotel, where Pierre finds Nicolas Goubert – head of motorcycle activity – and part of the team, dining on the terrace. The end of their dinner turns into a relaxed debriefing. With mischievous pleasure, Pierre recalls an article where Nicolas Goubert was rather disparaging about the performance of one of the manufacturers present in the top category. An impromptu meeting with three students from the Michelin School brings this informal evening to an end. We arrange to set off at 8 a.m. the following morning.

Life in yellow and blue

Friday, 9 a.m.: crowds of motorcyclists are heading for the racetrack. In the truck fitted out as an office, Pierre is finishing a 45-minute meeting with Andy Pope, head of Competition Communication. He pours himself a small coffee before starting a new meeting with Nicolas Goubert, who is just finishing a phone conversation in Japanese. The meeting is to examine the difficulties that might arise in the plants manufacturing tyres for competition. Outside, the team of tyre-fitters is working busily around the balancing machines. Some new members are learning the art of fitting big slick tyres onto ultra-wide rims...

It's exactly 10 a.m., the practice session is starting and the roar of the revving four-stroke engines fills the air. *"We'll have to go and see what they're up to"* decides Pierre. And we set off towards the box. Pierre spots the Yamaha Tech 3 pits and walks through the door in a decisive manner. Firm handshakes, friendly smiles and words of welcome show how much the man in the yellow and blue shirt commands respect... The man, but also the firm he has represented for more than forty years now. After a brief exchange with the Michelin technician and a quick glance at the screens, we head off to the neighbouring pits for a repeat performance. *"The tyre temperature is high"*, worries Pierre. *"It's a question of traction control. Here, the tyres are constantly sliding. Without skidding, there wouldn't be any tyre wear!"*
As we make our way towards the Honda Repsol pits, where Valentino Rossi is getting ready, our journey is interrupted by a long discussion with Alan Jenkins (or Jenkinson. To be checked. Ducati Corse) and a good joke with Carlo Pernat (Loris Capirossi's manager). It's 10.20 a.m., the lap times are coming in fast and, with his chin propped in his hand, Pierre analyses the progress of the RC211V. *"What Ducatti are achieving is fantastic. Their team is remarkably homogeneous and perhaps that's why they are establishing themselves as a real threat to Honda. The machines are getting more and more powerful. 300 horsepower will soon be a reality"*, declares Pierre. Valentino Rossi has just taken to the track. Television monitors show the current World Champion's front wheel. Wheelies, sharp braking and crazy angles... At the end of the lap, he registers the fastest time – a lead of six tenths of a second... At the end of the session, Pierre shares a joke with Gary Taylor (Suzuki) and, before leaving the Suzuki pits, has a quick look at the tyre temperature readings. Our marathon continues and, as we make our way back to the Michelin

workshop, Pierre suddenly stops in front of the Ducati 999, which decorates the entrance to the red team's hospitality suite. *"I really like the design of this part of the chassis where the rear cylinder appears"*, confides the keen motorcycle enthusiast who is also the head of competition. For nearly ten minutes, the Grand Prix is forgotten as we talk about the potential of the Italian diva and its ability to transform an experienced motorcyclist into an exceptional rider. Completely captivated, Pierre takes out his portable phone...and takes a picture of the 999! A fan of the Italian bike, Pierre Dupasquier also has a passionate interest in new technology. Will the *"old 916"* be replaced by the latest creation of the Bologna factories before Christmas? While we are waiting for the answer to that, we make our way back to the Michelin trucks for the meeting that traditionally takes place after every practice session. The technicians talk about the products *"driven on"* by *"their"* riders, without giving away any of the team's secrets. *"Super power take-up, great grip but it wobbles a bit"*. Michelin is preparing for the race. At the end of the meeting, Pierre tells us that they were a little worried about the tyre operating temperature but, by tomorrow, the ambient temperature should be lower. The fitters continue their delicate and crucial job.

A race against time

12.30 p.m. Pierre Dupasquier and Nicolas Goubert are eating local sandwiches on a corner of table, surrounded by Dutch motorcyclists. *"We've got an important meeting with the Yamaha Racing staff at one o'clock"*, whispers Pierre. Thirty minutes of quiet conversation to prepare the future and then we head off to look for the Eurosport France cabin for an unscheduled interview. Pierre Dupasquier is very much in demand. On the way, the mobile phone rings... *"We've got some problems at the Nürburgring. We've got bubbling"*. The boss makes a little grimace. *"I'm more often present for Formula 1 Grand Prix because there's a real battle going on. It calls for really fine analytical judgement"*.
In Eurosport's tiny cabin, Pierre forgets about his Formula 1 worries and gives lively answers to questions from Philippe Monneret and Rémy Tissier. He talks about *"the pleasure of riders, winding through the bends, Honda's sudden leap forward with their development of the RC211V, and the enormous job accomplished by Valentino Rossi – we really love him"*. Pierre unhitches himself from his headset and leaves the journalists to finish their live report. The marathon continues and Pierre Dupasquier sets off for another tour of the pits for the final session of time trials. For the

last five minutes, all the riders are out on the track and, in a final effort, Loris Capirossi manages to snatch pole position. *"Capi"*, Biaggi and Rossi are the only riders to break the two-minute barrier. Half an hour after the session and changed back into his *"civilian"* clothes again, Pierre says his goodbyes to the Michelin staff and we leave Assen to drive to the Nürburgring, on motorways that don't have a speed limit.

Competition according to Michelin

Pierre Dupasquier unfolds the map and plays the role of navigator. It's a family trait. Yves Dupasquier – his eldest son – has a long history as a sailor. Sailboat designer or yacht delivery skipper, he has already dragged Pierre into maritime adventures that had little to do with pleasure sailing. With his habitual verve, Pierre tells us about his *"fortunes at sea"*, while the motorway unwinds at a reasonable speed. The rush of the wind allows him to make a link between human relationships on board a yacht in the middle of the ocean and Michelin's principles on the racetrack.

"Service and high technology products are the tools we have to provide ourselves with in order to reach a simple objective – being perceived by the people we work with as the best in the world", is Pierre's sober analysis. *"Faultless service and particularly close attention to the people who use our tyres mean that we not only answer their questions, but also that we listen*

^
At lunchtime, there is no time to lose, so a quick sandwich is the order of the day.

^ <
Pierre Dupasquier still has a passion for motorbike racing.

<
Pierre and "his" bike tyres.

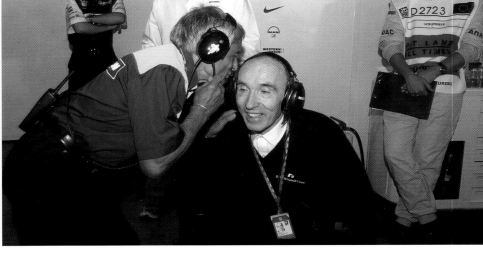

to what they have to say. This is vital in establishing a privileged relationship and it also allows us to find out what the tyre did and why it did it," continues Pierre. "These are our secrets, but they're not really secrets. It's a behaviour pattern to be followed at all times. This calls for total commitment from the people involved. You can never lower your guard because you might miss an element that allows you to understand a situation. It's a culture of competition that is perfectly in phase with our corporate culture. When all you have to do is make a better tyre than your competitors, it isn't really complicated", he concludes with the mischievous smile of a man who thrives on challenges.

For a long time now, the constructors and, above all the drivers, have perceived the strength of this philosophy, which stands out from the rest. "In Formula One, it was

our partners who came looking for us", recalls Pierre proudly "Toyota, with whom Michelin was already working in Rally and Endurance, called us in to tell us that they were in the final stages of a Formula 1 project and that they wanted us to work along side them ... And at that time, Michelin didn't really represent anything in F1. It was the same with BMW, at a time when Michelin was thinking of slackening off in Endurance" continues Pierre. "The people at BMW let us know that they didn't agree with our decision. They went on to tell us about their F1 agreement with Williams, saying that they wanted us with them." And in the recent past, the facts tend to confirm Professor Dupasquier's demonstration: Ford (Jaguar), Mercedes, Porsche and Renault have all embarked upon sizeable challenges... with Michelin working with them "Our partnerships stand the test of time because our agreements are based on long-term, technical collaboration and not on a marketing contract", concludes Pierre Dupasquier, with a final flourish.

Stepping into another world

With the relaxed atmosphere of Motorcycle Grand Prix racing behind us, the demands of the world of F1 begin to make themselves felt. Pierre is desperately trying to call Pascal Vasselon, head of F1 activity. He can't get through, but he'll get a roundup on events from José Nunez, one of the F1 team co-ordinators. The practice session was seriously disrupted by one of those downpours which are a feature of the Eifel hills. And what about the Ferraris? Did they start off with a lot of fuel on board?
As we negotiate another bend, the phone rings again. A muffled conversation ensues. "Thanks a lot for calling. Goodbye, Frank. It's Frank Williams. He's just signed a new, five-year contract with BMW", announces Pierre

in an exclusive scoop. We cover the last few miles in the rain, driving through pine forests. At around 7 p.m., we drop Pierre off outside the Dorint, the hotel favoured by many drivers and racing team personnel. As he slips on his FIA pass, his eyes creased with a smile, he tells us, "I hope I'll be able to find a nice little restaurant this evening ..."
Saturday morning. The Michelin team left the hotel at 6 a.m. to avoid traffic jams. It's a long working day in this business. Around 9 a.m., Pierre gives his first interview of the day in the Michelin Hospitality Suite. "It's a constant flow", says Pierre with a slightly rueful air. Journalists from the press, radio and television appreciate the Director of Competition for his availability and articulate communication. Furthermore, Michelin is gradually growing stronger. Alonso, Montoya, Räikkönen and Schumacher (Ralf) are starting to pose a growing threat to the talented driver at the wheel of the Ferrari. Nothing can be taken for granted and the men in yellow and blue know it – that's what gives them their quiet strength. "F1 is an extremely complex sport and the only way to make the tyres work

However, there's torrential rain at Assen and the start has to be postponed to give time to change the tyres on the starting grid. In the Michelin Hospitality suite, Pierre keeps a close eye on the television coverage of the event, worrying about *"his"* riders. Sete Gibernau and Max Biaggi surge into the lead, leaving the others behind. Under a menacing sky, Valentino Rossi manages third place. It's as fine as a motorcycle race can be. In the final lap, Sete Gibernau and his Honda score Michelin's 300th victory in the star category. Michelin's F1 press attaché, Séverine Ray, has waited for the end of the race to finish her press release. Pierre reads it carefully, changing a few words. *"Séverine manages to get the tone just right"*, comments Pierre. *"That's very important in this microcosm, where every word is subject to different interpretations".*

A few minutes later, Olivier Panis wanders in to eat a crêpe. It's a habit for the Panasonic Toyota Racing driver. Chocolate spread or maple syrup? No matter, Olivier has turned in a superb performance and the strict dietary restrictions of a Formula 1 driver are allowed to slip.

Everything is calm once again and the guests wander about the paddock amidst the *"tyremen"* and their trolleys. Our mission will be over in a few minutes. We'll have to leave Pierre after 72 hours sharing the daily life of the Michelin teams. One thing is very clear: both MotoGP and F1 are always flat out. There isn't a single moment of respite in Pierre Dupasquier's schedule, and it's the same for his team leaders, technicians and fitters. *"There's nothing extraordinary about that"*, smiles Pierre. *"We've got to get our tyres to work as well as possible and we've got tons of problems to solve. On top of that, we have to meet the press, discuss with our partners and keep an eye on everyone's performance ... ".* It doesn't seem all that complicated, but you have to be able to keep up the pace 365 days a year in a dozen disciplines as different as Formula One or MotoGP... And it has been like that for more than thirty years! On Sunday, we'll watch the first BMW WilliamsF1 Team double victory on TV. And we've got a date in a week's time, for the next Grand Prix.

An overloaded week-end

On Saturday June 28, Assen was the scene of the Dutch Motorcycle Grand Prix, while the F1 European Grand Prix took place at the Nürburgring the next day. This type of cohabitation is fairly normal when – like Michelin – you are involved in Formula One, Rally, Endurance, ALMS, Grand Prix Moto and Superbike, not forgetting Trial, Motocross, Enduro, etc.

This year, the busiest time for the Michelin logistics team was the weekend of June 14 & 15. The programme included the Le Mans 24-hour race, the Canadian Grand Prix in F1, the Catalonian Motorcycle Grand Prix, the Superbike event at Silverstone and, finally, the Cyprus Rally. (In fact, the Cyprus rally was the following week, but the men and equipment were already on the road). Altogether, this represented an army of 140 people and 15,000 tyres!

is to develop aerodynamic support. The people with cars working well have understood this; they've all hired aerodynamics specialists", jokes Pierre.

From the very start of this morning's session, Pierre makes his round of the pits. As in Assen, he takes a keen interest in the Michelin technicians' readings, the monitors showing partial lap times and the wear on the grooved tyres. Yet the atmosphere is hardly the same –there's more pressure, more restrictions and more VIP's. Pierre has the authority to enter the restricted access zones of the pits of partner racing teams (BMW WilliamsF1Team, Jaguar Racing, Renault F1 Team, Panasonic Toyota Racing et Team McLaren Mercedes). He observes, discusses and mulls things over – he even manages to make Frank Williams smile. The end of the session is the signal for a debriefing conference in the Michelin camp. As he trots through the paddock, Pierre bumps into Bernie Ecclestone, in the company of Paul Stoddart. The warm handshakes and cheerful conversation between the boss of F1 and Michelin's head of competition bring a flurry of activity to the paddock. In an instant, a crowd of photographers appears to immortalise the event and nourish the press. Pierre continues on his way, with the gleeful grin of kid who has just pulled something off. *"I've been friends with Bernie for 30 tears. Our friendships dates back to when Gordon Murray arrived in the Brabham pits with a briefcase*

that contained a Beatles cassette and some mint sweets. He used to wear pink sandals, which drove Bernie furious. And Bernie doesn't give people appointments. The only way to have a chat with him is to bump into him in the paddock".

The debriefing is positive, with the Michelin solutions seeming to give satisfaction and the afternoon's qualifying session looking set to go well. For Pierre, it's time for lunch, accompanied by a journalist. Passion, competition and responsibilities all whirl together in a tumultuous maelstrom... Fortunately, Pierre finds a way to get away from it all. But not before giving a television interview in front of the Bibendum at the Michelin Hospitality suite.

The result of a good job well done

2.50 p.m. In the Michelin workshop everything has calmed down and the fitters are watching the qualifying session on TV. As usual, Michael Schumacher is very fast, but Kimi Räikkönen (Team McLaren Mercedes) manages a perfect lap, making up lost time in the last part of the lap.

The young driver's pole position – at only 23 – is welcomed with whoops of joy in the Michelin tent. As in Assen the pole position goes to a Michelin partner – a good omen for the race.

Pierre Dupasquier: A fab-u-lous season

With seven wins this year, Michelin reaped a rich and abundant harvest in the 2003 Formula 1 season. Furthermore, the French rubber was unanimously regarded as the best.

-Pierre Dupasquier, how would you describe this championship?

Pierre Dupasquier: If one considers that when a car produces a great performance, it's because its tyres can do it – a simple principle which has been applied for many years – we can regard the season just gone as a vintage one for Michelin. What happened in 2003? The excellent Ferrari F2002 was running out of steam at the start of the season and had a hard time coping with the previous year's McLaren-Mercedes, the MP4-17. The tyre factor certainly played a part in this. Then, the team decided to concentrate on the MP4-18, slightly backing off the development of the car which was being raced. Immediately, the performance level showed signs of stagnation. At the same point of the season, BMW-Williams found the weak point on its FW25 and began to win on a regular basis.

- What role did Michelin play in this exceptional performance?

Pierre Dupasquier: It would not be insulting to our partners to say that their cars were not intrinsically dominant when up against the Ferraris. So a little boost had to be found from somewhere. Seeing a Renault win a grand prix and lap Mister Michael Schumacher in Hungary for a example, was cause for great satisfaction.

- Michelin won none of the last three grands prix. Is that connected to the clarification to the rules introduced by the FIA prior to Monza?

Pierre Dupasquier: Absolutely not. After Budapest, Ferrari and its partners realised that it could lose the title on the track and decided to use all the means at their disposal to bias the championship in their favour. We reacted by making very minor changes to our moulds...and found a performance gain! In Monza, Juan Pablo Montoya could have won the race, if he had made a better start. In Indianapolis we had the upper hand except on a damp to drying track. Finally, in Suzuka, Montoya was leading the race, four seconds ahead of Rubens Barrichello after just three laps. Unfortunately, he retired.

-In what areas do you still need to make progress?

Pierre Dupasquier: There is room for improvement in terms of the consistency of our tyres. Nevertheless, we know we are on the right track and we will be much better on this front next season.

-What are your aims for 2004?

Pierre Dupasquier: We are currently developing a range of tyres based on the same family of tyres which we used towards the end of the 2003 season. Thanks to new compounds, we have made a lot of progress, specifically eradicating some graining problems, while making performance gains. We are very confident and are impatient to see the cars that our partners will start testing this winter. Next year's championship has already begun.

SHARE THE SPIRIT

| BMW WILLIAMSF1 TEAM | TEAM McLAREN MERCEDES | RENAULT F1 TEAM | JAGUAR RACING | PANASONIC TOYOTA RACING |

Formula 1: a huge economic impact

The FIA presents a study which is the first systematic effort to quantify the economic importance of the Formula One races as a European Union-wide economic phenomenon. It shows that F1 is a sport without economic rivals.

This study is an analysis-first of its kind-of the local economic impact of a major professional sport – the Grands Prix Formula One races held in the European Union.

Virtually every conceivable facet of the economics of the sport was quantified–how many spectators, how many nonlocal spectators, how many days they stayed in the host locality, how much money they spent and on what, how many businesses benefited and which type of business, how many jobs were supported and in what businesses they were employed, where the affected businesses are located in the host community and what are the sizes of the local area benefiting from the race.

The findings in this regard are dramatic:
• More than two million spectators attended just eleven events;
• Almost $500 million was spent by spectators;
• Spending in 127,339 local businesses with 738,354 employees spread over 81,835 square kilometers.

It is the authors' view, based on the results of this study, that the European Union Grands Prix are probably unrivaled in the sporting world for creating economic benefits at the local level. The authors reached this conclusion after comparing the Grand Prix races in Europe to the economics of the premier American football, baseball, basketball and hockey team events. The authors also contrasted the local economic impact of European Grand Prix events with

> Bernie Ecclestone, F1's commercial rights holder. Here with the FIA's photographers' representative, Patrick Behar.

their closest motorsport rivals in America-the IndyCar and NASCAR racing events.

Unlike the major American team sport events, IndyCar and NASCAR events do create substantial local wealth for their host communities. But the difference between them and European Grand Prix events is one of kind, not degree. For example,

Formula One events generate on average much more than twice as much local wealth per event as do IndyCar events.

The book shows that Grand Prix-Formula One events are unusual amongst major professional sporting events in that so very great a percentage of the event spectators are nonlocals.

1997 European Union Grand Prix: Economic Impact Statistics

RACE	RACE WEEK ATTENDANCE	SUNDAY ATTENDANCE	NON-LOCAL ATTENDANCE	SPENDING (US DOLLARS)	NON-LOCAL SPENDING	BUSINESS	JOBS	TEMPORARY JOBS	AREA (SQ KMS)
Austria	234,500	110,000	96.5%	$36,988,250	98%	1,464	9,513	1,450	15,589
Belgium	203,000	81,000	93.0%	$33,225,000	93%	1,626	5,626	2,500	1,158
UK	182,000	90,000	80.0%	$50,151,000	90%	5,420	44,690	3,000	5,231
Europe	276,500	115,000	83.0%	$66,344,300	90%	3,037	14,887	800	8,289
France	184,500	75,000	92.0%	$53,660,800	98%	8,881	37,267	8,000	25,255
Germany	258,500	91,000	70.0%	$47,702,100	70%	3,632	17,271	–	4,531
Italy	188,000	90,000	65.0%	$43,860,800	70%	43,527	251,222	2,000	9,228
Monaco	222,432	66,505	60.0%	$71,493,200	80%	6,364	26,568	800	1,889
Portugal	55,600	37,300	50.0%	$10,704,000	60%	8,186	47,104	1,300	550
San Marino	176,975	81,353	78.0%	$42,195,200	85%	15,124	142,000	1,250	6,973
Spain (1998)	134,700	65,000	50.0%	$33,571,200	60%	30,078	142,207	–	3,142
TOTALS:	2,116,707	902,158	77.0%	$489,895,850	83%	127,339	738,354	21,100	81,835

Thus the money they spend in the local economy is "new money" or "outside money" coming into the local economy. This is economically important because these Formula One events stimulate spending in the local economy that would not occur without the presence of the Formula One event.

Equally important, the book shows that the nature of the non-local spectator at a Formula One event is critically different from other spectators at other professional sporting events in that the Formula One, non-local, spectator typically comes for more than one day. Thus the non-local spectator spends much of his money outside the racing facility and in the host community's retail outlets for lodging, food, beverages, apparel, transportation, etc.

This multi-day characteristic of the Formula One spectator is essential because it channels spectator expenditures into the local community's retail businesses and thereby contributes to the economic support of as much as 25 percent of the local area workforce that typically is employed in the local retail workforce.

The importance of the non-local, multi-day characteristics of the Formula One spectator cannot be overstated in terms of their impact on the local host economy.

The authors have done several studies of "repeat races with repeat sponsors"-the same race occurring in successive years at the same place, at approximately the same time and with the same sponsor. We have found that a "repeat" Grand Prix will increase total, non-local spending by nine percent or more. This appreciably large increase is due mainly to the greater numbers of non-local spectators who come for more than one day.

Total per day spending amounts were divided among the relevant three blocks of spectators:

- the largest spectator block: spectators who attend the races; eat, drink and shop in the area; and who stay overnight in local area hotels and motels;
- the second largest spectator block: spectators who attend the races; eat, drink and shop in the area; and who stay overnight with friends or in camp sites;
- the third largest spectator block: spectators who attend the races; eat and drink at the race facility; but return home or to lodging outside the local market area for the night.

The average spectator spends about $229 per day on tickets, parking, petrol, lodging, food, drink, entertainment, transportation and tourist retail.

The table below lists the ten types of local businesses typically most impacted by race spectator spending. These businesses are in addition to the racetrack facilities themselves.

Restaurants/Bars, Photo Shops, Lodging, Gift Shops, News Agents, Nightclubs/Discos, Transportation/Petrol, Booking/Travel, Drug Store, Local Retail Specialties.

Only Direct Spending Counted: This analysis does not quantify the indirect effects of the new but unknown millions of dollars pumped into the local economies because of the races. It is inevitable that the first round of "new" spending stimulates second, third and fourth rounds of spending.

In Conclusion: In looking at the Grand Prix phenomena across the European Union, two important conclusions bearing on economic impact are obvious. First, the local economic impacts are very large and very positive, probably unrivaled by any other professional sport. Second, the Grand Prix phenomena creates so much local wealth and in so many varied forms that virtually each of the eleven local host communities is a leading beneficiary of one or more revenue streams.

<
Max Mosley, FIA's President.

FIA representatives at Imola: Richard Woods (left) and Agnès Kaiser (right).
v

Ascari's nine in a row (1952-1953)

by Jacques Vassal
«Automobile historique»

Michael Schumacher ended the 2003 season having reached a grand total of seventy grand prix wins from 194 starts. It will be a difficult record to get close to, let alone beat. But did you know that a Ferrari driver once racked up 13 wins from 32 starts, including a run of nine victories in a row? He was called Alberto Ascari, a champion who was adored by the Italians and respected by all. He was twice crowned world champion and it all took place back in the Fifties.

Alberto Ascari was born on 13th July 1918 in Milan, the son of a great pre-war champion, Antonio Ascari. He had driven for the factory Alfa Romeo team, driving the "P2" in 1924 and '25, alongside Giuseppe Campari and Enzo Ferrari. Sadly, on 26th July 1925, while leading the French Grand Prix, Antonio Ascari was killed at Montlhery. At the age of seven, Alberto was an orphan. In Milan, he discovered motorbikes when he reached adolescence. He bought a Sertum, twin cylinder 500 cc machine and despite the protestations of his mother, began competing. In 1937, riding for the Scuderia Ambrosiana team, set up by a group of Milanese racers, which included Luigi Villoresi. He was spotted by the bosses of Bianchi and became their works rider in 1938 and '39, winning a few Italian championship rounds. He made his debut on four wheels in 1940, in

Antonio Ascari at the wheel of the Alfa Romeo P2, pushed by his mechanics before the start of the ACF and European Grand Prix at Lyon on 3rd August 1924.

>
∨

Jacques Vassal,
Journalist, writer and translator, as well as being an expert in singing and popular music, Jacques Vassal has worked for "Auto Passion" magazine for over eleven years. Since 2000, he has worked as a freelance for various specialist magazines, especially the monthly magazine "Automobile Historique", writing tests, portraits, interviews, retrospectives and articles on cars and motor sport of today and yesteryear. Along with Pierre Menard, he is also the co-author of "Legendes de la Formule 1", a new Chronosports publication.

Tripoli and in the Targa Florio, at the wheel of a single seater Maserati. He also drove a Sport 815 barchetta in the Mille Miglia, the car built in Modena in the Enzo Ferrari workshop.

The war put an end to all that. Alberto got by as best he could, running a petrol company supplying Africa, along with Villoresi. There were times when he had to hide to avoid demands from the German army. He found the time to get married in 1942 and to have a son and

then, in 1946 a daughter. That year, racing got underway again in Italy and France. Ascari was running a garage in Milan and at first he accompanied his friend Villoresi, who raced a Maserati 4CL, with a turbocharged 1500 cc engine. One day, during testing in Naples, he borrowed his friend's car, immediately setting lap times which impressed onlookers. From 1947, he was back in the saddle, driving a Scuderia Ambrosiana Maserati 4CL, then the 4CLT, which was the Trident marque's latest Formula 1 car. In 1948, they helped him to his first victories, in San Remo and then Turin for the Italian Grand Prix.

In the spring of 1949, Ascari signed his first works contract with Ferrari, partnered by Villoresi. In the 125 C (1500 cc supercharged V12) he won the Swiss GP in Berne and the Italian one in Monza. For the press and the tifosi, he was no longer just the son of his father, he now embodied all that was best about Italian motor sport. The World Championship was launched in 1950 and Ascari was to be one of its first stars. The Alfetta 158 cars won all the grands prix, but Ascari finished second in Monaco with an ageing Ferrari 125 C. In Belgium he brought along a 3.3 litre normally aspirated 275 F1. In Monza, Ferrari unveiled its latest World Championship weapon, the 4.5 litre normally aspirated 375 F1. That year, Ascari took on the mantle of the eternal challenger, up against a regal Fangio and the ever more powerful Alfetta, now putting out 425 horsepower! Argentina's Froilan

Gonzalez won the British GP, giving Ferrari its first ever World Championship victory, convincingly beating the Alfettas. But Ascari took the next two rounds, in Germany and Italy. The end of the season came in Spain, where he was robbed of almost certain victory by a bad choice of tyre from Ferrari. Fangio was world champion, with Ascari as runner-up.

The unbeaten run of nine

In 1952, Alfa Romeo had pulled out, Talbot-Lago had old fashioned equipment, while BRM and Osca were not ready. SO the CSI decided the world championship would be for two litre Formula 2 cars. Ferrari had the 500 F2 4 cylinder which was remarkably effective against the Maserati A6G and the A6GCM, the Gordinis, HWM, Connaught and Cooper-Bristol. Ascari missed the opening round, the Swiss GP, which was won by team-mate Piero Taruffi, as he was competing in the Indianapolis 500. He was going well until a wheel fell off at high speed. In Spa, on 22nd June, he won and better still, this was the start of a run of nine victories, a record that still remains unbroken in F1. The wins came over two seasons and helped Alberto to his two world championship titles. It should be pointed out that his main rival, Fangio, was out of action for most of the 1952 season, following a road accident in early June. Ascari's run of nine wins goes as follows:

22nd June 1952: Belgian and European Grand Prix run over 36 laps of the 14.080 km Spa-Francorchamps circuit. Ascari was driving a Ferrari 500 F2 and started from pole, but it was Behra who led the first lap, having passed Taruffi, then Farina and Ascari at Stavelot to lead Ascari by 1 second. On the next lap, Alberto fought back and re-passed Behra, who was also overtaken by Farina before having a long dice with Taruffi. The rain came and on lap 14, the Italian got into a slide, went off the track taking the Gordini driver with him. Two main competitors were thus eliminated, although happily uninjured. At this point, Robert Manzon in another Gordini was third behind Ascari and Farina. Ascari set the fastest race lap as he built his lead over Farina from 38" on lap 20 to 1'38 on lap 30 and 1'57 at the flag. It was a classy drive.

The following week, Ascari and Farina were both beaten by a majestic Behra in the Gordini at Reims, but it did not affect Ascari's winning run as this race did not count for the world title.

6th July 1952: ACF French Grand Prix at the 5.020 km Rouen-lesp-Essarts circuit. An interesting point is that this year the rules demanded drivers wear hard helmets, but the veteran Philippe Etancelin was given dispensation to race in a cycling helmet, rather than his usual back-to-front flat cap! Ascari wore a helmet in his favourite sky blue colour. 8000 spectators lined the magnificent track in the forest where they got a great view of the plunging descent to the Nouveau Monde hairpin. It had rained and the track was still wet when the flag dropped to start the race. Ascari led from Farina and the Gordinis of Manzon and Behra who had passed Taruffi's Ferrari. Behra spun on lap 3, managing to get back to the pits to repair bent steering and change a wheel before charging through the field to finish seventh. It was one less threat for Ascari to worry about. From then on, he and the other Ferrari drivers put on an impressive but frankly dull display, with Alberto's lead extending to 1'07 after the two hours of racing, as he beat the lap

record several times. When the rain arrived at half-distance, the positions remained unaltered and Ascari had a comfortable lead in the classification on 18 points, winning from Farina with Taruffi third, underlining Ferrari's dominance.

19th July 1952: British Grand Prix, Silverstone circuit. There were 31 cars at the start, ready to tackle 85 laps of the 4.710 km circuit, including of course our three works Ferrari 500 F2. This time, Farina took pole, although Ascari was credited with setting an identical time of 1'50 later in the session. At Silverstone, timing to a tenth of a second was not introduced until 1958! Once again, Ascari took off in the lead ahead of Farina and built up a lead. The Gordinis were hit with mechanical woes in the early laps, while the home crowd was delighted as the Connaughts of Dennis Poore and Ken Downing held Taruffi's Ferrari at bay, but he got past to reconstitute the eternal red triangle on lap 14. Second placed Farina had to stop to change spark plugs, losing a lot of time, eventually fighting back to 6th. By the end of the race, Ascari had lapped the entire field and set the fastest time in 1'52. Joining him on the podium were Taruffi and Mike Hawthorn, third in a

> ^
> Monza, 16th September 1951: Ascari and the Ferrari 375 F1 heading for his second win in a row at the Italian GP.

> ^ <
> Alberto Ascari and the Ferrari 125 C at the Swiss GP at Berne on 3rd July 1949 heading for his first international win.

> 22nd June 1952: Ascari and his 500 F2 won a Belgian Grand Prix hit by torrential rain. Here he tackles the La Source hairpin.
> ∨

Cooper-Bristol. The blonde Englishman's gritty drive was duly noted and he joined Scuderia Ferrari the following year.

3rd August 1952: The German Grand Prix, 18 laps of the 22.810 km Nurbrugring with 30 cars taking part. Ascari took pole in 10'04"9. It was a dry day at the 'Ring and Ascari took off in the lead chased by Manzon in the Gordini, ahead of Farina and Bonetto. Farina did not take long to get past Manzon, while Bonetto went off the road on the first lap followed by Trintignant and Pietsch. Despite an unscheduled stop at the end of lap 16 to top up his oil level, Ascari secured his fourth consecutive win, ahead of Farina. He was now way out ahead in the classification on 36 points, double the number of his closest pursuer Farina.

17th August 1952: The Dutch Grand Prix at the 4.193 km Zandvoort circuit. 18 drivers were on hand to tackle 90 laps, with Villoresi replacing Taruffi in the Ferrari camp, while ERA-Bristol was back with Stirling Moss. A minor sensation in qualifying, Mike Hawthorn had managed to put his Cooper-Bristol on the front row, alongside the Ferraris of pole man Ascari and Farina. It was raining at the start and Hawthorn managed to

slip between the two Ferraris, but only for one lap as Farina got past the Englishman as did Villoresi on lap 4. As the rain intensified, Ascari increased his lead to 26 seconds over Farina by one third distance, a minute at the two third point, despite stopping to change wheels. The rain stopped and the track dried, allowing Ascari to set the fastest time on the penultimate lap on his way to a straight fifth win. He now had 45 points to Farina's 24, but the leader would have to start dropping his worst scores which is difficult when they are all wins!

7th September 1952: The Italian Grand Prix. Ferrari brought out no less than five works 500 F2s for its home race, run over 80 laps of the 6.300 km circuit, which was also the final grand prix of the season. Somehow, four cars were squeezed onto each row of the grid and yet again, Ascari was on pole ahead of his team-mates Villoresi and Farina, with Trintignant's Gordini joining them on the front row. A convalescing Juan Manuel Fangio turned up to flag the race away. A surprise on the opening lap, as Gonzalez takes the lead, ahead of Trintignant and Ascari, with Manzon and Villoresi in close attendance. Ascari passed Trintignant on lap 3 to lie 7 seconds

behind Gonzalez, whose Maserati was on light tanks. For the first time this season, Ascari and the other Ferrari drivers appeared to have some opposition. On lap 37 however, Gonzalez had to pit to refuel and change his rear tyres, while the Ferraris were set to go the distance in one of the longest races of the year. The Argentine rejoined fifth, one minute down, making up one place at half distance, passing team-mate Bonetto. On cracking form, he also passed Farina to go third. Ascari realised he had to get his skates on and the two men traded fastest lap times, the two men eventually sharing the point that went with this honour. When Villoresi pitted on lap 62, Gonzalez went second but Ascari took the chequered flag ahead of the on-form "Pampas Bull." Alberto Ascari had taken six consecutive wins and six fastest race laps from six grands prix entered, if one excludes Indianapolis and was World Champion with a total of 53.5 points,

counting 36 of them, ahead of Farini on 24 and Taruffi on 22. The Ferrari 500 F2 was the dominant force but Ascari's talent must be recognised as the best of the Ferrari drivers, who managed to fend off the occasional attacks from the other marques. At the age of 34, he entered the F1 book of legends.

18th January 1953: The Argentine Grand Prix, held over 96 laps of the 4.02 km 17 de Octubre circuit. Faced with a threat from Maserati, Ferrari further developed its 500 F2, increasing power to 180 bhp with weight at 600 kilos, 20 more than the Maserati, which used more fuel. Ascari, Villoresi and Farina were all retained, to be joined by the young Mike Hawthorn. Fangio was back at Maserati alongside fellow countrymen, Froilan Gonzalez and Onofre Marimon. It was going to be a hot weekend in all senses of the word, as Argentina prepared to stage its first world championship race on the new circuit, around 40 kilometres from the centre of Buenos Aires. It drew a massive crowd of 400,000! General Peron himself was there and in a demagogic gesture aimed at pleasing the spectators, he ordered the barriers to be removed shortly before the start. The move would have dramatic consequences. Ascari walked the track, before setting the fastest qualifying time yet again. Fangio was next, ahead of Ascari and Farina. Ascari shot off into the lead as usual, followed by Farina and Fangio. On lap 32, a terrible drama unfolded: trying to avoid a child who was crossing the track, Farina lost control and his Ferrari ploughed into the crowd. There were nine dead and forty injured. To make matters worse, an ambulance on its way to the scene, also went into the crowd. The race was not stopped! The drivers somehow found their way through the mayhem. Fangio had been the only

one to pose a threat to Ascari and he retired with a broken transmission. Ascari set the fastest lap and won this terrible race, from Villoresi, Gonzalez and Hawthorn.

7th June 1953: Dutch Grand Prix at Zandvoort over 90 laps of the 4.185 km circuit. The Dutch track had been slightly modified. Wind and sand were as ever the main enemies for the drivers at the seaside track. Again Ascari was on pole and again Fangio was second ahead of Farina. Alberto got yet another fantastic start, followed by Fangio until the transmission let go again. Ascari was comfortably in the lead ahead of Farina, while Gonzalez took over from Bonetto in another Maserati and snatched third off Hawthorn. And for once, it was Villoresi who took the fastest lap.

21st June 1953: Belgian Grand Prix, over 36 laps of the 14.080 km Spa-Francorchamps circuit. This time the threat was real: not only did Ascari fail to take pole, but no Ferrari managed to set the fastest qualifying time, giving best to a Maserati; Fangio's of course, who was a full 2

seconds quicker than Ascari and Gonzalez, making the Ferrari the meat in the Maser sandwich! It certainly raised hopes of an interesting race and the crowd looked like getting one when, for once, Ascari did not take the lead at the start. The two Argentines in the Maseratis kicked off with a spectacular duel in the lead, while Alberto watched from a distance. But Gonzalez broke his accelerator on lap 11 and Fangio his engine on lap 13, leaving Ascari out in front, ahead of Hawthorn, Farina and Villoresi. But in the Maserati camp, the invited Belgian driver, Johnny Claes was called into the pits to hand over his car to Fangio, who drove like a maniac to climb from 8th to 5th place. Fangio inherited third when Hawthorn and Farina had mechanical problems and the Argentine began to attack Villoresi. Trying too hard, he spun at Stavelot and retired. But it had shown Ferrari that the Maseratis were now ready for a fight. Ascari had a comfortable lead over Villoresi at the flag, so Fangio would probably not have been able to stop him from taking his ninth consecutive win. A record which still stands fifty years later.

Double world champion

Then, at Reims for the French Grand Prix, Ascari faltered. It was one of the rare occasions when, with similar equipment and without any

Monza, 7th September 1952: only sixth place for Ascari in the Italian GP, but he had already taken the title. Note the paving stones and how close the photographers got to the action.
∨

> Spa-Francorchamps, 21st June 1953: Ascari takes the flag to win the Belgian GP in the Ferrari 500 F2. The ninth win in a run of nine. There are still two to come, in England and Switzerland, but in Reims and the Nurburgring the winning run was interrupted.

Monaco, 22nd May 1955: Ascari's last grand prix in the splendid Lancia D50, ahead of team-mate Eugenio Castellotti, who finished second. In a moment, Ascari would end up in the Monaco harbour. Four days later at Monza, he crashed and died.
v

Zandvoort, 7th June 1953: the drivers have fun before the start of the Dutch GP. From left to right, Alberto Ascari (the winner,) Juan Manuel Fangio, Nino Farina and "Gigi" Villoresi. Note the drivers' primitive clothing.
v
v

mechanical bothers, he did not dominate his team-mates and the rest of the opposition. It was blazing hot on the 5th July and Ascari let Hawthorn charge off in pursuit of Fangio's Maserati; a pursuit that ended in victory for the Englishman, with Gonzalez third. Ascari had to settle for 4th place, although it is worth noting that the top four were covered by just 4.6 seconds. In England, Ascari was back to his winning ways ahead of Fangio. But in Germany, even though he led from the start from pole position (in 9'59"8, the first man to lap the 'Ring in under 10 minutes) on lap 5, a wheel came off his Ferrari. Feeling it coming, he managed to nurse the car back to the pits. He rejoined a long way down, but then took over Villoresi's car and beat the lap record on his way to 8th place. Farina won, saving the day for Ferrari, but Fangio, second again, had looked very strong.

After mourning the death of Tazio Nuvolari, in Mantua on 11th August, Ascari was in action at the Swiss Grand Prix to continue his domination of the championship. Fangio took pole, but Alberto led as he pleased up to two thirds

distance. He then stopped for new plugs and rejoined with the bit between his teeth. Proving that he could race from behind, he shot up the order to win. That just left Italy. On this 13th September, the Monza circuit was the scene of one of the most closely fought grand prix in the history of the championship. For most of the race there was a fantastic dice, as Ascari and Farina battled with Fangio and Marimon. The last mentioned spun and the final stages were fought out between the three title contenders, as they constantly slipstreamed past one another.

Just before the finish, Ascari was caught out by a backmarker and skidded, to be hit by Marimon. Fangio pulled off a masterly win from Farina at the line. The superstitious Ascari pointed out that the race took place on the 13th. He was very slightly injured and lifted off the track by the marshals. But he got to his feet and walked back to his pits and made it on time to stand on the podium and congratulate Fangio. Alberto was beaten at home, but World Champion for the second year in a row. He was the first double world champion in the history of the sport.

The Death of a hero

In 1954, a new 2.5 litre formula was adopted for the grands prix. Mercedes were back and on paper, the Lancia D50 looked promising. As Ferrari's programme did not look too tempting and the salary was not that good either, Ascari was tempted to switch to Lancia, which he did once he knew his pal Villoresi was going there too. But the new car had all sorts of problems and its F1 debut was delayed. Ascari consoled himself by winning the Mille Miglia in a Lancia D24 sports car. He then raced in the French and British Grands Prix for Maserati, but without success. He also retired from the Italian GP, where he made a one-off appearance for his previous employer, Ferrari. The Lancias were only ready in time for the penultimate round of the season in Spain, but here again Ascari retired.

The start of the 1955 championship looked more promising as Ascari started the first round, the Monaco Grand Prix, from the front row alongside Fangio in the Mercedes on pole and ahead of Moss in the second Mercedes. Both the German cars retired, leaving Ascari in the lead. He slid on a patch of oil at the Port chicane and his car flew into the sea. He swam to shore, with just a few bruises and a cut nose. Four days later at Monza, he turned up to chat with his fellow drivers at the circuit bar. Eugenio Castellotti was trying the brand new 3 litre Ferrari 750 sports car which he was due to race on the Sunday. Ascari had turned up in a suit and tie, but he could not resist the temptation and borrowed Castellotti's helmet, gloves and goggles to give it a quick spin. He did one warm up lap and then stepped up the pace. On his third lap, the car skidded and went off the road at the Vialone turn. The car flipped over and the driver was thrown out. He was seriously injured and died a few minutes later, at the side of the track, in the arms of his friend Villoresi. Italy had just lost a hero, a great driver and a good man. Since Ascari, no Italian has ever won the Formula 1 Drivers' World Championship.

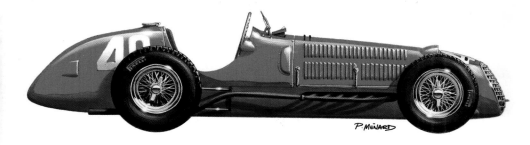

< Ferrari 125 C, 1950

P. MENARD

< Ferrari 375 F1, 1951

P. MENARD

< Ferrari 500 F2, 1952

< Ferrari 625 F1, 1954

P. MENARD

< Maserati 250 F 1954

P. MENARD

< Lancia D 50, 1955

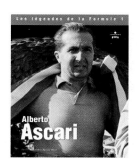

Discover Juan Manuel Fangio; his life, his career, his races, his cars and a complete and detailed record of his racing, as well as exclusive eye-witness accounts, including those of the five times world champion himself, in "Juan Manuel Fangio – La course faite homme". The book features 150 photos (black and white and colour) and profiles of all the F1 cars he drove in the World Championship. This 160 page volume came out in 2002 and is the No. 1 book in the "Les Legendes de la Formule 1" written by Pierre Menard and Jacques Vassal, published by Chronosports. Also available: "Ayrton Senna – Au-dela de l'exigence", "Stirling Moss – Le champion sans couronne" and "Alain Prost- La science de la course."

ATMOSPHERE

No matter how many words, they cannot match a good photo. So why not dozens of photos? Nothing like it to convey the atmosphere of a Grand Prix weekend.

The feminine touch

Formula 1, an exclusively male sport? Luckily, these two pages will convince you otherwise. And if these young ladies do not look too busy, more and more women are now occupying key roles in the paddock. Working as press officers or engineers, they are not only efficient but charming too.

Black is black

What could be more graphic than a back-lit Formula 1 tyre? Much coveted, these cylinders of synthetic rubber were one of the main talking points this season. With Michelin scoring 408 points to 216 for Bridgestone, the French marque was the dominant force by a long way. In the end, the title escaped them only because of the superiority and consistency of Michael Schumacher and his Ferrari.

With courage

The season for the yellow team did not live up to expectations. But what expectations? The team fought on with a small budget, without throwing in the towel, seizing any opportunity that came its way. Including this fantastic win in Brazil.

Savour the detail

There is no doubt that F1 cars are beautiful pieces of kit. Viewed from certain angles, that beauty is enhanced. These little gems prove that point.

Deliverance

The podium ceremony is the moment when all the tension built up during the race is finally released. The drivers let themselves go, while the crowd rushes in from all round the circuit, to be anointed with the victory champagne as they get close to their idols.

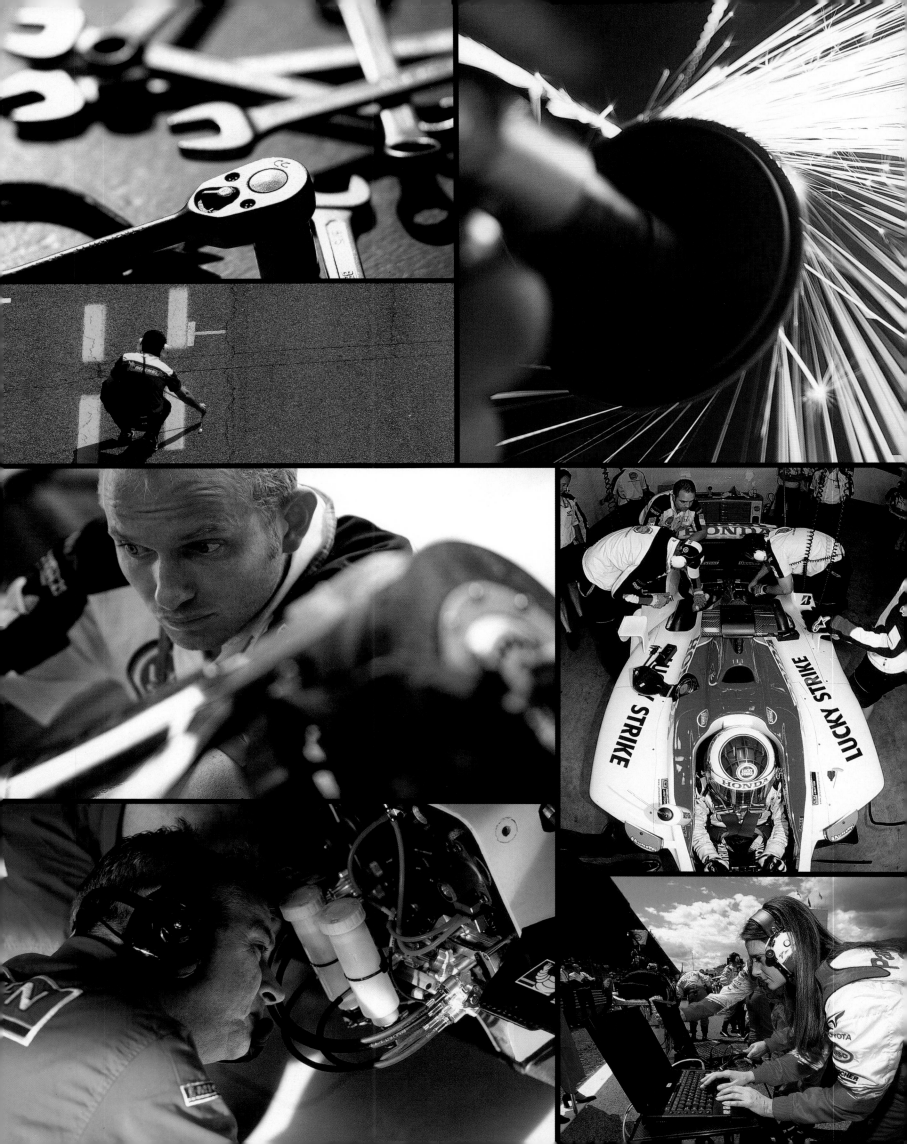

To work

Running two cars for 90 minutes on a Sunday afternoon demands a colossal amount of work, both for the team and their suppliers. Several thousand people work like ants in the hope of seeing their cars finish the race and in some cases, win it.

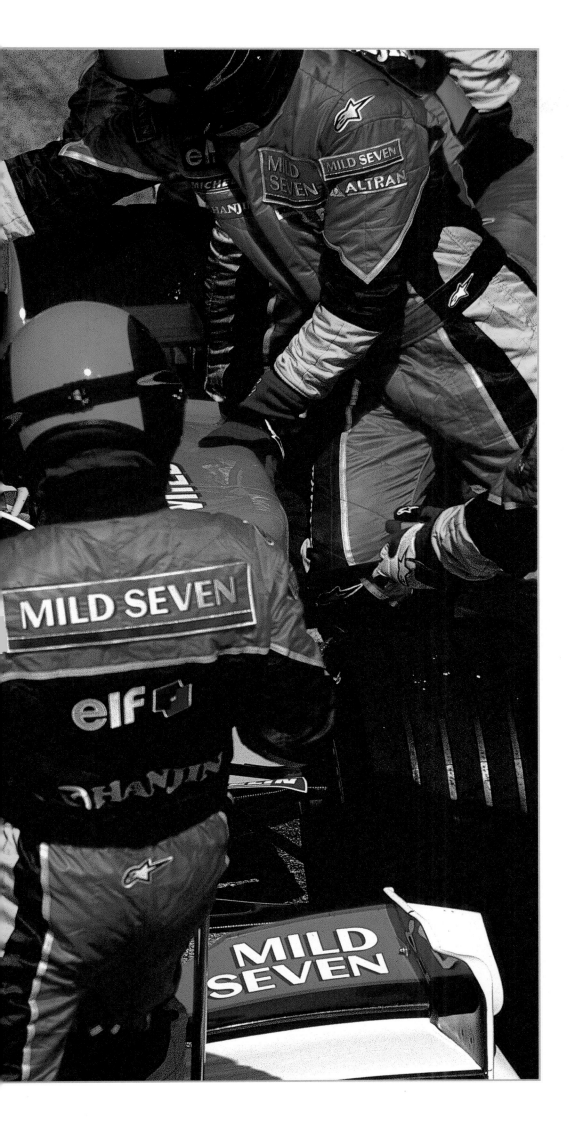

THE 16 GRANDS PRIX

From Melbourne to Suzuka, the
16 Grands Prix in 2003 were packed
with all sorts of excitement.

THE FIRST WILL BE THE LAST

A great start! The first grand prix of the 2003 season was exciting from beginning to end, mainly because the track was still damp at the start. The result: numerous overtaking moves and several crashes.

When the chequered flag was hung out, David Coulthard was first to see it waved, after there had been six changes of leader. He was not to know it yet, but this would be the Scotsman's first and last win of the season. In fact, several drivers had looked like taking victory, including Kimi Räikkönen, who was penalised for speeding in the pit lane, Juan Pablo Montoya, who spun ten laps from the finish and then there were the Ferrari drivers who got it all wrong. No red car finished on the podium for the first time since...September 1999, after 53 consecutive podium finishes!

New rules: satisfactory for all bar one lone voice...

After the 2002 season had been dominated to the point of boredom by Ferrari, the FIA had decided on some drastic changes over the winter, aimed at making F1 more interesting. The changes had been made virtually without consultation and without the usual unanimous approval of the teams. They included a test session on Friday mornings for those who signed the "Heathrow Agreement," one lap qualifying and parc ferme to prevent work on the cars (except in the case of a failure or accident.) The rules had changed so much that team bosses were not able to take them all on board at once. They met on Wednesday in Melbourne to ask for some details to be modified as soon as possible.

Therefore a press release clarifying some points in the rule book was published the same day, specifying that drivers would only have a 30 second window to take to the track when it was their turn to qualify. Any driver who broke down or was unable to complete his timed lap would start from the back of the grid. If a driver went off the track, causing it to be shut, the other driver, who would then be on his warm-up lap could

come into the pits to refuel and change tyres. Further rules banned teams from putting screens up in their garages to conceal all or part of the cars, so that photographers could do their job and the public opposite the pits would get a better view of what used to be a hidden world. Finally, the use of the spare car was forbidden, with teams only allowed to use two cars, unless a car was written off in an accident.

The FIA reserved the right to change these rules after the first grand prix. In this respect, the Melbourne race was fulfilling the role of Guinea Pig. The first field trial therefore duly went ahead on Friday, when the first qualifying session for the Australian Grand Prix went off without a hitch.

The majority of observers went so far as to agree that the new format actually made the session more interesting, particularly as it afforded spectators a better view of all the cars. For the drivers, there was more stress as the slightest error could be fatal as there are no longer any second chances.

While Ron Dennis and Frank Williams admitted they were satisfied with the way the session went, Jean Todt, Ferrari's managing director, did not hide his hostility to the changes. "*To be honest, we were opposed to these changes,*" he admitted. "*Obviously, as we won everything last year, we had no interest in seeing these rules applied. Having said that, we will deal with it.*"

Michael Schumacher was quickest in the afternoon, but he made a mistake in the morning's free practice. "*It's almost become a tradition at this circuit,*" he commented. "*In fact, this morning, my engineer said he was worried because I had not gone off the track yet. Now it's done!*"

∨

Saturday: take the same ones...

Had it been worth all the histrionics! The rules regarding qualifying procedure had been turned on their head, but the result stayed the same with two Ferrari back on the front row again!

In Melbourne, after qualifying, everyone was asking themselves if the changes had been worth all the hassle. "*Surely people did not expect to see our cars in the middle of the grid just because of the new rules?*" asked world champion Michael Schumacher. "*You can make all the changes you want, but you cannot stop the best from being quickest,*" added Williams technical director Patrick Head.

The most disappointed man on the day seemed to be Rubens Barrichello. The new rules were supposed to ensure that every driver made his run on a clear track with absolutely no traffic, so he was

surprised to see yellow flags warning him that Kimi Räikkönen was driving slowly around the circuit. Having been quickest on Friday, he now set the second best time on the grid. Behind him came Juan Pablo Montoya's Williams in third place; a worthy performance after a difficult start to the weekend.

But the surprise came in the shape of the two Saubers, with Heinz-Harald Frentzen fourth and Nick Heidfeld seventh. The other teams reckoned the Swiss cars had qualified virtually on empty tanks, something Peter Sauber refused to confirm. "*It is the first time we have tackled qualifying in this format and I am keen to find out if we have made the right choice. But so far, our strategy seems to be working.*"

In brief

> BMW motorsport director Gerhard Berger announced in Melbourne that he planned to retire from Formula 1 after this race. "*I will stay on as an advisor to BMW for certain strategic decisions, but I will no longer attend all the grands prix.*" The Austrian explained that he wanted to concentrate on other business activities and spend more time with his family.

> 1.3 seconds: the time difference on Friday between the quickest man and Mark Webber, the last driver not to have any problems. The grid looked very close as the season got underway.

> It was also the first time for the Friday morning test session for the "Heathrow Agreement" teams and marked the return of Allan McNish, driving for Renault with the number 34 on his car.

>
The first parc ferme of the season, with an impressive collection of slumbering cars. "*There's a small fortune in there,*" commented a marshal.

Paul Stoddart is angry

The week prior to the Australian Grand Prix, Ron Dennis and Frank Williams had accused Minardi of lacking professionalism. Paul Stoddart was apoplectic with rage: *"Frank is forgetting that his team was once refused an entry at Silverstone because it did not have enough money. And Ron should remember that he went bust three times before creating a winning team. Minardi's budget is probably not big enough to cover the top teams' catering costs, but at least we are fighting. It is a disgrace to criticise us in our position."*

On Saturday afternoon, the Minardi team again grabbed the headlines, by refusing to complete a qualifying lap. This way, the Italian cars returned to the pits without having to go into parc ferme, allowing the team to take its time preparing them for the race and more specifically, alter the fuel load. The two Minardis were therefore relegated to the back row, where no doubt they would have ended up anyway. It was a trick they probably planned to pull off at other races during the season, but for the fact that this ruse was banned as from the next grand prix.

∧
Olivier Panis qualified his Toyota in fifth place, an excellent result for the Frenchman, who would not do as well until the very end of the season. In Melbourne, he even set the second highest top speed at 310.7 km/h, just before the braking area for the first chicane.

<
A pensive David Coulthard. Only eleventh at the end of qualifying, the Scotsman had plenty to think about. His team-mate, Kimi Räikkönen had done even worse, in 15th spot, but at least he had the excuse of having gone off the track during his timed lap.

<<
Melbourne city centre is a bustling place, packed with shops and glass fronted malls. It is a magnificent city where good weather always seems to be on the agenda.

Starting grid

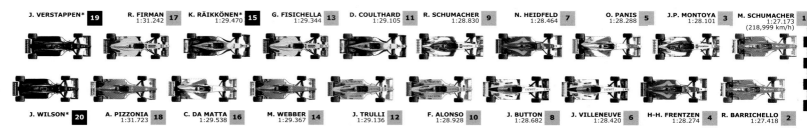

Pos	Driver	No	Time
	J. VERSTAPPEN*	19	1:31.242
	R. FIRMAN	17	1:29.470
	K. RÄIKKÖNEN*	15	1:29.344
	G. FISICHELLA	13	1:29.105
	D. COULTHARD	11	1:28.830
	R. SCHUMACHER	9	1:28.464
	N. HEIDFELD	7	1:28.288
	O. PANIS	5	1:28.101
	J.P. MONTOYA	3	1:27.173 (218,999 km/h)
	M. SCHUMACHER	1	

Pos	Driver	No	Time
	J. WILSON*	20	1:31.723
	A. PIZZONIA	18	1:29.538
	C. DA MATTA	16	1:29.367
	M. WEBBER	14	1:29.136
	J. TRULLI	12	1:28.928
	F. ALONSO	10	1:28.682
	J. BUTTON	8	1:28.420
	J. VILLENEUVE	6	1:28.274
	H-H. FRENTZEN	4	1:27.418
	R. BARRICHELLO	2	

*K. RÄIKKÖNEN, J. VERSTAPPEN and J. WILSON start from the pit lane

^
Ron Dennis looks smug on the podium and with just cause as both his drivers were there with him.

9.482: the number of seconds separating fourth placed Michael Schumacher from the winner David Coulthard as they crossed the finish line. It shows how close was the racing and who knows if the German might have won but for his unusual wing geometry!

Champagne for David Coulthard. Starting from 11th on the grid, he had not expected such a party.
V

David wins, Ferrari makes the wrong tyre choice and falls short of the podium

Scuderia Ferrari had not tasted failure on this scale since the 2002 Monaco Grand Prix! It had always got at least one of its drivers onto the podium since the 1999 European Grand Prix.

But in Melbourne, for the first time in almost four years, no red car finished in the top three. Michael Schumacher had made a good start, going into the lead from pole position. At the very start of the race, the red cars even pulled out such a lead that it looked as though the outcome of the 2003 season was a foregone conclusion. They had a 7 second advantage over their pursuers by the end of the opening lap and over 11 seconds at the end of lap 2. The figures were misleading. The Ferraris had started on intermediate tyres because of the damp track, while all their rivals, with the exception of David Coulthard had risked starting on dry weather tyres. As soon as the cars had dried out the racing line, those on dry tyres were back in control. David Coulthard pitted to change his tyres on lap two, but Michael Schumacher waited until lap 7 to do the same. It was already too late. Team-mate Rubens Barrichello did not even get that far, going off the track on lap six, having jumped the start and he was due to come in for a drive-through penalty. "*It was not my day,*" commented the Brazilian. "*I am not sure what happened at the start. I was pushing hard on the brake pedal, but my car was determined to move forward. I was talking to the team on the radio about my penalty when I lost control of the car.*"
Out in front, Juan Pablo Montoya, Kimi Räikkönen

and Michael Schumacher took turns at leading, as the pit stops changed the order. The world champion might well have won, but for the fact he damaged his Ferrari, driving over the kerbs. "*There were bits hanging off and the handling was terrible,*" he reported. "*It felt like I had a puncture. Under the circumstances, I am happy to have finished fourth and picked up five points.*" For Scuderia boss Jean Todt, the Australian Grand Prix had ended in failure. "*It was a strange race and not just because of the new

rules, but also because of the weather,*" was his analysis. "*The safety car was deployed, there were different strategies and these factors make it difficult to draw any conclusions. We know this season will be tough, but we think we have everything in place to achieve our objectives.*"
Come the end of the season, Michael Schumacher indeed had cause to be grateful for those five Australian points and the championship was possibly won because of them.

Bad luck strikes Kimi and Juan Pablo in Melbourne

Both Kimi Räikkönen and Juan Pablo Montoya had victory within their grasp in Melbourne. But the chance of winning the first race of the season and in Kimi's case, the first of his career, eluded them. Leading from lap 17 to 32, then engaged in a race long duel with Michael Schumacher, whom he pushed into making a mistake at the chicane (photo below,) Räikkönen was one of the stars of the season opener. Starting from the pits to take the opportunity to fit dry tyres instead of the intermediates chosen earlier, the Finn should have won the race, if he had not been

forced to come in for a drive-through penalty, having been caught speeding in the pit lane at his pit stop. "*I don't know what happened, because I operated the speed limiter in the usual way,*" regretted the McLaren man. The penalty dropped him to third place.

Another potential winner spoilt his chances with no external assistance. Juan Pablo Montoya had every intention of winning this race with his Williams-BMW. The Columbian found himself leading from laps 7 to 16, then from 33 to 41 and finally from 46 to

47. It was as he began his 48th lap that he got it wrong at the first chicane. His car took off in a spin, but luckily the engine kept spinning too. The Colombian got back on track just ahead of Kimi Räikkönen, but David Coulthard had slipped through. "*It was entirely my fault,*" admitted Montoya. "*But I was really out of luck today. My strategy was the right one, but every time I got into the lead, the safety car wiped out my advantage.*"

^
But for an error on lap 48, Juan Pablo Montoya should have won. Instead, he finished second.

"*See if you can get by on the grass!*" Kimi Räikkönen duels with Michael Schumacher at the first chicane.
v

Race summary

> It's the start of a new season. Michael Schumacher leads, but only for another six laps. The winner in waiting, David

Coulthard is at the back of the pack (**1**).

> Further back, the battle rages. Alonso and R. Schumacher

will end up in the points but Pizzonia will finish 13th (**2**).

> Montoya finds himself leading on lap 7. He

will lead three times but throw away the win with a spin ten laps from home (**3**).

> Kimi Räikkönen fights

off Michael Schumacher, pushing him onto the grass (**4**).

> Very consistent, H.H.

Frentzen will finish sixth (**5**).

> Surprise winner of this first Grand Prix, David Coulthard is cheered

by his team (**6**).

> No Ferraris on the podium. It had not happened for 53 races (**7**).

At home

Mark Webber had given the crowds plenty to cheer about in Melbourne in 2002, when he finished in the points at the wheel of the humble Minardi.In 2003, he moved to Jaguar. A bigger budget but less success as the Australian was forced to retire with a suspension problem, after he had been running fifth for a while.

> Renault on the attack. Starting from 10th on the grid, Fernando Alonso took just seven laps to climb up t second place. He was followed by team-mate Jarno Trulli, who climbed from twelfth on the grid to second after ten laps. It was the big surprise of the weekend. The two Renaults finally finished in the points; the first of Alonso's career after a season as the team's test driver.

Rule changes: McLaren and Williams attack the FIA

The Lausanne International Chamber of Commerce will face the difficult task of judging the conflict between the Federation Internationale de l'Automobile (the FIA) and the McLaren and Williams teams.

The week before the Australian Grand Prix, the two English teams had indeed lodged a complaint in Lausanne against the FIA and the rules of the Concorde Agreement. The two team principals, Ron Dennis and Frank Williams maintained that the FIA President, Max Mosley had not respected the correct procedures for modifying the Formula 1 rule book. "*We are all bound by the Concorde Agreement,*" explained Ron Dennis. "*It provides for certain procedures and these were not followed in respect of the banning of electronics, the timetable for qualifying and the placing of cars in parc ferme this season.*"

Signed by twelve parties, the ten teams, the FIA and the F1 commercial rights holder, Bernie Ecclestone, the Concorde Agreement calls for a unanimous vote from its members for any last minute decisions which do not involve safety. Last December, pushed by the FIA to come up with cost reduction ideas, the teams

tried to put forward suggestions for 2003, which Max Mosley described as "laughable." He then single-handedly pushed through a raft of drastic measures and it was this procedure which was being contested by Ron Dennis and Frank Williams. "*Other teams share our views, but have not dared speak out,*" added Dennis. "*The arbitration of the chamber of commerce is not a classic judicial procedure, which would be decided in a public and noisy session,*" specified Williams. "*The arbitration from Lausanne takes place behind closed doors, usually in a big hotel*

Not far from the track, the beach. On Thursday, a BAR team sponsor, Brunotti, launched a new line of swimwear on the Melbourne seafront.
> v

Ralf Firman was pretty relaxed for his first grand prix. The Irishman qualified 17th but went off the track on lap twelve.
v

with a Swiss judge calling witnesses. There is no unnecessary procedure. The judge will then decide who is right; Max Mosley or us and it ends there." The procedure will take at least a year.

Not all the team owners approved of this action. "*Conflict is the last thing Formula 1 needs right now,*" declared BAR boss David Richards. "*On the contrary, we should be joining forces to make F1 successful.*"

Weekend gossip

> FIA President Max Mosley had been expected in Melbourne on Thursday for a press conference where he would justify the changes to the rule introduced for this season. Unfortunately, "because of problems with flights" Max Mosley cancelled his plans at the last minute. It was a strange excuse given that all the teams, the press and the spectators had all managed to make it to Melbourne.

> Kimi Räikkönen turned up with a brand new livery on his helmet. A Finnish painter had come up with the design. He was thus breaking the superstition that drivers never change their helmet design.

> Jacques Villeneuve was not a happy boy after the race. The points system had been altered to allocate points down to eighth place and he finished ninth!

results

Practice

All the time trials

N°	Driver	N° Chassis - Engine	Private testing	Pos.	Practice friday	Pos.	Qualifying friday	Pos.	Practice saturday	Pos.	Warm-up	Pos.	Qualifying saturday	Pos.
1.	Michael Schumacher	Ferrari F2002 225			1:27.666	6	1:27.103	4	1:27.517	4	1:27.844	2	1:27.173	1
2.	Rubens Barrichello	Ferrari F2002 222			1:27.459	4	1:26.372	1	1:27.558	5	1:27.738	1	1:27.418	2
3.	Juan Pablo Montoya	Williams FW25 04 - BMW			1:27.929	9	1:27.450	10	1:27.700	6	1:30.325	16	1:28.101	3
4.	Ralf Schumacher	Williams FW25 03 - BMW			1:27.982	10	1:28.266	16	1:27.814	7	1:28.895	7	1:28.830	9
5.	David Coulthard	McLaren MP4-17D 06 - Mercedes			1:26.988	2	1:27.242	6	1:28.090	9	1:28.692	5	1:29.105	11
6.	Kimi Räikkönen	McLaren MP4-17D 09 - Mercedes			1:26.529	1	1:26.551	2	1:28.564	14	1:28.903	8	1:29.470	15
7.	Jarno Trulli	Renault R23-03	1:28.125	1	1:27.286	3	1:27.411	9	1:26.928	1	1:28.654	4	1:29.136	12
8.	Fernando Alonso	Renault R23-02	1:28.339	4	1:27.671	7	1:27.255	7	1:27.424	3	1:28.142	3	1:28.928	10
9.	Nick Heidfeld	Sauber C22-01 - Petronas			1:27.918	8	1:27.510	12	1:28.049	8	1:29.653	12	1:28.464	7
10.	Heinz-Harald Frentzen	Sauber C22-03 - Petronas			1:28.207	12	1:27.563	13	1:28:590	15	1:29.485	11	1:28.274	4
11.	Giancarlo Fisichella	Jordan EJ13-04 - Ford	1:28.225	3	1:29.327	16	1:27.633	14	1:28.619	16	1:29.888	13	1:29.344	13
12.	Ralph Firman	Jordan EJ13-02 - Ford	1:30.325	6	1:29.531	17	1:29.977	17	1:29.814	17	1:32.229	18	1:31.242	17
14.	Mark Webber	Jaguar R4-01	1:28.213	2	1:27.654	5	1:27.675	15	1:28:421	12	1:29.991	14	1:29.367	14
15.	Antonio Pizzonia	Jaguar R4-03	1:30.502	8	1:28.092	11	1:30.092	19	1:30.551	18	1:32.414	19	1:31.723	18
16.	Jacques Villeneuve	BAR 005-2 - Honda			1:31.529	20	1:26.832	3	1:28.509	13	1:28.694	6	1:28.420	6
17.	Jenson Button	BAR 005-4 - Honda			1:28.493	14	1:27.159	5	1:27.415	2	1:29.205	9	1:28.682	8
18.	Justin Wilson	Minardi PS03/04 - Cosworth	1:31.187	9	1:30.606	19	1:30.479	20	1:30.857	19	1:31.063	17	DNF	
19.	Jos Verstappen	Minardi PS03/01 - Cosworth	1:30.458	7	1:30.198	18	1:30.053	18	1:31.066	20	1:30.288	15	DNF	
20.	Olivier Panis	Toyota TF103/03			1:28.362	13	1:27.352	8	1:28.360	11	1:29.346	10	1:28.288	5
21.	Cristiano da Matta	Toyota TF103/02			1:28.698	15	1:27.478	11	1:28.177	10		20	1:29.538	16
34.	Allan McNish	Renault R23-01	1:29.557	5										

Maximum speed

N°	Driver	P1 Qualifs	Pos.	P1 Race	Pos.	P2 Qualifs	Pos.	P2 Race	Pos.	Finish Qualifs	Pos.	Finish Race	Pos.	Trap Qualifs	Pos.	Trap Race	Pos.
1.	M. Schumacher	285,7	2	288,1	1	294,4	6	302,3	2	297,4	3	304,9	1	311,1	1	318,4	1
2.	R. Barrichello	288,2	1	273,6	17	296,2	1	293,9	16	297,6	2	293,4	17	310,2	3	304,9	17
3.	J.P. Montoya	284,8	3	287,2	3	294,1	8	296,5	12	295,1	8	296,6	11	308,3	8	311,2	9
4.	R. Schumacher	280,2	14	285,0	7	294,9	5	300,0	7	295,1	7	300,2	5	308,8	6	314,4	4
5.	D. Coulthard	284,1	4	288,0	2	293,9	9	301,1	4	295,8	5	300,0	7	309,5	5	314,8	3
6.	K. Räikkönen	281,1	11	287,0	5	295,4	3	302,2	3	294,7	10	300,2	6	307,8	9	316,4	2
7.	J. Trulli	281,6	8	281,6	13	290,5	16	292,9	18	290,4	18	293,9	16	304,8	15	309,1	15
8.	F. Alonso	281,3	9	283,0	11	288,8	18	295,3	14	290,5	17	296,1	13	305,1	12	313,5	5
9.	N. Heidfeld	280,5	12	271,7	19	292,1	12	296,4	13	293,3	13	291,4	18	306,7	10	309,9	12
10.	H-H. Frentzen	282,5	7	283,0	10	294,1	7	296,8	11	294,5	11	296,3	12	308,7	7	310,3	11
11.	G. Fisichella	280,3	13	281,1	14	289,3	17	295,0	15	292,1	15	299,3	8	304,9	14	309,1	14
12.	R. Firman	272,7	19	270,2	20	286,9	19	293,2	17	286,8	20	288,6	19	301,3	19	304,8	18
14.	M. Webber	282,9	5	284,7	8	293,6	10	300,6	5	293,7	12	302,0	3	306,2	11	313,4	6
15.	A. Pizzonia	270,5	20	282,7	12	291,5	14	297,1	10	292,2	14	294,2	15	304,7	16	308,9	16
16.	J. Villeneuve	281,2	10	287,1	4	291,8	13	297,2	9	295,0	9	299,0	9	304,9	13	312,1	8
17.	J. Button	282,5	6	285,7	6	293,4	11	300,6	6	295,9	4	301,4	4	303,7	17	312,6	7
18.	J. Wilson	275,5	17	275,0	15	285,7	20	292,1	19	288,8	19	294,5	14	300,6	20	303,9	19
19.	J. Verstappen	273,9	18	274,5	16	291,1	15	287,0	20	291,1	16	288,6	20	301,9	18	301,7	20
20.	O. Panis	278,7	16	283,5	9	295,9	2	303,1	1	297,6	1	304,1	2	310,7	2	310,7	10
21.	C. Da Matta	280,0	15	273,3	18	295,1	4	298,5	8	295,2	6	298,4	10	310,0	4	309,8	13

Race

Classification & Retirements

Pos.	Driver	Team	Lap	Time	Average	
1.	D. Coulthard	McLaren Mercedes	58	1:34:42.124	194,868 km/h	
2.	J.P. Montoya	Williams BMW	58	+ 8.675	194,571 km/h	
3.	K. Räikkönen	McLaren Mercedes	58	+ 9.192	194,553 km/h	
4.	M. Schumacher	Ferrari	58	+ 9.482	194,543 km/h	
5.	J. Trulli	Renault	58	+ 38.801	193,546 km/h	
6.	H-H. Frentzen	Sauber Petronas	58	+ 43.928	193,373 km/h	
7.	F. Alonso	Renault	58	+ 45.074	193,334 km/h	
8.	R. Schumacher	Williams BMW	58	+ 45.745	193,312 km/h	
9.	J. Villeneuve	BAR Honda	58	+ 1:05.536	192,646 km/h	
10.	J. Button	BAR Honda	58	+ 1:05.974	192,631 km/h	
11.	J. Verstappen	Minardi Cosworth	57	1 lap	188,473 km/h	
12.	G. Fisichella	Jordan Ford	52	6 laps	190,863 km/h	Gearbox prob
13.	A. Pizzonia	Jaguar	52	6 laps	189,664 km/h	Broken rear suspension

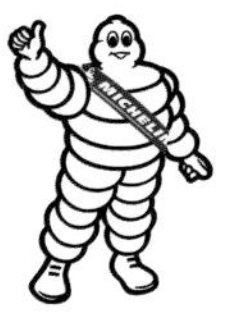

Driver	Team		Reason
O. Panis	Toyota	32	Fuel pressure problem, pump failure
N. Heidfeld	Sauber Petronas	21	Broken front right suspension after collision in the pack
J. Wilson	Minardi Cosworth	17	Radiator holed by stone
M. Webber	Jaguar	16	Broken right rear suspension
C. Da Matta	Toyota	8	Misses 100 m board, brakes late and ends up in the gravel trap
R. Firman	Jordan Ford	7	Goes off on Barrichello's oil
R. Barrichello	Ferrari	6	Goes off, distracted by his radio and having problems with HANS

Fastest laps

	Driver	Time	Lap	Average
1.	K. Räikkönen	1:27.724	32	217,623 km/h
2.	M. Schumacher	1:27.759	27	217,536 km/h
3.	J. Montoya	1:27.942	39	217,083 km/h
4.	F. Alonso	1:28.170	35	216,522 km/h
5.	D. Coulthard	1:28.272	28	216,272 km/h
6.	J. Button	1:28.600	57	215,471 km/h
7.	R. Schumacher	1:28.617	37	215,430 km/h
8.	J. Trulli	1:28.638	44	215,379 km/h
9.	J. Villeneuve	1:28.770	57	215,059 km/h
10.	H.-H. Frentzen	1:29.096	35	214,272 km/h
11.	A. Pizzonia	1:29.217	37	213,981 km/h
12.	G. Fisichella	1:29.274	49	213,845 km/h
13.	O. Panis	1:29.694	23	212,843 km/h
14.	M. Webber	1:29.697	14	212,836 km/h
15.	J. Verstappen	1:31.785	29	207,994 km/h
16.	J. Wilson	1:33.139	13	204,971 km/h
17.	N. Heidfeld	1:33.519	14	204,138 km/h
18.	C. Da Matta	1:33.753	7	203,628 km/h
19.	R. Firman	1:36.644	6	197,537 km/h
20.	R. Barrichello	1:37.086	5	196,638 km/h

Pit stops

	Driver	Time	Lap	Stop n°
1.	D. Coulthard	24.591	2	1
2.	J. Villeneuve	25.720	4	1
3.	J. Button	24.144	5	1
4.	H-H. Frentzen	27.516	6	1
5.	M. Schumacher	31.490	7	1
6.	N. Heidfeld	27.059	7	1
7.	O. Panis	28.585	8	1
8.	G. Fisichella	29.533	8	1
9.	A. Pizzonia	31.893	8	1
10.	J. Wilson	26.599	8	1
11.	F. Alonso	28.606	10	1
12.	J.P. Montoya	26.782	17	1
13.	J. Trulli	27.757	17	1
14.	R. Schumacher	40.515	17	1
15.	J. Villeneuve	31.230	25	2
16.	J. Button	44.291	25	2
17.	M. Schumacher	26.060	29	2
18.	O. Panis	14.862	30	2
19.	J. Verstappen	38.452	31	1
20.	D. Coulthard	28.352	32	2
21.	K. Räikkönen	28.877	33	1
22.	G. Fisichella	41.765	33	2
23.	H-H. Frentzen	27.758	36	2
24.	K. Räikkönen	14.699	39	2
25.	F. Pizzonia	28.896	39	2
26.	J. Button	25.625	39	3
27.	R. Schumacher	26.039	41	2
28.	J. Villeneuve	26.134	41	3
29.	J.P. Montoya	25.135	42	2
30.	F. Alonso	25.269	42	2
31.	J. Trulli	24.729	45	2
32.	M. Schumacher	26.463	46	3

The table of „ Leading Gaps „ is based on the lap by lap information, but only for some selected drivers (for ease of understanding). It adds-in the gaps between these drivers. The line marked „0" represents the winner's average speed. In general, this starts at a slower speed than its eventual average speed, because of the weight of fuel carried on board the car. Then, it goes above the average, before dropping again during the refueling pit stops. This graph therefore allows one to see at any given time the number of seconds (vertically) seperating the drivers on every lap (horizontally)

Race leaders

Driver	Laps in the lead	Nber of Laps
M. Schumacher	1 > 6	6
J.P. Montoya	7 > 16	10
K. Räikkönen	17 > 32	16
J.P. Montoya	33 > 41	9
M. Schumacher	42 > 45	4
J.P. Montoya	46 > 47	2
D. Coulthard	48 > 58	11

Driver	Nber of Laps	Kilometers
J.P. Montoya	21	111,363 km
K. Räikkönen	16	84,848 km
D. Coulthard	11	58,333 km
M. Schumacher	10	53,030 km

Lap chart

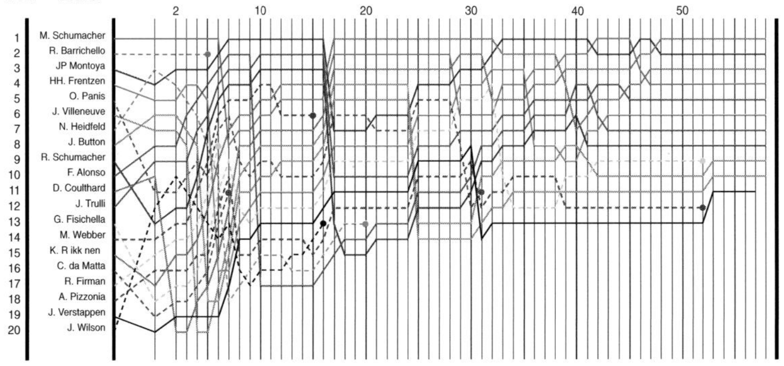

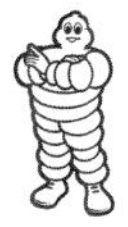

Gaps on the leader board

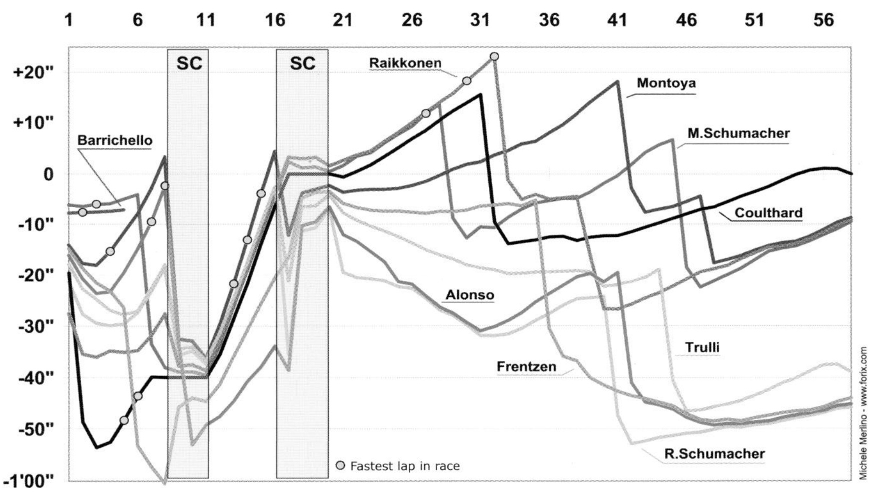

Championship after one round

Drivers

1. D. Coulthard ....(1 win) 10
2. J.P. Montoya 8
3. K. Räikkönen 6
4. M. Schumacher...5
5. J. Trulli 4
6. H-H. Frentzen..3
7. F. Alonso...2
8. R. Schumacher 1
9. J. Villeneuve...0
10. J. Button...0
11. J. Verstappen 0
12. G. Fisichella..0
13. A. Pizzonia 0

O. Panis ....-
N. Heidfeld ....-
J. Wilson ....-
M. Webber...-
C. da Matta...-
R. Firman ....-
R. Barrichello ....-

Constructors

1. West McLaren Mercedes........(1 win).........16
2. BMW WilliamsF1 Team...............................9
3. Mild Seven Renault F1 Team.......................6
4. Scuderia Ferrari Marlboro...........................5
5. Sauber Petronas 3
6. Lucky Strike BAR Honda 0
7. European Minardi Cosworth........................0
8. Jordan Ford..0
9. Jaguar Racing...0

Panasonic Toyota Racing...............................-

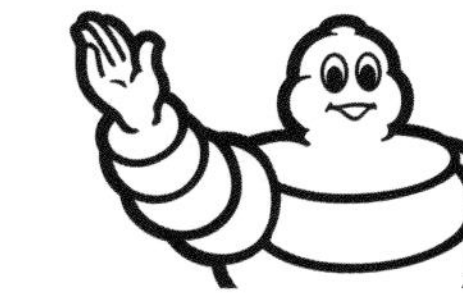

The circuit

Name	Albert Park, Melbourne
Date	March 9th 2003
Length	5303 meters
Distance	58 laps, 307,574 km
Weather	cloudy, 17-21°c
Track temperature	17-19°c (humid track at the start, then dry)

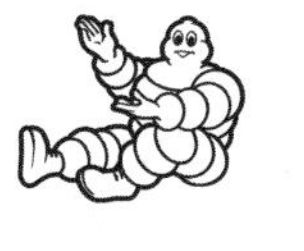

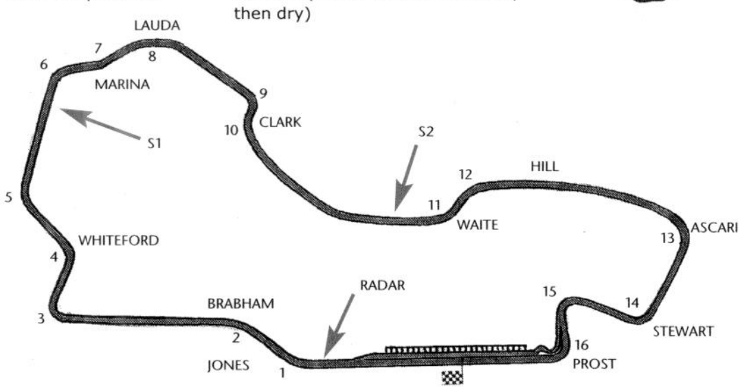

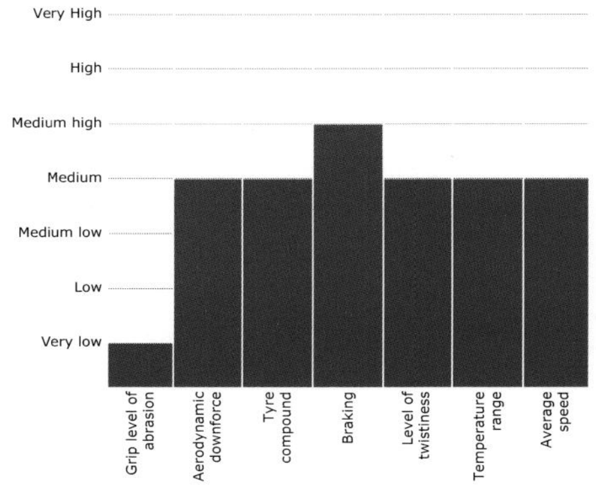

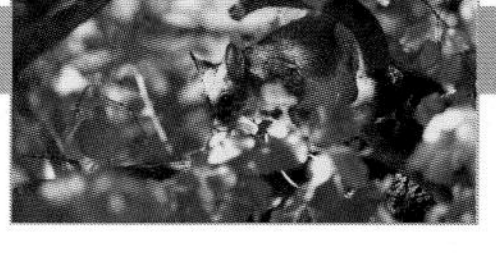

THE YOUNGSTERS ARE GROWING UP

The Malaysian Grand Prix was run under a rather tense international backdrop as the war in Iraq had just begun two days before qualifying. With a 23 year old winner in the shape of Kimi Räikkönen and pole position going to the 21 year old Fernando Alonso, the Sepang weekend consecrated the careers of two new F1 talents. And what talent! For a long time now, Kimi Räikkönen had shown that he had the potential to be very good and only a day before, Fernando Alonso had taken pole position to put his own name in the record books. Indeed, apart from three laps, they were the only two drivers to lead the race in Sepang. For Kimi Räikkönen, who was still in the running for the championship right up to the final race in Suzuka, this win was strangely enough, his only one of a season which saw him finish in second place no less than seven times.

Renault sprung a surprise in qualifying

> An all yellow and blue front row was a nice novelty in Sepang and it was down to the talent of the two Renault drivers and also had something to do with the new rules aimed at jazzing up the grid. On Saturday, Ron Dennis insinuated that the two Renaults had qualified on virtually empty tanks. He had to eat his words after the race, apologising in his own unique way to the Anglo-French team.

Fernando Alonso is easy to miss. If he was not wearing a race suit, no one would pay much attention to this quiet little lad. He had made his Formula 1 debut at the age of 19, with Minardi in 2001, but failed to score any points. With a somewhat mournful expression, his self-effacing personality means he keeps out of the limelight. A lover of football and cycling, coming from a family of modest means, he started off in karting, when he won the world junior championship in 1996. When Renault team bosses Flavio Briatore and Patrick Faure announced in July 2002 that they planned to replace Jenson Button with Fernando Alonso, the news was met with disbelief: why sack a more than promising Brit for a young kid who had done nothing of note?

Fernando Alonso started to write the answer to this question on the tarmac. Behind the wheel, he is fearless. In Melbourne, a fortnight earlier, in his first grand prix for Renault, the Spaniard had scored the first two points of his career. Then, in Sepang, aged 21, he became the youngest driver in history to take pole position. He thus did better than Rubens Barrichello, who had taken pole at Spa in 1994, aged 22.

With Jarno Trulli also qualified on the front row, the Renaults seemed particularly well suited to this circuit. *"The team did a magnificent job. The car was very easy to drive, very efficient, especially in the quick corners,"* enthused Alonso. *"Being on pole is a fantastic feeling. But of course the race is the important thing."* Suffering from the 'flu on Friday, the Spaniard was a bit better on Saturday. *"But I am planning to go back to the hotel early to sleep as much as possible,"* he concluded.

> 17th in qualifying, Ralf Schumacher, who won here in 2002, was way off the pace. *"I am still not very happy with the balance of the car and I made some small mistakes, but it should not have been penalised so badly,"* he regretted. *"It seems I still have to get used to the new qualifying format."* For his part, Juan Pablo Montoya was eighth on the grid, but also complained about the balance on his car.

Second on the grid, Jarno Trulli shared his feelings of optimism. *"The car has gone well all weekend,"* he suggested. *"When we started work on it this winter, there were some reliability problems, but they have now been resolved. It will be a great year for us."*

In Melbourne, both Renaults were impressive in the early stages of the race, when they climbed through the field in the opening laps. In Sepang, they would not have to do that. Third on the grid, Michael Schumacher was going to have his work cut out getting past them.

In brief

> Two accidents in two weeks was a complete coincidence according to Rubens Barrichello, on the subject of the Ferrari F2003-GA. The new Ferrari was due to appear at Imola in a month's time, but it still lacked reliability and had just been involved in two big crashes. Ferrari's test driver Luca Badoer had been injured, so it was Felipe Massa who turned up here as third driver.

> The FIA President, Max Mosley, had not shown up in Melbourne two weeks ago and there was no sign of him here in Malaysia. In Melbourne it was a flight problem which kept him in England. Here, Max Mosley was giving no explanations. *"I don't think my presence in Sepang would be of any use and would constitute a distraction from the important matter of the on-track action,"* he stated in a press release.

> David Coulthard was fined 500 dollars for exceeding the 60 km/h pit lane speed limit by 1.2 km/h. The FIA was definitely not being light handed when it came to dishing out fines.

> Michael Schumacher's contract with Scuderia Ferrari was due to expire at the end of 2004. The week after the Australian Grand Prix, the team fixed him up with a two year extension, but dropped his salary by 7 million Euros per year, in an attempt to reduce the team's monstrous budget. The driver's reaction had not been made public.

Starting grid

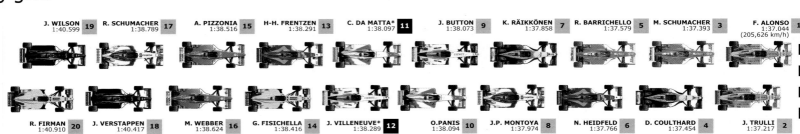

*J. VILLENEUVE forced to retire on the formation lap.

*C. DA MATTA starts from the pit lane.

Position	Driver	Time
19	J. WILSON	1:40.599
17	R. SCHUMACHER	1:38.789
15	A. PIZZONIA	1:38.516
13	H-H. FRENTZEN	1:38.291
11	C. DA MATTA*	1:38.097
9	J. BUTTON	1:38.073
7	K. RÄIKKÖNEN	1:37.858
5	R. BARRICHELLO	1:37.579
3	M. SCHUMACHER	1:37.393
1	F. ALONSO	1:37.044 (205,626 km/h)
20	R. FIRMAN	1:40.910
18	J. VERSTAPPEN	1:40.417
16	M. WEBBER	1:38.624
14	G. FISICHELLA	1:38.416
12	J. VILLENEUVE*	1:38.289
10	O. PANIS	1:38.094
8	J.P. MONTOYA	1:37.974
6	N. HEIDFELD	1:37.766
4	D. COULTHARD	1:37.454
2	J. TRULLI	1:37.217

Kimi's only win

"Of course, I am very happy, but I have not yet realised what this means. I think I will only realise tomorrow that I have won." Kimi Räikkönen was still a bit stunned when he stepped off the podium after the race, thanks to the heat and the emotion of having finally taken his first F1 win. *"At least this win will make my life easier. I won't have to answer questions from journalists who were always asking me when I was going to take my first win!"*

For once, he even seemed to have lost some of his icy exterior. *"I don't think I will need a plane tonight to fly home to Switzerland. Today, I feel I could fly there on my own!"*

The youngest man in history to take pole position, Fernando Alonso, also had reason to be proud, standing on the third step of the podium. *"It's the best weekend of my life,"* exulted the Renault man. *"But the race was really difficult. It was like 56 laps of qualifying. On my first set of tyres, I had to keep an eye on Kimi who was right behind me. On the second set, I was fighting with Rubens (Barrichello) and on the third, I had gearbox problems."* Those problems forced the Spaniard to change gear manually, while the bad case of 'flu he had been suffering with all weekend did not make his task any easier as it worsened towards the end of the race. It's a hard life being a driver.

Is Michael Schumacher losing his cool?

Was something going on inside Michael Schumacher's head? In Melbourne, two weeks earlier, he had given the kerbs a pasting, ending his hopes of victory.

In Sepang, he did even worse. After the start, as he came to the second part of the hairpin, he tried an impossible move, a suicidal attack up the inside of Jarno Trulli. It ended in a spin for the Italian, while the German went over the grass, taking a penalty from the stewards. It was a rare mistake from Michael Schumacher.

After the race, observers reckoned he was losing his cool. It was a somewhat hasty appraisal, as this was only the second race of the 2003 season. Michael Schumacher had no doubt succumbed to his old demons, which brought out his aggressive nature. *"I made a mistake,"* he admitted. *"I hit Jarno and I apologise to him for that."*

< And it's in the bag for Kimi Räikkönen! McLaren had the perfect score of two wins from two starts and led the Constructors' classification on 26 points to Ferrari's 16. No way was the Woking squad going to risk bringing out the MP4-18.

After Melbourne, this was another poor weekend for Ferrari. In Sepang, Rubens Barrichello saved face with second place. The Brazilian led for just three laps, during the pit stops.
V

Race summary

> Boosted by starting from pole, Fernando Alonso leads the pack into the first corner. He would keep the lead for 13 laps **(1)**.

> At the first corner, Michael Schumacher misjudges his braking and collides with Trulli, who stops to change his front wing. Schumacher does the same on lap 3 **(2)**.

> On lap 9, Michael Schumacher is given a drive-through penalty **(3)**.

> After Alonso refuels, Kimi Räikkönen takes the lead **(4)**.

> At the end of a superb race, Jenson Button drops two places in the final corner as his rear tyres are shot from too much oversteer **(5)**.

> First win for Räikkönen, cheered on by his team **(6)**.

> A very wet podium **(7)**.

Make way for youth

By taking pole position at Sepang at the age of 21, Fernando Alonso became the youngest ever driver in the history of the sport to do so. "*It would be nice if I could also become the youngest winner of a grand prix and the youngest world champion in history,*" joked the Spaniard. The win was not too far off in coming, so why not the world title too??

> Several drivers had their hopes dashed immediately after the start, when Michael Schumacher hit Jarno Trulli, causing chaos in the pack. The collision also cost Montoya dear. "*Of course my race was ruined at that point,*" recounted the Colombian. "*I was hit from behind by Pizzonia's Jaguar and I had to stop to change my rear wing. More bad luck, a mechanical problem slowed the process and I got going three laps down on the leaders. There was nothing more I could do.*"

Jacques and Jenson at loggerheads

Trouble and strife within the BAR-Honda team. Over the winter, Jacques Villeneuve had tossed various barbed comments in the direction of his new team-mate, Jenson Button. In Melbourne, things got worse as the Canadian got in the way of the Englishman's pit stop. Villeneuve claimed that a radio fault caused a misunderstanding, but team boss David Richards denied there had been any technical problem. "*I don't know what happened,*" reckoned Button in Sepang. "*Jacques has his own take on motor sport. I always thought he was a difficult team-mate and today I see that I was right.*"

Of course, Villeneuve denied having deliberately hindered his team-mate. "*Jenson got it wrong in Melbourne. He should have stopped one lap earlier and now he is trying to blame someone else. That's the story of his career.*"

Richards was going to have to intervene between his drivers so that their spat did not affect the team's performance. "*We will have to talk about the problem*" he confirmed in Sepang. "*In future, so that Jacques can hear us better, we will just turn up the volume and shout down the radio. And if that doesn't work, we'll fit some old Grundig speakers in the cockpit with big round volume knobs. We're working on it.*"

> Stay calm and take a cold drink. Like every year in Sepang, the heat was literally unbearable in the paddock. The faces of some of the drivers said it all!

The end is nigh for the single rain tyre

It was a case of classic Malaysian weather at the track: a sunny morning, followed by cloudy skies around midday, then incredibly heavy storms around three in the afternoon.

Ideal conditions for trying out the rain tyres. Up until 2002, the manufacturers brought along a variety of wet weather tyres, to deal with varying degrees of water on track. However, this year, the new rules limited the tyre suppliers to just one type of rain tyre. "*That means we have had to make some compromises,*" explained Pascal Vasselon, Michelin's F1 boss. "*Naturally, we cannot cover all eventualities. We are trying to come up with a tyre which works in light rain and then can carry on being used on a dry track. We have noticed that in heavy rain, the organisers bring out the safety car to neutralise the race, so we have not paid too much attention to these conditions.*" However, the monsoon which hit Brazil a fortnight later, causing a raft of accidents, led the FIA to change the rules to allow for two types of rain tyre.

"*Cheers Fernando*". On the podium, the two young heroes of the race did not stint on the Champagne.

F1 world is unconcerned

There was a dead calm on Wednesday at the Sepang circuit. With four days to go before the Malaysian Grand Prix, those in the paddock were going about their business as usual. F1 logos were being painted, the press room was being cleaned and of course the dreadful Malaysian heat did not exactly inspire too much activity.

No team owners and very few drivers were at the track on Wednesday and the war in Iraq seemed to have little effect on those who were there. "It's business as usual" said the man from the FIA. Nick Heidfeld however was concerned about events in the Middle East. "*I feel safe here, but I am worried,*" he said. "*I do not agree with this war which poses a threat to the lives of so many people.*"

Michael Schumacher turned up and was of the same opinion. "*I respect my country's position. I am against the conflict. But Malaysia is the only Muslim country where I feel safe during this time of war.*" Cristiano Da Matta reckoned the war would be bad for the world economy and that F1

would no doubt suffer the consequences. He was right, as several sponsors had already cancelled their trip to Malaysia for their guests, while some French journalists had failed to make the trip because of safety concerns. Only one man looked on the positive side: Didier, a French security guard working at the track: "*I reckon I prefer to be stuck here for a few more days than go back to Paris. At least here, the hotel has a swimming pool!*"

On Thursday, Rubens Barrichello suggested that F1 should continue, allowing people to forget war for a moment while they watched the race. Juan Pablo Montoya agreed. "*In Colombia we have been in a state of civil war for the past 30 to 40 years. There are murders every day, bombs and kidnapping. I often think about my home country. Each time I win a race, I give Colombians the chance to think about something else and smile a little.*" Let the show go on!

results

Practice

All the time trials

N°	Driver	N° Chassis - Engine	Private testing	Pos.	Practice friday	Pos.	Qualifying friday	Pos.	Practice satruday	Pos.	Warm-up	Pos.	Qualifying saturday	Pos.
1.	Michael Schumacher	Ferrari F2002 225			1:37.313	7	1:34.980	1	1:36.990	4	1:39.483	16	1:37.393	3
2.	Rubens Barrichello	Ferrari F2002 222			1:37.497	9	1:35.681	2	1:37.422	9	1:38.060	3	1:37.579	5
3.	Juan Pablo Montoya	Williams FW25 01 - BMW			1:36.998	4	1:35.939	3	1:37.218	7	1:38.615	8	1:37.974	8
4.	Ralf Schumacher	Williams FW25 03 - BMW			1:37.045	5	1:36.805	13	1:37.436	10	1:38.640	10	1:38.789	17
5.	David Coulthard	McLaren MP4-17D 08- Mercedes			1:36.102	1	1:36.297	5	1:36.777	2	1:37.848	2	1:37.454	4
6.	Kimi Räikkönen	McLaren MP4-17D 09 - Mercedes			1:38.515	15	1:36.038	4	1:36.557	1	1:37.506	1	1:37.858	7
7.	Jarno Trulli	Renault R23-03	1:37.851	3	1:36.372	3	1:36.301	6	1:37.198	6	1:38.443	6	1:37.217	2
8.	Fernando Alonso	Renault R23-02	1:37.693	1	1:36.231	2	1:36.693	10	1:36.849	3	1:38.122	4	1:37.044	1
9.	Nick Heidfeld	Sauber C22-01 - Petronas			1:37.906	12	1:36.407	7	1:38.090	16	1:38.700	12	1:37.766	6
10.	Heinz-Harald Frentzen	Sauber C22-03 - Petronas			1:37.951	13	1:36.615	8	1:37.751	13	1:38.933	15	1:38.291	13
11.	Giancarlo Fisichella	Jordan EJ13-04 - Ford	1:37.815	2	1:37.847	11	1:36.759	12	1:37.443	11	1:41.202	18	1:38.416	14
12.	Ralph Firman	Jordan EJ13-02 - Ford	1:40.296	5	1:38.516	16	1:38.240	17	1:38.282	17	1:42.884	20	1:40.910	20
14.	Mark Webber	Jaguar R4-01	1:49.907	9	1:38.870	18	1:37.669	16	1:37.980	15	1:38.680	11	1:38.624	16
15.	Antonio Pizzonia	Jaguar R4-03	1:40.784	6	1:38.839	17			1:37.947	14	1:38.907	14	1:38.516	15
16.	Jacques Villeneuve	BAR 005-2 - Honda			1:37.357	8	1:37.585	15	1:38.329	18	1:38.621	9	1:38.289	12
17.	Jenson Button	BAR 005-4 - Honda			1:37.060	6	1:36.632	9	1:37.418	8	1:38.468	7	1:38.073	9
18.	Justin Wilson	Minardi PS03/04 - Cosworth	1:41.929	8	1:39.695	20	1:39.354	19	1:40.638	20	1:40.588	17	1:40.599	19
19.	Jos Verstappen	Minardi PS03/01 - Cosworth	1:40.923	7	1:39.183	19	1:38.904	18	1:40.382	19	1:41.458	19	1:40.417	18
20.	Olivier Panis	Toyota TF103/05			1:37.748	10	1:36.995	14	1:37.623	12	1:38.187	5	1:38.094	10
21.	Cristiano da Matta	Toyota TF103/02			1:37.992	14	1:36.706	11	1:37.093	5	1:38.876	13	1:38.097	11
34.	Allan McNish	Renault R23-01	1:38.851	4										

Maximum speed

N°	Driver	P1 Qualifs	Pos.	P1 Race	Pos.	P2 Qualifs	Pos.	P2 Race	Pos.	Finish Qualifs	Pos.	Finish Race	Pos.	Trap Qualifs	Pos.	Trap Race	Pos.
1.	M. Schumacher	293,0	4	302,7	2	148,9	7	157,9	1	268,7	10	274,8	2	300,2	3	311.5	3
2.	R. Barrichello	294,7	1	302,9	1	147,6	12	156,1	2	270,5	3	275,5	1	301,6	1	311,8	2
3.	J.P. Montoya	290,2	10	297,2	10	147,8	10	151,3	13	269,7	7	269,8	9	296,7	14	317,2	1
4.	R. Schumacher	292,2	5	297,8	8	148,5	8	153,0	8	268,1	13	271,8	6	297,6	12	302,7	16
5.	D. Coulthard	292,0	6	294,5	15	149,5	5	150,1	15	271,5	1	269,7	10	297,1	13	298,6	18
6.	K. Räikkönen	292,0	7	300,9	3	152,2	2	154,7	4	270,4	4	272,6	4	298,6	9	309,9	5
7.	J. Trulli	287,6	18	297,9	7	151,0	4	153,8	6	265,9	19	268,9	14	295,5	17	305,5	10
8.	F. Alonso	290,0	11	299,0	4	153,1	1	154,7	3	266,4	17	269,5	13	298,2	10	306,4	8
9.	N. Heidfeld	290,4	9	294,3	16	146,4	13	149,5	16	268,2	12	265,9	18	299,1	7	303,2	15
10.	H-H. Frentzen	289,3	12	295,7	12	146,2	17	151,8	11	266,7	16	267,5	17	298,9	8	307,2	7
11.	G. Fisichella	288,4	15			147,9	9			265,9	18			294,6	19		
12.	R. Firman	283,3	20	293,3	17	145,3	19	153,2	7	263,8	20	267,7	16	295,8	16	304,1	13
14.	M. Webber	288,0	17	297,0	11	147,7	11	151,0	14	266,9	15	269,9	8	299,3	5	304,5	12
15.	A. Pizzonia	288,7	14	294,7	14	148,9	6	147,6	18	270,2	5	269,7	11	294,1	20	301,9	17
16.	J. Villeneuve	290,6	8			146,4	14			269,0	9			296,5	15		
17.	J. Button	288,0	16	298,1	6	143,3	20	149,1	17	268,3	11	270,6	7	299,2	6	306,2	9
18.	J. Wilson	286,5	19	293,0	18	146,3	15	152.0	10	267,4	14	268,5	15	294,7	18	305,0	11
19.	J. Verstappen	289,3	13	295,1	13	145,7	18	154,0	5	269,5	8	272,5	5	299,5	4	303,7	14
20.	O. Panis	294,4	2	298,9	5	146,2	16	152,5	9	271,0	2	274,6	3	300,7	2	308,7	6
21.	C. Da Matta	293,2	3	297,6	9	151,9	3	151,4	12	269,7	6	269,5	12	297,6	11	310,5	4

Race

Classification & Retirements

Pos.	Driver	Team	Lap	Time	Average
1.	K. Räikkönen	McLaren Mercedes	56	1:32:22.195	201,629 km/h
2.	R. Barrichello	Ferrari	56	+ 39.286	200,210 km/h
3.	F. Alonso	Renault	56	+ 1:04.007	199,327 km/h
4.	R. Schumacher	Williams BMW	56	+ 1:28.026	198,476 km/h
5.	J. Trulli	Renault	55	1 lap	197,918 km/h
6.	M. Schumacher	Ferrari	55	1 lap	197,804 km/h
7.	J. Button	BAR Honda	55	1 lap	197,797 km/h
8.	N. Heidfeld	Sauber Petronas	55	1 lap	196,888 km/h
9.	H-H. Frentzen	Sauber Petronas	55	1 lap	194,926 km/h
10.	R. Firman	Jordan Ford	55	1 lap	194,880 km/h
11.	C. Da Matta	Toyota	55	1 lap	194,871 km/h
12.	J.P. Montoya	Williams BMW	53	3 laps	190,234 km/h
13.	J.Verstappen	Minardi Cosworth	52	4 laps	185,995 km/h

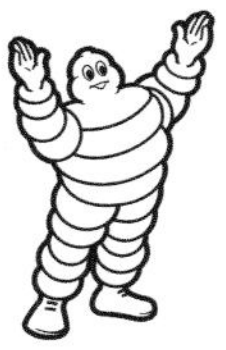

Driver	Team		Reason
A. Pizzonia	Jaguar	43	Brake problems, goes off track
J. Wilson	Minardi Cosworth	42	Unbearable pain in shoulder, nerve trapped by HANS
M. Webber	Jaguar	36	Called in by team: too heavy oil consumption
O. Panis	Toyota	13	Fuel pressure problem
D. Coulthard	McLaren Mercedes	3	Engine cut out by electrical problem
G. Fisichella	Jordan Ford	0	Takes up incorrect grid position, selects reverse which overheats clutch at start
J. Villeneuve	BAR Honda	0	Electronic failure damages gearbox (formation lap)

Fastest laps

	Driver	Time	Lap	Average
1.	M. Schumacher	1:36.412	45	206,974 km/h
2.	R. Barrichello	1:36.542	24	206,695 km/h
3.	K. Räikkönen	1:36.764	10	206,221 km/h
4.	F. Alonso	1:37.078	12	205,554 km/h
5.	J. Trulli	1:37.484	53	204,698 km/h
6.	J.P. Montoya	1:37.787	26	204,063 km/h
7.	D. Coulthard	1:38.021	2	203,576 km/h
8.	R. Schumacher	1:38.071	24	203,472 km/h
9.	C. Da Matta	1:38.156	35	203,296 km/h
10.	O. Panis	1:38.176	7	203,255 km/h
11.	J. Button	1:38.413	10	202,765 km/h
12.	M. Webber	1:38.464	6	202,660 km/h
13.	N. Heidfeld	1:38.528	9	202,529 km/h
14.	A. Pizzonia	1:38:572	3	202,438 km/h
15.	H-H. Frentzen	1:39.287	19	200,980 km/h
16.	R. Firman	1:39.665	14	200,218 km/h
17.	J. Verstappen	1:39.667	3	200,214 km/h
18.	J. Wilson	1:39.752	12	200,044 km/h

Pit stops

	Driver	Time	Lap	Stop n°
1.	J.P. Montoya	4:06.282	1	1
2.	A. Pizzonia	54.484	1	1
3.	J. Verstappen	2:46.858	1	1
4.	M. Schumacher	37.480	3	1
5.	M. Schumacher	24.113	9	2
6.	O. Panis	34.161	12	1
7.	J. Verstappen	37.912	10	2
8.	N. Heidfeld	50.283	13	1
9.	J. Wilson	50.327	13	1
10.	F. Alonso	36.520	14	1
11.	M. Webber	1:07.590	15	1
12.	J. Trulli	35.894	16	1
13.	J. Button	35.888	17	1
14.	C. Da Matta	37.502	17	1
15.	H-H. Frentzen	46.067	17	1
16.	K. Räikkönen	37.350	19	1
17.	A. Pizzonia	37.044	19	2
18.	R. Barrichello	35.338	22	1
19.	R. Schumacher	35.099	22	1
20.	R. Firman	55:468	22	1
21.	M. Schumacher	34.705	26	3
22.	J.P. Montoya	38.546	28	2
23.	C. Da Matta	42.491	33	2
24.	J. Verstappen	39.098	31	3
25.	J. Button	38.422	34	2
26.	N. Heidfeld	35.669	34	2
27.	F. Alonso	36.418	35	2
28.	H-H. Frentzen	35.623	35	2
29.	J. Wilson	39.556	35	2
30.	J. Trulli	50.029	36	2
31.	R. Barrichello	34.879	38	2
32.	A. Pizzonia	37.199	38	3
33.	K. Räikkönen	35.234	40	2
34.	R. Schumacher	34.311	40	2
35.	M. Schumacher	35.171	43	4
36.	C. Da Matta	36.382	48	3

Race leaders

Driver	Laps in the Lead	Nber of Laps
F. Alonso	1 > 13	13
K. Räikkönen	14 > 19	6
R. Barrichello	20 > 22	3
K. Räikkönen	23 > 56	34

Driver	Nber of Laps	Kilometers
K. Räikkönen	40	221,720 km
F. Alonso	13	72,059 km
R. Barrichello	3	16,629 km

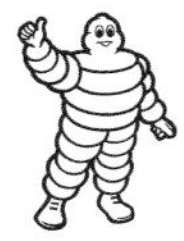

Lap Chart

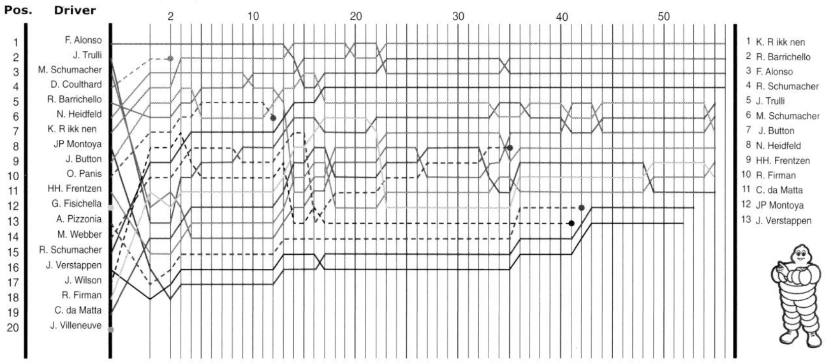

Gaps on the leader board

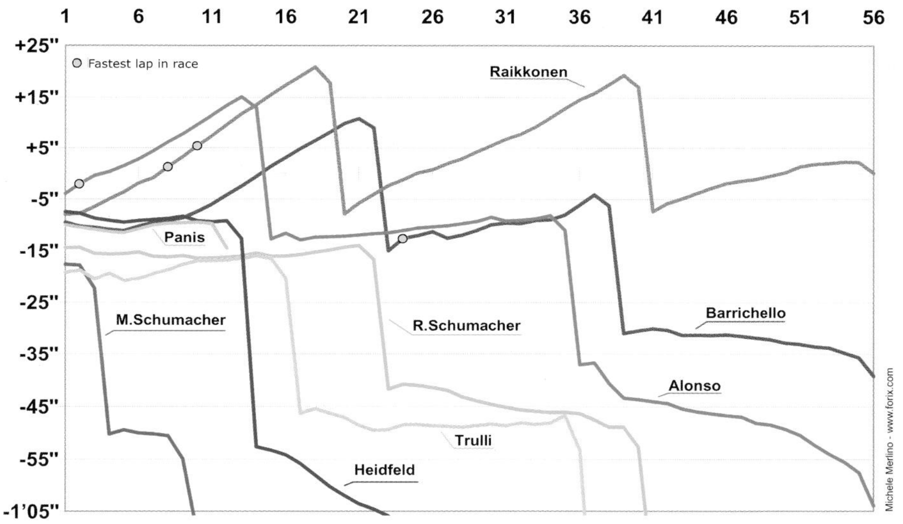

Championship after two rounds

Drivers

1. K. Räikkönen ....(1 win) 16
2. D. Coulthard ....(1 win) 10
3. J.P. Montoya 8
4. R. Barrichello..8
5. F. Alonso 8
6. M. Schumacher..8
7. J. Trulli 8
8. R. Schumacher 6
9. H-H. Frentzen..3
10. J. Button...2
11. N. Heidfeld...1
12. J. Villeneuve...0
13. R. Firman..0
14. J. Verstappen 0
15. C. Da Matta...0
16. G. Fisichella..0
17. A. Pizzonia 0

J. Wilson ....-
M. Webber...-
O. Panis ....-

Constructors

1. West McLaren Mercedes........(2 wins) 26
2. Scuderia Ferrari Marlboro 16
3. Mild Seven Renault F1 Team 16
4. BMW Williams F1 Team 14
5. Sauber Petronas 4
6. Lucky Strike BAR Honda 2
7. Jordan Ford...0
8. European Minardi Cosworth........................0
9. Panasonic Toyota Racing 0
10. Jaguar Racing...0

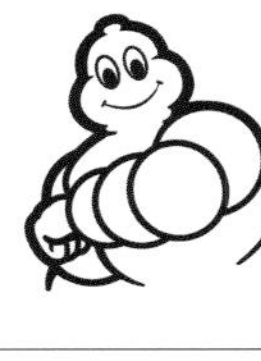

The circuit

Name	Sepang, Kuala Lumpur
Date	March 23rd, 2003
Length	5543 meters
Distance	56 laps, 310,408 km
Weather	sunny and very hot, highly humid 33-36°c
Track temperature	39-41°c

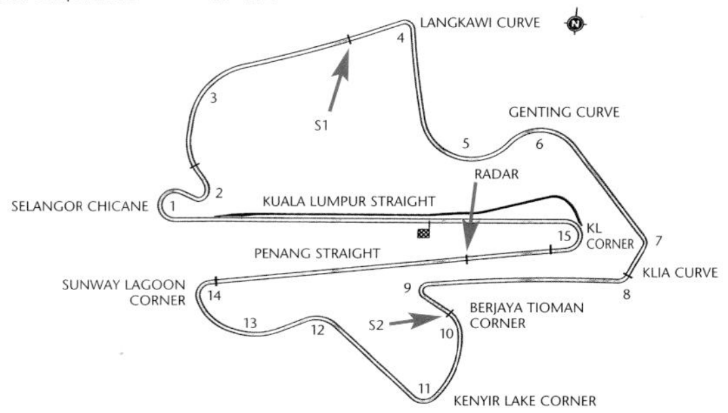

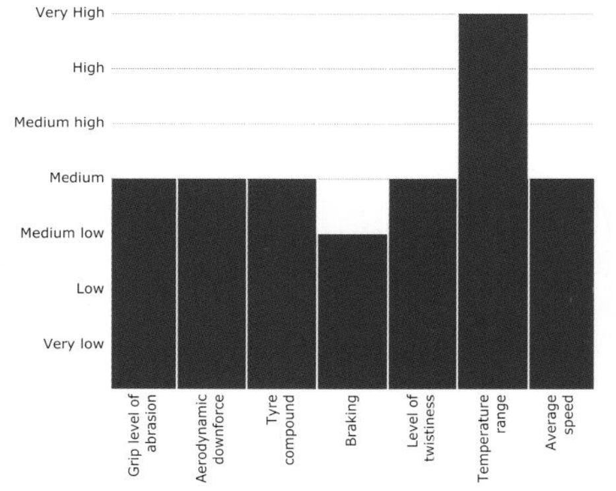

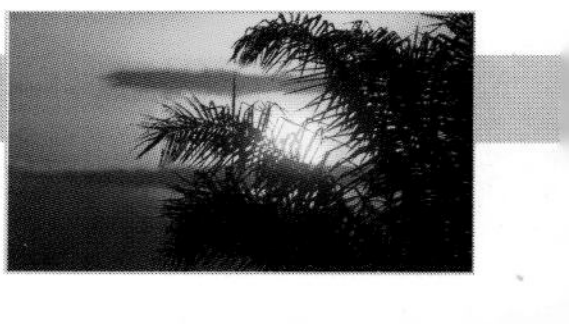

CHAOS AT INTERLAGOS

Incredible, mad, unbelievable, fabulous: adjectives come thick and fast to describe this Brazilian Grand Prix.

It rained at the start and the race was run in a downpour, drying out towards the end and it was, by a long chalk, the most action packed race of the last few years. The madness did not even end until the Friday following the grand prix, when an error in the way the timing screen was analysed was discovered and rectified, thus handing victory to Giancarlo Fisichella, after Kimi Räikkönen had stood on the top step of the podium on the Sunday. This messy affair at least served to remind everyone that while Formula 1 might be a technically sophisticated environment, it is still run by human beings. And like all human beings, they are capable of making mistakes, especially when the end of a race is as chaotic as the one in Interlagos.

Rubinho keeps his promise to his home crowd

"Bar-ri-chel-lo, Bar-ri-chel-lo." On Saturday afternoon, the number "1" has just appeared alongside Rubens Barrichello's name on the giant scoreboard. The crowds massed in the grandstands leap into the air as one with joy and begin chanting the name of their hero to the backbeat of a frantic Samba rhythm.

Not since Ayrton Senna, back in 1991, had the Interlagos crowd been able to cheer a Brazilian driver on pole position. No surprise then that come Sunday, a huge crowd was hustling around the ticket booths at the Sao Paulo track.

Rubens Barrichello was delighted. The seventh pole position of his career was finally the right one. "*To be honest, I have always dreamed of this moment,*" he admitted after the session. "*Ever since I was a child, when I lived here near the circuit, I have dreamed of having a good car and to do a lap of honour of the track after taking pole position and raising my hands in the air as the crowd cheered me. I have just experienced a wonderful moment.*" His qualifying lap went very well. "*I concentrated*

on not pushing too hard and was careful not to make any mistakes," he continued. "*Normally, I can see the split times on my steering wheel, but today I wanted to concentrate to the maximum and I asked the team not to put them up.*"

But Rubens' biggest challenge was still to come. "*All of Sunday will be a big test for me. I know there will be a lot of pressure on my shoulders of course, but I don't mind. After all, in football, teams always have their best games at home.*"

A further concern for "Rubinho" was the weather. If it was fine on Saturday, then rain was expected to arrive at the Interlagos circuit for the race. "*Rain? Let's think about that later,*" he added. "*I will ask my grandmother for the forecast.*" Barrichello had started the Brazilian Grand Prix eight times and posted eight retirements. Could it be that 2003 was finally going to be his year?

In the other Ferrari, Michael Schumacher had not put together a good lap and was sixth. That far down the grid, his start was likely to be as hot as the weather.

A surprise from Mark Webber

Mark Webber was a surprising third for Jaguar in qualifying, thus confirming that his fastest time on Friday was no fluke. "*We have been competitive in every session so far this weekend, which is a good sign,*" commented the Australian, thus silencing critics who reckoned he had qualified on just a whiff of fuel. "*I am especially happy for the team. Everyone has worked very hard after the disaster in Malaysia.*" In Sepang, Webber qualified 16th before retiring with a lubrication problem.

Qualifying had been very tight, with only 59 thousandths of a second separating the top four. There were only 11 thousandths splitting Rubens Barrichello and David Coulthard, 33 thousandths between the Scotsman and Mark Webber and Kimi Räikkönen was only a further 15 thousandths behind.

Taking the average speed of the pole position lap, 59 thousandths represented a bit less than three and a half metres, or less than the length of a Formula 1 car.

In brief

> Juan Pablo Montoya had a different helmet design this weekend. "*I organised a competition for Colombian children,*" he explained. "*There were two categories: 6 to 12 years and 13 to 16. The helmet I am wearing this weekend was designed by Ivonne, a 16 year old girl who is my guest this weekend.*"

> Pedro de la Rosa had just signed a test driver contract with the McLaren-Mercedes team, backing up Alexander Wurz, who also

filled the role of third driver. Apparently there is a distinction between these two roles, even if neither man ever drove in a grand prix this year!

> The FIA had decided to take the European Commission to court over its anti-tobacco advertising laws. Originally, the ban should have come into force on 1st October 2006, but now it had been brought forward to 31st July 2005. The change was giving the teams a few headaches.

> Antonio Pizzonia suffered with brake problems and a lack of balance on his car. Qualified down in 17th spot, there was plenty to worry about.

Starting grid

Pos	Driver	Time		Pos	Driver	Time
1	R. BARRICHELLO	1:13.807 (210.175 km/h)		2	D. COULTHARD	1:13.818
3	M. WEBBER	1:13.851		4	K. RÄIKKÖNEN	1:13.866
5	J. TRULLI	1:13.953		6	R. SCHUMACHER	1:14.124
7	M. SCHUMACHER	1:14.130		8	G. FISICHELLA	1:14.191
9	J.P. MONTOYA	1:14.223		10	F. ALONSO	1:14.384
11	J. BUTTON	1:14.504		12	N. HEIDFELD	1:14.631
13	J. VILLENEUVE	1:14.668		14	H-H. FRENTZEN*	1:14.839
15	O. PANIS	1:14.839		16	R. FIRMAN*	1:15.240
17	A. PIZZONIA*	1:15.317		18	C. DA MATTA	1:15.641
19	J. VERSTAPPEN*	1:16.542		20	J. WILSON	1:16.586

* H-H. FRENTZEN, R. FIRMAN, A. PIZZONIA and J. VERSTAPPEN start from the pit lane.

< A damp atmosphere on the grid. The predicted rain had well and truly arrived.

Carnage at Interlagos

When it rains during a race, the result is always unpredictable. The Brazilian Grand Prix was certainly no exception to this rule. Synopsis: at the start, it is raining too hard to let the pack go. The start is therefore delayed and given behind the safety car.

This situation is maintained for 8 laps until a dryish line begins to appear. As the race begins for real, David Coulthard takes the lead ahead of Rubens Barrichello, who is soon passed by Kimi Räikkönen.

On lap 18, Ralph Firman watches a wheel fly off his Jordan as he travels down the main straight. The Englishman is now just a passenger as his car hits Olivier Panis' Toyota. On lap 25, Juan Pablo Montoya and Antonio Pizzonia go off the track at the same point, with the Jaguar crashing into the

Williams which had only just come to rest. Two laps later, again at the same point, Michael Schumacher skids off into the tyre barrier in his Ferrari, signalling the retirement of the five times world champion. This corner claimed yet another victim when Jenson Button crashed his BAR on lap 33.

But it was on lap 54, when the rain had been gone for over an hour that the most serious accident occurred. Mark Webber lost control of his Jaguar coming onto the main straight and hit the concrete wall at over 300 km/h. His car literally exploded, losing three wheels in the middle of the track.

The marshals barely had time to get out the yellow flags when Fernando Alonso, running third in the Renault, crashed into one of these wheels. His

Renault then bounced off into the tyre barrier before spinning like a top and hitting the wall. The Spaniard got out of the cockpit, but obviously hurt, he collapsed at the side of the track. He was taken by helicopter to a Sao Paulo hospital where he was found to have bruising and a twisted ankle. He still finished third, even though he never made it to the podium...

In the end, everyone survived this grand prix which was peppered with spins, slides and crashes. At first, Kimi Räikkönen came off best, as a second consecutive win saw him charge off into the lead of the championship with an 11 point advantage over team-mate David Coulthard. Or so it seemed until the following Friday...
(see page 107.)

A pensive Heinz-Harald Frentzen. At Interlagos, the German made the most of the confusion to score three points for fifth place. Not bad, considering the weaknesses of the Sauber chassis.

∨

(above, left and right)
Ralph Firman goes to console Olivier Panis after their coming together, which happened as a result of the Jordan losing a wheel and careering out of control at the end of the straight.

(below right)
The race had to be run behind the safety car on several occasions. It was not enough to prevent numerous spins coming out of the Senna chicane.

(below left)
The most serious accident happened when Mark Webber's Jaguar hit the wall, followed by Fernando Alonso's Renault crashing into the debris, hidden by a slight crest in the road.

The carnage in numbers

The Brazilian Grand Prix will forever be remembered in the annals of motorsport for a variety of reasons. Here are some figures from the race:
- 9 drivers went off the track and wrecked their cars, including Michael Schumacher.
- The safety car came out five times, at the start and then while wrecks were cleared away.

- 6 drivers led the race with three changes in the last 8 laps.
- The race was stopped 18 laps ahead of schedule.
- Between qualifying and the start of the race, held in the rain, drivers lost over 120 km/h down the main straight. On Sunday, Nick Heidfeld was clocked at 188.2 km/h before braking for the first chicane, as against 311.0 km/h on Saturday.

Sunday 6th April: what's going on!

When the race director decided to stop the race, Giancarlo Fisichella had just started his 55th lap. At first, the result was therefore fixed as at the end of lap 54, or just after the Italian had taken the lead in his Jordan. A quarter of an hour later, the timing screens in the press room showed a new finishing order: the race result had been taken at the end of lap 53, which made Kimi Räikkönen the winner.

According to article 154 of the F1 sporting regulations, "*in the event of a race being stopped, the result will be taken from the end of the penultimate lap, taken as being two laps prior to the one on which the race was stopped.*" The problem was that lap 53 fell just short of the 75% race distance (originally scheduled for 71 laps) giving a 75% figure of 53.25 laps. Therefore, only half points should have been allocated. However,

the championship table showed full points being given to the drivers. "*It's because over 75% of the race had been completed, as Fisichella had started his 55th lap,*" offered FIA press delegate Agnes Kaiser by way of explanation.
It was not a very convincing explanation as the rule governing points is the same as the one which centres on a race being stopped and that Fisichella was not the winner, or at least not quite yet!

Wednesday 9th April: Giancarlo in court

"*The FIA has received proof which suggests that, contrary to the information provided by the timekeepers at Interlagos, car number 11 (Giancarlo Fisichella) had started his 56th lap before the race was stopped. If this is the case, the race result should be calculated as at the end of lap 54 (victory for Fisichella, Ed.) and not on lap 53 as published.*" The official release from the FIA on the Wednesday after

the race was something of a bombshell.
At Jordan, press officer Helen Temple was delighted: "*When we spoke to them, the FIA people officially confirmed they had been mistaken. We are the ones who have won the race,*" she said.
On Sunday, the positions on lap 55 had never been shown on the timing screens, which would have been the case if Fisichella had really started his 56th lap.

On Wednesday, at TAG Heuer, F1's official timekeepers, there was some surprise that FIA was questioning the result three days later. All the more so as a meeting had taken place between the timekeepers and the race director, just after the finish to analyse the situation.

Friday 11th April: there was a mistake...

Giancarlo Fisichella was delirious with delight on Friday when his boss Eddie Jordan called him to give him the news that he had just taken his first career win after 110 attempts. "*I always thought I had won,*" explained the Italian. "*But with all the confusion after the race, it was exhausting for me. I am still very disappointed not to have been able to enjoy this great moment from the top of the podium. But I am satisfied that it is clear that I have taken my first grand prix win.*"
It had taken five days to learn the name of the winner of the Brazilian Grand Prix and all that

without there being any protests or disqualifications – a first in the history of F1. Quite simply, the stewards had misread the timing information. As they met again in Paris to re-examine all the elements, they reversed their Sunday decision. "*Having studied all the data supplied by the timekeepers, the stewards are certain that car number 11 (Giancarlo Fisichella) had crossed the finish line having completed his 55th lap before the instruction to stop the race had been given,*" explained the FIA. That meant that the Jordan driver was indeed on his 56th lap,

which means the result should have been fixed as of the end of lap 54, two laps earlier and not on lap 53, as had originally been decided.
One little lap made all the difference, as it propelled Fisichella from second to first place. For the Jordan team, it was a great way to celebrate its 200th grand prix. "*The evidence proves beyond doubt that Fisichella is the winner,*" admitted Ron Dennis. "*It's a shame that neither Giancarlo nor the team were able to celebrate the win in Brazil. But if I know Eddie, I am sure that the pints of Guinness will be flowing today.*"

Race summary

> The start is givent under rainy conditions. After many laps behind the Safety Car, Barrichello takes the lead. He will drop from

the race, in the lead during lap 47 **(1)**.

> Michael Schumacher goes off at the same spot as Montoya and

Pizzonia **(2)**.

> Ralph Firman's suspension brakes at the beginning of lap 18. He hits the Toyota

of Olivier Panis and they both retire **(3)**.

> The track is drying and the rithm picks up. Mark Webber hits

the wall and leaves debris all over the track. The race is red flagged **(4)**.

> Coming up at full

speed, Fernando Alonso does not see all of Webber's debris and slams violently into the wall. He will be unhurt **(5)**.

> Fisichella is on fire in the parc ferme **(6)**.

> Räikkönen celebrates his victory. Fisichella is not convinced **(7)**.

For better or for worse

Making the most of his experience, Jacques Villeneuve finished sixth in Interlagos and scored his first points of the season. He does not know it yet, but this would be his best result of the year as he would only score once more, in Monza.

Rubens cursed at Interlagos

^
Rubens Barrichello charges on through the rain. He would have won the race but for running out of fuel because of a pick-up problem.

To say that the Interlagos circuit is situated in the Barrichello family's backyard would be more than a euphemism. From the second floor of the press room, behind the grandstands on the back straight, one can see a little karting track. The one where little Rubens learned his trade. And behind the kart track, hidden in the trees, alongside the little Interlagos lake, one can spot the magnificent Barrichello family home.

No wonder the man everyone here calls Rubinho feels at home at the Brazilian Grand Prix: a grand prix which nevertheless, he has never won, despite having taken five wins to date. "*It's been pointed out to me that Brazilian drivers have won here in 1973, 1983 and 1993. It would seem to be my turn this year,*" joked Rubens on Thursday before the race. "*Unfortunately, I don't believe in this sort of statistic as Formula 1 changes too fast for them to mean anything. But I will be working flat out to win the race. I am at the top of my game, the car is perfect and everything is in place. I think that winning "my" grand prix would be a bit like winning the world championship! If I do it, I will jump into the crowd from the podium..*"

The little Brazilian definitely believed it was his weekend and indeed, in the race, he nearly pulled it off. Except that there really does seem to be a curse preventing Rubens Barrichello from winning the Brazilian Grand Prix. "Rubinho" had avoided all the pitfalls on offer that day, to find himself leading on lap 45. He was pulling out a big lead over the pack when his car gave up on him two laps later....it had run out of fuel. The biggest disappointment of his career!

>
Nor was it a success for Williams. At Interlagos the two Anglo-German cars came home with two little points courtesy of Ralf Schumacher's seventh place. Juan Pablo Montoya finished in the tyre barriers at the exit to the Senna chicane.

>
Kimi Räikkönen really thought he had won his second grand prix in a row. Never mind. Even with just the eighth points for second place, the Finn still had a handy lead in the championship classification.

results

Practice

All the time trials

N°	Driver	Chassis n°. – Engine	Private testing	Pos.	Practice friday	Pos.	Qualifying friday	Pos.	Practice saturday	Pos.	Warm-up	Pos.	Qualifying saturday	Pos.
1.	Michael Schumacher	Ferrari F2002 225			1:28.060	1	1:25.585	5	1:13.546	2	1:14.166	3	1:14.130	7
2.	Rubens Barrichello	Ferrari F2002 223			1:31.462	6	1:23.249	2	1:13.993	7	1:14.002	2	1:13.807	1
3.	Juan Pablo Montoya	Williams FW25 04 - BMW			1:30.885	5	1:27.961	17	1:13.929	5	1:14.321	5	1:14.223	9
4.	Ralf Schumacher	Williams FW25 03 - BMW			1:35.013	12	1:26.709	13	1:14.192	9	1:14.719	8	1:14.124	6
5.	David Coulthard	McLaren MP4-17D 08 - Mercedes			1:28.188	2	1:24.655	4	1:13.893	4	1:14.253	4	1:13.818	2
6.	Kimi Räikkönen	McLaren MP4-17D 09 - Mercedes				17	1:24.607	3	1:13.946	6	1:13.886	1	1:13.866	4
7.	Jarno Trulli	Renault R23-03	1:14.262	1	1:29.607	4	1:26.577	12	1:13.621	3	1:14.863	11	1:13.953	5
8.	Fernando Alonso	Renault R23-02	1:14.680	4		20	1:26.203	9	1:14.209	10	1:14.934	13	1:14.384	10
9.	Nick Heidfeld	Sauber C22-01 - Petronas			1:38.728	14	1:27.111	16	1:14.744	15	1:14.773	10	1:14.631	12
10.	Heinz-Harald Frentzen	Sauber C22-03 - Petronas			1:33.131	10	1:26.375	10	1:14.921	17	1:15.291	15	1:14.839	14
11.	Giancarlo Fisichella	Jordan EJ13-04 - Ford	1:15.092	5	1:32.603	9	1:26.726	14	1:14.224	11	1:14.913	12	1:14.191	8
12.	Ralph Firman	Jordan EJ13-02 - Ford	1:16.559	8	1:57.783	16	1:28.083	18	1:15.475	18	1:16.115	18	1:15.240	16
14.	Mark Webber	Jaguar R4-01	1:14.492	3	1:33.714	11	1:23.111	1	1:14.102	8	1:14.584	6	1:13.851	3
15.	Antonio Pizzonia	Jaguar R4-03	1:14.464	2		18	1:25.764	8	1:14.511	13	1:15.245	14	1:15.317	17
16.	Jacques Villeneuve	BAR 005-2 - Honda			1:48.359	15	1:25.672	7	1:14.523	14	1:14.768	9	1:14.658	13
17.	Jenson Button	BAR 005-4 - Honda			1:28.903	3		20	1:14.464	12	1:14.690	7	1:14.504	11
18.	Justin Wilson	Minardi PS03/04 - Cosworth	1:16.615	9		19	1:28.317	19	1:16.067	20	1:16.935	20	1:16.586	20
19.	Jos Verstappen	Minardi PS03/01 - Cosworth	1:16.322	7	1:37.226	13	1:26.886	15	1:15.610	19	1:16.744	19	1:16.542	19
20.	Olivier Panis	Toyota TF103/05			1:31.518	7	1:25.614	6	1:13.457	1	1:15.401	17	1:14.839	15
21.	Cristiano da Matta	Toyota TF103/02			1:31.548	8	1:26.554	11	1:14.819	16	1:15.352	16	1:15.641	18
34.	Allan McNish	Renault R23-01	1:16.087	6										

Maximum speeds

N°	Driver	P1 Qualifs	Pos.	P1 Race	Pos.	P2 Qualifs	Pos.	P2 Race	Pos.	Finish Qualifs	Pos.	Finish Race	Pos.	Trap Qualifs	Pos.	Trap Race	Pos.
1.	M. Schumacher	303,5	13	298,9	9	250,2	16	231,7	1	311,2	12	307,4	9	306,2	13	275,5	7
2.	R. Barrichello	303,8	12	305,2	2	250,7	15	230,6	2	313,0	6	315,9	3	304,0	15	276,9	6
3.	J.P. Montoya	307,3	2	305,8	1	251,5	12	216,5	13	314,9	2	318,9	2	317,5	1	262,3	13
4.	R. Schumacher	306,3	4	300,3	5	257,6	1	230,2	3	311,6	11	310,9	6	312,6	2	289,6	1
5.	D. Coulthard	307,1	3	304,8	3	252,7	8	229,4	5	315,6	1	314,1	4	312,4	3	289,0	2
6.	K. Räikkönen	305,8	5	303,1	4	255,2	2	227,8	7	314,1	4	322,2	1	301,8	19	267,5	10
7.	J. Trulli	299,3	19	298,8	10	252,7	7	225,9	8	307,3	15	306,5	11	310,5	6	284,9	4
8.	F. Alonso	298,5	20	297,2	14	251,7	11	229,1	6	305,6	19	311,4	5	302,6	18	275,4	8
9.	N. Heidfeld	304,2	10	213,3	20	248,2	18	135,3	20	313,4	5	241,5	20	311,0	5	188,2	20
10.	H-H. Frentzen	305,0	8	298,5	11	250,8	14	225,7	9	312,7	7	306,9	10	308,0	10	267,8	9
11.	G. Fisichella	305,7	6	298,4	12	252,7	6	224,2	10	311,9	8	306,3	13	312,3	4	266,7	11
12.	R. Firman	304,1	11	290,6	18	251,2	13	216,9	12	311,7	10	301,2	15	309,3	8	251,9	15
14.	M. Webber	301,0	16	299,0	8	253,8	3	229,6	4	307,6	14	310,6	7	310,1	7	277,8	5
15.	A. Pizzonia	301,3	15	298,1	13	251,9	10	215,3	16	306,2	18	305,6	14	307,5	12	262,1	14
16.	J. Villeneuve	304,9	9	300,3	6	252,8	5	220,5	11	311,9	9	309,3	8	302,9	16	286,7	3
17.	J. Button	308,4	1	292,8	15	252,8	4	212,6	19	314,3	3	299,3	17	308,3	9	249,6	17
18.	J. Wilson	301,3	14	287,7	19	239,5	20	213,2	18	307,1	16	296,7	19	295.0	20	240,7	18
19.	J. Verstappen	299,7	18	291,6	16	244,3	19	216,1	14	306,4	17	299,2	18	307,6	11	250,1	16
20.	O. Panis	305,2	7	291,5	17	252,3	9	215,5	15	310,7	13	300,6	16	302,8	17	236,5	19
21.	C. Da Matta	300,0	17	300,0	7	248,5	17	214,1	17	305,5	20	306,5	12	304,3	14	264,7	12

Race

Classification & Retirements

Pos.	Driver	Team	Lap	Time	Average	
1.	G. Fisichella	Jordan Ford	54	1:31:17.748	152,902 km/h	
2.	K. Räikkönen	McLaren Mercedes	54	+ 0.945	152,876 km/h	
3.	F. Alonso	Renault	54	+ 6.348	152,725 km/h	Hit Webber's debris
4.	D. Coulthard	McLaren Mercedes	54	+ 8.096	152,676 km/h	
5.	H-H. Frentzen	Sauber Petronas	54	+ 8.642	152,661 km/h	
6.	J. Villeneuve	BAR Honda	54	+ 16.054	152,455 km/h	
7.	R. Schumacher	Williams BMW	54	+ 38.526	151,834 km/h	
8.	J. Trulli	Renault	54	+ 45.927	151,631 km/h	
9.	M. Webber	Jaguar	53	1 lap	151,858 km/h	Big accident
10.	C. Da Matta	Toyota	53	1 lap	149,029 km/h	

Driver	Team		Reason
R. Barrichello	Ferrari	47	Fuel feed problem causing car to run out of fuel
J. Button	BAR Honda	33	Crash (turn 3)
J.Verstappen	Minardi Cosworth	31	Spin (turn 3)
M. Schumacher	Ferrari	27	Crash (turn 3)
J.P. Montoya	Williams BMW	25	Crash (turn 3)
A. Pizzonia	Jaguar	25	Crash (hits Montoya's wreck (turn 3)
O. Panis	Toyota	18	Hit by an out of control Firman
R. Firman	Jordan Ford	18	Front right suspension breaks suddenly, hits Panis
J. Wilson	Minardi Cosworth	16	Spins and stalls (turn 3)
N.Heidfeld	Sauber Petronas	9	Engine breaks with lubrication problem

Fastests Laps

	Driver	Time	Lap	Average
1.	R. Barrichello	1:22.032	46	189,101 km/h
2.	H.H. Frentzen	1:23.089	53	186,696 km/h
3.	D. Coulthard	1:23.132	40	186,599 km/h
4.	G. Fisichella	1:23.454	51	185,879 km/h
5.	F. Alonso	1:23.770	41	185,178 km/h
6.	M. Schumacher	1:24.040	18	184,583 km/h
7.	K. Räikkönen	1:24.104	39	184,443 km/h
8.	J. Villeneuve	1:24.463	48	183,659 km/h
9.	R. Schumacher	1:24.778	46	182,976 km/h
10.	M. Webber	1:24.956	50	182,593 km/h
11.	J. Trulli	1:25.036	43	182,421 km/h
12.	J.P. Montoya	1:25.814	24	180,767 km/h
13.	J. Button	1:26.042	17	180,288 km/h
14.	C. Da Matta	1:27.080	47	178,139 km/h
15.	A. Pizzonia	1:27.990	24	176,297 km/h
16.	J. Verstappen	1:28.010	25	176,257 km/h
17.	J. Wilson	1:28.023	15	176,231 km/h
18.	R. Firman	1:29.159	13	173,985 km/h
19.	O. Panis	1:30.494	17	171,419 km/h
20.	N. Heidfeld	2:11.396	4	118,058 km/h

Pit stops

	Driver	Time	Lap	Stop n°
1.	O. Panis	36.664	1	1
2.	G. Fisichella	40.673	7	1
3.	R. Firman	41.684	8	1
4.	D. Coulthard	33.545	19	1
5.	M. Schumacher	36.051	19	1
6.	J.P. Montoya	38.542	19	1
7.	R. Barrichello	36.631	19	1
8.	F. Alonso	39.002	19	1
9.	M. Webber	41.050	19	1
10.	J. Button	41.265	19	1
11.	J. Trulli	56.111	19	1
12.	R. Schumacher	36.873	19	1
13.	J. Villeneuve	45.299	19	1
14.	F. Alonso	36.074	20	2
15.	K. Räikkönen	38.447	27	1
16.	C. Da Matta	41.233	27	1
17.	M. Webber	36.654	33	2
18.	C. Da Matta	45.236	35	2
19.	F. Alonso	24.129	42	3
20.	C. Da Matta	37.154	45	3
21.	R. Schumacher	35.639	48	2
22.	D. Coulthard	35.023	52	2

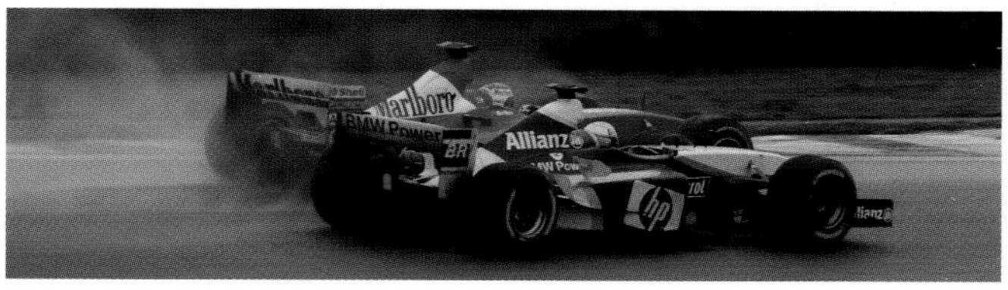

Race leaders

Driver	Laps in the lead	Nbr of Laps
R. Barrichello	1 >8	8
D. Coulthard	9 > 10	2
K. Räikkönen	11 > 26	16
D. Coulthard	27 > 44	18
R. Barrichello	45 > 46	2
D. Coulthard	47 > 52	6
K. Räikkönen	53	1
G. Fisichella	54	1

Driver	Nbr of Laps	Kilometers
D. Coulthard	26	112,034 km
K. Räikkönen	17	73,253 km
R. Barrichello	10	43,090 km
G. Fisichella	1	4,279 km

Lap chart

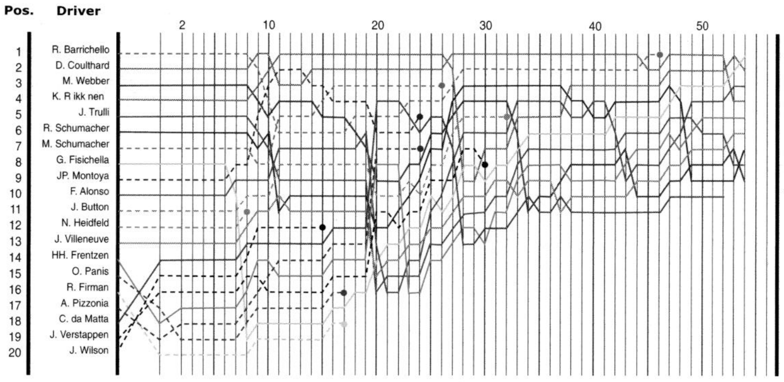

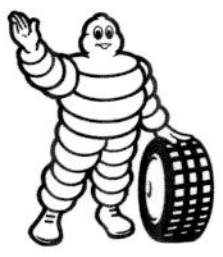

Gaps on the leader board

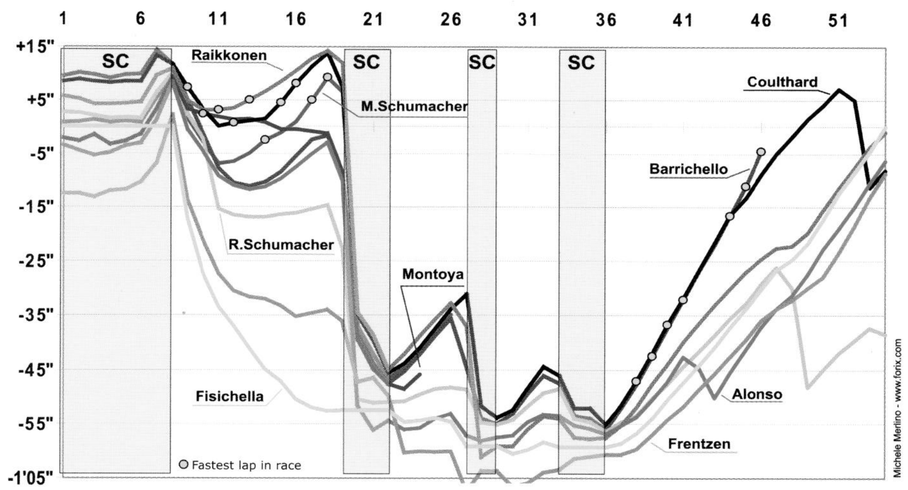

Championship after three rounds

Drivers

1. K. Räikkönen ....(1 win) 24
2. D. Coulthard ....(1 win) 15
3. F. Alonso 14
4. G. Fisichella ....(1 win) 10
5. J. Trulli 9
6. J.P. Montoya 8
7. R. Barrichello..8
8. M. Schumacher 8
9. R. Schumacher 8
10. H.H. Frentzen 7
11. J. Villeneuve...3
12. J. Button...2
13. N. Heidfeld..1
14. M. Webber 0
15. C. Da Matta...0
16. R. Firman..0
17. J. Verstappen 0
18. A. Pizzonia 0
J. Wilson ....-
O. Panis ....-

Constructors

1. West McLaren Mercedes ....(2 wins) 39
2. Mild Seven Renault F1 Team 23
3. Scuderia Ferrari Marlboro 16
4. BMW Williams F1 Team 16
5. Jordan Ford.........................(1 win).........10
6. Sauber Petronas 8
7. Lucky Strike BAR Honda 5
8. Jaguar Racing..0
9. Panasonic Toyota Racing 0
10. European Minardi Cosworth.......................0

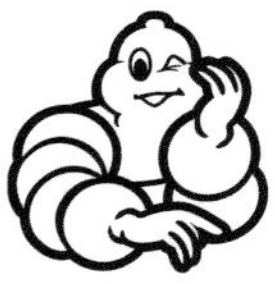

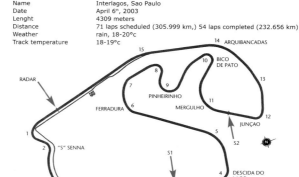

The circuit

Name	Interlagos, Sao Paulo
Date	April 6th, 2003
Lenght	4309 meters
Distance	71 laps scheduled (305.999 km,) 54 laps completed (232.656 km)
Weather	rain, 18-20°c
Track temperature	18-19°c

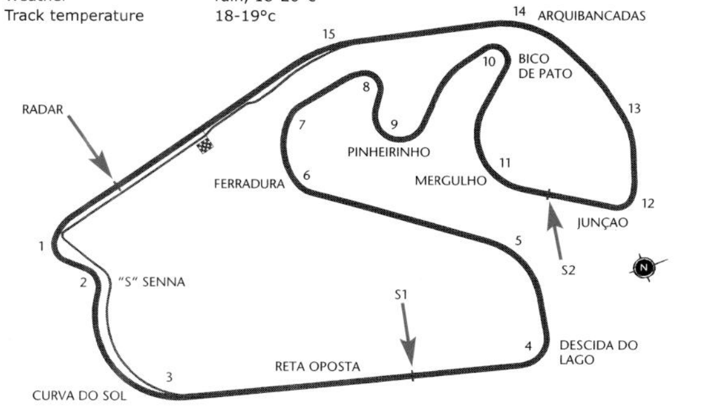

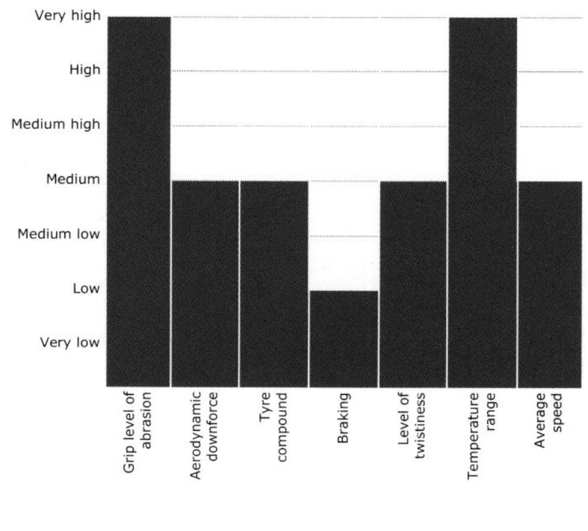

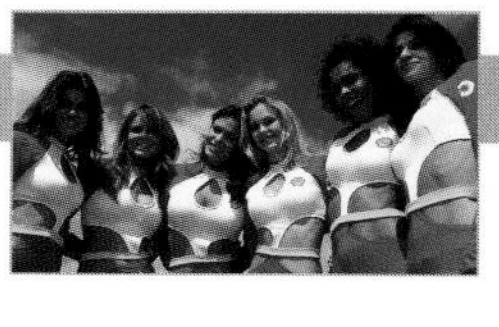

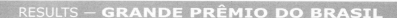

A SPECIAL WIN

Michael Schumacher took victory at Imola just a few hours after the death of his mother in a Cologne hospital. The two Schumacher brothers had visited Elizabeth Schumacher the night before, by which time she was already unconscious. It was a huge emotional wrench for the five times world champion. On the podium, he looked gaunt as the traditional champagne stayed in the bottle. Michael was also excused the usual post-race press conference.

It was also the first win of the year for Scuderia Ferrari after the early part of the season had been riddled with bad luck. Thanks to this win, Michael Schumacher moved up to third place in the championship, behind the two McLaren drivers.

In the early hours of Friday morning, the Ferrari camp is still wracked with indecision: the 2002 car or the new F2003-GA.

Allan McNish, happy in his role as third Renault driver on Friday mornings.

Not as a good as a real podium ceremony, but at Imola on Friday morning, Giancarlo Fisichella finally got his hands on the winner's trophy from the Brazilian Grand Prix.

Michael and Ralf vanish after qualifying

It was the first time it had happened in the history of the sport: a few minutes after qualifying, the two drivers who had put their cars on the front row of the grid had left the circuit.

Around 15h15, Bernie Ecclestone's Maybach pulled up outside the Ferrari motorhome to pick up the two drivers. A few minutes later, the car reappeared in the car park: apparently the Scuderia felt that seeing its driver go off in a Mercedes car was not the right image. So it was that Michael and Corinna Schumacher left in a black Maserati, along with Cora and Ralf. They were heading for Forli airport, around thirty kilometres from the circuit, where Ralf's private jet was waiting to take the family members to

Cologne, where Elizabeth Schumacher, the mother of the two drivers, was in hospital.

At the circuit, rumours were doing the rounds that Mrs. Schumacher was in a coma, hence the worried expressions which could be read on the faces of her sons during the press conference after qualifying. The drivers were back at Imola on Sunday.

The race looked like going well for the world champion who had taken his second pole position of the season. "*This season is tougher than last year, but I was expecting that and there are still 13 races to go for me to make up the 16 points deficit. We can do it.*" At the time, he was only eighth in the championship.

Mark Webber impresses

Evidently, his third place on the grid in Brazil was not down to luck. In Imola, Mark Webber qualified in fifth place. "*In some ways, my lap was quite conservative,*" he commented. "*I did not want to take the risk of making a stupid mistake. Controlling your aggression over one lap is not easy and the margin between the quickest and the slowest was very small.*" As far as his fuel load was concerned, Webber had clear views: "*Even if the cynics reckon we ran virtually on empty, I say wait and see. We will show them in the race. The car has made enormous progress. It's as simple as that.*"

Starting grid

Pos	Driver	Time
1	M. SCHUMACHER	1:22.327 (215.710 km/h)
2	R. SCHUMACHER	1:22.341
3	R. BARRICHELLO	1:22.557
4	J.P. MONTOYA	1:22.789
5	M. WEBBER	1:23.015
6	K. RÄIKKÖNEN	1:23.148
7	J. VILLENEUVE	1:23.160
8	F. ALONSO	1:23.169
9	J. BUTTON	1:23.381
10	O. PANIS	1:23.460
11	N. HEIDFELD	1:23.700
12	D. COULTHARD	1:23.818
13	C. DA MATTA	1:23.838
14	H-H. FRENTZEN	1:23.932
15	A. PIZZONIA	1:24.147
16	J. TRULLI	1:24.190
17	G. FISICHELLA	1:24.317
18	J. WILSON**	1:25.826
19	R. FIRMAN*	1:26.357
20	J. VERSTAPPEN*	

*R. FIRMAN and J. VERSTAPPEN start from the pit lane.

**J. WILSON comes into the pits after the formation lap to refuel. So he starts from the pit lane.

A victory with no champagne and no press conference

It was clear that Michael Schumacher was affected. As he stepped from his car and then on the podium, the reigning champion kept a straight face and showed no signs of delight at his victory. Within minutes of the podium ceremony, he left the circuit without saying a word. It was not the moment for celebration as he was in mourning for his mother, who had died a few hours earlier in the night of Saturday to Sunday, from complications with sclerosis of the liver. For Ferrari, this was a very special win, especially as luck had not been with the Scuderia up until now. *"It really is a very special win,"* commented Jean Todt after the race.

In the absence of his driver, it was Todt who took his place in the press conference. *"Michael has proved yet again what many people refuse to accept, that he is a very special man. Despite being in mourning, he wanted to race. It was his decision. At Ferrari, we have never forced anyone to race. But he insisted on doing so, for the team and for his fans. He then wanted to go onto the podium to thank them. It is at moments like these that you realise what a close family Ferrari is."*

The race was a straightforward one for the German. Apart from a handful of laps during the pit stops, he was never challenged for the lead. Rubens Barrichello would no doubt have finished second, if he had not lost time at the first pit stop. *"We knew that with this new points system reliability would be the key. That is why we decided to run the F2002,"* concluded Jean Todt.

Kimi ekes out his lead

Thanks to a daring two stop strategy, McLaren did well out of Imola, with a second place for Kimi Räikkönen and fifth for David Coulthard. Indeed, most of the opposition opted for three stops, which seemed logical given that rain had been expected before the end of the race, although it actually never materialised.

On the other hand, a two stop strategy allowed the team to get the most out of the Michelin tyres, which tend to work better on longer runs. Thanks to his second place, Räikkönen increased his lead in the world championship, which he now led by 13 points, ahead of team-mate David Coulthard. *"The championship is looking pretty good,"* said the delighted Finn. *"But we have to wait for the MP4-18 in order to think about winning races on a regular basis."*

∧
Kimi Räikkönen in full flow at Imola, before leaving the circuit with a comfortable lead in the championship. He said that in order to win, he was waiting for the MP4-18 to make its appearance at the Austrian Grand Prix. But to what year was he referring?

<
Both Williams finished in the points, but a long way back in 4th and 7th places.

Race summary

> Before the race, Fisichella and Jordan received their winner trophies from the Brazilian Grand Prix after a richly deserved victory (1).

> Ralf is about to pass his brother at the start and take the lead (2).

> The opening laps are hectic with the Schumacher brothers locked in mortal combat. Further back, Barrichello waits patiently for the pit stops to start (3).

> Behind the leading trio, Räikkönen will only make two stops before taking 2nd place, despite being harried by Barrichello in the closing stages (4)

> Montoya's race was spoilt by a refuelling problem, requiring 4 stops (5).

> Button brings BAR a ray of sunshine with 8th place (6).

> Rubens and Michael in parc ferme (7).

On your marques

Behind the big names like Ferrari, BMW-Williams, McLaren-Mercedes and Renault, a battle was also raging for the minor places amongst the smaller teams like Jordan and those with pretensions to join the big boys of F1, like Toyota and Jaguar.

paddock

Max Mosley says he is happy and does not want to change anything

Rubens Barrichello sweeps the gravel at Tosa corner during practice. In the race, the Brazilian finished where he started, in third spot.

The FIA President, Max Mosley, had not attended any of the first three grands prix of the season, contrary to his original plans. On Thursday however, he made a surprise appearance in the Imola paddock, for a meeting with all the team owners.

These had been complaining since the start of the season about the new race weekend timetable. Several team principals were against the new one lap qualifying format, as well as the parc ferme restrictions which prevent the mechanics from working on the cars between qualifying and the race.

At the end of the meeting, Max Mosley came to the media centre to give a resume of what had taken place. *"We have now obtained agreement from everyone that the 2003 season will continue with exactly the same format with which it started,"* revealed the FIA president. *"The only change

After three retirements from the first three starts, Olivier Panis finally finished a grand prix, in ninth place.

which we have admitted is to authorise the use of spare cars up until Saturday midday. The teams have also insisted that the banning of electronic traction control, launch control and electronic gearbox control, scheduled for next year, not be applied. They are very insistent on this point, but we at the FIA are equally keen on banning electronic aids and I hope we will manage to convince everyone in the weeks that follow."* This ban had originally been scheduled to take effect as from the British Grand Prix and had already been delayed until the start of 2004.

Indeed, for the 2004 season, Mosley reaffirmed that the FIA planned to introduce standard rear wings, another cause for discussion within the teams. *"We will do this very correctly,"* insisted the Englishman. *"We will carry out tests and do some research. On this point also, I hope we will reach agreement with the teams."*

Pessimistic

As for the long term future, namely 2008 and the expected schism between SLEC and the GPWC, Mosley seemed relatively pessimistic. *"I have always felt that the threat of a parallel championship organised by the constructors is a bluff and that everyone will finally reach an agreement. But it seems that is not the case. It seems more and more likely that we will have two championships when the current agreement expires."* The Concorde Agreement which governs the commercial aspects of Formula 1 is due to finish at the end of 2007 and the majority of the major constructors in F1 (Fiat-Ferrari, BMW, Mercedes, Renault, Jaguar) seem to want to start their own championship called the GPWC. *"It would not be Formula 1, which would continue with the remaining teams,"* concluded Mosley. *"But the FIA would still be in charge of safety matters for this new championship."*

Weekend gossip

> Back in Europe after three "Flyaway" grands prix, Formula 1 rediscovered its beloved paddock and motorhomes. Not much new this year, except on the technical front. *"Budgets are dropping so it's not the time to invest in follies,"* admitted a member of the BAR team. However, the Scuderia had an extra motorhome, paid for by sponsor Vodafone.

> Apart from Sauber, Williams, Minardi and Toyota, all the other Formula 1 teams were supported financially by tobacco companies this year. Williams was definitely out on its own, as in Imola it announced a sponsorship deal with a nicotine substitute manufacturer, NiQuitin, which held a press conference where it distributed patches and gum to anyone who wanted them in the paddock.

> McLaren cannot help itself from doing better than the rest. Last year, also at this circuit, the British team unveiled its new glass and steel palace; the Communications Centre. This year, it was the technical side of the team which got a face lift. Imola marked the debut of three new trailer units which have two floors for transporting the cars and equipment. They are true mobile workshops and include several briefing rooms and all the machine tools necessary to work on

parts of the car or produce new bits. The economic crisis appeared to have had no effect on David Coulthard and Kimi Räikkönen's team.

> Fernando Alonso had recovered completely from his terrible accident in Brazil, two weeks previously. *"I am a hundred percent fit,"* he claimed. *"Usually after a big impact like the one I had, you have slight pains in the neck. But this time, nothing. I have to thank the new HANS system for protecting my head. I think it is the reason why I have come out of the crash so well."*

> With just 52,000 paying spectators on Sunday, there were clear indications that F1 was losing its appeal. In total, 82,000 people turned up over the course of the weekend, which is a long way off the 198,000 in 1999 and the 120,000 in 2002. It was the smallest crowd ever since Imola first staged a grand prix.

> Ferrari took a long time making up its mind in deciding whether to use the 2002 car or the new F2003-GA. In the end, the Scuderia went for the first option here in Imola, as there were doubts over engine reliability on the new car.

results

Practice

All the time trials

N°	Driver	Chassis n°. – Engine	Private testing	Pos.	Practice friday	Pos.	Qualifying friday	Pos.	Practice saturday	Pos.	Warm-up	Pos.	Qualifying saturday	Pos.
1.	Michael Schumacher	Ferrari F2002 223			1:23.057	10	1:20.628	1	1:22.974	5	1:23.452	2	1:22.327	1
2.	Rubens Barrichello	Ferrari F2002 225			1:23.057	9	1:21.082	2	1:22.819	1	1:26.198	19	1:22.557	3
3.	Juan Pablo Montoya	Williams FW25 04 - BMW			1:21.409	2	1:21.490	4	1:23.769	8	1:23.509	3	1:22.789	4
4.	Ralf Schumacher	Williams FW25 02 - BMW			1:21.335	1	1:21.193	3	1:22.897	2	1:23.514	4	1:22.341	2
5.	David Coulthard	McLaren MP4-17D 08 - Mercedes			1:22.121	4	1:22.326	9	1:23.198	7	1:23.349	1	1:23.818	12
6.	Kimi Räikkönen	McLaren MP4-17D 06 - Mercedes			1:23.557	13	1:22.147	8	1:22.962	4	1:24.019	8	1:23.148	6
7.	Jarno Trulli	Renault R23-03	1:24.003	5	1:23.051	8	1:23.100	16	1:24.322	13	1:25:554	16	1:24.190	16
8.	Fernando Alonso	Renault R23-05	1:24.298	6	1:22.561	5	1:22.809	13	1:23.042	6	1:24.002	7	1:23.169	8
9.	Nick Heidfeld	Sauber C22-03 - Petronas			1:23.834	14	1:22.911	14	1:24.747	15	1:24.377	12	1:23.700	11
10.	Heinz-Harald Frentzen	Sauber C22-04 - Petronas			1:22.714	7	1:22.531	10	1:25.332	17	1:24.527	13	1:23.932	14
11.	Giancarlo Fisichella	Jordan EJ13-04 - Ford	1:23.239	2	1:23.267	11	1:22.724	11	1:24.132	11	1:25.191	15	1:24.317	17
12.	Ralph Firman	Jordan EJ13-03 - Ford	1:23.885	4	1:24.007	15	1:24.360	17	1:24.763	16	1:26.191	18	1:26.357	19
14.	Mark Webber	Jaguar R4-04	1:23.457	3	1:22.056	3	1:21.669	5	1:22.958	3	1:24.231	10	1:23.015	5
15.	Antonio Pizzonia	Jaguar R4-03	1:23.099	1	1:23.426	12	1:22.919	15	1:26.195	20	1:25.029	14	1:24.147	15
16.	Jacques Villeneuve	BAR 005-2 - Honda			1:25.153	18	1:21.926	7	1:24.098	9	1:24.028	9	1:23.160	7
17.	Jenson Button	BAR 005-4 - Honda			1:22.669	6	1:21.891	6	1:24.178	12	1:23.750	5	1:23.381	9
18.	Justin Wilson	Minardi PS03/04 - Cosworth	1:26.374	9	1:25.706	20	1:25.195	20	1:25.945	19	1:26.169	17	1:25.826	18
19.	Jos Verstappen	Minardi PS03/01 - Cosworth	1:25.905	8	1:25.180	19	1:24.990	19	1:25.745	18	1:26.746	20		20
20.	Olivier Panis	Toyota TF103/05			1:24.565	17	1:22.765	12	1:24.099	10	1:23.893	6	1:23.460	10
21.	Cristiano da Matta	Toyota TF103/02			1:24.117	16	1:24.854	18	1:24.683	14	1:24.332	11	1:23.838	13
34.	Allan McNish	Renault R23-01	1:25.264	7										
39.	Matteo Bobbi	Minardi PS03/02 - Cosworth	1:29.433	10										

Maximum speeds

N°	Driver	P1 Qualifs	Pos.	P1 Race	Pos.	P2 Qualifs	Pos.	P2 Race	Pos.	Finish Qualifs	Pos.	Finish Race	Pos.	Trap Qualifs	Pos.	Trap Race	Pos.
1.	M. Schumacher	227,3	1	225,5	2	263,4	5	266,7	3	181,5	4	174,1	6	300,8	6	310,5	1
2.	R. Barrichello	224,6	4	224,7	4	263,3	8	271,0	1	183,9	1	175,1	4	303,1	4	310,3	2
3.	J.P. Montoya	224,5	5	227,9	1	267,2	1	267,5	2	183,7	2	176,0	2	303,2	3	308,4	3
4.	R. Schumacher	223,4	9	222,0	9	265,2	2	266,6	6	179,6	11	170,9	14	303,8	2	307,6	4
5.	D. Coulthard	217,4	20	220,7	14	263,0	9	266,7	4	179,4	13	174,7	5	304,3	1	306,3	6
6.	K. Räikkönen	220,9	12	223,4	6	263,3	7	266,7	5	181,2	5	173,1	9	300,4	7	306,2	7
7.	J. Trulli	218,5	16	218,3	19	253,8	20	258,0	20	180,6	8	175,8	3	291,6	20	296,4	20
8.	F. Alonso	224,1	7	225,3	3	257,0	19	259,8	19	181,1	6	177,0	1	293,2	19	298,2	19
9.	N. Heidfeld	219,7	14	219,0	17	259,8	16	260,0	18	179,5	12	171,9	11	298,1	15	303,0	15
10.	H-H. Frentzen	224,2	6	220,8	13	261,1	13	260,8	16	173,2	20	170,5	15	299,1	13	303,2	14
11.	G. Fisichella	219,2	15	220,6	15	260,4	14	263,6	9	178,8	16	171,0	13	295,9	16	305,2	9
12.	R. Firman	218,0	17	219,8	16	259,8	15	262,0	13	180,0	10	169,8	17	293,3	18	299,8	18
14.	M. Webber	217,8	18	224,2	5	263,8	4	265,0	7	175,7	19	173,4	8	299,4	11	303,8	12
15.	A. Pizzonia	223,8	8	222,3	8	259,3	17	264,1	8	179,1	14	168,1	19	299,6	9	304,9	11
16.	J. Villeneuve	226,7	2	221,4	12	262,9	10	261,1	14	182,5	3	167,9	20	300,1	8	307,3	5
17.	J. Button	225,6	3	221,8	11	264,5	3	260,9	15	180,8	7	168,8	18	299,2	12	303,3	13
18.	J. Wilson	217,5	19	218,8	18	261,5	12	260,6	17	180,4	9	172,3	10	301,3	5	304,9	10
19.	J. Verstappen	220,3	13	216,9	20	259,2	18	262,1	12	175,9	18	171,6	12	295,7	17	300,8	17
20.	O. Panis	223,3	10	222,4	7	262,0	11	263,4	11	178,9	15	170,5	16	299,5	10	302,5	16
21.	C. Da Matta	221,7	11	221,9	10	263,3	6	263,4	10	177,2	17	174,0	7	299,0	14	305,2	8

Race

Classification & Retirements

Pos.	Driver	Team	Lap	Time	Average
1.	M. Schumacher	Ferrari	62	1:28:12.058	207,894 km/h
2.	K. Räikkönen	McLaren Mercedes	62	+ 1.882	207,821 km/h
3.	R. Barrichello	Ferrari	62	+ 2.291	207,805 km/h
4.	R. Schumacher	Williams BMW	62	+ 8.803	207,549 km/h
5.	D. Coulthard	McLaren Mercedes	62	+ 9.411	207,525 km/h
6.	F. Alonso	Renault	62	+ 43.689	206,192 km/h
7.	J.P. Montoya	Williams BMW	62	+ 45.271	206,131 km/h
8.	J. Button	BAR Honda	61	1 lap	204,500 km/h
9.	O. Panis	Toyota	61	1 lap	203,778 km/h
10.	N.Heidfeld	Sauber Petronas	61	1 lap	203,705 km/h
11.	H-H. Frentzen	Sauber Petronas	61	1 lap	203,663 km/h
12.	C. Da Matta	Toyota	61	1 lap	202,651 km/h
13.	J. Trulli	Renault	61	1 lap	202,200 km/h
14.	A. Pizzonia	Jaguar	60	2 laps	198,491 km/h
15.	G. Fisichella	Jordan	57	5 laps	202,936 km/h Hydraulic prob. engine failure

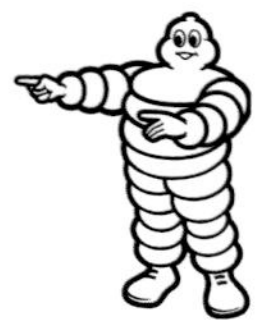

Driver	Team		Reason
M. Webber	Jaguar	55	Broken half shaft
R. Firman	Jordan	52	Engine breaks because of clutch problem
J. Verstappen	Minardi	39	Engine dies after short-circuit
J. Wilson	Minardi	24	Problem with refuelling rig
J. Villeneuve	BAR Honda	20	Engine damaged after minor fire at 1st refuelling

Fastests Laps

	Driver	Time	Lap	Average
1.	M. Schumacher	1:22.491	17	215,281 km/h
2.	R. Barrichello	1:22.775	49	214,543 km/h
3.	K. Räikkönen	1:22.810	21	214,452 km/h
4.	J.P. Montoya	1:22.946	32	214,100 km/h
5.	D. Coulthard	1:23.200	20	213,447 km/h
6.	R. Schumacher	1:23.265	29	213,280 km/h
7.	F. Alonso	1:23.844	60	211,807 km/h
8.	J. Button	1:23.972	15	211,484 km/h
9.	J. Villeneuve	1:24.108	16	211,142 km/h
10.	M. Webber	1:24.258	30	210,766 km/h
11.	C. Da Matta	1:24.705	15	209,654 km/h
12.	G. Fisichella	1:24.730	27	209,592 km/h
13.	A. Pizzonia	1:24.733	36	209,585 km/h
14.	H-H. Frentzen	1:24.874	34	209,237 km/h
15.	O. Panis	1:25.123	36	208,625 km/h
16.	N. Heidfeld	1:25.329	38	208,121 km/h
17.	J. Trulli	1:25.444	13	207,841 km/h
18.	R. Firman	1:25.539	45	207,610 km/h
19.	J. Wilson	1:26.354	23	205,651 km/h
20.	J. Verstappen	1:26.835	35	204,512 km/h

Pit stops

	Driver	Time	Lap	Stop n°
1.	O. Panis	26.612	11	1
2.	N. Heidfeld	25.349	13	1
3.	C. Da Matta	24.740	13	1
4.	F. Alonso	26.324	14	1
5.	M. Webber	24.663	15	1
6.	J. Trulli	26.570	15	1
7.	R. Schumacher	25.393	16	1
8.	J. Button	27.611	16	1
9.	R. Barrichello	25.315	17	1
10.	J.P. Montoya	29.592	17	1
11.	M. Schumacher	24.827	18	1
12.	J. Villeneuve	28.809	18	1
13.	G. Fisichella	37.301	18	1
14.	H-H. Frentzen	26.467	18	1
15.	A. Pizzonia	28.111	18	1
16.	M. Webber	14.784	20	2
17.	J. Werstappen	27.784	20	1
18.	D. Coulthard	25.917	21	1
19.	J. Wilson	35.085	21	1
20.	K. Räikkönen	25.217	22	1
21.	R. Firman	26.939	26	1
22.	O. Panis	24.767	27	2
23.	C. Da Matta	24.757	28	2
24.	J.P. Montoya	27.849	30	2
25.	N. Heidfeld	24.270	30	2
26.	R. Schumacher	24.250	31	2
27.	M. Webber	26.814	31	3
28.	J.P. Montoya	24.109	32	3
29.	R. Barrichello	25.105	33	2
30.	M. Schumacher	24.015	34	2
31.	J. Button	28.317	37	2
32.	G. Fisichella	28.138	37	2
33.	A. Pizzonia	41.989	38	2
34.	F. Alonso	26.920	39	2
35.	H-H. Frentzen	32.173	40	2
36.	J. Trulli	26.163	40	2
37.	O. Panis	24.797	43	3
38.	K. Räikkönen	27.564	44	2
39.	D. Coulthard	23.896	45	2
40.	N. Heidfeld	24.741	45	3
41.	C. Da Matta	24.722	45	3
42.	M. Webber	24.499	47	4
43.	R. Firman	25.529	47	2
44.	R. Schumacher	23.352	48	3
45.	M. Schumacher	23.988	49	3
46.	J.P. Montoya	23.944	49	4
47.	R. Barrichello	30.115	50	3

Race leaders

Driver	Laps in the lead	Nbr of Laps
R. Schumacher	1 > 15	15
M. Schumacher	16 > 18	3
K. Räikkönen	19 > 22	4
M. Schumacher	23 > 49	27
R. Barrichello	50	1
M. Schumacher	51 > 62	12

Driver	Nbr of Laps	Kilometers
M. Schumacher	42	207,186 km
R. Schumacher	15	73,758 km
K. Räikkönen	4	19,732 km
R. Barrichello	1	4,933 km

Lap chart

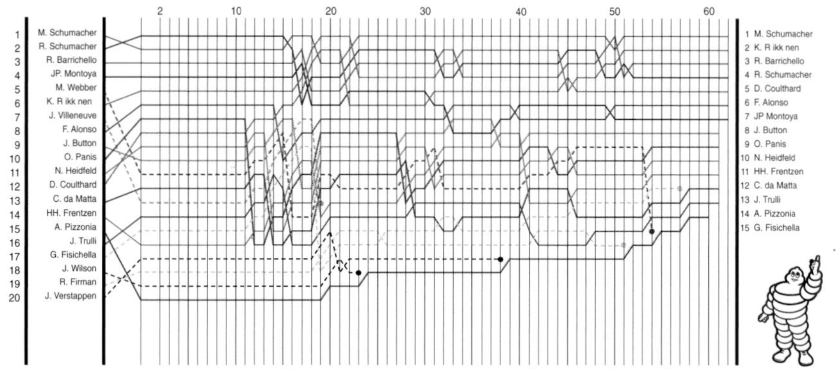

Gaps on the leader board

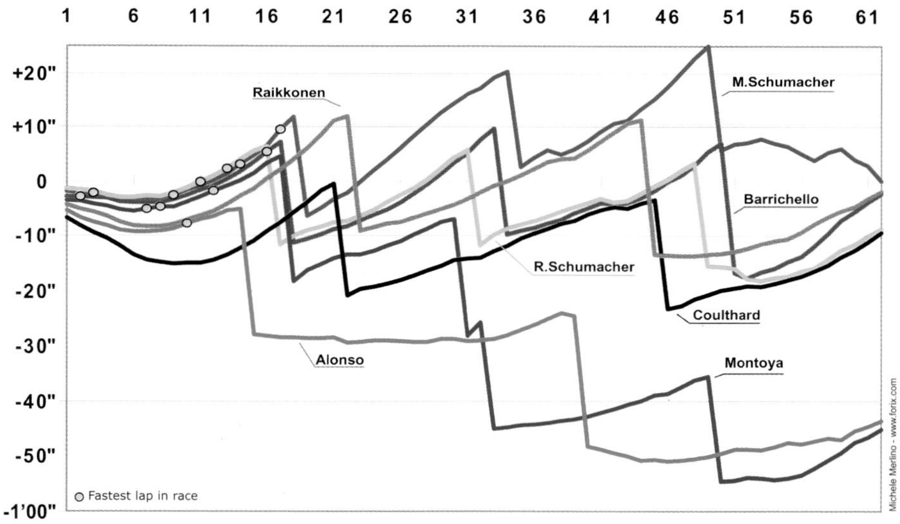

Championship after four rounds

Drivers

1. K. Räikkönen ....(1 win) 32
2. D. Coulthard ....(1 win) 19
3. M. Schumacher ....(1 win) 18
4. F. Alonso 17
5. R. Barrichello 14
6. R. Schumacher 13
7. G. Fisichella ....(1 win) 10
8. J.P. Montoya 10
9. J. Trulli 9
10. H-H. Frentzen 7
11. J. Villeneuve 3
12. J. Button 3
13. N. Heidfeld 1
14. M. Webber 0
15. O. Panis 0
16. C. Da Matta 0
17. R. Firman 0
18. J. Verstappen 0
19. A. Pizzonia 0

J. Wilson ....-

Constructors

1. West McLaren Mercedes........(2 wins) 51
2. Scuderia Ferrari Marlboro ......(1 win).........32
3. Mild Seven Renault F1 Team 26
4. BMW Williams F1 Team 23
5. Jordan Ford.........................(1 win).........10
6. Sauber Petronas 8
7. Lucky Strike BAR Honda 6
8. Panasonic Toyota Racing 0
9. Jaguar Racing..0
10. European Minardi Cosworth.........................0

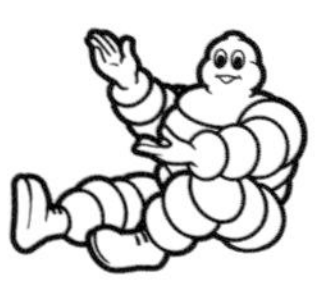

The circuit

Name	Autodromo Enzo & Dino Ferrari, Imola
Date	April 20th, 2003
Lenght	4933 meters
Distance	62 laps, 305,609 km
Weather	Cloudy but hot, 18-19°c
Track temperature	21-24°c

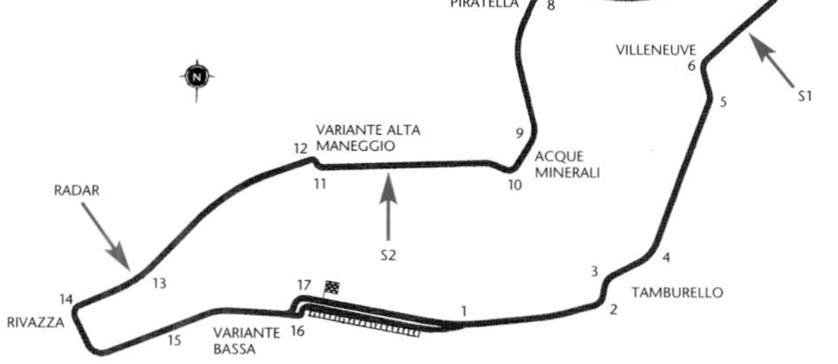

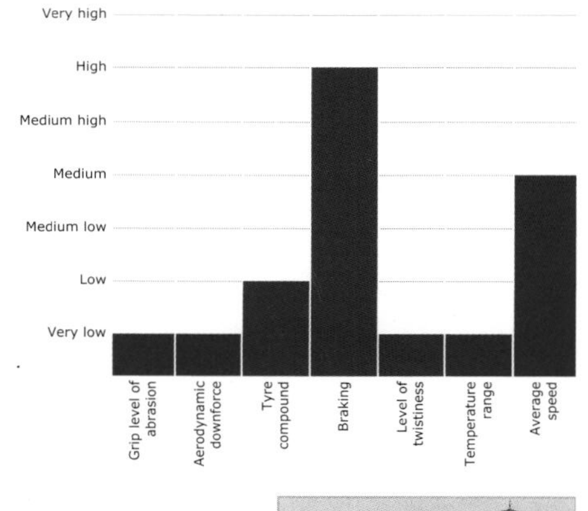

All results : © 2003 Formula One Administration Ltd,
6 Princes Gate, London, SW7 1QJ, England

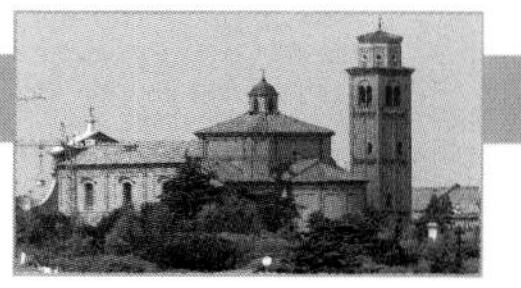

THE F2003-GA GETS OFF TO A GOOD START

The new Ferrari, the F2003-GA, finally made its official debut in Barcelona.
In qualifying, it was good enough to get both its drivers onto the front row. In the race, it was good enough to win, but it was definitely not dominant. This performance reassured the Scuderia's rivals, who had previously been frightened by what they had heard. "*If we had believed what people were telling us about this car, we would not even have bothered to come and race here,*" said Flavio Briatore. Michael Schumacher led pretty much from start to finish. But behind him, local hero Fernando Alonso finished second ahead of Rubens Barrichello, much to the delight of the Spanish crowd.

^ The new F2003-GA was quick and looked fantastic under the Catalan sun.

The front row for the Scuderia's new monster

The Scuderia's new car was not pussyfooting around on its official grand prix debut: after Saturday's qualifying, Michael Schumacher and Rubens Barrichello had monopolised the front row of the grid.

After four rounds of the 2003 championship, Schumacher was only third on points. Apart from some serious bad luck, the delay in introducing the new car was partly to blame for this situation. The Scuderia kicked off the year with the F2002, while development testing of the F2003-GA was not going to plan. After two big shunts, the F2003-GA ("GA" in honour of Giovanni Agnelli, the Fiat patriarch who had died earlier in the year) suffered from several reliability problems which had delayed its appearance until this Spanish Grand Prix. So finally the beast was let out of the factory. *"We delayed the appearance of the new car until now, because we were uncertain about its reliability,"* confirmed Ross Brawn. *"In any case, we had started its development very late last season and we knew we would have to begin the season with the old chassis. But after the past couple of weeks, we no longer have any concerns*

about the F2003-GA, which has covered over 3000 trouble free kilometres. It is time to bring it to races, where you can learn more about a car than in testing."*
Michael Schumacher could not hide his feelings on Saturday. One only had to look at his face during

Kimi plum last

He was still running away in the lead of the world championship, but on Saturday, Kimi Räikkönen got it all wrong. When it was time for his one quick lap, the Finn got into a slide and ended up in the gravel.
Back on track, he had lost over four seconds. The team therefore got on the radio and told him to come into the pits, rather than finish the lap, in

the press conference to see satisfaction written all over it. "It was not easy," explained the German. *"I had never driven on this circuit with this car and I had to find the right set-up. Everything had to be checked and double checked. But for sure the 2003 car has more neutral handling and is quicker."*

order to save a few kilometres-worth of fuel, as refuelling before the race is banned. Ever since the Australian Grand Prix, all the cars have to go to parc ferme after qualifying. The rule was brought in after Melbourne, where the two Minardis made no attempt to qualify before pitting in order to change engines.

"Not all at once please." The good natured Juan Pablo Montoya signs autographs on his way into the circuit.
>

>> Third place on the grid for the kid from Oviedo, Fernando Alonso. *"Of course it's great to fight with the best, especially here in front of my home crowd. I hope to score a few points, even if in theory we are not in the hunt for victory."*

Starting grid

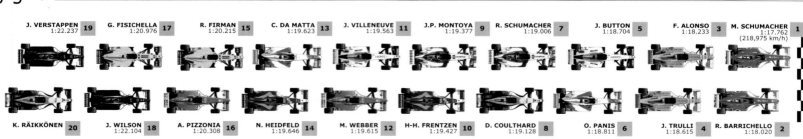

Position	Driver	Time
19	J. VERSTAPPEN	1:22.237
17	G. FISICHELLA	1:20.976
15	R. FIRMAN	1:20.215
13	C. DA MATTA	1:19.623
11	J. VILLENEUVE	1:19.563
9	J.P. MONTOYA	1:19.377
7	R. SCHUMACHER	1:19.006
5	J. BUTTON	1:18.704
3	F. ALONSO	1:18.233
1	M. SCHUMACHER	1:17.762 (218,975 km/h)
20	K. RÄIKKÖNEN	1:22.104
18	J. WILSON	1:20.308
16	A. PIZZONIA	1:19.646
14	N. HEIDFELD	1:19.615
12	M. WEBBER	1:19.427
10	H-H. FRENTZEN	1:19.128
8	D. COULTHARD	1:18.811
6	O. PANIS	1:18.615
4	J. TRULLI	1:18.020
2	R. BARRICHELLO	

Michael Schumacher wins in the new car, taking a second consecutive victory, bringing him to within 4 points of Kimi Räikkönen in the championship.

Michael Schumacher would not have won with the old car

But behind all Scuderia Ferrari's claims for the new car, what was the F2003-GA really like?

Yes, it made for an all-red front row of the grid and finished the race in first and second place. But looked at more closely, Michael Schumacher's lead over Fernando Alonso's Renault was not very impressive. And coming home third, Rubens Barrichello had been powerless against the Spanish youngster. In contrast, the previous year, the two Ferraris had also taken the front row, before Schumacher was the runaway winner of the race.

Was the F2003-GA as good as they said? *"It really is a good car,"* insisted the five times world champion after the race. *"If we had stuck with the 2002 car today, we would not have won. We really owe the win to the new car. It has improved in all areas, which is what makes it special. In the early stages, I was able to pull out a slight lead which was enough, but only just."* While he did not win by a huge margin, Schumacher had nothing bad to say about the car. *"This car is really surprising. It is beautiful and works very well. I love it. It is much more neutral than the old one. Drivers always want neutral handling cars. Having said that, we knew the race would be difficult, which was no surprise looking at the times that the Renaults did in qualifying."*

The F2003-GA was only in the early stages of its development. As it learnt more about the car there was no doubt that the team would be able to improve its performance. But what was left to discover, given that it had already worked it way through 7530 kilometres in testing – the equivalent to 25 Grands Prix!

After five races, the mystery surrounding the new Ferrari had now been partly lifted. It therefore seemed that the outcome of the 2003 season might well depend on the qualities of the new McLaren MP4-18, which was currently expected to show up for the Monaco Grand Prix!

If the Woking wonder was not up to the job and while the Williams-BMW seemed to be wide of the mark at this early stage of the year, it looked as though the name of the 2003 world champion would be the same one seen on the trophy in 2000, 2001 and 2002!

<
(on left)
First corner collision, as Jarno Trulli runs into David Coulthard.

(under)
lap 18: Coulthard again, this time fighting off Jenson Button, by shutting the door... and crashing. The BAR gets going again but has to pit for a new nose.

Race summary

> The pack heads for the first chicane. Alonso already looks threatening and splits the two Ferraris **(1)**.

> Having made a mess of qualifying, Raikkonen starts from the back row. He is about to hit Pizzonia on the grid **(2)**.

> The first chicane is always problematic. Once again, several drivers are forced to run wide **(3)**.

> Trulli and Coulthard touch on the opening lap. Trulli retires while Coulthard continues **(4)**.

> The battle rages. Button and Coulthard fight it out until both men retire after colliding **(5)**.

> Alonso passes Barrichello before putting Michael Schumacher under constant pressure, following the winning

Ferrari all the way to the flag **(6)**.

> 3rd podium of the season for Alonso **(7)**.

paddock

Weekend gossip

> "A new car is a bit like a baby. You know when it is due to come into the world, but it can be a bit early or a bit late." So said David Coulthard on the subject of the arrival of the new McLaren MP4-18, which was due very shortly. It seems that even in F1, sometimes babies never come at all…

> Glory for Michael Schumacher! In Barcelona the reigning world champion unveiled a plaque in his honour on the "Avenue of Champions," an area behind the main grandstand. The plaque marked the German's four wins at this circuit.

> It was only the fifth grand prix of the 2003 season, but the driver transfer rumours had already started. It seemed that Antonio Pizzonia would not finish the season at Jaguar. He could be replaced by Alexander Wurz, third driver at McLaren,

as Ron Dennis was apparently ready to let him go for the tidy sum of a million dollars.

> This year, 96,000 spectators had poured into the circuit, against 98,000 in 2002. The drop in numbers might have been even greater if the Alonso phenomenon had not drawn in large numbers of Spaniards this year.

^
A quiet but effective race from Juan Pablo Montoya, who finished fourth and picked up another five points. "The race was fun today," he remarked. "At the start, the car was quite difficult to drive because we had gone for different settings from usual. But at the end, with more rubber on the track, it was much better. I enjoyed myself."
>

>
A Spaniard on the podium and the crowd goes wild. For Kimi Räikkönen however, there was less to smile about. On the grid, the Finn ran into the back of Antonio Pizzonia, when the Jaguar's launch control failed to work properly.

Viva Fernando!

The Spanish spectators only had eyes for him and they got their money's worth: Fernando Alonso, all of 21 years old, finished second, just over five seconds down on Michael Schumacher. It was not a big gap after 65 laps of racing.
It was the best result of his Formula 1 career and it was his fifth podium finish from five grands prix! "It's really fantastic," he enthused. "This is the best place to finish second. The whole weekend went perfectly for the team. The race was quite easy, because the gaps between Michael, Rubens and me were always

quite big. I was going quickly, but without much pressure. I cannot dream of anything better at the moment. In fact I think I am dreaming now while I'm awake."
The dream looked like continuing for quite some time. In Barcelona, rumours were flying round the paddock that Ferrari was interested in the young Spaniard, no doubt in a bid to groom a successor to Michael Schumacher as another rumour would have us believe that the German was planning to hang up his helmet at the end of the 2004 season.

The FIA backs down

Traction control was supposed to be banned as from the British Grand Prix, but this had been put back to the start of the 2004 season. Then, just prior to the Spanish Grand Prix, the FIA announced that this move had been cancelled for the foreseeable future. However, launch control and fully automatic gearboxes will be banned in 2004.
Several planned changes were reviewed in a meeting held in London between the FIA and the team bosses. The latter were keen to avoid take a backward technological step, which would have been very costly and time consuming, especially as far as returning to manual gearboxes was concerned. The idea of having just one rear wing type was also delayed until 2006 after a series of tests.
On the engine side, the FIA stuck to its guns as regards its idea of running just one engine per race weekend as from 2004, but agreed not to go any further (one engine for two grands prix in 2005 and one engine for six grands prix in 2006.) This would be in exchange for the engine suppliers selling their V10s to the smaller teams at a reasonable price, fixed at 10 million dollars per year.

Practice

All the time trials

N°	Driver	Chassis n° – Engine	Private testing	Pos.	Practice friday	Pos.	Qualifying friday	Pos.	Practice saturday	Pos.	Warm-up	Pos.	Qualifying saturday	Pos.
1.	Michael Schumacher	Ferrari F2003-GA 229			1:18.738	15	1:17.130	1	1:18.623	4	1:19.260	4	1:17.762	1
2.	Rubens Barrichello	Ferrari F2003-GA 228			1:18.303	10	1:17.218	3	1:18.214	2	1:18.872	1	1:18.020	2
3.	Juan Pablo Montoya	Williams FW25 04 - BMW			1:17.897	6	1:18.607	14	1:19.819	15	1:19.958	8	1:19.377	9
4.	Ralf Schumacher	Williams FW25 05 - BMW			1:17.015	1	1:18.409	11	1:19.846	16	1:19.439	6	1:19:006	7
5.	David Coulthard	McLaren MP4-17D 09 - Mercedes			1:17.209	4	1:18.060	9	1:19.150	7	1:20.127	12	1:19.128	8
6.	Kimi Räikkönen	McLaren MP4-17D 06 - Mercedes			1:19.337	18	1:17.862	8	1:19.012	6	1:19.419	5		20
7.	Jarno Trulli	Renault R23-03	1:17.706	1	1:17.138	2	1:17.149	2	1:18.263	3		18	1:18.615	4
8.	Fernando Alonso	Renault R23-04	1:18.048	3	1:17.184	3	1:18.100	10	1:17.670	1	1:18.928	2	1:18.233	3
9.	Nick Heidfeld	Sauber C22-03 - Petronas			1:19.219	17	1:19.050	17	1:20.349	18	1:20.116	11	1:19.646	14
10.	Heinz-Harald Frentzen	Sauber C22-04 - Petronas			1:18.691	13	1:18.909	16	1:19.729	13		19	1:19.427	10
11.	Giancarlo Fisichella	Jordan EJ13-04 - Ford	1:17.991	2	1:18.954	16	1:18.879	15	1:19.773	14			1:20.976	17
12.	Ralph Firman	Jordan EJ13-03 - Ford	1:18.761	7	1:18.639	12	1:19.195	18	1:20.298	17	1:20.478	14	1:20.215	15
14.	Mark Webber	Jaguar R4-04	1:18.731	6	1:17.933	7	1:17.793	7	1:19.172	9	1:20.405	13	1:19.615	12
15.	Antonio Pizzonia	Jaguar R4-02	1:18.699	5	1:18.350	11	1:18.528	13	1:19.262	10	1:20.836	15	1:20.308	16
16.	Jacques Villeneuve	BAR 005-3 - Honda			1:18.731	14	1:18.461	12	1:19.525	12	1:19.998	9	1:19.563	11
17.	Jenson Button	BAR 005-4 - Honda			1:17.966	8	1:17.613	5	1:19.159	8	1:19.245	3	1:18.704	5
18.	Justin Wilson	Minardi PS03/03 - Cosworth	1:21.036	8	1:20.264	19	1:21.100	20	1:21.960	20	1:22.002	17	1:22.104	18
19.	Jos Verstappen	Minardi PS03/01 - Cosworth	1:21.294	9	1:20.559	20	1:20.822	19	1:21.945	19	1:21.997	16	1:22.237	19
20.	Olivier Panis	Toyota TF103/05			1:17.220	5	1:17.746	6	1:18.985	5	1:19.792	7	1:18.811	6
21.	Cristiano da Matta	Toyota TF103/02			1:18.101	9	1:17.443	4	1:19.342	11	1:20.039	10	1:19.623	13
34.	Allan McNish	Renault R23-01	1:18.625	4										

Maximum speeds

N°	Driver	P1 Qualifs	Pos.	P1 Race	Pos.	P2 Qualifs	Pos.	P2 Race	Pos.	Finish Qualifs	Pos.	Finish Race	Pos.	Trap Qualifs	Pos.	Trap Race	Pos.
1.	M. Schumacher	292,6	1	291,9	1	302,9	2	304,9	2	291,5	2	289,6	2	322,2	2	331,5	1
2.	R. Barrichello	290,4	3	291,1	2	304,0	1	307,9	1	293,4	1	290,8	1	325,4	1	328,2	2
3.	J.P. Montoya	289,0	7	285,7	5	297,9	5	299,1	9	286,3	5	285,9	7	311,6	9	320,8	9
4.	R. Schumacher	291,4	2	287,3	3	298,6	4	298,1	11	287,8	4	287,1	3	313,4	7	319,1	12
5.	D. Coulthard	287,6	9	280,0	11	294,1	12	300,3	6	282,7	13	283,4	10	308,2	13	327,9	3
6.	K. Räikkönen	289,9	4			296,2	11			286,3	6			316,4	3		
7.	J. Trulli	285,7	10			291,4	17			282,4	15			309,1	11	291,0	18
8.	F. Alonso	289,3	6	285,9	4	292,2	14	294,6	14	283,6	12	283,5	9	307,7	14	317,6	15
9.	N. Heidfeld	284,8	12	278,2	12	297,0	8	299,6	8	285,3	9	281,7	12	314,4	6	323,1	8
10.	H-H. Frentzen	284,3	13	277,4	13	297,5	6	297,1	12	284,5	10	280,6	14	312,2	8	320,1	10
11.	G. Fisichella	280,8	18	269,7	16	289,5	18	295,4	13	276,2	20	280,7	13	306,2	18	320,1	11
12.	R. Firman	283,9	16	282,3	9	291,8	15	293,9	15	277,9	18	279,4	16	307,0	15	317,8	13
14.	M. Webber	284,2	15	283,3	7	291,5	16	300,0	7	282,7	14	284,1	8	306,6	17	323,4	7
15.	A. Pizzonia	285,4	11			293,8	13			281,6	16			304,8	19		
16.	J. Villeneuve	284,2	14	268,5	17	297,4	7	298,4	10	283,6	11	282,5	11	308,3	12	316,4	16
17.	J. Button	288,2	8	280,5	10	299,0	3	301,7	3	288,1	3	286,4	6	310,9	10	325,9	4
18.	J. Wilson	281,1	17	270,8	15	288,4	20	293,7	16	277,0	19	278,6	17	306,7	16	316,4	17
19.	J. Verstappen	280,3	19	276,2	14	289,3	19	293,6	17	278,2	17	279,4	15	302,6	20	317,6	14
20.	O. Panis	289,9	5	282,7	8	296,8	9	300,7	5	286,1	8	287,0	5	315,6	4	324,2	5
21.	C. Da Matta	274,3	20	283,9	6	296,4	10	301,0	4	286.3	7	287,1	4	315,1	5	323,6	6

Race

Classification & Retirements

Pos.	Driver	Team	Lap	Time	Average
1.	M. Schumacher	Ferrari	65	1:33:46.933	196,619 km/h
2.	F. Alonso	Renault	65	+ 5.716	196,420 km/h
3.	R. Barrichello	Ferrari	65	+ 18.001	195,992 km/h
4.	J.P. Montoya	Williams BMW	65	+ 1:02.022	194,476 km/h
5.	R. Schumacher	Williams BMW	64	1 Lap	193,289 km/h
6.	C. Da Matta	Toyota	64	1 Lap	193,277 km/h
7.	M. Webber	Jaguar	64	1 Lap	193,044 km/h
8.	R. Firman	Jordan Ford	63	2 Laps	190,207 km/h
9.	J. Button	BAR Honda	63	2 Laps	189,792 km/h
10.	N.Heidfeld	Sauber Petronas	63	2 Laps	189,761 km/h
11.	J. Wilson	Minardi Cosworth	63	2 Laps	188,221 km/h
12.	J. Verstappen	Minardi Cosworth	62	3 Laps	185,894 km/h

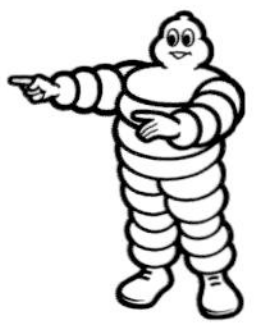

Driver	Team		Reason
G. Fisichella	Jordan Ford	44	Broken engine
O. Panis	Toyota	42	Gearbox prob.
H-H. Frentzen	Sauber Petronas	39	Broken left front pushrod
D. Coulthard	McLaren Mercedes	18	Speared by Button (turn 1)
J. Villeneuve	BAR Honda	13	Minor fire in engine wiring
J. Trulli	Renault	0	Hits Coulthard's left rear wheel, crashes
A. Pizzonia	Jaguar	0	Prob. with launch control, stays glued to the grid and his hit by Räikkönen
K. Räikkönen	McLaren Mercedes	0	Hits the back of Pizzonia's Jaguar

Fastests Laps

	Driver	Time	Lap	Average
1.	R. Barrichello	1:20.143	52	212,470 km/h
2.	M. Schumacher	1:20.307	51	212,036 km/h
3.	F. Alonso	1:20.476	42	211,591 km/h
4.	R. Schumacher	1:20.798	8	210,747 km/h
5.	O. Panis	1:20.803	14	210,734 km/h
6.	C. Da Matta	1:20.935	22	210,391 km/h
7.	J. Button	1:21.300	7	209,446 km/h
8.	J.P. Montoya	1:21.448	21	209,065 km/h
9.	H-H. Frentzen	1:21.791	32	208,189 km/h
10.	M. Webber	1:21.967	20	207,742 km/h
11.	J. Villeneuve	1:22.175	9	207,216 km/h
12.	N. Heidfeld	1:22.568	34	206,230 km/h
13.	D. Coulthard	1:22.577	10	206,207 km/h
14.	R. Firman	1:22.719	29	205,853 km/h
15.	G. Fisichella	1:22.900	17	205,404 km/h
16.	J. Verstappen	1:22.942	16	205,300 km/h
17.	J. Wilson	1:23.222	7	204,609 km/h

Pit stops

	Driver	Time	Lap	Stop n°
1.	R. Firman	32.192	1	1
2.	H-H. Frentzen	32.386	1	1
3.	D. Coulthard	33.970	1	1
4.	N. Heidfeld	30.677	4	1
5.	J. Button	28.762	14	1
6.	J. Werstappen	31.056	14	1
7.	O. Panis	32.495	16	1
8.	J. Wilson	33.799	16	1
9.	F. Alonso	29.523	17	1
10.	C. Da Matta	29.231	17	1
11.	R. Schumacher	31.452	18	1
12.	M. Webber	33.604	18	1
13.	J. Button	54.419	18	2
14.	M. Schumacher	29.897	19	1
15.	J.P. Montoya	31.909	19	1
16.	R. Barrichello	29.688	20	1
17.	G. Fisichella	46.797	22	1
18.	R. Firman	32.171	25	2
19.	J. Verstappen	31.240	28	2
20.	C. Da Matta	29.513	29	2
21.	H-H. Frentzen	30.821	30	2
22.	N. Heidfeld	29.315	32	2
23.	M. Schumacher	28.980	35	2
24.	R. Barrichello	28.926	36	2
25.	F. Alonso	28.245	37	2
26.	J. Wilson	33.994	38	2
27.	R. Schumacher	31.021	41	2
28.	O. Panis	31.879	41	2
29.	J.P. Montoya	30.795	42	2
30.	R. Firman	37.230	43	3
31.	M. Webber	31.880	44	2
32.	J. Button	31.437	44	3
33.	N. Heidfeld	29.286	44	3
34.	J. Verstappen	1:21.735	44	3
35.	C. Da Matta	29.981	48	3
36.	M. Schumacher	29.051	49	3
37.	F. Alonso	28.928	50	3
38.	R. Barrichello	28.998	50	3
39.	N. Heidfeld	19.919	53	4

Race leaders

Driver	Laps in the lead	Nbr of Laps
M. Schumacher	1 > 18	18
R. Barrichello	19 > 20	2
M. Schumacher	21 > 35	15
F. Alonso	36 > 37	2
M. Schumacher	38 > 49	12
F. Alonso	50	1
M. Schumacher	51 > 65	15

Driver	Nbr of Laps	Kilometers
M. Schumacher	60	283,674 km
F. Alonso	3	14,190 km
R. Barrichello	2	9,460 km

Lap chart

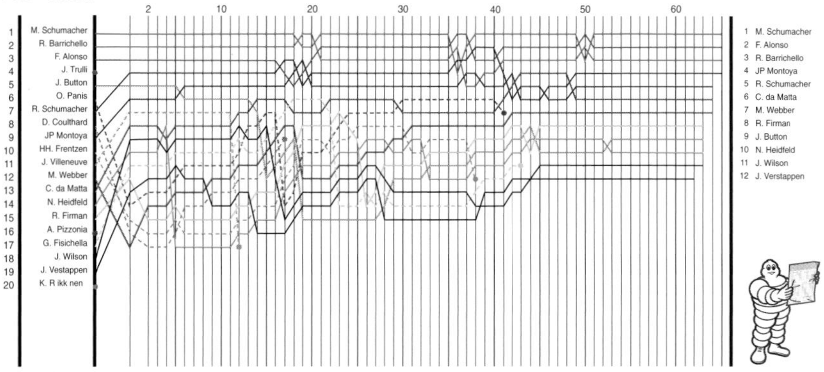

Gaps on the leader board

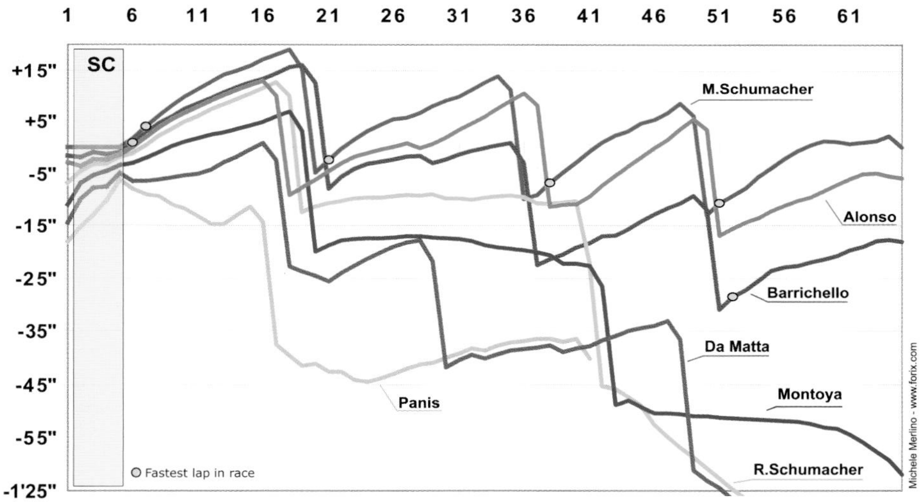

Championship after five rounds

Drivers

1. K. Räikkönen ....(1 win) 32
2. M. Schumacher ....(2 wins)................28
3. F. Alonso 25
4. R. Barrichello.......................................20
5. D. Coulthard ....(1 win) 19
6. R. Schumacher 17
7. J.P. Montoya 15
8. G. Fisichella ....(1 win) 10
9. J. Trulli 9
10. H-H. Frentzen..7
11. J. Villeneuve 3
12. C. Da Matta...3
13. J. Button...3
14. M. Webber 2
15. N. Heidfeld..1
16. R. Firman..1
17. O. Panis..0
18. J. Verstappen 0
19. J. Wilson...0
20. A. Pizzonia 0

Constructors

1. West McLaren Mercedes........(2 wins).......51
2. Scuderia Ferrari Marlboro......(2 wins).......48
3. Mild Seven Renault F1 Team 34
4. BMW Williams F1 Team 32
5. Jordan Ford..........................(1 win).........11
6. Sauber Petronas 8
7. Lucky Strike BAR Honda 6
8. Panasonic Toyota Racing 3
9. Jaguar Racing...2
10. European Minardi Cosworth........................0

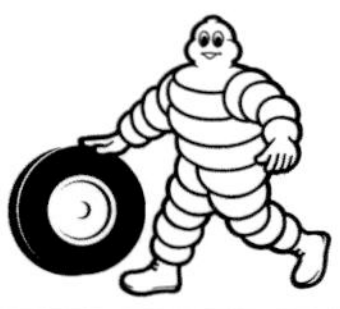

The circuit

Name	Circuit de Catalunya, Barcelona
Date	May 4th, 2003
Lenght	4730 meters
Distance	65 laps, 307,324 km
Weather	Sunny and hot, 23-26°c
Track temperature	26-32°c

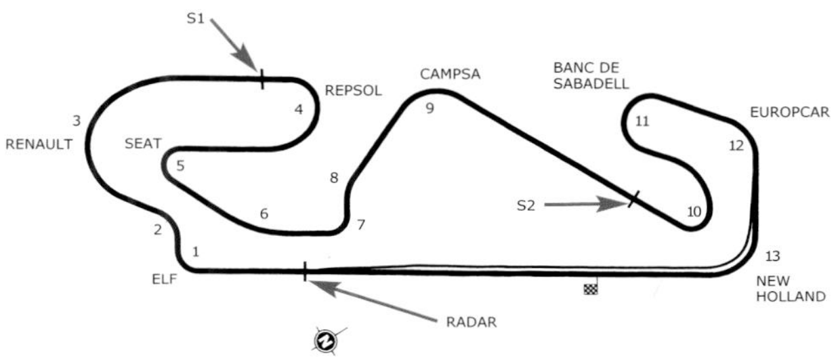

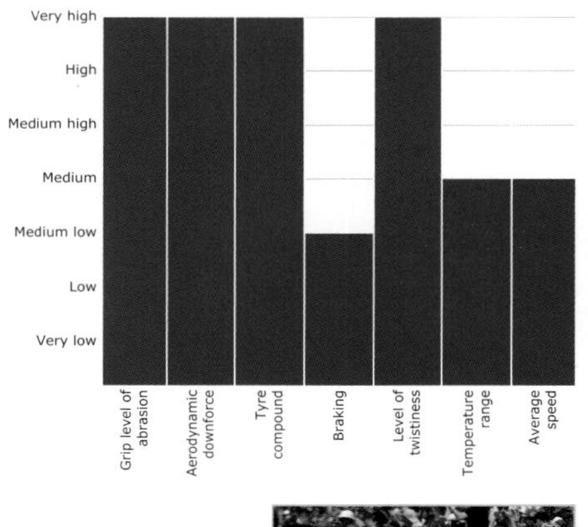

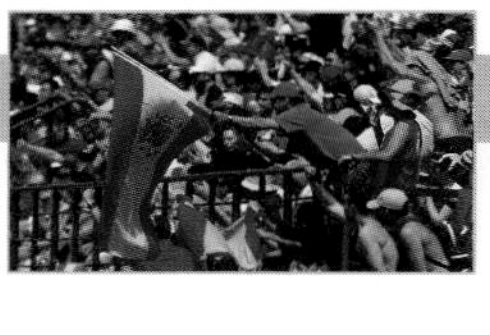

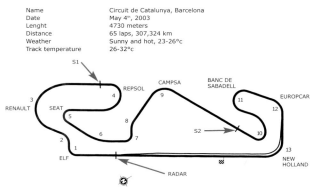

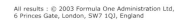

MICHAEL TURNS UP THE HEAT

Michael Schumacher pulled off another stunning exploit in Zeltweg. He won the Austrian Grand Prix even though his car caught fire during his first pit stop. The incident cost him 20 seconds, but the Ferrari man remained calm in the cockpit while the mechanics put out the flames. "*I guess the guys thought I was feeling the cold and decided to warm me up a bit,*" he joked after the race. "*It was not much fun seeing the flames in the mirrors. But I stayed in the car because I realised immediately that the guys seemed to have the situation under control.*"

A third consecutive win meant that the reigning world champion had now closed to within just two points of championship leader Kimi Räikkönen, who finished second.

> And that's pole! The entire Ferrari team explodes with delight after yet another star performance from Michael Schumacher. He predicted that the best of the F2003-GA was yet to come.

Michael on pole with the Saubers surprising

(below)
Kimi Räikkönen was second quickest in qualifying, just 39 thousandths slower than Michael Schumacher. "*I am particularly happy, especially after the disaster at the last grand prix.*" (he was 20th on the grid.)

(bottom)
A packed crowd around the Zeltweg circuit for the final Austrian Grand Prix. The race has disappeared from the 2004 calendar.
v

But how did Nick Heidfeld do that? The Saubers had been struggling to get onto the top half of the grid in this first half of the season since the Malaysian Grand Prix, but here was Nick Heidfeld setting the fourth fastest time in qualifying for the Austrian Grand Prix. It was a minor miracle given his performance up until then – 12th on Friday and 11th on Saturday morning.

His return to form was even more of a miracle, given that the German had to leap into his spare car after his race car developed a problem in the fifteen minute warm-up session held just before qualifying. "*I am really happy with this result,*" he rejoiced afterwards. "*Especially in these circumstances. I really have to thank the team as when I had to take the spare, I thought it would*

be a compromise. But actually, the spare was identical to my race car, except that it was quicker! Fantastic!" Peter Sauber was impressed. "*I am very proud of Nick. It takes some doing to take the spare, having driven the other car all weekend. He only had one lap to get used to it and I can tell you that it takes nerves of steel and enormous confidence to attack flat out in a car*

which you have not tested. I really admire Nick for this performance." In fact, Sauber has a tradition of going well at this Zeltweg circuit. In 1998, Jean Alesi was second quickest, starting from the front row! "*We know this track particularly well,*" continued Peter Sauber. "*We are in the habit of being quick here because we know what settings work well.*"

The MP4-18 really does exist!

Former Formula 1 driver and commentator for British television on ITV, Martin Brundle, had seen it the previous week. And he is happy to tell anyone who will listen that "she" is absolutely fantastic, surprising and revolutionary. "She" is the new McLaren MP4-18, which should have appeared earlier this season, but

was running behind schedule. Now finally in one piece, it was due to make its track debut later in the week at the Castellet circuit, prior to making its race debut one month later at the Canadian Grand Prix. In Monaco however, McLaren decided to err on the side of caution and run the current MP4-17D.

Starting grid

| F. ALONSO* 19 1:20.113 | M. WEBBER* 17 1:11.662 | H-H. FRENTZEN* 15 1:11.307 | C. DA MATTA** 13 1:10.834 | O. PANIS 11 1:10.402 | G. FISICHELLA 9 1:10.105 | J. BUTTON 7 1:09.935 | R. BARRICHELLO 5 1:09.784 | J.P. MONTOYA 3 1:09.391 | M. SCHUMACHER 1 1:09.150 (225,214 km/h) |
| J. VERSTAPPEN 20 | J. WILSON 18 1:14.508 | R. FIRMAN 16 1:11.505 | D. COULTHARD 14 1:10.893 | J. VILLENEUVE 12 1:10.618 | R. SCHUMACHER 10 1:10.279 | A. PIZZONIA 8 1:10.045 | J. TRULLI 6 1:09.890 | N. HEIDFELD 4 1:09.725 | K. RÄIKKÖNEN 2 1:09.189 |

< One podium ceremony follows the next and they all look the same for Michael Schumacher, who won in Austria for a third consecutive time. The only difference between this one and Barcelona two weeks earlier was that Kimi Räikkönen was alongside him, rather than Fernando Alonso. It meant the Finn managed to hang onto his championship lead as he headed home from Austria.

Three starts, one fire, one big moment: a hectic afternoon in Zeltweg

This third win of the season did not exactly come easy for Michael Schumacher. Three starts, a fire, rain wetting the track and one off-track excursion: the German braved them all to take his third win in a row. The race was so busy that Ferrari team boss Jean Todt claimed it was a miracle: "*What a race!*" he exclaimed. "*I think it will figure in the Ferrari history books.*"
At the start, Cristiano da Matta stalled his car not once but twice, so that the cars all had to regroup on two further occasions.
Then, a few drops of rain made the track very slippery. "*When you are in the lead, it is not easy,*" explained Michael Schumacher. "*It was*

raining a lot at Turns 1 and 2 for a while, but less on the rest of the track and I never knew what to expect. It is easier when you are following someone, because you can see what their car is doing." The German's biggest problem occurred on lap 23 when he made his first pit stop. When his team-mate, Rubens Barrichello, had made his first visit to the pits, there was a problem with his refuelling rig and the team switched to using Schumacher's. Then, when the German arrived, a few drops of fuel had remained in the nozzle from the rig and caught fire when they dropped onto the hot Ferrari. The fire only lasted a matter of seconds and was rapidly brought under control

by the team, but it cost Michael two places. He rejoined the track behind Juan Pablo Montoya and Kimi Räikkönen, before retaking the lead nine laps later, when the Colombian suffered an engine failure on his Williams. Schumacher's race should have been a steady run to the flag from then on, but for the fact he slid off the track having found a patch of oil on lap 45! "*I think this was quite a busy and exciting race,*" he joked as he stepped off the podium. "*But it all ended well.*" With this third win, Schumacher closed to within two points of Kimi Räikkönen in the championship. It would not be long before he swallowed the Finn's lead completely.

And they're off. At the first corner, Michael Schumacher maintains his pole advantage, ahead of Juan Pablo Montoya, Kimi Räikkönen and Rubens Barrichello.
∨

Weekend gossip

> Juan Pablo Montoya was definitely out of luck. The Colombian had not made it to the podium since the Australian Grand Prix. Here, he made a good start before running into bother with a lack of hydraulic pressure which forced him to retire on lap 33. But he was not that disappointed: "*Everything was going to plan,*" he explained. "*I was catching Michael at a rate of around two seconds a lap, which shows the potential of the FW25 and that everything is moving in the right direction and the Michelin tyres are working well. Then I began to lose water pressure and I knew it was over.*" Maybe he was not too comfortable on the track, but he was certainly going well on the road. The previous week, he had been

flashed by a speed camera doing almost 200 km/h on a motorway on the Cote d'Azur not far from Monaco. His driving license was confiscated by the French authorities and he was due to appear in court shortly.

> On Saturday night, the McLaren team was authorised by the FIA to change certain vital components on the Mercedes engine in Kimi Räikkönen's car. After the race, the other teams complained, affirming that McLaren had therefore effectively modified the car in parc ferme, which is strictly forbidden. The Finn was not disqualified, but the situation had to be cleared up before the next grand prix.

Race summary

> The race finally gets underway at the third attempt (**1**).

> As Michael Schumacher refuels,

his car catches fire. The team puts out the flames and sends the driver on his way. He is now 3rd (**2**).

> Montoya is now out on his own in the lead, but his engine explodes. Another easy win slips from his grasp (**3**).

> Schumacher catches Räikkönen and gets past. With Montoya out, he is back in the lead (**4**).

> The minor places are hard fought. Button fends off Ralf Schumacher. At the finish, Coulthard slots in between the two of

them (**5**).

> Barrichello catches 2nd placed Räikkönen, but cannot get past (**6**).

> M. Schumacher is jubilant and cannot believe it (**7**).

Visible anguish

Being a mechanic during a grand prix is not an enviable task. Having spent hours preparing the cars, they are reduced to the role of spectator, with butterflies in their stomach, hoping that no mechanical woes will sideline "their" car. The worst moment comes when it is time for the pit stops. At this point, everything depends on them and a mistake is always a possibility. On Sunday, it's just two hours of anguish...

Di Montezemolo leads the revolt

> ^
> Nothing new under the sun in Austria: Rubens Barrichello finished third, while his team-mate won the race, just as happened in the previous two grands prix...

> >
> Smile, you're on camera! In Austria, the Michelin drivers were brought together for a family photo. The French company's press officer had to overcome the difficulty of getting them all together in the same place.

On Thursday, while the teams went about their business in the Zeltweg paddock in the cool of the Austrian mountains, the atmosphere was unusually hot behind the closed doors of the motorhomes. The future of Formula 1 was up for discussion. Secure in the short term, it was still under threat from a parallel championship due to get underway in 2008. At the root of the problem, Bernie Ecclestone's dictatorial control of the financial aspects of the sport. Ever since he became boss of the constructors' association in the Seventies, the Englishman had turned F1 from a minority interest sport into a global business watched by millions of television viewers. Its success had attracted several major car constructors. Today, all the big players have thrown their hat in the ring, with the exception of VAG (Volkswagen-Audi) and General Motors. The car companies invest fortunes in F1, but reckon they do not get as much out of it as they should. "*I know of no other sport where the participants are deprived of the main sources of revenue,*" explained Ferrari president, Luca di Montezemolo. "*In F1, the teams get none of the revenue from circuit advertising and we only get 47% of the television rights. Bernie must be made to see that without the constructors there is no Formula 1. We must get more.*" Grouped together in a "pirate" organisation, the GPWC, the major constructors

were now putting pressure on Ecclestone to share the cake differently. "*We are still negotiating, but if we do not reach agreement before 1st January 2004, we will organise our own parallel championship starting in 2008,*" concluded the Italian. The date having been fixed, there was now just seven months to save

F1 from what would undoubtedly be a devastating schism for F1. No one was too optimistic and negotiations between the constructors, Bernie Ecclestone and the banks, which own 75% of his company, had already been dragging on for three years, so far without reaching a successful conclusion.

The Williams-BMW marriage: the couple are bickering

Gerhard Berger, the director of BMW's F1 programme, who was due to leave the job at the end of June, had caused consternation earlier in the week, with a quote in the German newspaper, "Bild" that the German engine supplier "*would never win a world championship if it stayed with Williams.*"
On Thursday, BMW's other boss, Mario Theissen, confirmed these reservations. "*We are not happy with the current situation. We are fourth in the*

constructors' classification and that falls well short of our expectations," he affirmed. "*We have to do something to fix the problem. Especially, we need to look at how the team operates.*" BMW evidently had plans to infiltrate the Williams organisational structure, which to date was under the sole control of its two owners, Frank Williams and Patrick Head. "*If we look at the way the team is structured, how its research department is organised, one realises that there is a lot to do,*"

continued Theissen. "*There is also a problem with the ability of the staff, as well as with the available budget.*" The contract with the English team was due to expire at the end of 2004 and, for the time being, BMW did not seem prepared to extend it. "*We are currently looking at our options,*" concluded Theissen. "*If we continue with Williams, it would be with guarantees of winning, which is definitely not the case at the moment.*"

> >
> Jacques Villeneuve had a quiet race in Austria: starting from twelfth on the grid, he finished twelfth having lost a lot of time during a pit stop. But after two consecutive retirements, the result could be considered as progress.

Practice

All the time trials

N°	Driver	N° Chassis - Engine	Private testing	Pos.	Practice friday	Pos.	Qualifying friday	Pos.	Practice saturday	Pos.	Warm-up	Pos.	Qualifying saturday	Pos.
1.	Michael Schumacher	Ferrari F2003-GA 229			1:08.968	4	1:07.908	1	1:09.331	3	1:09.639	3	1:09.150	1
2.	Rubens Barrichello	Ferrari F2003-GA 228			1:09.826	12	1:08.187	2	1:09.241	1	1:10.852	13	1:109.784	5
3.	Juan Pablo Montoya	Williams FW25 06 - BMW			1:09.530	10	1:08.839	6	1:09.301	2	1:09.323	1	1:09.391	3
4.	Ralf Schumacher	Williams FW25 05 - BMW			1:09.961	13		20	1:09.418	4	1:12.560	19	1:10.279	10
5.	David Coulthard	McLaren MP4-17D 08 - Mercedes			1:08.836	1	1:08.947	7	1:10.222	15	1:10.184	7	1:10.893	14
6.	Kimi Räikkönen	McLaren MP4-17D 09 - Mercedes			1:10.019	14	1:08.978	8	1:09.870	7	1:09.628	2	1:09.189	2
7.	Jarno Trulli	Renault R23-03	1:10.338	4	1:08.944	2	1:09.450	11	1:09.704	5	1:09.973	4	1:09.890	6
8.	Fernando Alonso	Renault R23-04	1:10.380	5	1:09.071	6	1:09.680	13	1:09.923	9	1:10.108	5	1:20.113	19
9.	Nick Heidfeld	Sauber C22-02 - Petronas			1:09.374	8	1:09.479	12	1:10.044	11	1:10.413	10	1:09.725	4
10.	Heinz-Harald Frentzen	Sauber C22-03 - Petronas			1:09.800	11	1:10.055	15	1:10.456	17	1:10.961	14	1:11.307	15
11.	Giancarlo Fisichella	Jordan EJ13-04 - Ford	1:09.781	1	1:10.089	15	1:09.281	10	1:10.018	10	1:10.552	11	1:10.105	9
12.	Ralph Firman	Jordan EJ13-03 - Ford	1:10.763	7	1:10.296	16	1:11.171	19	1:11.413	18	1:12.045	17	1:11.505	16
14.	Mark Webber	Jaguar R4-04	1:10.036	3	1:09.023	5	1:08.512	3	1:09.891	8	1:10.153	6	1:11.662	17
15.	Antonio Pizzonia	Jaguar R4-03	1:09.907	2	1:08.961	3	1:09.024	9	1:10.057	12	1:10.202	8	1:10.045	8
16.	Jacques Villeneuve	BAR 005-3 - Honda			1:09.429	9	1:08.680	4	1:09.708	6	1:10.702	12	1:10.618	12
17.	Jenson Button	BAR 005-4 - Honda			1:09.374	7	1:08.831	5	1:10.212	14	1:10.243	9	1:09.935	7
18.	Justin Wilson	Minardi PS03/04 - Cosworth	1:11.280	8	1:11.060	20	1:11.056	18	1:11.936	20	1:12.817	20	1:14.508	18
19.	Jos Verstappen	Minardi PS03/03 - Cosworth	1:11.717	9	1:10.903	19	1:10.894	17	1:11.546	19	1:12.230	18		20
20.	Olivier Panis	Toyota TF103/05			1:10.504	18	1:09.764	14	1:10.076	13	1:11.243	16	1:10.402	11
21.	Cristiano da Matta	Toyota TF103/07			1:10.494	17	1:10.370	16	1:10.370	16	1:10.988	15	1:10.834	13
34.	Allan McNish	Renault R23-00	1:10.395	6										

Maximum speed

N°	Driver	P1 Qualifs	Pos.	P1 Race	Pos.	P2 Qualifs	Pos.	P2 Race	Pos.	Finish Qualifs	Pos.	Finish Race	Pos.	Trap Qualifs	Pos.	Trap Race	Pos.
1.	M. Schumacher	307,9	4	318,8	2	211,5	1	215,0	1	278,7	3	285,9	1	308,3	2	316,0	1
2.	R. Barrichello	305,9	9	319,2	1	210,7	2	214,2	3	275,5	10	285,2	2	309,0	1	314,0	2
3.	J.P. Montoya	309,0	3	309,2	14	207,7	9	208,3	9	281,7	1	283,1	6	307,9	4	309,6	7
4.	R. Schumacher	306,4	8	314,4	5	207,4	10	208,2	10	280,7	2	283,3	5	308,0	3	312,0	4
5.	D. Coulthard	304,9	12	313,9	6	203,1	17	209,9	7	276,5	7	283,0	7	302,9	11	310,7	6
6.	K. Räikkönen	309,1	2	308,3	15	207,4	11	214,9	2	276,4	8	281,6	8	305,5	7	308,2	8
7.	J. Trulli	305,5	10	309,9	12	206,0	13	206,5	14	274,8	13	276,9	16	302,6	12	306,0	15
8.	F. Alonso	307,8	5	309,3	13	209,9	3	209,3	8	276,2	9	277,2	15	302,4	13	304,5	16
9.	N. Heidfeld	306,5	7	306,9	16	208,2	7	208,0	11	275,0	12	276,3	17	305,1	8	307,5	11
10.	H-H. Frentzen	306,5	6			205,5	15			271,4	18			300,2	17		
11.	G. Fisichella	304,5	13	310,4	10	208,0	8	205,3	15	276,7	6	278,6	14	304,9	9	306,9	13
12.	R. Firman	300,2	17	310,0	11	192,2	19	202,1	17	272,3	17	279,5	10	300,9	16	307,3	12
14.	M. Webber	296,5	20	313,3	7	209,6	4	213,4	4	272,5	16	280,3	9	301,2	15	307,8	9
15.	A. Pizzonia	302,0	16	311,8	8	208,5	6	210,1	6	273,7	14	278,9	12	301,2	14	306,9	14
16.	J. Villeneuve	303,5	14	315,4	4	205,0	16	207,6	12	277,4	5	283,8	3	307,9	5	313,1	3
17.	J. Button	305,0	11	316,0	3	206,0	14	206,6	13	275,2	11	283,5	4	307,2	6	310,8	5
18.	J. Wilson	297,6	18	304,6	17	196,1	18	202,3	16	270,6	20	273,2	18	295,4	19	303,0	17
19.	J. Verstappen	296,9	19			184,0	20			270,8	19			278,4	20		
20.	O. Panis	309,7	1	303,7	18	209,1	5	199,4	18	277,4	4	278,7	13	304,4	10	302,6	18
21.	C. Da Matta	303,2	15	310,7	9	206,3	12	211,3	5	273,6	15	279,1	11	299,3	18	307,6	10

Race

Classification & Retirements

Pos.	Driver	Team	Lap	Time	Average
1.	M. Schumacher	Ferrari	69	1:24:04.888	213,003 km/h
2.	K. Räikkönen	McLaren Mercedes	69	+ 3.362	212,861 km/h
3.	R. Barrichello	Ferrari	69	+ 3.951	212,836 km/h
4.	J. Button	BAR Honda	69	+ 42.243	211,234 km/h
5.	D. Coulthard	McLaren Mercedes	69	+ 59.740	210,510 km/h
6.	R. Schumacher	Williams BMW	68	1 lap	209,589 km/h
7.	M. Webber	Jaguar	68	1 lap	209,300 km/h
8.	J. Trulli	Renault	68	1 lap	208,504 km/h
9.	A. Pizzonia	Jaguar	68	1 lap	208,270 km/h
10.	C. Da Matta	Toyota	68	1 lap	208,012 km/h
11.	R. Firman	Jordan Ford	68	1 lap	207,845 km/h
12.	J. Villeneuve	BAR Honda	68	1 lap	207,817 km/h
13.	J. Wilson	Minardi Cosworth	67	2 laps	205,216 km/h

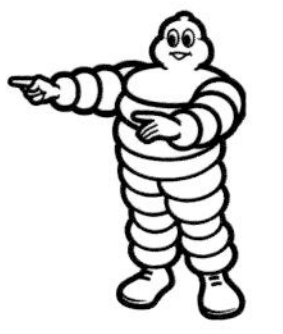

Driver	Team		Reason
G. Fisichella	Jordan Ford	61	Fuel pressure problem
N. Heidfeld	Sauber Petronas	47	Loss of engine power
F. Alonso	Renault	45	Engine failure
J.P. Montoya	Williams BMW	33	Engine failure after water loss
O. Panis	Toyota	7	Left front suspension damaged after a puncture
J. Verstappen	Minardi Cosworth	0	Launch control problem
H-H. Frentzen	Sauber Petronas	0	Clutch problem at second start

Fastest laps

	Driver	Time	Lap	Average
1.	M. Schumacher	1:08.337	41	227,894 km/h
2.	R. Barrichello	1:08.913	44	225,989 km/h
3.	M. Webber	1:08.966	68	225,815 km/h
4.	K. Räikkönen	1:09.423	45	224,329 km/h
5.	D. Coulthard	1:09.626	64	223,675 km/h
6.	J. Villeneuve	1:09.764	64	223,232 km/h
7.	J. Button	1:09.828	22	223,028 km/h
8.	A. Pizzonia	1:09.978	67	222,549 km/h
9.	J.P. Montoya	1:10.112	28	222,124 km/h
10.	R. Schumacher	1:10.246	40	221,700 km/h
11.	J. Trulli	1:10.358	68	221,347 km/h
12.	C. Da Matta	1:10.466	67	221,008 km/h
13.	N. Heidfeld	1:10.516	12	220,852 km/h
14.	F. Alonso	1:10.526	34	220,820 km/h
15.	R. Firman	1:10.659	68	220,405 km/h
16.	G. Fisichella	1:11.019	60	219,287 km/h
17.	J. Wilson	1:11.267	67	218,524 km/h
18.	O. Panis	1:13.097	6	213,053 km/h

Pit stops

	Driver	Time	Lap	Stop n°
1.	O. Panis	31.636	2	1
2.	J. Wilson	28.223	3	1
3.	N. Heidfeld	29.585	13	1
4.	A. Pizzonia	32.997	14	1
5.	R. Firman	31.482	14	1
6.	R. Schumacher	29.586	15	1
7.	G. Fisichella	32.909	15	1
8.	M. Webber	33.410	15	1
9.	J. Trulli	29.922	17	1
10.	C. Da Matta	31.217	18	1
11.	J.P. Montoya	28.787	20	1
12.	D. Coulthard	29.509	20	1
13.	R. Barrichello	39.880	21	1
14.	J. Villeneuve	39.710	22	1
15.	M. Schumacher	40.755	23	1
16.	K. Räikkönen	29.337	23	1
17.	J. Button	28.541	23	1
18.	J. Wilson	32.162	24	2
19.	M. Webber	31.315	30	2
20.	F. Alonso	29.838	37	1
21.	C. Da Matta	30.632	37	2
22.	J. Trulli	28.316	38	2
23.	N. Heidfeld	30.581	39	2
24.	M. Schumacher	32.330	42	2
25.	R. Firman	31.379	42	2
26.	R. Schumacher	28.357	43	2
27.	G. Fisichella	29.567	45	2
28.	J. Wilson	29.946	45	3
29.	J. Button	30.913	47	2
30.	A. Pizzonia	29.496	47	2
31.	K. Räikkönen	29.103	49	2
32.	J. Villeneuve	1:31.533	49	2
33.	R. Barrichello	30.925	50	2
34.	D. Coulthard	27.516	50	2
35.	M. Webber	29.357	54	3

Race leaders

Driver	Laps in the lead	Nber of Laps
M. Schumacher	1 > 23	23
J.P. Montoya	24 > 31	8
M. Schumacher	32 > 42	11
K. Räikkönen	43 > 49	7
R. Barrichello	50	1
M. Schumacher	51 > 69	19

Driver	Nber of Laps	Kilometers
M. Schumacher	53	229,278 km
J.P. Montoya	8	34,608 km
K. Räikkönen	7	30,282 km
R. Barrichello	1	4,326 km

Lap chart

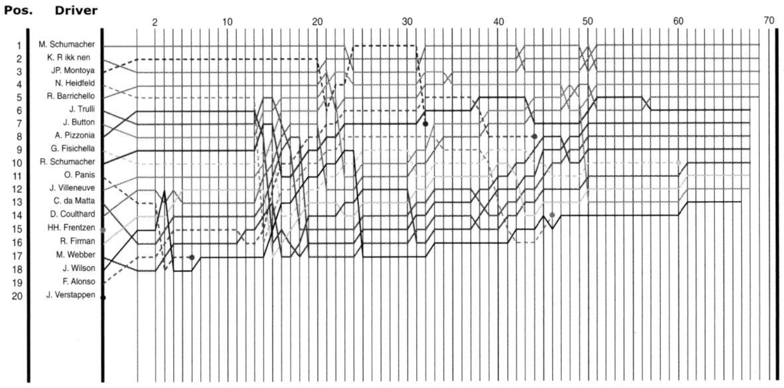

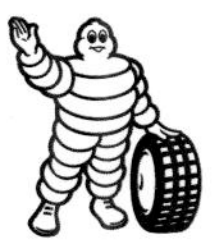

Gaps on the leader board

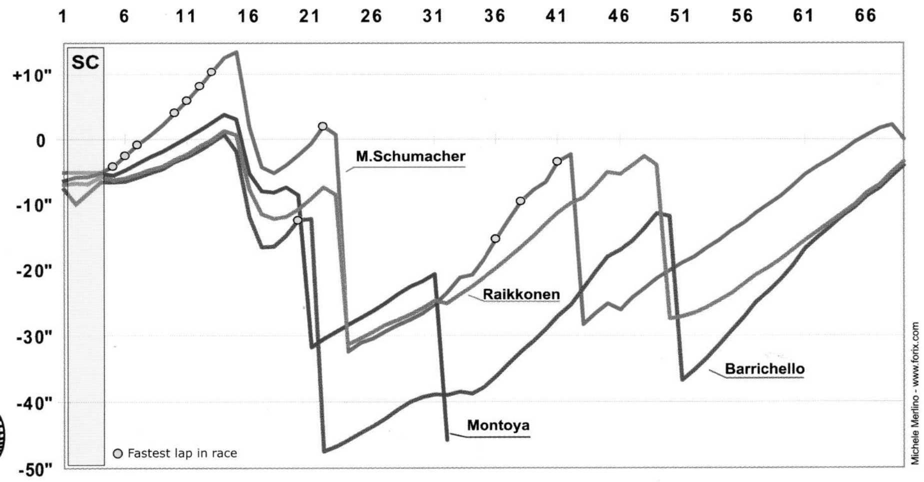

Championship after six rounds

Drivers

1. K. Räikkönen ....(1 win) 40
2. M. Schumacher ....(3 wins)................38
3. R. Barrichello...26
4. F. Alonso 25
5. D. Coulthard ....(1 win) 23
6. R. Schumacher 20
7. J.P. Montoya 15
8. G. Fisichella ....(1 win) 10
9. J. Trulli...10
10. J. Button..8
11. H-H. Frentzen..7
12. M. Webber 4
13. J. Villeneuve...3
14. C. Da Matta...3
15. N. Heidfeld...1
16. R. Firman..1
17. A. Pizzonia 0
18. O. Panis..0
19. J. Verstappen 0
20. J. Wilson...0

Constructors

1. Scuderia Ferrari Marlboro ......(3 wins) 64
2. West McLaren Mercedes ....(2 wins) 63
3. Mild Seven Renault F1 Team 35
4. BMW Williams F1 Team 35
5. Jordan Ford........................(1 win).........11
6. Lucky Strike BAR Honda..........................11
7. Sauber Petronas 8
8. Jaguar Racing..4
9. Panasonic Toyota Racing 3
10. European Minardi Cosworth.......................0

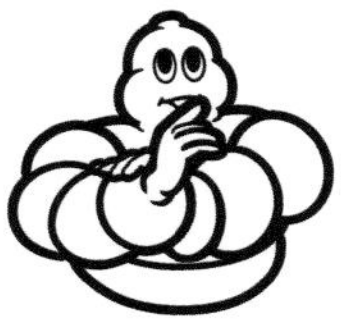

The circuit

Name	A1 Ring, Spielberg
Date	May 18, 2003
Length	4326 meters
Distance	71 laps scheduled (307.146 km,) 69 laps completed (298.494 km)
Weather	good weather with clear skies 19-22 C
Track temperature	20-31°c

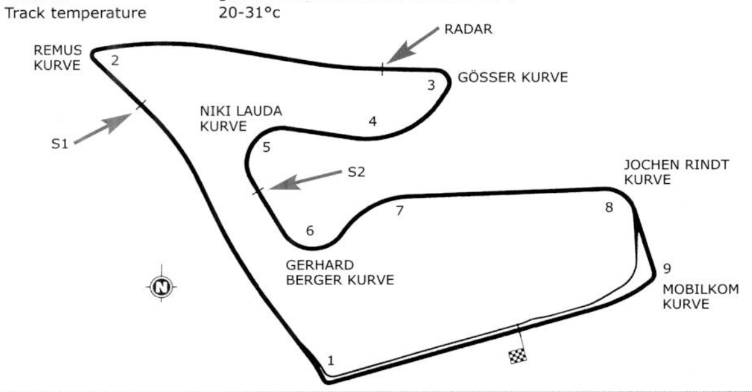

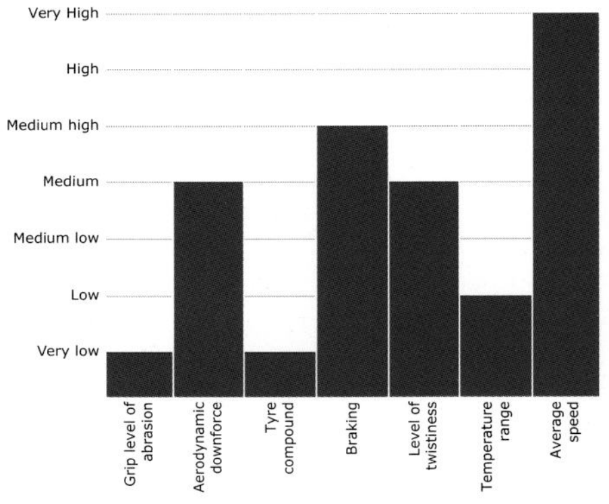

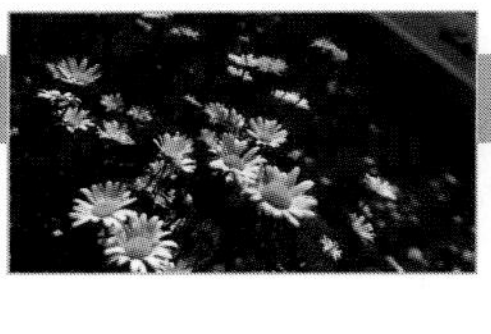

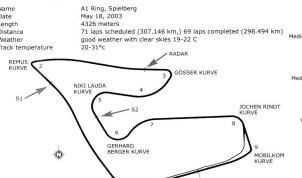

PRINCELY JUAN PABLO

Starting from third place on the grid, Juan Pablo Montoya won the Monaco Grand Prix in true style. Second already at the first corner, the Colombian propelled his Williams-BMW into the lead on lap 21, two laps before making his first pit-stop. After a second visit to the pits, he retook the lead and kept it all the way to the chequered flag.

Colombia's Juan Pablo Montoya thus took the second win of his F1 career, after a long gap dating back to the 2001 Italian Grand Prix.

Pole on Saturday, courtesy of Ralf Schumacher, the win on Sunday with Montoya; the Williams team had royally dominated the 2003 Monaco Grand Prix. As for Ralf Schumacher, he finished in fourth place.

> Ralf Schumacher attacks. His first pole position awaited at the end of the lap.

> Kimi Räikkönen qualified on the front row. "*It's very important here at Monaco. I am a little disappointed to have missed out on pole by just 36 thousandths of a second, but I guess my turn will come one day. I might have lost a bit of time at the swimming pool, because I hit the kerb a bit too hard. We will have to wait and see for the race.*"

Michelin take the top four places on the grid

Kimi Räikkönen benefited from some charming support in Monaco, which might have motivated him to get on the front row.

He was very surprised to find himself on pole, was Ralf Schumacher. In fact, as soon as the session was over, it was party time in the Williams camp, mainly because this was the first time all season that one of its cars had taken the top slot. "*Really, I didn't expect to find myself first!*" exclaimed the German after the session. "*Driving at Monaco is always a challenge, but it's also a real pleasure when the car is perfectly balanced.*" In third place, Montoya confirmed that the Anglo-German car was going well. "*We have gone through a few difficult weeks and I am happy to see that we have started to get a better understanding of how the FW25 reacts,*" was the Colombian's reaction. "*My car is well balanced, but it was bottoming on the track in some places, which cost me some time.*"

With Kimi Räikkönen third and Jarno Trulli fourth, Michelin made a clean sweep of the top four places on the grid. Indeed, tyres were the dominant factor in qualifying. "*Michelin has come up with an excellent compound here, which is very consistent,*" confirmed Ralf Schumacher. For his part, Pierre Dupasquier was back in a good mood again. "*It is really satisfying to see that our five partner teams have at least one car in the top ten,*" he commented. "*The only thing they have in common is their tyres and their collective performance shows we have come up with a very good product for this circuit.*"

Michelin had already won here in 2002 with Scotsman, David Coulthard. This year however, there were still some doubts that the tyres would perform consistently over a race distance. Nevertheless, Dupasquier was optimistic. "*In 2002, our tyres lost performance after a few laps, before coming back again a few laps later. This season, we have reached a higher performance level, while combining it with better consistency. The tyres reach their optimum after one lap, but they don't drop off after that. At least not for the next 20 laps.*" Given that no testing takes place at Monaco, there was a chance that the 78 laps of the race would still serve up a few surprises.

The Monegasque myth revisited

The Monte Carlo circuit is in itself a legend. It is, by a long way, the most difficult, the slowest and the most demanding of the season from a mechanical point of view. On the twists and turns of Monaco, any error is fatal. Here there is no running slightly onto the grass verge, nor taking a trip through the gravel trap before getting back on track. The slightest error ends up in a collision or a heavy crash into the barriers.

Every year, a few drivers complain that the track is totally unsuited to the demands of a modern Formula 1 car, marvels of modern technology turned into objects of ridicule as they tackle the mean streets of the Principality.

Aware of the problem, the organisers really have no margin to improve the circuit. Year after year, they make little modifications and this year they remodelled the port chicane and the entry to the swimming pool section. For 2003, they completely changed the pit lane exit (which now came out after the Ste. Devote chicane) and the entry to the Rascasse corner was speeded up, by opening it out to 45 degrees rather than a right angle. "*The new entry to Rascasse should make it easier to overtake,*" commented David Coulthard. "*I think it's an improvement, even if it is a shame to have changed one of the most difficult corners on the circuit. I think it is less demanding now, but I don't want to say that too often, in case I go off there!*"

On Wednesday, Michael Schumacher was not in a position to comment on the new configuration: "*I tried to see what they have done,*" he said with a grin, "*but there are so many cars on the track that I have not been able to get a clear picture of the changes yet. No doubt I will find out in practice.*"

The modifications since last year:
- 5000 square metres of land reclaimed from the sea, by piling in 400 ten tonne concrete blocks
- Circuit moved 10 metres nearer to the sea between the swimming pool exit and the entry to Rascasse
- New exit chicane at the swimming pool
- Track shortened by 30 metres to 3,340 metres

The modifications cost 20 million Euros.

Ferrari hides its disappointment

With Michael Schumacher fifth and Rubens Barrichello seventh, long faces were the order of the day in the Ferrari camp after qualifying. Jean Todt kept his head down in his notes, his teeth clenched, while the word "desastro" was echoing round the VIP guest area. The source of the problem was of course, the tyres. On Thursday, when the two Ferraris had been quickest at the end of the day, they had apparently run on the softer of the two types of tyre. On Saturday, in final qualifying, they were using the harder tyres which they planned to use in the race and they seemed less well suited to the track. The team still refused to give up hope, to the point of not excluding the possibility of a win. "*Of course, it is our worst qualifying performance of the season on a circuit where grid position is the most important factor,*" observed Todt, the Scuderia's managing director. "But we will have to see how much fuel our rivals had on board. If we can stay out on track longer than they can, we could be in the hunt for the win at the end.*"

The unique atmosphere of Monaco
V

Starting grid

Juan Pablo at the Prince's table

And they're off. Charging through from third place, Juan Pablo Montoya takes the first corner in second place.

In Monaco, it is considered bad form to splash the royal family. The champagne ceremony therefore takes place on the track at the foot of the steps to the royal box.

Waiting for the start, Michael Schumacher finds time to sign autographs for the marshals.

There is no doubt that Juan Pablo Montoya is one of the most talented drivers in Formula 1. His seven pole positions in 2002 proved, if proof was necessary, that he had plenty of speed and aggression.

He brought all these talents to bear in winning the most coveted grand prix of the season in Monaco. Starting from third on the grid, Montoya immediately went second behind Ralf Schumacher, by passing Kimi Räikkönen at the first corner.

The lead came his way on lap 21, when his team-mate made his first pit-stop, two laps before he came in for his own refuelling. After his second stop, he retook the lead and kept it all the way to the flag. "*At the start of the race, I tried to pull away from Kimi (Räikkönen)*" he explained. The worst moment came when the team asked me to push even harder before pitting! Then it was just a question of settling into a rhythm. Towards the end, Kimi was very close, but I was not worried. I just had to make sure I made no mistakes."

The Colombian thus took the second win of his F1 career, his first for a long time: since the 2001 Italian Grand Prix to be precise. "*Yes, it's been a long wait,*" he agreed. "*Last year I was on pole seven times and none of them turned into victories. It was hard to swallow. The car went well today and in fact it has been excellent since Thursday. The team did a very good job.*"

The win was partly down to the Michelin tyres, clearly superior to their Japanese rivals here in Monaco.

"*I really needed this win,*" continued Montoya. "*It's fantastic, it's almost unreal. There have been some races where I came very close to winning,* like Australia this year for example where I made a mess of it. I was a bit worried about getting it wrong again. But I've finally done it! And of course, winning in Monaco is very special. There is no other race like it in F1. It's a bit like winning the Indy 500 in the United States. It's the first time I have finished this race and I've come home in first place!" The victory meant that, according to tradition, he got to sit at Prince Rainier's table for the Sunday night Gala Dinner.

Fifth in the championship, 23 points down on the leader (who was still Kimi Räikkönen,) the Colombian admitted he was rethinking his championship chances. "*At the moment, I am quite a way back in the order, but if the car continues to go the way it has done in Austria and here, then why not? It seems that the new Ferrari has not brought them the advantage they had last year.*"

One winner and a lot of disappointed people

As it is every year, the Monaco Grand Prix was the object of all desires. Juan Pablo Montoya's victory meant failure and disappointment for many drivers.

In the McLaren camp, Kimi Räikkönen extended his championship lead over Michael Schumacher, by finishing second ahead of the German. Now, the Finn was on 48 points against 44 for the Ferrari driver. Qualified on the front row, Räikkönen lost a place to Montoya at the first corner and never managed to make up any ground after that. "*I'm definitely not having much luck*", regretted the Finn. "*It seems that all my starts have been bad this season. My race consisted of following Juan Pablo in the hope he would make a mistake, but he did not and I had no chance of passing him. On top of that, after my pit stops, even if I managed to stay out a bit longer, I always seemed to come up against traffic and so I could not get any advantage.*"

There was no joy to be had at Ferrari either. Third place for Michael Schumacher and eighth for

Rubens Barrichello was not up to the required standard, after the Scuderia failed to make up for its problems in qualifying when it came to the race. "*I could have finished higher if I had not been blocked by Trulli at the start of the race,*" regretted the reigning world champion. Ralf Schumacher was equally disappointed. Having started from pole, he could have expected to do better than fourth. He was still the only driver to have finished every 2003 grand prix in the points, but it was not enough to bring a smile to his face. In Monaco, the champion's little brother had a rather busy afternoon. He led for the first twenty laps, but never regained the lead after the pit stops. "*The balance of the car changed after the first pit stop,*" he reported. "*I don't know why, but I couldn't match the pace of the front runners.*" On lap 52, he missed his braking at Rascasse, selected reverse and lost a dozen seconds or so pulling off the manoeuvre. From then on, there was no chance of him attacking his brother.

As for David Coulthard, the Scotsman who won in

2002, brought his McLaren home seventh for two points. "*I was blocked behind Jarno Trulli for most of the race and, unfortunately, he was on the same pit-stop strategy as me.*"

Continuing down the list of those who got it wrong, Heinz-Harald Frentzen did it big time, as his Sauber did not even finish the opening lap! "*I am so sorry Peter,*" was the first phrase uttered by the German when he got back to his pits. He had quite simply got it wrong at the swimming pool chicane. Going too quickly, he rode over the kerb, causing the car to spin and crash into the barrier.

Nick Heidfeld finished eleventh, well out of the points, having been stuck for six laps behind Jos Verstappen's Minardi after his first pit-stop. As for Renault, both drivers scored points: Fernando Alonso finished fifth and Jarno Trulli was sixth after a trouble-free race. The Italian seemed disappointed at having been held up badly by backmarkers. He had qualified on the second row and had not made the most of it.

Race summary

> Jenson Button does not take part in the race, following his serious accident on Saturday **(1)**.

> A clean start sees Montoya make the most of it to get ahead of Raikkonen and set off in pursuit of Ralf **(2)**.

> Michael Schumacher makes a late refuelling stop and catches the lead duo. He is stuck behind Trulli after the second

stop **(3)**.

> Alonso makes up two positions at the start and uses the same pit stop strategy as

Michael Schumacher. He finishes 5th ahead of Trulli **(4)**.

> Raikkonen tries to close on Montoya but

it is futile and the Colombian is unbeatable **(5)**.

> Montoya on his lap of honour **(6)**.

> Patrick Head on the podium. It had been 20 years since a Williams last won at Monaco (Rosberg '83.) **(7)**.

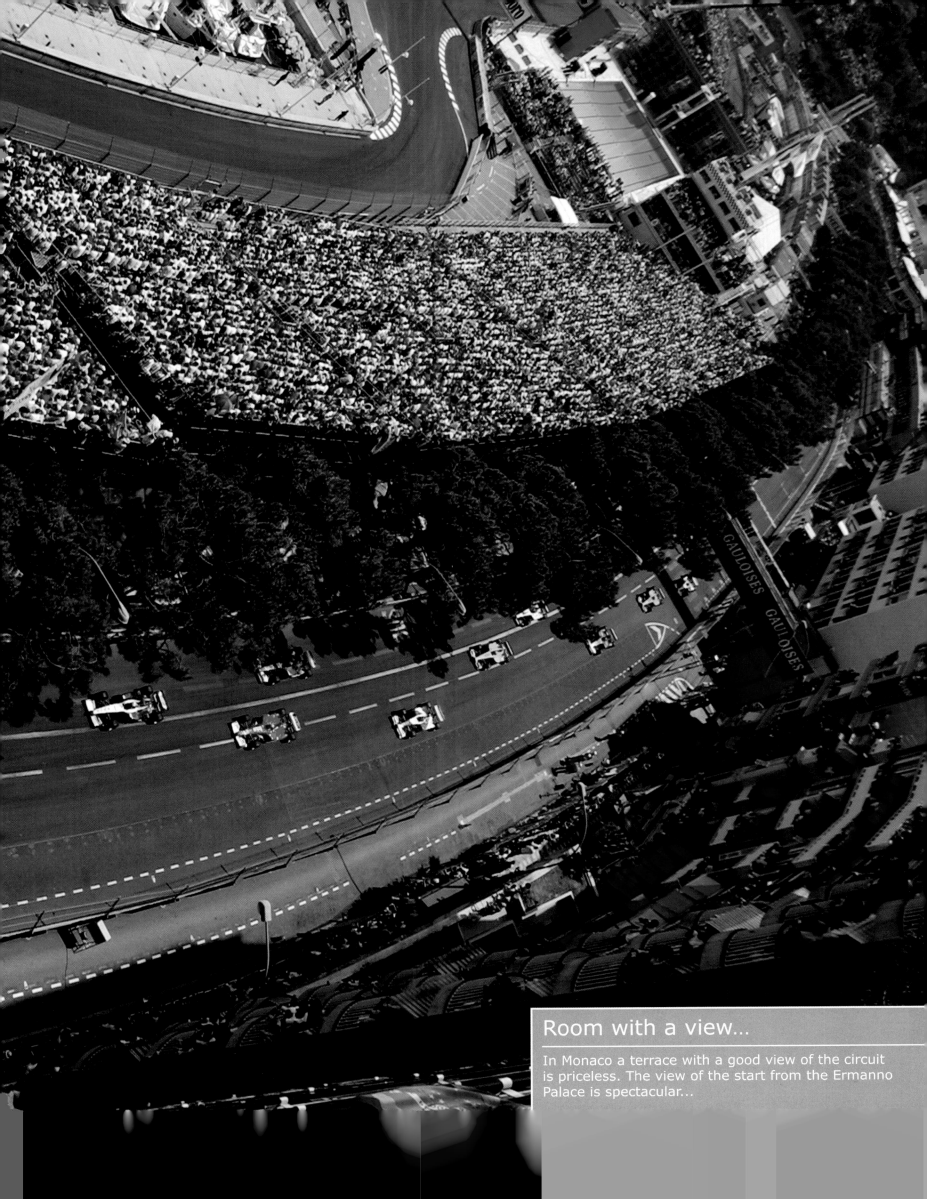

Room with a view...

In Monaco a terrace with a good view of the circuit
is priceless. The view of the start from the Ermanno
Palace is spectacular...

> Giancarlo Fisichella finished 10th in Monaco, having qualified 12th.

>> In Monaco, the track is not the only place to spot some beautiful chassis...

Renault backtracks with its V10

The Renault team is doing quite nicely thank you. In 2002, it had finished fourth in the Constructors' classification. In 2003, in Monaco, Renault found itself lying third on 35 points. In Malaysia, the two French cars had monopolised the front row of the grid and to date, Fernando Alonso had three podium finishes to his name. Front of house, everything seemed rosy, but round the back of the kitchens, a few pots were boiling over. The result was that Renault Sport boss, Jean-Jacques His had just left the team to join the Ferrari group. No one had yet been fingered as his replacement, which proved something was not quite right and that the departure had been a hasty one.

The cause of the departure centred on Renault's decision to abandon the wide angled, 110 degree V10. "*We have realised that we needed a lot of time and testing to make our engine reliable with this angle,*" explained Renault vice-president Patrick Faure. "*For 2004, given the new regulations (which require one engine to be used for an entire race weekend, practice, qualifying and race, Ed.) we have decided to return to a more classic configuration. This decision is, I think, the reason why Jean-Jacques His has decided to leave us. He would have preferred to continue with the 110 degree engine. But I think ours is the better decision and even a sort of insurance for the future.*" Even more of an insurance given that there were moves afoot to insist that, starting in 2005, the major manufacturers had to supply more than one team, as a result of a decision taken by the FIA aimed at helping the smaller teams.

The matter had upset several of the major players. "*We have to achieve three targets to be able to supply another team,*" analysed Faure. "*Firstly, we need a powerful and reliable engine, secondly we do not want to lose money and thirdly, we want to work with a team which would be a partner rather than just a customer.*"

The FIA had suggested a figure of 10 million dollars per season as the maximum cost a constructor could ask a team to pay for an engine supply deal. It was not enough according to some of the engine specialists. "*We have done our own sums,*" continued Faure. "*In order not to lose money, we would need around 15 million dollars. Ten would not meet our costs.*"

From this point on, Renault had two teams of engine specialists at work: one continuing with the 2003 engine and the other on the next V10 with a smaller V angle. The French constructor was certainly making it clear that it was in F1 for the long haul.

In the Toyota camp, Cristiano da Matta finished just out of the points in 9th place, while Olivier Panis was last man home in 13th spot. The Frenchman admitted to being very disappointed, after a weekend spent fighting traction control problems.
>v

Shadows and light on Mark Webber's Jaguar. In the race, the Australian retired with engine failure on lap 14.
v

Weekend gossip

> 8 to 10! The number of years that it would take Jaguar to reach the same level as Ferrari in Formula 1. "*I don't really see how we could do it any quicker,*" admitted new team boss, Tony Purnell.

> "*If my friends pay the rate, they get a room. If not, then for them, the hotel is full!*" A comment from David Coulthard about his mates who expect to get a free room in his own hotel, the Columbus, in Fontvieille, behind the big rock in Monaco. He is a real Scotsman after all...

> "*There is nothing really special about the new McLaren.*" A comment from Michael Schumacher on the subject of the new MP4-18, which had made its test debut a week earlier. Harsh words for what the English team maintained was a revolutionary machine. "*I don't know what Michael meant by that,*" counter-attacked McLaren's technical director Adrian Newey. He did hint that it might not be seen at the races before 2004 given some serious reliability problems. At the time, he did not know how right he was.

results

Practice

All the time trials

N°	Driver	N° Chassis - Engine	Private testing	Pos.	Practice friday	Pos.	Qualifying friday	Pos.	Practice saturday	Pos.	Warm-up	Pos.	Qualifying saturday	Pos.
1.	Michael Schumacher	Ferrari F2003-GA 229			1:16.915	6	1:16.305	1	1:15.255	3	1:16.127	5	1:15.644	5
2.	Rubens Barrichello	Ferrari F2003-GA 228			1:17.372	10	1:16.636	2	1:15.861	7	1:16.313	6	1:15.820	7
3.	Juan Pablo Montoya	Williams FW25 06 - BMW			1:17.173	8	1:17.108	8	1:15.098	2	1:17.002	10	1:15.415	3
4.	Ralf Schumacher	Williams FW25 05 - BMW			1:18.039	15	1:17.063	6	1:15.303	4	1:16.754	8	1:15.259	1
5.	David Coulthard	McLaren MP4-17D 06 - Mercedes			1:16.505	3	1:17.059	5	1:14.747	1	1:15.596	1	1:15.700	6
6.	Kimi Räikkönen	McLaren MP4-17D 09 - Mercedes			1:17.218	9	1:17.926	11	1:15.604	6	1:15.798	2	1:15.295	2
7.	Jarno Trulli	Renault R23-03	1:16.888	1	1:16.800	5	1:16.905	4	1:15.517	5	1:16.052	4	1:15.500	4
8.	Fernando Alonso	Renault R23-04	1:18.600	5	1:16.578	4	1:18.370	14	1:17.290	14	1:15.931	3	1:15.884	8
9.	Nick Heidfeld	Sauber C22-02 - Petronas			1:18.660	17	1:17.912	10	1:18.167	18	1:17.463	12	1:17.176	14
10.	Heinz-Harald Frentzen	Sauber C22-04 - Petronas			1:17.550	11		20	1:17.232	15	1:17.316	11	1:17.402	15
11.	Giancarlo Fisichella	Jordan EJ13-04 - Ford	1:17.569	2	1:16.930	7	1:17.080	7	1:16.311	9	1:19.431	16	1:16.967	12
12.	Ralph Firman	Jordan EJ13-03 - Ford	1:18.714	6	1:18.133	16	1:18.286	13	1:17.986	16	1:20.670	19	1:17.452	16
14.	Mark Webber	Jaguar R4-04	1:18.420	3	1:16.373	1	1:17.637	9	1:15.886	8	1:16.434	7	1:16.237	9
15.	Antonio Pizzonia	Jaguar R4-03	1:19.521	7	1:17.913	14	1:18.967	15	1:17.113	12	1:18.053	13	1:17.103	13
16.	Jacques Villeneuve	BAR 005-2 - Honda			1:17.710	12	1:18.109	12	1:16.810	10	1:16.986	9	1:16.755	11
17.	Jenson Button	BAR 005-4 - Honda			1:16.476	2	1:16.895	3	1:16.895	11				
18.	Justin Wilson	Minardi PS03/04 - Cosworth	1:19.923	8	1:18.952	18	1:19.680	17	1:18.606	20	1:19.517	17	1:20.063	19
19.	Jos Verstappen	Minardi PS03/03 - Cosworth	1:19.978	9	1:19.026	19	1:19.421	16	1:18.425	19	1:19.705	18	1:18.706	18
20.	Olivier Panis	Toyota TF103/04			1:17.811	13	1:19.903	18	1:18.101	17	1:18.745	15	1:17.464	17
21.	Cristiano da Matta	Toyota TF103/07			1:19.956	20	1:20.374	19	1:17.686	15	1:18.123	14	1:16.744	10
34.	Allan McNish	Renault R23-00	1:18.438	4										

Maximum speed

N°	Driver	P1 Qualifs	Pos.	P1 Race	Pos.	P2 Qualifs	Pos.	P2 Race	Pos.	Finish Qualifs	Pos.	Finish Race	Pos.	Trap Qualifs	Pos.	Trap Race	Pos.
1.	M. Schumacher	204,3	14	214,8	1	222,4	2	230,4	1	265,4	5	272,3	3	288,0	6	300,0	3
2.	R. Barrichello	210,7	4	214,7	2	197,4	18	221,4	7	265,0	6	272,7	2	288,8	4	299,7	4
3.	J.P. Montoya	201,3	16	213,6	4	216,5	4	222,3	4	270.0	1	271,6	5	290,5	3	298,0	6
4.	R. Schumacher	210,1	5	212,1	6	213,3	7	221,9	5	269,7	2	270,6	6	291,2	1	298,4	5
5.	D. Coulthard	210,0	6	211,1	8	202,8	14	222,6	3	265,6	4	273,0	1	288,0	5	300,4	2
6.	K. Räikkönen	209,3	9	213,6	5	216,0	5	218,7	9	265,7	3	272,3	4	290,7	2	300,9	1
7.	J. Trulli	206,0	12	209,5	10	223,2	1	224,0	2	257,1	17	260,4	16	279,4	18	287,9	18
8.	F. Alonso	211,8	1	211,7	7	220,6	3	221,8	6	256,8	18	260,3	17	281,9	14	289,0	16
9.	N. Heidfeld	199,7	18	210,2	9	198,8	16	213,2	12	259,5	13	263,0	14	282,7	12	291,4	13
10.	H-H. Frentzen	204,4	13	150,3	19	214,0	6	181,4	19	258,2	16			282,5	13	254,7	19
11.	G. Fisichella	206,6	11	207,8	12	207,0	10	221,3	8	260,8	12	262,9	15	281,3	16	290,2	15
12.	R. Firman	209,5	7	207,2	13	198,3	17	209,1	14	258,6	15	264,2	12	279,8	17	292,3	11
14.	M. Webber	211,0	3	204,1	14	209,7	9	205,7	16	262,0	11	265,2	11	284,3	10	292,8	10
15.	A. Pizzonia	209,4	8	201,9	15	205,7	12	207,6	15	262,6	9	265,2	10	284,8	9	294,1	9
16.	J. Villeneuve	207,9	10	208,8	11	212,2	8	215,8	11	262,6	10	268,3	7	285,7	8	295,8	7
17.	J. Button																
18.	J. Wilson	192,3	19	200,5	17	187,0	19	198,0	18	255,5	19	260,1	18	277,5	19	288,0	17
19.	J. Verstappen	200,1	17	200,8	16	199,0	15	199,5	17	258,7	14	263,1	13	281,6	15	291,7	12
20.	O. Panis	202,4	15	195,9	18	206,4	11	210,5	13	263,6	7	267,5	8	283,9	11	290,6	14
21.	C. Da Matta	211,2	2	214,7	3	202,9	13	217,6	10	263,5	8	267,2	9	285,8	7	295,0	8

Race

Classification & Retirements

Pos.	Driver	Team	Lap	Time	Average
1.	J.P. Montoya	Williams BMW	78	1:42:19.010	152,772 km/h
2.	K. Räikkönen	McLaren Mercedes	78	+ 0.602	152,757 km/h
3.	M. Schumacher	Ferrari	78	+ 1.720	152,729 km/h
4.	R. Schumacher	Williams BMW	78	+ 28.518	152,066 km/h
5.	F. Alonso	Renault	78	+ 36.251	151,875 km/h
6.	J. Trulli	Renault	78	+ 40.972	151,759 km/h
7.	D. Coulthard	McLaren Mercedes	78	+ 41.227	151,753 km/h
8.	R. Barrichello	Ferrari	78	+ 53.266	151,458 km/h
9.	C. Da Matta	Toyota	77	1 lap	149,221 km/h
10.	G. Fisichella	Jordan Ford	77	1 lap	149,185 km/h
11.	N. Heidfeld	Sauber Petronas	76	2 laps	148,291 km/h
12.	R. Firman	Jordan Ford	76	2 laps	147,685 km/h
13.	O. Panis	Toyota	74	4 laps	143,815 km/h

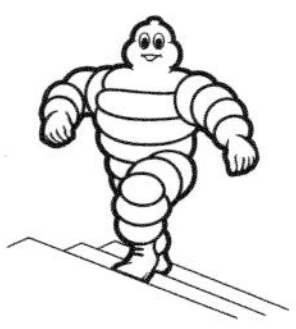

Driver	Team		Reason
J. Villeneuve	BAR Honda	64	Engine failure
J. Wilson	Minardi Cosworth	30	Fuel vaporisation problem
J. Verstappen	Minardi Cosworth	29	Fuel vaporisation problem
M. Webber	Jaguar	17	Loss of air from engine pneumatic system
A. Pizzonia	Jaguar	11	Engine cuts out with electrical problem
H-H. Frentzen	Sauber Petronas	1	Straight on into the barrier (turn 16)

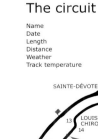

Fastest laps

	Driver	Time	Lap	Average
1.	K. Räikkönen	1:14.545	49	161,298 km/h
2.	M. Schumacher	1:47.707	30	160,948 km/h
3.	R. Schumacher	1:14.768	77	160,817 km/h
4.	J.P. Montoya	1:14.902	47	160,529 km/h
5.	R. Barrichello	1:15.307	59	159,666 km/h
6.	F. Alonso	1:15.397	58	159,475 km/h
7.	D. Coulthard	1:15.439	51	159,387 km/h
8.	J. Trulli	1:15.679	51	158,881 km/h
9.	C. Da Matta	1:16.282	51	157,625 km/h
10.	J. Villeneuve	1:16.292	50	157,604 km/h
11.	G. Fisichella	1:16.647	72	156,875 km/h
12.	N. Heidfeld	1:16.835	75	156,491 km/h
13.	R. Firman	1:17.208	51	155,735 km/h
14.	O. Panis	1:17.777	70	154,595 km/h
15.	M. Webber	1:18.004	13	154,145 km/h
16.	J. Verstappen	1:19.146	25	151,921 km/h
17.	J. Wilson	1:19.169	19	151,877 km/h
18.	A. Pizzonia	1:19.437	8	151,365 km/h

Pit stops

	Driver	Time	Lap	Stop n°
1.	M. Webber	28.775	14	1
2.	R. Schumacher	29.120	21	1
3.	C. Da Matta	28.820	22	1
4.	N. Heidfeld	28.302	22	1
5.	J.P. Montoya	28.512	23	1
6.	R. Firman	31.621	24	1
7.	K. Räikkönen	28.970	25	1
8.	G. Fisichella	30.685	25	1
9.	J. Trulli	28.359	27	1
10.	D. Coulthard	28.878	27	1
11.	F. Alonso	28.684	29	1
12.	R. Barrichello	29.762	30	1
13.	J. Villeneuve	28.197	30	1
14.	M. Schumacher	29.321	31	1
15.	O. Panis	33.741	33	1
16.	N. Heidfeld	28.681	43	2
17.	R. Schumacher	29.032	48	2
18.	J.P. Montoya	28.692	49	2
19.	C. Da Matta	29.002	49	2
20.	K. Räikkönen	29.138	53	2
21.	J. Villeneuve	28.464	54	2
22.	J. Trulli	26.942	56	2
23.	D. Coulthard	26.870	56	2
24.	R. Firman	29.217	55	2
25.	G. Fisichella	29.077	57	2
26.	M. Schumacher	27.462	59	2
27.	R. Barrichello	27.739	60	2
28.	F. Alonso	26.117	61	2

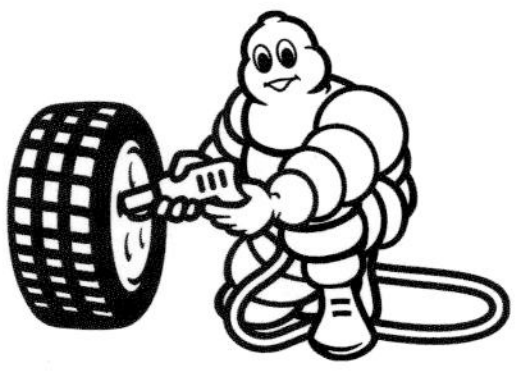

Race leaders

Driver	Laps in the lead	Nber of Laps
R. Schumacher	1 > 20	20
J.P. Montoya	21 > 22	2
K. Räikkönen	23 > 24	2
J. Trulli	25 > 26	2
M. Schumacher	27 > 30	4
J.P. Montoya	31 > 48	18
K. Räikkönen	49 > 52	4
M. Schumacher	53 > 58	6
J.P. Montoya	59 > 78	20

Driver	Nber of Laps	Kilometers
J.P. Montoya	40	133,600 km
R. Schumacher	20	66,800 km
M. Schumacher	10	33,400 km
K. Räikkönen	6	20,040 km
J. Trulli	2	6,680 km

Gaps on the leader board

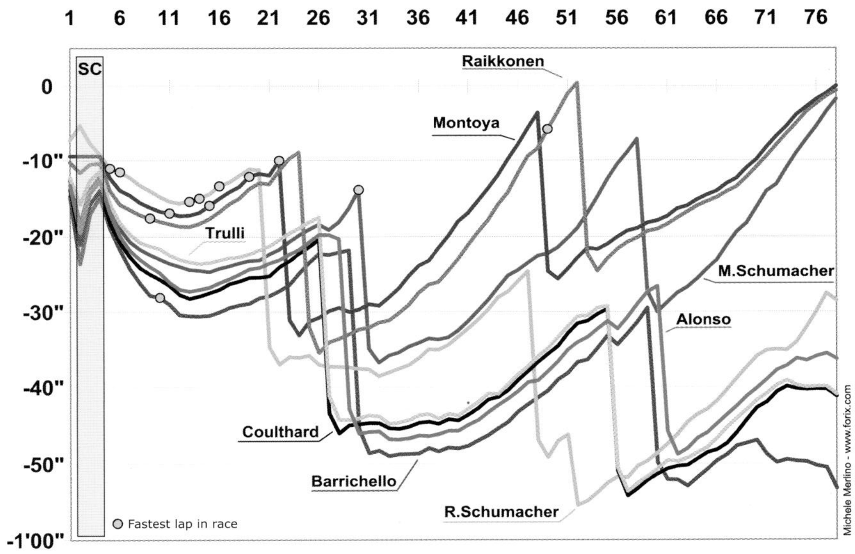

Lap chart

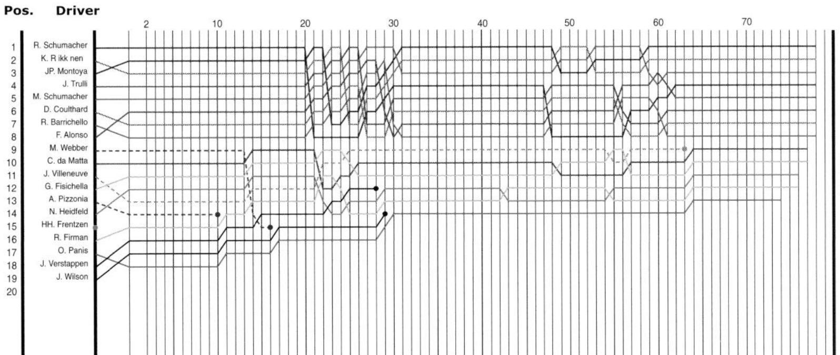

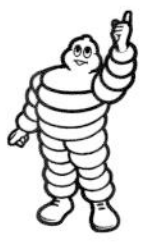

Championship after seven rounds

Drivers

1. K. Räikkönen ....(1 win) 48
2. M. Schumacher ....(3 wins)................44
3. F. Alonso 29
4. R. Barrichello 27
5. J.P. Montoya.............(1 win) 25
6. D. Coulthard ....(1 win) 25
7. R. Schumacher 25
8. J. Trulli 13
9. G. Fisichella ....(1 win) 10
10. J. Button...8
11. H-H. Frentzen..7
12. M. Webber 4
13. J. Villeneuve..3
14. C. Da Matta...3
15. N. Heidfeld...1
16. R. Firman...1
17. A. Pizzonia 0
18. O. Panis...0
19. J. Verstappen 0
20. J. Wilson..0

Constructors

1. West McLaren Mercedes........(2 wins) 73
2. Scuderia Ferrari Marlboro ......(3 wina).......71
3. BMW Williams F1 Team ....(1 win).........50
4. Mild Seven Renault F1 Team 42
5. Jordan Ford.........................(1 win).........11
6. Lucky Strike BAR Honda............................11
7. Sauber Petronas 8
8. Jaguar Racing..4
9. Panasonic Toyota Racing 3
10. European Minardi Cosworth.........................0

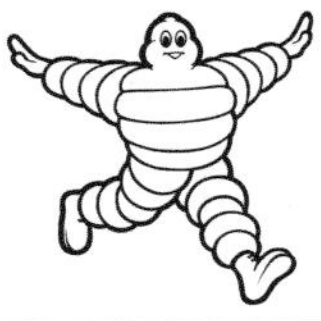

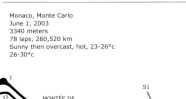

The circuit

Name	Monaco, Monte Carlo
Date	June 1, 2003
Length	3340 meters
Distance	78 laps, 260,520 km
Weather	Sunny then overcast, hot, 23-26°c
Track temperature	26-30°c

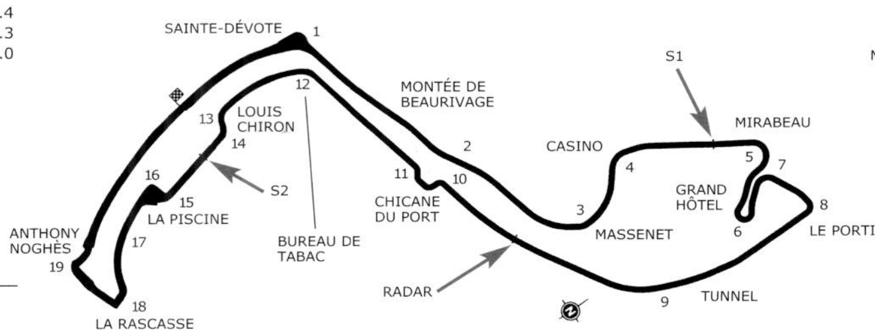

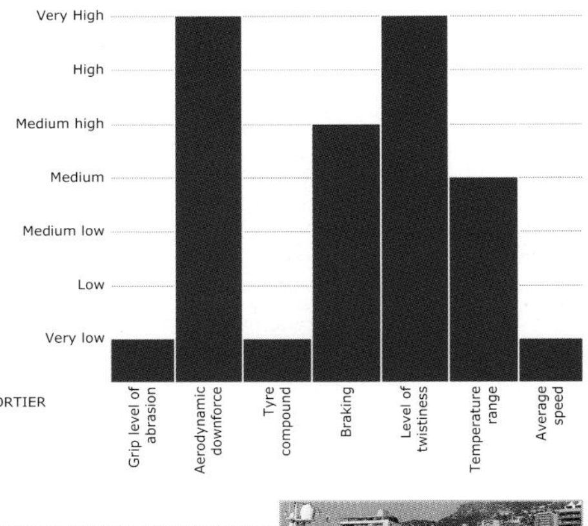

All results : © 2003 Formula One Administration Ltd,
6 Princes Gate, London, SW7 1QJ, England

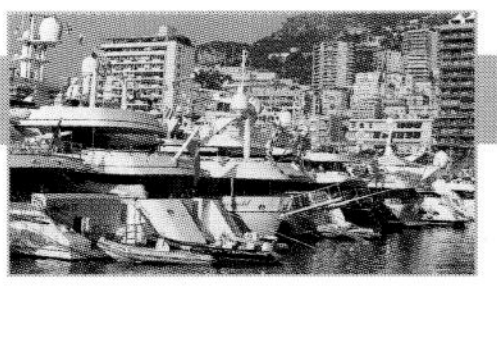

BET ON RED

In Montreal, Michael Schumacher took his fourth grand prix win of the season and finally moved to the head of the drivers' classification. Just a few days earlier, he had renewed his contract with Ferrari for a further two seasons.

However, behind this apparently triumphal tableau, all was not rosy in the garden. Michael Schumacher had won, but only just. He had to fight all the way to hold off an apparently quicker Williams.

For Ferrari, the danger had shifted. Now, the threat no longer came from McLaren, but from the redoubtable BMW-Williams team.

Michael Schumacher re-signs with Ferrari to the end of 2006

> ^
> In Montreal, Ralf Schumacher took his second consecutive pole, following on from the one in Monaco.

The news broke on the Monday prior to the Canadian Grand Prix: Michael Schumacher had extended his contract with Ferrari for a further two years, which meant he would sit in the red car until the end of 2006.

In Montreal, the German explained his decision: "*This contract makes me very happy,*" he confided. "*I will feel at home in the Ferrari family for another three years and that is a good thing.*"

It was also a good thing for the German's manager, Willy Weber, who could therefore continue selling his Ferrari-red merchandise. "*I am very happy to have renewed my contract, as much for myself as for the team and the tifosi,*" continued

Schumacher. "*In 2001, when I had signed a contract to the end of 2004, I thought I would retire then at the age of 35. But, a few weeks ago, when I was asked to stay on for an additional two years, I did not say no. Because the atmosphere within the team is really great. I love working in this environment. It's fantastic.*"

Of course, the five times world champion was heavily influenced in his decision by the fact that the rest of the current "dream team;" technical director Ross Brawn, chief designer Rory Byrne, engine specialists Paolo Martinelli and Gilles Simon, as well as managing director Jean Todt, had also signed up for the long ride. "*Before*

signing, I made sure I would be working with the same people," admitted Schumi. "*That's why I am still very optimistic for the future.*"

At the end of the contract, the German might well consider a well-deserved retirement. "*This contract means I will end my career in red, even though I don't want to talk about retirement,*" he concluded. "*I will then be 37 and in any case, no other top team would be interested in me by then!*" And money? According to Weber, Schumacher had signed up for the same fee he was on for the past two years. "*No more, no less,*" which amounts to around thirty million dollars. A good deal for everyone.

A 100% Williams-BMW front row

> >
> Good looking guy that David Coulthard! However, on track, he was not looking so good this year. In Montreal he qualified down in 11th place. At least it was better than his team-mate Kimi Räikkönen who ended up 20th after spinning at the first corner. He broke the rear wing and started from last on the grid.

> >
> Friday's first qualifying session took place in heavy showers. Conditions were difficult right from the start of the session and then got worse after the first few cars had made their runs. The changeable conditions meant the Ferraris topped the time sheet at the end of the day.

After a rainy Friday, it rained again on Saturday morning in Montreal. The showers stopped around midday and the qualifying session took place on a dry track.

For the drivers, it was not easy to find the right set-up in these conditions, as all the other sessions had taken place on a wet track. However, while practice had been dominated up until then by the Bridgestone tyres, it was the Michelins which clearly had the upper hand in the dry. That fact saw the fastest time fall to Ralf Schumacher, who took his second consecutive pole position after Monaco.

"*I did not expect this, running so early in the session,*" said the world champion's little brother. His team-mate, Juan Pablo Montoya, who made a slight mistake at the third chicane, would start alongside him on the front row, while Michael Schumacher was back in third place. "*I made one or two small mistakes, but in any case, I don't think I could have beaten the Williams,*" analysed the Ferrari man. In fourth place came Fernando Alonso, who was beaten to third spot by Michael Schumacher by just a thousandth of a second- the equivalent of 5.73 centimetres!

Starting grid

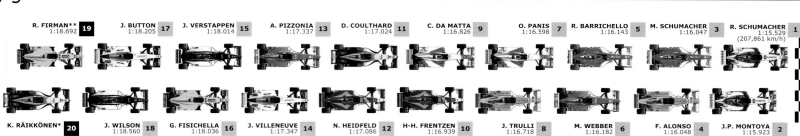

* K. RÄIKKÖNEN starts from the pit lane.

** R. FIRMAN Comes into the pits after the formation lap to refuel. So he starts from the pit lane.

| R. FIRMAN** 19 1:18.692 | J. BUTTON 17 1:18.205 | J. VERSTAPPEN 15 1:18.014 | A. PIZZONIA 13 1:17.337 | D. COULTHARD 11 1:17.024 | C. DA MATTA 9 1:16.826 | O. PANIS 7 1:16.598 | R. BARRICHELLO 5 1:16.143 | M. SCHUMACHER 3 1:16.047 | R. SCHUMACHER 1 1:15.529 (207,861 km/h) |

| K. RÄIKKÖNEN* 20 1:18.560 | J. WILSON 18 1:18.036 | G. FISICHELLA 16 1:18.036 | J. VILLENEUVE 14 1:17.347 | N. HEIDFELD 12 1:17.086 | H-H. FRENTZEN 10 1:16.939 | J. TRULLI 8 1:16.718 | M. WEBBER 6 1:16.182 | F. ALONSO 4 1:16.048 | J.P. MONTOYA 2 1:15.923 |

< Start. The two Williams make perfect getaways. Juan Pablo got it all wrong on the second lap when he spun into the famous Quebec wall.

Victory for Michael Schumacher: in Montreal the slowest man wins!

A Ferrari won again, but this time, the Italian cars were not the quickest. At the finish, Michael Schumacher was holding up a train of cars made up of the two Williams and Fernando Alonso's Renault. Three cars, manifestly quicker and yet unable to get past? "*It's not surprising,*" commented Michael Schumacher after the race. "*The cars are so closely matched today that overtaking is very difficult, even on a circuit where you can pass like this one.*"
Michael Schumacher built this victory in the pits, at his first refuelling. While the German found himself behind the two Williams in the early laps, Juan Pablo Montoya knocked himself out of the running by sliding off at the final chicane. "*It was my fault,*" admitted the Colombian. "*I was following Ralf too closely, I lost downforce and spun off like a top.*" He then set off on a long road back to the front, but it took him the best part of 60 laps to get in touch with the lead group. "*I had brake problems,*" added Montoya, who finished third.

Ahead of him, Ralf Schumacher might well have harboured hopes of winning the grand prix if it had not been for the fact that he refuelled one lap before his big brother. That one lap made all the difference, as Michael made the most of it to lift the pace and rejoin the track in the lead.
From then on, it was all over, even if Ralf stayed glued to the back of the Ferrari. "*I think I was a bit quicker than him, but I could not get close enough to Michael to try and pass,*" explained the Williams man. "*In 2001, I won here thanks to a quicker pit-stop. Today, it was Michael's turn. That's life*"
It was now the mid-point of the season and Michael Schumacher was finally heading the standings with a three point lead over Kimi Räikkönen, who finished sixth here after a puncture. "*For the moment, my main rival is still Kimi, but we have to keep an eye on the Williams,*" commented the winner on the day. "*It is a very difficult season. Today, I had major brake problems and I could not go any quicker.*"

Paul Stoddart receives support from Bernie Ecclestone

The dirty washing was washed in public in Montreal. During a press conference, Minardi owner Paul Stoddart complained openly about the attitude of Ron Dennis, Frank Williams and Jean Todt, the bosses of McLaren, Williams and Ferrari respectively. They were blocking the transfer of funds which had been decided back in January to help the smaller teams survive. Ron Dennis was also in the conference and was absolutely furious that these matters were being discussed in open court. Bernie Ecclestone was watching proceedings from the back of the room and seemed to be in agreement with Stoddart's views. On Saturday evening, "Mr. E" decided to help out the Italian team, investing a "non-returnable" loan of four million pounds; enough to see the Faenza squad survive through to 2004.

Fourth place for Fernando Alonso, who finished right on the tail of the top three. "*For the first time this season, we were really fighting on equal terms with the leaders and it's a great feeling. It was a very positive weekend and I had no problems with the car.*"
<

< "*Yes, the Ferraris are red.*" A visibly amused Jean Todt explains what happens on the grid to singer Ozzy Osbourne.

Race summary

> Starting from pole, Ralf Schumacher has the upper hand as the race gets underway. Montoya and M. Schumacher follow (**1**).

> Barrichello loses his front wing on the opening lap. He drops down the order and finishes over a minute down (**2**).

> Still on the first lap, Pizzonia and Trulli collide at the hairpin. Both retire (**3**).

> Montoya spins at the end of lap 2. Luckily, he does not hit anything and continues to finish 3rd (**4**).

> Having started from pit lane, Raikkonen suffers a puncture. A great charge sees him finish 6th (**5**).

> Michael Schumacher passes Ralf during the pit-stops and Ralf is unable to fight back (**6**).

> 6th Canadian win for Michael Schumacher, which sees him take the lead in the Drivers' Championship (**7**).

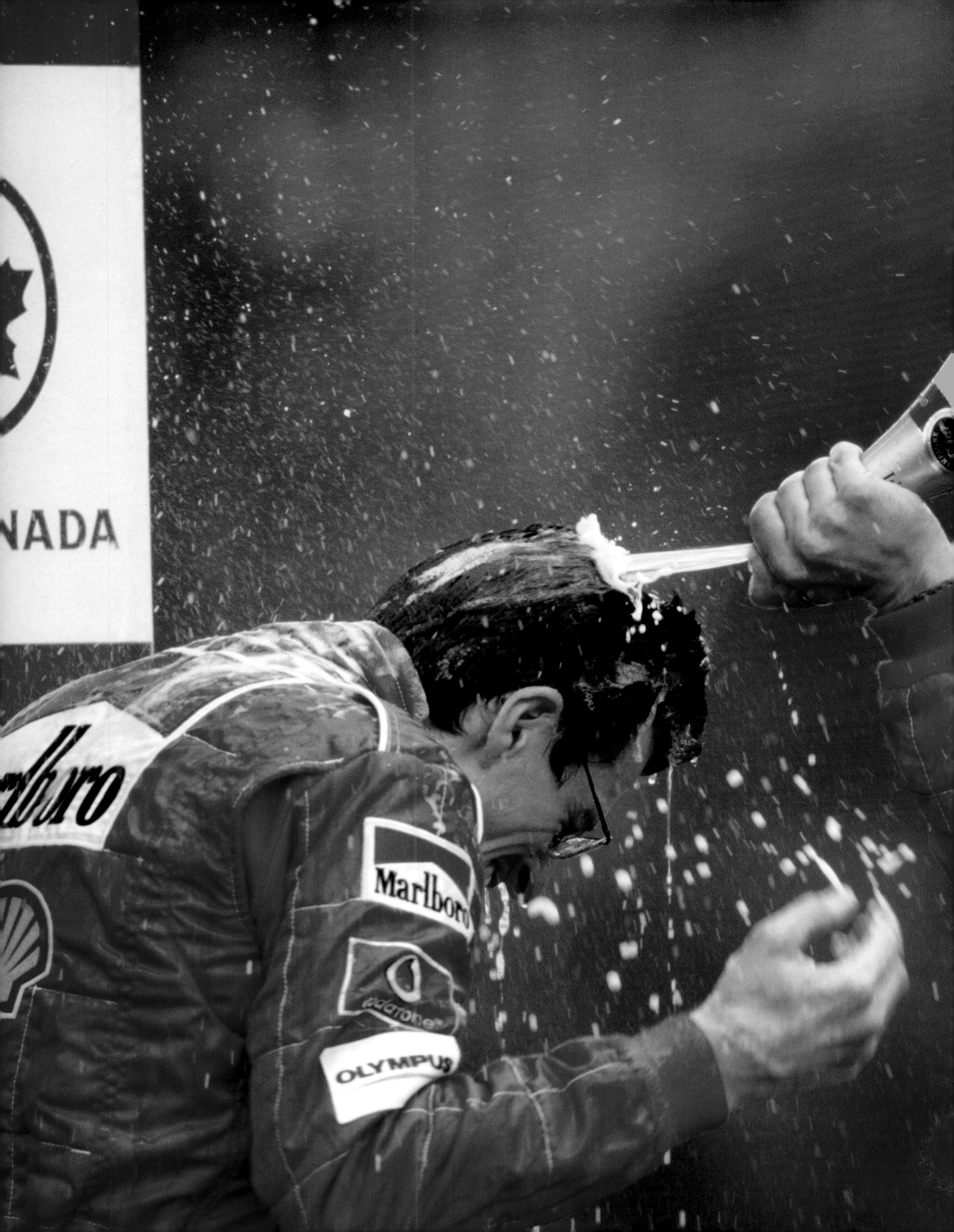
NADA
Marlboro
OLYMPUS

Cheers!

In Montreal, Michael Schumacher took his fourth win from five grands prix and finally took the lead in the championship. It merited cracking open the champagne to celebrate a race which seemed to put him in the driving seat for the title. He did not know that the road would be long and hard and that he would not win again until... Monza.

Kimi Räikkönen finishes sixth and scores three points, having staged a great climb through the field. Starting from the pits, he even had to contend with a puncture, having run over some debris. "*In the end, this result is far from being a disaster,*" commented the Finn. "*After around ten laps, the team asked me to look after the brakes and so I was not able to attack as hard as I would have liked, which meant I did not make up as many places as I thought I would.*"

In the Toyota camp, Olivier Panis took the single point for eighth place. "*It's my first point of the season and it marks a new start for me,*" rejoiced the Frenchman. Cristiano da Matta (photo) had to retire six laps from the flag with a suspension problem. He was still classified eleventh and last.

>

Jacques Villeneuve will therefore never be a prophet in his own land. The Canadian has never won the Canadian Grand Prix and he was a long way off it this time. Having held up a queue of cars in the early stages, the man from Quebec retired as early as lap 15, having lost brake fluid.

>v

Paul Stoddart with Ron Dennis. In Montreal, the two bosses mixed about as well as oil and water.

v

Craig Pollock reassures Quebec as to Jacques' future in Formula 1.

For the past few months now, Canadian race fans have been getting worried. The contract linking Jacques Villeneuve to the BAR team was due to expire at the end of the season and the local press was asking itself where the Canadian would hang his hat to continue his career.

So far, every conceivable rumour had been round the block from retirement to a move back to the States and Champ Cars or even a drive with Ferrari.

This year was the first time that Villeneuve did not hold his traditional pre-weekend press conference in his "Newtown" restaurant, to give the local media the benefit of his pearls of wisdom. It was only on Thursday, in a Bridgestone press conference that the driver finally spoke on the subject: "*I cannot yet say what I will be doing next season,*" he stated. "*All I know is that I would like to be in a position to win races.*"

The wish would be hard to grant. The good seats are both rare and expensive. Ferrari had the "No Vacancies" sign hanging on its door, as did Williams. In the McLaren camp, there was a chance David Coulthard might retire, but boss Ron Dennis was not interested in the troublesome Villeneuve, even if he came free of charge! There were possibilities with Jaguar, Toyota or even Renault, but there were no guarantees that the Canadian would be in a position to win races with this last trio.

Jacques Villeneuve had not won a grand prix since 1997 and his market value and appeal had dropped considerably. Another problem was that, this season, he had so far been beaten in qualifying four to two by his team-mate Jenson Button, who was paid considerably less than the man from Quebec. In 2002, when it came to talking about 2003, BAR boss David Richards had asked his driver to reduce

his salary demands – around 20 million dollars per year. Jacques Villeneuve dug his heels in, relying on a cast iron contract, drawn up by Craig Pollock back in the days when he was still in charge at BAR.

Since then, there was no love lost between the driver and Richards. If Villeneuve wanted to continue trying his luck with BAR, he would have to accept a substantial pay cut. In the end, he even offered to drive free of charge, but that did not work either. "*I would like to stay with BAR,*" added the 1997 world champion. "*Because after all the effort I have put in, it would hurt me to someone else win in this car and get the benefit of my efforts.*"

According to his manager Craig Pollock, Jacques Villeneuve would be absolutely definitely on the starting grid in 2004. He was quite firm on this point. "*I am in discussion with several teams and Jacques will be in F1 next year,*" he assured anyone prepared to listen. He would not be so well paid, that was certain. "*The price does not matter. The important thing is that his contract is satisfactory for both parties. It will be a contract for one, two or three years and it might not even be Jacques' last contract. Everything after that will depend on his motivation.*" Craig Pollock continued to picture his driver at Ferrari, alongside Michael Schumacher. "*That would add a bit of excitement to F1,*" he concluded.

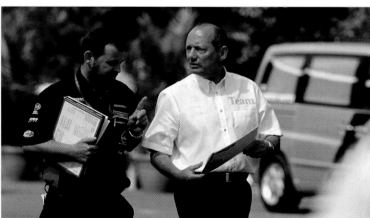

Practice

All the time trials

N°	Driver	N° Chassis - Engine	Private testing	Pos.	Practice friday	Pos.	Qualifying friday	Pos.	Practice saturday	Pos.	Warm-up	Pos.	Qualifying saturday	Pos.
1.	Michael Schumacher	Ferrari F2003-GA 229			1:17.228	3	1:31.969	2	1:23.385	1	1:18.845	17	1:16.047	3
2.	Rubens Barrichello	Ferrari F2003-GA 228			1:18.240	10	1:30.925	1	1:23.677	2	1:18.579	16	1:16.143	5
3.	Juan Pablo Montoya	Williams FW25 06 - BMW			1:17.216	2	1:37.479	12	1:28.225	16	1:17.799	8	1:15.923	2
4.	Ralf Schumacher	Williams FW25 05 - BMW			1:17.894	6	1:38.210	15	1:25.668	5	1:16.236	1	1:15.529	1
5.	David Coulthard	McLaren MP4-17D 07 - Mercedes			1:18.165	9	1:36.463	8	1:25.839	7	1:17.313	3	1:17.024	11
6.	Kimi Räikkönen	McLaren MP4-17D 09 - Mercedes			1:18.155	8	1:35.373	6	1:26.771	13	1:16.697	2		20
7.	Jarno Trulli	Renault R23-05 & 03	1:16.629	4	1:32.552	20	1:41.413	19	1:25.961	9	1:17.560	4	1:16.718	8
8.	Fernando Alonso	Renault R23-04	1:15.483	1	1:31.658	19	1:35.173	5	1:25.382	4	1:17.651	5	1:16.048	4
9.	Nick Heidfeld	Sauber C22-02 - Petronas			1:23.061	15	1:32.778	3	1:26.537	11	1:17.979	11	1:17.086	12
10.	Heinz-Harald Frentzen	Sauber C22-01 - Petronas			1:19.765	14	1:35.776	7	1:29.190	18	1:18.339	14	1:16.939	10
11.	Giancarlo Fisichella	Jordan EJ13-04 - Ford	1:17.156	6	1:28.141	17	1:38.617	18	1:25.240	3	1:18.328	13	1:18.036	16
12.	Ralph Firman	Jordan EJ13-03 - Ford	1:17.426	7	1:17.973	7	1:34.759	4	1:26.690	12	1:20.594	20	1:18.692	19
14.	Mark Webber	Jaguar R4-04	1:16.469	3	1:17.344	4	1:36.699	9	1:26.440	10	1:17.807	9	1:16.182	6
15.	Antonio Pizzonia	Jaguar R4-03	1:16.253	2	1:16.621	1	1:38.255	17	1:27.145	15	1:17.930	10	1:17.337	13
16.	Jacques Villeneuve	BAR 005-3 - Honda			1:18.716	13	1:44.702	20	1:25.704	6	1:17.689	7	1:17.347	14
17.	Jenson Button	BAR 005-5 - Honda			1:28.872	18	1:38.109	14	1:25.902	8	1:18.439	15	1:18.205	17
18.	Justin Wilson	Minardi PS03/04 - Cosworth	1:18.495	9	1:18.586	12	1:38.088	13	1:27.018	14	1:18.893	18	1:18.560	18
19.	Jos Verstappen	Minardi PS03/03 - Cosworth	1:17.852	8	1:24.571	16	1:37.426	11	1:28.246	17	1:19.588	19	1:18.014	15
20.	Olivier Panis	Toyota TF103/05			1:17.464	5	1:37.313	10	1:30.410	20	1:17.676	6	1:16.598	7
21.	Cristiano da Matta	Toyota TF103/04			1:18.559	11	1:38.244	16	1:29.215	19	1:17.983	12	1:16.826	9
34.	Allan McNish	Renault R23-03	1:16.726	5										

Maximum speed

N°	Driver	P1 Qualifs	Pos.	P1 Race	Pos.	P2 Qualifs	Pos.	P2 Race	Pos.	Finish Qualifs	Pos.	Finish Race	Pos.	Trap Qualifs	Pos.	Trap Race	Pos.
1.	M. Schumacher	270,0	2	275,6	3	296,9	4	303,6	2	298,1	4	306,0	3	333,9	3	348,4	1
2.	R. Barrichello	270,6	1	275,7	2	298,0	2	302,8	4	299,0	3	305,3	4	334,3	2	344,8	3
3.	J.P. Montoya	264,3	9	274,6	4	297,1	3	303,0	3	299,8	1	306,9	2	334,4	1	342,4	5
4.	R. Schumacher	269,7	3	270,8	6	298,0	1	304,7	1	299,5	2	307,8	1	333,8	4	341,8	6
5.	D. Coulthard	265,7	4	265,8	14	293,5	5	298,7	7	294,7	6	303,6	6	327,9	5	343,2	4
6.	K. Räikkönen	213,3	20	271,8	5	287,0	18	302,0	5	293,7	8	303,3	7	270,3	20	345,0	2
7.	J. Trulli	263,0	11	257,9	18	287,3	16	289,0	19	289,8	17	293,2	19	326,1	9	332,3	17
8.	F. Alonso	264,9	6	270,3	7	289,9	9	298,4	8	291,4	12	299,3	12	325,7	12	338,9	8
9.	N. Heidfeld	263,5	10	266,1	13	287,6	13	294,4	14	287,6	19	296,8	16	320,6	16	333,6	15
10.	H-H. Frentzen	265,0	5	256,5	20	288,9	12	292,3	17	290,2	14	293,4	18	322,6	14	337,0	11
11.	G. Fisichella	257,0	17	267,5	10	284,7	19	294,1	16	290,6	13	298,6	13	321,6	15	334,2	14
12.	R. Firman	254,2	18	260,9	17	283,6	20	285,2	20	284,6	20	289,8	20	316,2	18	326,4	20
14.	M. Webber	261,8	12	267,9	9	287,5	15	292,1	18	289,0	18	296,2	17	315,6	19	331,0	18
15.	A. Pizzonia	260,3	16	269,2	8	287,1	17	295,2	13	290,0	15	297,5	14	316,3	17	329,2	19
16.	J. Villeneuve	260,6	15	264,4	15	289,1	11	296,6	10	292,3	11	301,3	9	325,8	11	338,2	10
17.	J. Button	264,5	8	267,2	11	289,9	8	298,0	9	293,1	10	303,7	5	326,1	10	339,9	7
18.	J. Wilson	233,7	19	261,2	16	287,5	14	294,2	15	290,0	16	296,9	15	326,2	8	333,0	16
19.	J. Verstappen	261,1	13	257,8	19	289,6	10	296,0	11	293,3	9	300,9	10	326,9	6	334,4	13
20.	O. Panis	260,8	14	266,2	12	291,7	7	295,4	12	293,9	7	299,5	11	325,6	13	335,7	12
21.	C. Da Matta	264,8	7	276,0	1	292,7	6	301,8	6	294,7	5	303,2	8	326,6	7	338,6	9

Race

Classification & Retirements

Pos.	Driver	Team	Lap	Time	Average	
1.	M. Schumacher	Ferrari	70	1:31:13.591	200,777 km/h	
2.	R. Schumacher	Williams BMW	70	+ 0.784	200,748 km/h	
3.	J.P. Montoya	Williams BMW	70	+ 1.355	200,727 km/h	
4.	F. Alonso	Renault	70	+ 4.481	200,612 km/h	
5.	R. Barrichello	Ferrari	70	+ 1:04.261	198,447 km/h	
6.	K. Räikkönen	McLaren Mercedes	70	+ 1:10.502	198,223 km/h	
7.	M. Webber	Jaguar	69	1 lap	196,767 km/h	
8.	O. Panis	Toyota	69	1 lap	196,252 km/h	
9.	J. Verstappen	Minardi Cosworth	68	2 laps	193,586 km/h	
10.	A. Pizzonia	Jaguar	66	4 laps	191,784 km/h	Brake prob.
11.	C. Da Matta	Toyota	64	6 laps	196,524 km/h	Suspension prob.

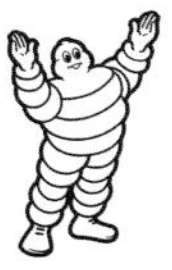

Driver	Team		Reason
J. Wilson	Minardi Cosworth	61	Broken gearbox
J. Button	BAR Honda	52	Loss of 4th, 6th and 7th gears
D. Coulthard	McLaren Mercedes	48	Loss of 4th, 6th and 7th gears
N. Heidfeld	Sauber Petronas	48	Engine failure
J. Trulli	Renault	23	Car damaged after collision with Pizzonia at the start
G. Fisichella	Jordan Ford	21	Gearbox prob (unable to select 1st gear)
R. Firman	Jordan Ford	21	Minor fire caused by oil leak
J. Villeneuve	BAR Honda	15	Loss of brake fluid
H-H. Frentzen	Sauber Petronas	7	Electrical prob. between engine and gearbox

Fastest laps

	Driver	Time	Lap	Average
1.	F. Alonso	1:16.040	53	206,465 km/h
2.	J.P. Montoya	1:16.349	39	205,629 km/h
3.	R. Barrichello	1:16.368	35	205,578 km/h
4.	M. Schumacher	1:16.378	46	205,551 km/h
5.	R. Schumacher	1:16.599	48	204,958 km/h
6.	K. Räikkönen	1:16.699	67	204,691 km/h
7.	D. Coulthard	1:17.088	23	203,658 km/h
8.	G. Fisichella	1:17.186	20	203,399 km/h
9.	A. Pizzonia	1:17.324	54	203,036 km/h
10.	J. Button	1:17.562	22	202,413 km/h
11.	M. Webber	1:17.592	45	202,335 km/h
12.	N. Heidfeld	1:17.769	44	201,874 km/h
13.	C. Da Matta	1:17.787	38	201,828 km/h
14.	O. Panis	1:17.904	40	201,524 km/h
15.	J. Wilson	1:18.039	42	201,176 km/h
16.	J. Verstappen	1:18.521	38	199,941 km/h
17.	J. Trulli	1:18.696	16	199,496 km/h
18.	R. Firman	1:19.453	18	197,596 km/h
19.	J. Villeneuve	1:19.780	6	196,786 km/h
20.	H-H. Frentzen	1:20.043	3	196,139 km/h

Pit stops

	Driver	Time	Lap	Stop n°
1.	A. Pizzonia	44.208	1	1
2.	R. Barrichello	36.600	2	1
3.	J. Trulli	38.598	2	1
4.	J. Trulli	1:00.709	4	2
5.	J. Verstappen	33:290	11	1
6.	J. Vilson	33.313	13	1
7.	J. Villeneuve	39.101	14	1
8.	O. Panis	31.295	15	1
9.	C. Da Matta	30.917	16	1
10.	N. Heidfeld	31.847	18	1
11.	J.P. Montoya	32.110	19	1
12.	M. Webber	33.900	19	1
13.	R. Schumacher	31.248	20	1
14.	M. Schumacher	32.485	21	1
15.	J. Button	34.620	23	1
16.	D. Coulthard	31.086	24	1
17.	F. Alonso	31.187	26	1
18.	A. Pizzonia	31.102	29	2
19.	K. Räikkönen	36.936	33	1
20.	R. Barrichello	33.860	39	2
21.	J. Verstappen	33.672	40	2
22.	O. Panis	31.526	42	2
23.	J. Wilson	33.895	43	2
24.	C. Da Matta	30.862	44	2
25.	J.P. Montoya	31.143	45	2
26.	R. Schumacher	30.229	46	2
27.	N. Heidfeld	30.884	45	2
28.	M. Webber	31.606	46	2
29.	M. Schumacher	31.428	48	2
30.	J. Button	31.462	47	2
31.	A. Pizzonia	31.246	52	2
32.	F. Alonso	28.502	55	2

Race leaders

Driver	Laps in the lead	Nber of Laps
R. Schumacher	1 > 19	19
M. Schumacher	20	1
F. Alonso	21 > 25	5
M. Schumacher	26 > 48	23
F. Alonso	49 > 54	6
M. Schumacher	55 > 70	16

Driver	Nber of Laps	Kilometers
M. Schumacher	40	174,440 km
R. Schumacher	19	82,859 km
F. Alonso	11	47,971 km

Gaps on the leader board

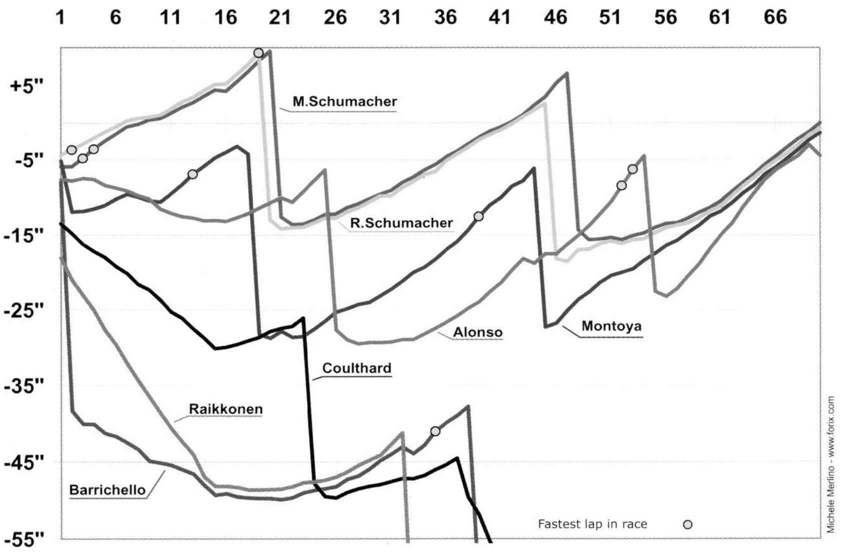

Lap chart

Pos. Driver

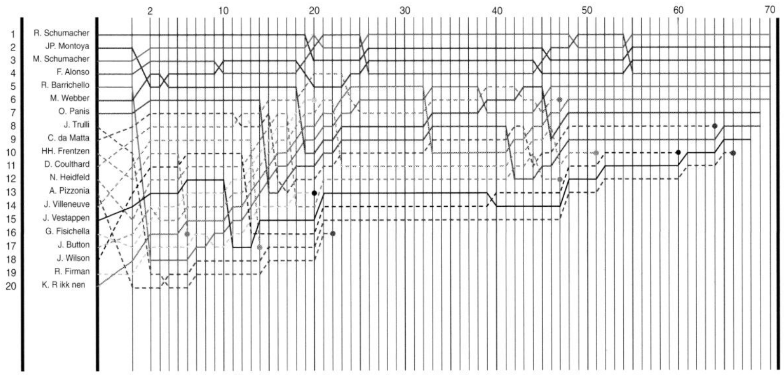

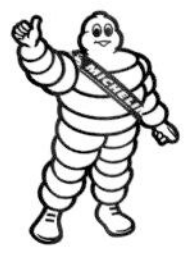

Championship after eight rounds

Drivers

1. M. Schumacher ....(4 wins)................54
2. K. Räikkönen ....(1 win) 51
3. F. Alonso 34
4. R. Schumacher 33
5. J.P. Montoya.............(1 win) 31
6. R. Barrichello..31
7. D. Coulthard ....(1 win).................25
8. J. Trulli 13
9. G. Fisichella ....(1 win) 10
10. J. Button..8
11. H-H. Frentzen...7
12. M. Webber 6
13. C. Da Matta..3
14. J. Villeneuve...3
15. O. Panis...1
16. N. Heidfeld...1
17. R. Firman...1
18. A. Pizzonia 0
19. J. Verstappen 0
20. J. Wilson 0

Constructors

1. Scuderia Ferrari Marlboro ......(4 wins) 85
2. West McLaren Mercedes........(2 wins) 76
3. BMW Williams F1 Team ....(1 win).........64
4. Mild Seven Renault F1 Team 47
5. Jordan Ford.........................(1 win).........11
6. Lucky Strike BAR Honda...........................11
7. Sauber Petronas 8
8. Jaguar Racing..6
9. Panasonic Toyota Racing 4
10. European Minardi Cosworth........................0

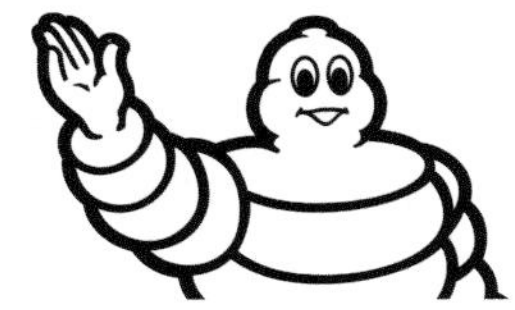

The circuit

Name	Gilles Villeneuve, Montréal
Date	June 15, 2003
Length	4361 meters
Distance	70 laps, 305,270 km
Weather	Sunny and hot, 20-22°c
Track temperature	28-32°c

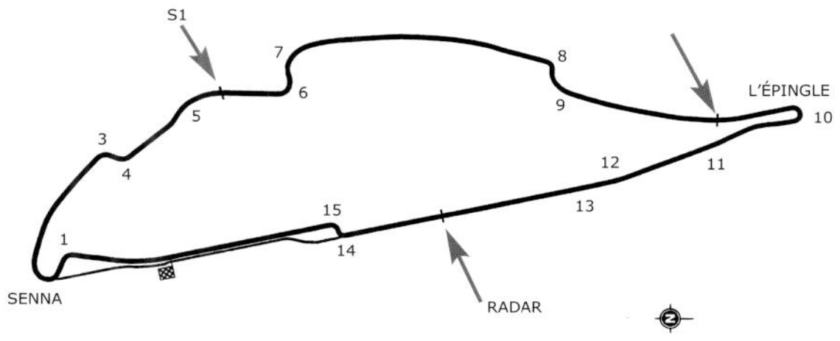

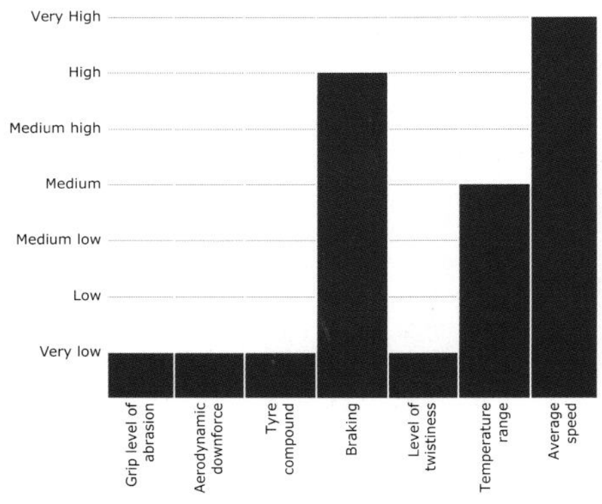

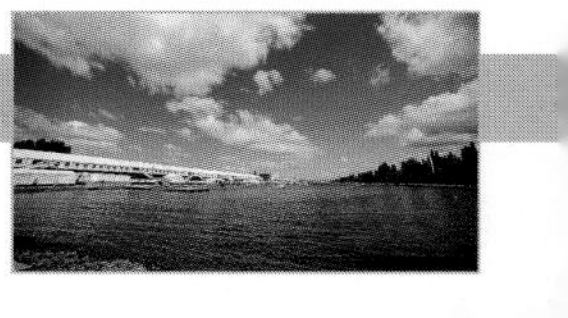

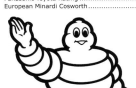

SCHUMACHER AND MONTOYA ARE AT IT AGAIN

Juan Pablo Montoya and Michael Schumacher engaged in a merciless battle yet again at the Nürburgring. On lap 43, after the second run of pit-stops, Montoya attacked Schumacher with a daring move around the outside of the Dunlop hairpin. It was a stunning manoeuvre which ended with both cars touching. The Williams kept going, but the Ferrari was tipped into a slide before coming to rest in the gravel trap. But a shove from the marshals got it going again.

The stewards met after the race to investigate the incident. There were rumours that Michael Schumacher would be disqualified for shutting the door, while others reckoned Montoya would be penalised for having caused an avoidable accident, but both men escaped censure.

Out in front, Ralf Schumacher took the win having dominated 40 of the 60 laps. The BMW-Williams team did the double on the same weekend that the two companies announced they were extending their partnership until the end of 2009.

> Kimi Räikkönen took pole at the Nürburgring. He would not do it again until... Indianapolis.

Kimi's first

Kimi Räikkönen swept round the Nürburgring to take his McLaren-Mercedes to pole position after a closely contested session. The Finn beat Michael Schumacher in the Ferrari by 32 thousandths of a second and Ralf Schumacher's Williams-BMW by just 96 thousandths!

At the age of 23, Räikkönen thus recorded his first ever Formula 1 pole position after 42 attempts. "*I am very happy,*" he commented the moment he stepped from the cockpit. "*Especially after the last race in Canada (where he had started from the back of the grid.) The car was almost perfect and I just tried to put together a good lap, without looking at what times the others had done.*"

Still as tight-lipped as ever, the Finn raised his left eyebrow by all of a quarter of a millimetre when he learned that fellow countryman Mika Hakkinen had also recorded his first career pole at this circuit, back in 1997, opening the door to a career which saw him crowned champion twice. "*It's good to know,*" he commented. "*But I have to thank the team which worked very well to produce such an efficient car.*" The end!

The bad times continue at Sauber

Sauber's 2003 season was turning into a nightmare. As always, the Zurich-based team had got off to a good start in the early races, when its rivals were less well prepared.

While this strategy had worked well enough over the past two years, it was no longer working in 2003. On the one hand, the major constructors whjich Sauber had been in the habit of beating (Toyota, Jaguar, Honda and Renault) were now clearly better prepared. On the other hand, the Swiss team's major asset, its fabled reliability, was no longer evident. Since the start of the 2003 championship, the two Saubers had totalled sixteen starts of which seven had ended in mechanical failure: one clutch problem, two suspension failures and four engine failures. And when the Saubers did manage to reach the finish line, it was usually well outside the points.

On Saturday, this black run continued. In the warm-up, both Heinz-Harald Frentzen and Nick Heidfeld came back to the pits with the same comment, even though they had not conferred.

Their engine was making a strange noise at high revs. The Ferrari engineers attached to the team decided to send Frentzen out in the spare car and to change Heidfeld's engine. In an incredible show of efficiency, they managed to switch motors in just 28 minutes. But when Heidfeld set off for his qualifying lap, a hydraulic problem reared its head in the gearbox department and he ended up off the track. "*The situation is not clear,*" is all Peter Sauber was giving away about the explanations supplied by Ferrari on the subject of these endless failures.

> The Toyota factory in Cologne is less than 100 kilometres from the circuit as the crow flies, so there was a large contingent of the team's employees at the Nürburgring. Somehow, two outsiders had managed to infiltrate the ranks.

> Juan Pablo Montoya qualified fourth. He complained a bit about the balance of the car, but he was confident that he had chosen the best strategy for the race.

Starting grid

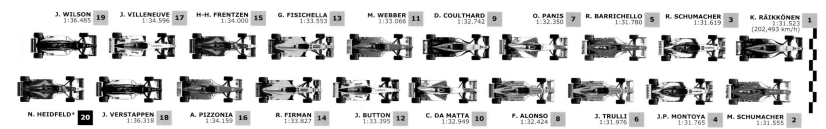

J. WILSON 1:36.485 19	J. VILLENEUVE 1:34.596 17	H-H. FRENTZEN 1:34.000 15	G. FISICHELLA 1:33.553 13	M. WEBBER 1:33.066 11	D. COULTHARD 1:32.742 9	O. PANIS 1:32.350 7	R. BARRICHELLO 1:31.780 5	R. SCHUMACHER 1:31.619 3	K. RÄIKKÖNEN 1:31.523 1 (202,493 km/h)
N. HEIDFELD* 20	J. VERSTAPPEN 1:36.318 18	A. PIZZONIA 1:34.159 16	R. FIRMAN 1:33.827 14	J. BUTTON 1:33.395 12	C. DA MATTA 1:32.949 10	F. ALONSO 1:32.424 8	J. TRULLI 1:31.976 6	J.P. MONTOYA 1:31.765 4	M. SCHUMACHER 1:31.555 2

* N. HEIDFELD starts from the pit lane.

An incident-packed race

Ralf Schumacher was due to celebrate his 28th birthday on the day after the European Grand Prix. But he had already offered himself the best possible present in the form of a win at the Nürburgring.

It was his first of the 2003 season and it put him back on course in the fight for the world championship title, as he was now just 15 points behind his brother Michael. "*It's great to win again after such a long time,*" he enthused. "*And especially after two pole positions which did not lead to much. We had a perfect car today with perfect tyres. Considering that we did our run with around 10 kilos more fuel than the others, it is a very good performance.*"

In second place, Juan Pablo Montoya had a busier afternoon than his team-mate. Starting from fourth on the grid, the Colombian began by getting past Rubens Barrichello during the pit stops, before trying to pass Michael Schumacher on the track. It was a daring move round the outside of the Dunlop corner and it promoted him to second place. "*I don't know what happened to Michael, but he was very slow in the tight corners. I had new tyres and I knew I could not waste any time if I wanted to make use of the extra grip that they would give me for a few laps. I put my nose to the right of Michael, he closed the door, so I switched to the left and went for it. I left him enough room to get through and I stayed off the kerb, but he probably came into the corner too quickly. He slid and we touched.*"

On Sunday night, Michael Schumacher confirmed that it was nothing more than a simple racing accident. "*Juan Pablo was quicker than me and he gave me just enough room to survive. I guess I could have done with a bit more room, but I have no complaints about him.*" Second place meant eight more points for Juan Pablo which kept him in contact with the championship leaders. "*I am very pleased, especially as I was only fifth at the first corner. After my second pit-stop, the car was definitely better on the new tyres.*"

The one-two was a good sign for the Anglo-German squad, coming just a fortnight before the French Grand Prix as none of the teams would have much time to make any significant changes to their cars. "*I really like the Magny-Cours circuit and I hope we will be on the pace there. The car is really fantastic now.*"

A black day for McLaren-Mercedes

For the McLaren-Mercedes team, it was all going so well, until it turned into a nightmare. Kimi Räikkönen looked set fair for the win, as he was leading Ralf Schumacher by almost five seconds until his engine let go on lap 26. "*I am very disappointed, because I think I could have won today,*" confirmed the Finn when he returned to the garage.

For his part, David Coulthard spent the best part of the race trying to get past a Renault – first it was Jarno Trulli's and then Fernando Alonso's.

Towards the end of the race he was duelling with the Spaniard and with three laps remaining, the Scot misread the situation and ended up in the gravel. "*It's been a very frustrating weekend for the team,*" admitted David. "*I was going to score points. But suddenly, I had to move onto the grass to avoid Fernando when he braked incredibly early. I will be talking to him about it.*"

After the race, McLaren boss Ron Dennis went to see his opposite number at Renault, Flavio Briatorie, to give him his views on the incident. It achieved nothing and, as usual, the haughty Flavio was unperturbed.

Behind the scenes, things were not going much better at McLaren. The MP4-18 had just failed the FIA crash test, which meant a new modified chassis would have to be built. For his part, Norbert Haug confirmed that Mercedes would supply an additional team with its engines in 2004, although he did not specify which one.

Race summary

> The pack hurtles through the first turn with Räikkönen and Ralf Schumacher leading the way (1).

> Räikkönen's McLaren appears to be toying with the opposition in the early stages as he pulls out a lead over his pursuers (2).

> On lap 24, drama as the Finn's engine blows up. He would pay heavily for this retirement come the end of the season (3).

> M. Schumacher and Montoya stage another memorable duel. It will turn to the advantage of the Colombian (4).

> Coulthard follows Alonso closely. A moment's inattention and Coulthard has to take avoiding action. He slides off and ends his race in the gravel (5).

> R. Schumacher wins at home to the cheers of his team (6).

> His mechanics in parc ferme (7).

A minor miracle

Sometimes, at the height of a storm one can spot a patch of blue sky. Just when everything seemed to be going wrong for the Sauber team and its chances had been written off, the Swiss crew came home from the Nürburgring with one more point in the bank. The last point on offer fell to Nick Heidfeld after a steep climb through the order, as the German had started from the pit lane.

Williams and BMW together until 2009

It was said that the BMW bosses were tired of the eccentricities displayed by Frank Williams and Patrick Head, the two men at the top of the team. A month ago, the German marque's competitions boss, Mario Theissen, had openly criticised the two men, accusing them of doing a bad job of running their technical team, which had suffered several defections in recent weeks.

Over in the Williams camp, technical director Patrick Head was quick to refute claims that the BMW engine was the most powerful in the paddock. The atmosphere between the two partners was far from the sweetness and light necessary to fight for the Drivers' world championship.

The situation was aggravated by the fact that their marriage contract was due to expire at the end of the 2004 season. In F1 terms, that was as good as saying it was due to end tomorrow. There were all sorts of rumours about what would happen next, including a suggestion that car giant BMW would quite simply buy the Williams team to run its own chassis.

But in the end, on Thursday at the 'Ring, the partnership was extended to the end of the 2009 season. The BMW men were keen to point out that, from now on, they would be involved in much more than simply providing the engines. "*For us it is a case of getting the most out of both our companies, to use all Williams' expertise in order to obtain perfect integration with our side of the operation,*" explained Burkhard Goschel, a member of the BMW board with responsibility for Formula 1. The Bavarian company had apparently decided to invest millions of dollars in the Williams team, primarily financing the building of a second wind tunnel due to be operational in time for the start of the 2004 season. "*BMW is now investing in our team at an unprecedented level,*" underlined Frank Williams. "*Obviously, that can only be a good thing for our partnership.*"

This season, having overcome its teething troubles, the Williams-BMW FW25 now seemed capable of winning races on a regular basis. With its future now decided, the team could put all its efforts into concentrating on the 2003 championshp.

results

Practice

All the time trials

N°	Driver	N° Chassis - Engine	Private testing	Pos.	Practice friday	Pos.	Qualifying friday	Pos.	Practice 1 saturday	Pos.	Practice 2 saturday	Pos.	Warm-up	Pos.	Qualifying saturday	Pos.
1.	Michael Schumacher	Ferrari F2003-GA 229			1:32.560	10	1:30.353	2	1:32.852	6	1:32.652	9	1:31.981	1	1:31.555	2
2.	Rubens Barrichello	Ferrari F2002-GA 230			1:32.607	12	1:30.842	5	1:32.039	2	1:33.010	10	1:32.097	2	1:31.780	5
3.	Juan Pablo Montoya	Williams FW25 06 - BMW			1:32.590	11	1:30.376	3	1:32.477	4	1:31.366	2	1:32.252	4	1:31.765	4
4.	Ralf Schumacher	Williams FW25 07 - BMW			1:32.170	8	1:30.522	4	1:32.891	7	1:31.305	1	1:32.547	7	1:31.619	3
5.	David Coulthard	McLaren MP4-17D 07 - Mercedes			1:31.918	7	1:30.903	6	1:32.471	3	1:31.608	4	1:32.114	3	1:32.742	9
6.	Kimi Räikkönen	McLaren MP4-17D 09 - Mercedes			1:31.260	3	1:29.989	1	1:32.803	5	1:32.021	5	1:32.385	5	1:31.523	1
7.	Jarno Trulli	Renault R23-05	1:32.085	1	1:31.513	4	1:31.143	7	1:33.707	10	1:32.356	7	1:33.029	8	1:31.976	6
8.	Fernando Alonso	Renault R23-04	1:32.311	2	1:31.750	5	1:31.533	8	1:34.179	12	1:32.391	8	1:33.068	9	1:32.424	8
9.	Nick Heidfeld	Sauber C22-01 - Petronas			1:32.901	16	1:52.300	13	1:34.784	16	1:33.698	15		20		20
10.	Heinz-Harald Frentzen	Sauber C22-03 - Petronas			1:32.792	14	1:32.201	10	1:34.775	15	1:34.090	18		19	1:34.000	15
11.	Giancarlo Fisichella	Jordan EJ13-04 - Ford	1:34.579	7	1:32.692	13	1:32.196	9	1:35.332	18	1:33.214	12	1:34.229	14	1:33.553	13
12.	Ralph Firman	Jordan EJ13-03 - Ford	1:33.019	4	1:33.643	18	1:53.893	14	1:34.967	17	1:34.827	17	1:34.373	15	1:33.827	14
14.	Mark Webber	Jaguar R4-04	1:33.174	5	1:31.224	2	1:35.972	12	1:34.564	13	1:33.635	14	1:34.164	13	1:33.065	11
15.	Antonio Pizzonia	Jaguar R4-05	1:32.965	3	1:31.794	6	1:57.435	18	1:33.127	8	1:33.076	11	1:34.746	16	1:34.159	16
16.	Jacques Villeneuve	BAR 005-3 - Honda			1:33.602	17		20	1:34.127	11	1:34.085	16	1:34.114	12	1:34.596	17
17.	Jenson Button	BAR 005-5 - Honda			1:32.841	15	1:32.479	11	1:34.582	14	1:33.474	13	1:33.780	11	1:33.395	12
18.	Justin Wilson	Minardi PS03/04 - Cosworth	1:35.455	9	1:35.525	20	1:54.546	15	1:37.001	20	1:36.026	19	1:36.559	17	1:36.485	19
19.	Jos Verstappen	Minardi PS03/03 - Cosworth	1:34.857	8	1:34.947	19	1:55.921	16	1:36.845	19	1:36.381	20	1:37.181	18	1:36.318	18
20.	Olivier Panis	Toyota TF103/05			1:31.197	1	1:57.327	17	1:31.181	1	1:31.190	3	1:32.545	6	1:32.350	7
21.	Cristiano da Matta	Toyota TF103/04			1:32.492	9		19	1:33.140	9	1:32.057	6	1:33.306	10	1:32.949	10
34.	Allan McNish	Renault R23-00	1:33.935	6												

Maximum speed

N°	Driver	P1 Qualifs	Pos.	P1 Race	Pos.	P2 Qualifs	Pos.	P2 Race	Pos.	Finish Qualifs	Pos.	Finish Race	Pos.	Trap Qualifs	Pos.	Trap Race	Pos.
1.	M. Schumacher	273,9	6	276,1	6	227,3	4	227,5	1	254,8	2	253,8	7	304,7	2	311,2	6
2.	R. Barrichello	274,5	4	277,2	4	231,0	1	231,3	2	253,4	4	256,4	1	303,7	6	310,7	8
3.	J.P. Montoya	276,3	1	279,2	1	224,7	11	231,2	3	258,0	1	254,9	4	304,4	4	313,1	1
4.	R. Schumacher	275,0	3	278,7	2	226,8	6	229,7	5	250,9	9	255,1	2	304,4	3	321,8	3
5.	D. Coulthard	274,3	5	277,9	3	221,9	15	228,9	7	251,4	7	254,2	5	304,2	5	311,9	4
6.	K. Räikkönen	275,3	2	276,0	7	229,4	2	232,3	1	254,1	3	255,0	3	304,9	1	308,1	12
7.	J. Trulli	273,5	7	274,3	12	225,5	9	224,9	14	249,8	14	249,7	15	302,9	8	307,1	16
8.	F. Alonso	272,9	8	273,4	16	223,6	13	227,3	11	248,8	16	249,1	16	298,8	15	307,3	15
9.	N. Heidfeld	240,0	20	274,6	10	198,6	20	223,6	17	252,3	5	253,4	8	298,9	14	311,4	5
10.	H-H. Frentzen	269,8	13	272,3	17	225,7	8	223,5	18	250,5	10	249,8	14	302,9	7	308,6	11
11.	G. Fisichella	267,6	17	272,3	18	226,0	7	226,2	12	245,7	19	248,5	18	292,8	20	305,3	18
12.	R. Firman	264,9	19	270,0	19	224,5	12	223,8	16	245,3	20	247,0	19	297,1	18	304,5	19
14.	M. Webber	268,7	16	273,9	15	225,3	10	229,4	6	250,2	11	251,4	10	299.0	13	306,6	17
15.	A. Pizzonia	270,4	12	273,9	14	220,0	16	226,0	13	248,1	17	249,0	17	299,9	12	307,7	13
16.	J. Villeneuve	270,8	11	275,0	8	216,4	19	224,7	15	250,1	12	250,5	12	298,0	17	310,2	9
17.	J. Button	269,3	15	274,3	11	226,9	5	227,4	10	252,0	6	250,0	13	298,7	16	307,6	14
18.	J. Wilson	269,3	14	274,2	13	219,9	18	222,2	19	249,8	13	251,3	11	301,0	11	310,7	7
19.	J. Verstappen	266,0	18	269,4	20	220,1	17	222,0	20	245,9	18	246,9	20	295,0	19	301,0	20
20.	O. Panis	272,5	9	276,9	5	227,5	3	227,5	8	251,2	8	253,8	6	301,5	10	309,3	10
21.	C. Da Matta	272,1	10	274,8	9	222,8	14	230,8	4	248,9	15	253,0	9	301,5	9	321,9	2

Race

Classification & Retirements

Pos.	Driver	Team	Lap	Time	Average	
1.	R. Schumacher	Williams BMW	60	1:34:43.622	195,826 km/h	
2.	J.P. Montoya	Williams BMW	60	+ 16.821	195,056 km/h	
3.	R. Barrichello	Ferrari	60	+ 39.673	194,277 km/h	
4.	F. Alonso	Renault	60	+ 1:05.731	193,396 km/h	
5.	M. Schumacher	Ferrari	60	+ 1:06.162	193,382 km/h	
6.	M. Webber	Jaguar	59	1 lap	192,014 km/h	
7.	J. Button	BAR Honda	59	1 lap	191,509 km/h	
8.	N. Heidfeld	Sauber Petronas	59	1 lap	190,779 km/h	
9.	H.H Frentzen	Sauber Petronas	59	1 lap	190,147 km/h	
10.	A. Pizzonia	Jaguar	59	1 lap	190,124 km/h	
11.	R. Firman	Jordan Ford	58	2 laps	188,456 km/h	
12.	G. Fisichella	Jordan Ford	58	2 laps	187,658 km/h	
13.	J. Wilson	Minardi Cosworth	58	2 laps	186,833 km/h	
14.	J. Verstappen	Minardi Cosworth	57	3 laps	185,040 km/h	
15.	D. Coulthard	McLaren Mercedes	56	4 laps	193,452 km/h	Caught out by Alonso braking, crashes

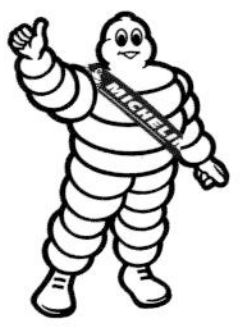

Driver	Team		Reason
C. Da Matta	Toyota	54	Engine failure after oil leak
J. Villeneuve	BAR Honda	52	Broken gearbox
J. Trulli	Renault	38	Fuel pressure prob.
O. Panis	Toyota	38	Spin after locking brakes, engine stalled
K. Räikkönen	McLaren Mercedes	26	Engine failure

Fastest laps

	Driver	Time	Lap	Average
1.	K. Räikkönen	1:32.621	14	200,092 km/h
2.	R. Schumacher	1:32.826	34	199,650 km/h
3.	M. Schumacher	1:32.904	34	199,483 km/h
4.	J.P. Montoya	1:33.094	59	199,076 km/h
5.	R. Barrichello	1:33.200	15	198,849 km/h
6.	D. Coulthard	1:33.236	12	198,773 km/h
7.	F. Alonso	1:33.307	17	198,621 km/h
8.	J. Trulli	1:33.348	13	198,534 km/h
9.	C. Da Matta	1:33.398	15	198,428 km/h
10.	O. Panis	1:33.583	8	198,035 km/h
11.	H-H. Frentzen	1:33.994	33	197,170 km/h
12.	M. Webber	1:34.191	37	196,757 km/h
13.	J. Button	1:34.208	14	196,722 km/h
14.	N. Heidfeld	1:34.541	23	196,029 km/h
15.	G. Fisichella	1:34.656	29	195,791 km/h
16.	A. Pizzonia	1:34.915	47	195,256 km/h
17.	J. Villeneuve	1:35.100	45	194,876 km/h
18.	R. Firman	1:35.328	29	194,410 km/h
19.	J. Wilson	1:36.709	19	191,634 km/h
20.	J. Verstappen	1:37.365	3	190,343 km/h

Pit stops

	Driver	Time	Lap	Stop n°
1.	M. Webber	34.777	14	1
2.	H-H. Frentzen	32.552	14	1
3.	J. Villeneuve	38.246	14	1
4.	J. Trulli	32.703	15	1
5.	J. Button	33:965	15	1
6.	O. Panis	34.210	15	1
7.	J. Verstappen	36.754	15	1
8.	K. Räikkönen	33.876	16	1
9.	M. Schumacher	32.609	16	1
10.	C. Da Matta	33.246	16	1
11.	A. Pizzonia	35.463	16	1
12.	J. Wilson	35.394	16	1
13.	R. Barrichello	33.019	17	1
14.	J.P. Montoya	32.933	18	1
15.	F. Alonso	32.431	18	1
16.	D. Coulthard	33.308	18	1
17.	N. Heidfeld	32.518	20	1
18.	R. Schumacher	32.103	21	1
19.	C. Da Matta	39.236	24	2
20.	R. Firman	32.879	26	1
21.	G. Fisichella	31.568	27	1
22.	H-H. Frentzen	30.880	31	2
23.	M. Schumacher	34.067	36	2
24.	O. Panis	33.771	36	2
25.	R. Barrichello	33.339	37	2
26.	J. Wilson	34.582	36	2
27.	J. Button	35.974	37	2
28.	N. Heidfeld	32.864	37	2
29.	F. Alonso	32.549	38	2
30.	M. Webber	33.354	38	2
31.	J. Verstappen	34.648	37	2
32.	J.P. Montoya	32.493	40	2
33.	R. Schumacher	33.044	41	2
34.	A. Pizzonia	33.999	40	2
35.	D. Coulthard	33.769	42	2
36.	R. Firman	33.152	41	2
37.	J. Villeneuve	33.387	41	2
38.	C. Da Matta	32.075	43	3
39.	A. Pizzonia	22.040	43	3
40.	G. Fisichella	33.598	43	2
41.	H-H. Frentzen	30.766	44	3
42.	G. Fisichella	40.872	53	3

Race leaders

Driver	Laps in the lead	Nber of Laps
K. Räikkönen	1 > 16	16
R. Schumacher	17 > 21	5
K. Räikkönen	22 > 25	4
R. Schumacher	26 > 60	35

Driver	Nber of Laps	Kilometers
R. Schumacher	40	205,920 km
K. Räikkönen	20	102,943 km

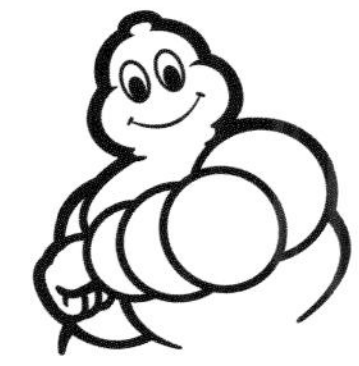

Lap chart

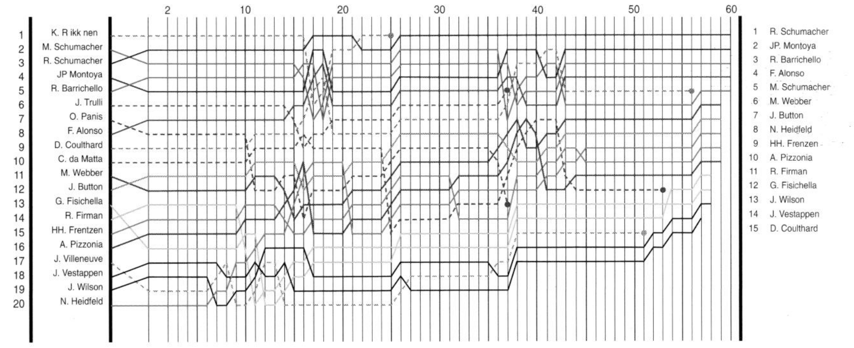

Gaps on the leader board

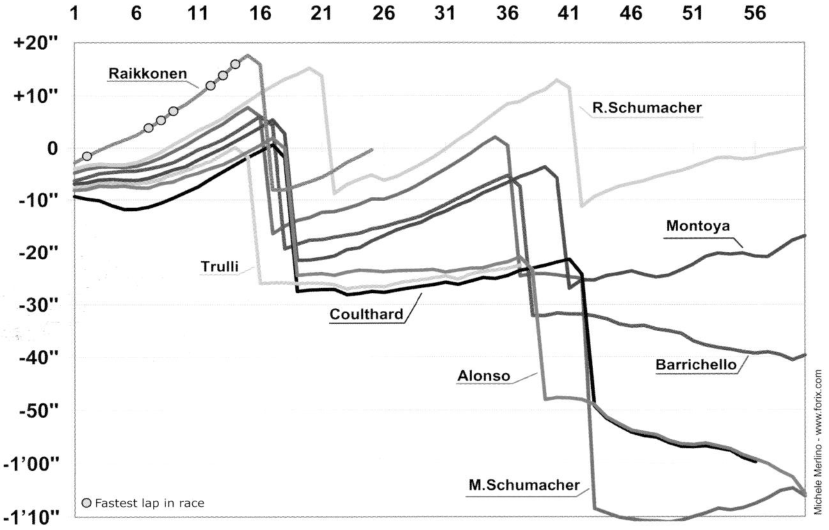

Championship after nine rounds

Drivers

1. M. Schumacher ....(4 wins)................58
2. K. Räikkönen ....(1 win) 51
3. R. Schumacher...........(1 win) 43
4. J.P. Montoya..............(1 win) 39
5. F. Alonso 39
6. R. Barrichello 37
7. D. Coulthard ....(1 win) 25
8. J. Trulli 13
9. G. Fisichella ....(1 win) 10
10. J. Button 10
11. M. Webber 9
12. H-H. Frentzen..7
13. C. Da Matta...3
14. J. Villeneuve..3
15. N. Heidfeld..2
16. O. Panis...1
17. R. Firman..1
18. A. Pizzonia 0
19. J. Verstappen 0
20. J. Wilson..0

Constructors

1. Scuderia Ferrari Marlboro ......(4 wins) 95
2. BMW Williams F1 Team ....(2 wins) 82
3. West McLaren Mercedes.........(2 wins) 76
4. Mild Seven Renault F1 Team 52
5. Lucky Strike BAR Honda...........................13
6. Jordan Ford..........................(1 win).........11
7. Sauber Petronas 9
8. Jaguar Racing..9
9. Panasonic Toyota Racing 4
10. European Minardi Cosworth........................0

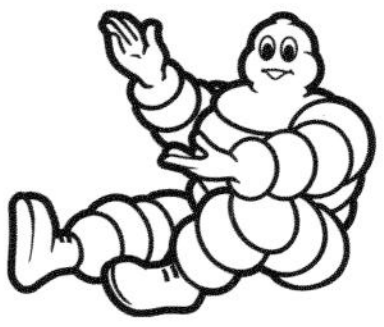

The circuit

Name	Nürburgring
Date	June 29, 2003
Length	5148 meters
Distance	60 laps, 308,863 km
Weather	Sunny with a few clouds, 24-26°c
Track temperature	29-33°c

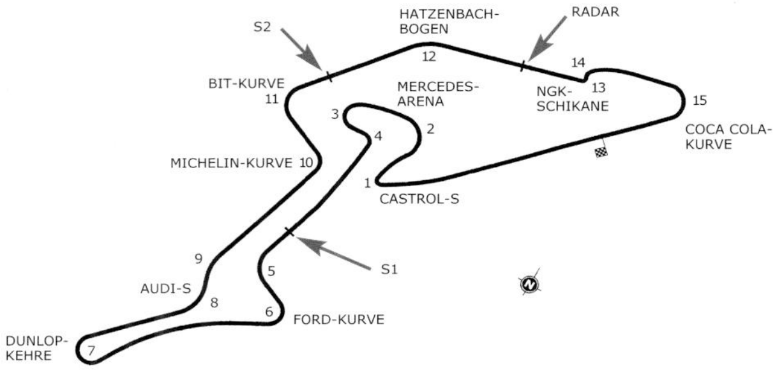

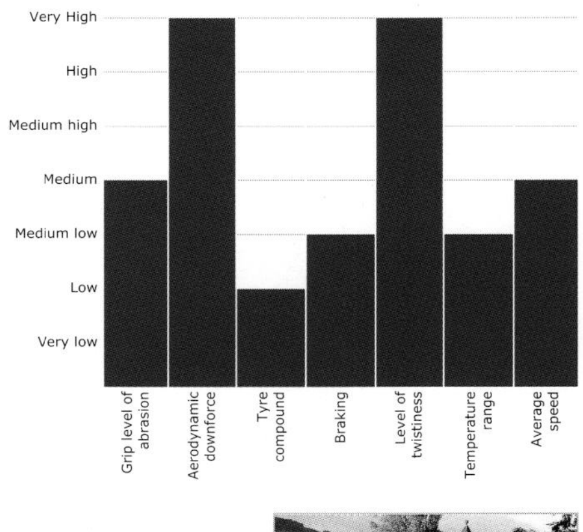

All results : © 2003 Formula One Administration Ltd,
6 Princes Gate, London, SW7 1QJ, England

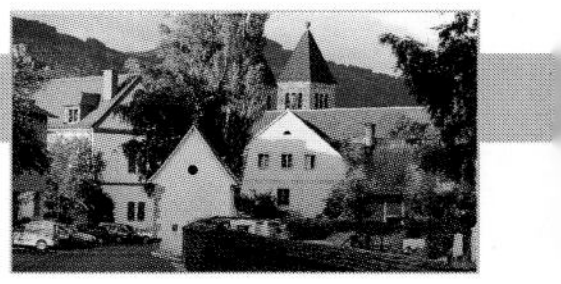

A SECOND ONE-TWO FOR WILLIAMS

In Magny-Cours, the BMW-Williams team scored its second consecutive one-two finish, following hot on the heels of the one in the European Grand Prix. The drivers triumphed in the same order, with Ralf Schumacher ahead of Juan Pablo Montoya.

In the world championship, the younger Schu had closed to within 11 points of his big brother. He was now only giving away three points to Kimi Raikkonen.

Michael Schumacher finished third, powerless against the Anglo-German cars. There was a serious malaise in the Scuderia Ferrari camp, where the Bridgestone tyres were being blamed for the poor performance.

> Jos Verstappen took provisional pole on Friday! Thanks to the new rules...

Plenty of star guests in the Magny-Cours paddock: Flavio Briatore is seen here with girlfriend Heidi Klum and Renault President, Louis Schweitzer.
v

A first for a Friday: a Minardi on pole position!

The results of the first qualifying session for the French Grand Prix were, to put it mildly, unexpected. Heavy showers hit the track throughout Friday morning and qualifying got underway on a damp track, which gradually dried out as the cars went round and the sun came out. Exceptional circumstances which produced equally exceptional results, as it was the two Minardis, the only cars to run on "dry" tyres, which set the fastest times, with Jos Verstappen ahead of Justin Wilson. The tail-enders had become the quickest.

Unfortunately for the little Faenza squad, post-qualifying scrutineering revealed that Justin Wilson's car was under the minimum weight of 605 kilos, by 2.5 kilos.

The error occurred as the team made the last minute switch to "dry" tyres which weigh less than the "rain" tyres. That meant the Englishman was disqualified. *"It's a shame for Justin, but it is still a memorable day for the team,"* triumphed Paul Stoddart. *"It was a risky decision going out on dry tyres and the mechanics simply forgot to add fuel to compensate for the weight of the tyres."*

On Saturday, it was back to reality for the Italian team and back to the back of the grid as usual.

Jean Todt: 10 years as leader of the Scuderia

New helmet design for Jarno Trulli. The artwork was not quite finished and would not be until Silverstone, a fortnight later.
>v

President Schweitzer had definitely not come on his own...
v

When Jean Todt got the call from Scuderia Ferrari at the start of 1993, the patient was in intensive care. The Italian team was still a cult object for the tifosi, but its two drivers at the time, Gerhard Berger and Jean Alesi had to make do with a dreadful car, part designed in England and built in Italy.

It took Jean Todt months, or in fact years to clear out the dead wood, saddle up the prancing horse and get it moving forward again. His masterstroke was to convince Michael Schumacher in mid-1995 to join the team, bringing with him the engineers who had helped him win with Benetton. Along came technical director Ross Brawn and the designer, Rory Byrne. It was a "dream team" which survives to this day. *"I do not like looking to the past,"* he commented. *"I tend to look to the future. I always try and produce extraordinary moments with those I have chosen and with whom I like to work. We are all happy to work for Ferrari. When one loves motor sport, it is the most extraordinary marque."*

A third for Ralf!

After taking pole in Monaco and Canada, Ralf Schumacher took his third pole of the season at Magny-Cours.

This performance was all the more unexpected as the German was one of the early runners in the session, because of the strange order imposed by the result of Friday's qualifying session. It meant that all the big names were amongst the first to try their luck on Saturday. *"I am especially happy to be on pole having been the fourth driver to make my run, when the track conditions were still not at their best,"* said a smiling Ralf Schumacher. *"I had a bit of understeer in the third sector, but I am happy to see the gap we have to our rivals."*

Juan Pablo Montoya was second, just 117 thousandths behind his team-mate. But both Williams were around half a second ahead of Michael Schumacher's Ferrari.

Starting grid

Pos	Driver	Time
20	J. WILSON*	1:19.619
18	R. FIRMAN	1:18.514
16	H-H. FRENTZEN	1:17.562
14	J. BUTTON	1:17.077
12	J. VILLENEUVE	1:16.990
10	O. PANIS	1:16.345
8	R. BARRICHELLO	1:16.166
6	J. TRULLI	1:15.967
4	K. RÄIKKÖNEN	1:15.533
2	J.P. MONTOYA	1:15.136
19	J. VERSTAPPEN	1:18.709
17	G. FISICHELLA	1:18.431
15	N. HEIDFELD	1:17.445
13	C. DA MATTA	1:17.068
11	A. PIZZONIA	1:16.965
9	M. WEBBER	1:16.308
7	F. ALONSO	1:16.087
5	D. COULTHARD	1:15.628
3	M. SCHUMACHER	1:15.480
1	R. SCHUMACHER	1:15.019 (211,674 km/h)

Williams-BMW totally invincible

Magny-Cours is a rural spot situated bang in the centre of France, just a short drive from Michelin headquarters in Clermont-Ferrand.

This weekend, over 600 of its employees were invited to watch the French Grand Prix. They had no regrets come Sunday evening as their tyres were fitted to no less than six of the top eight finishers.

With his Michelin-shod Williams-BMW, Ralf Schumacher led the race from start to finish. Starting from pole, the German thus took his second win in a row, after his victory at the Nurburgring. Since the start of the season, he had scored points in every grand prix and was now lying third in the championship, eleven points behind his elder brother and three down on Kimi Raikkonen.

In Magny-Cours, he had a sensational start to the race, immediately clearing off into the distance ahead of the chasing pack, led by team-mate Juan Pablo Montoya. "At the start of the race, the car was working really well," commented the winner. *"I tried to push hard right from the beginning, as we had planned and everything went well. Then, on my second set of tyres, my settings were not so good and I was held up by backmarkers and I could not match my earlier pace."* The only scary moment for the German was a little slide, five laps from home. *"I braked a bit late,"* he admitted. In fact, throughout the race, the only driver who might have bothered him was his team-mate, Juan Pablo Montoya, who was only sixth tenths back after the third pit-stop. *"When I saw Juan*

< Ralf Schumacher was happy and with good cause. "Our car is very good, but the Williams FW25 is really strong this season," commented the winner's big brother.

Pablo pit and then go very quickly, I decided to come in one lap earlier than planned," continued Ralf Schumacher. *"The team was very efficient and reacted very quickly."* The decision certainly made sure of the win for the German.

As for Montoya, he lost a lot of time at his first pit-stop. The left rear wheel caused a problem which resulted in a full four seconds longer stop than his team-mate.

The Colombian's hopes of victory went out the window at this point. *"Up to my first pit-stop, my car wasn't that good, but afterwards, I was able to step up the pace,"* he explained. *"I was quite*

aggressive in the traffic, the car was perfect and it went quite well, which meant I could close on Ralf. Towards the end, I tried everything, but Ralf came out of his third pit-stop just ahead of me. There was nothing I could do from then on. I missed out on taking the lead by one little second."

It was a glorious performance from the two Williams, which were clearly superior to their rivals over the past four grands prix. The following week, they were due to test at Barcelona to try some new parts which would produce even more improvements.

Unease confirmed in the Red camp

There was no sign of a party under the Ferrari awning come Sunday night. Around 18h00, Jean Todt held a brief press conference to explain the events of the weekend. In the space of a few races, the Italian team appeared to have lost its shine. The Brigestone tyres stood accused, seemingly unable to match the Michelins. *"We are not quick enough, but for several reasons and not just one,"* insisted Todt. *"It is the whole chassis-engine-tyre*

package which is at fault and we have to make progress in all areas."

The Scuderia's technical director, Ross Brawn, had a more radical view: *"We have to rethink everything. We have to turn our situation around through a full 360 degrees. We are not competitive enough."* For his part, Michael Schumacher felt it was too early to talk of a crisis in the camp.

"Smile, you're on camera." In Formula 1, nothing escapes the attention of the hundreds of photographers. Especially not the podium ceremony.
<

Refuelling stop for Rubens Barrichello. In Magny-Cours, the Brazilian could do no better than seventh place.
∨

Race summary _____

> Ralf Schumacher makes a good start, ahead of his team-mate. M. Schumacher is swallowed up by

Coulthard at the first corner. But the German gets him back round the outside of the long right hander to

maintain 4th spot **(1.)**
> M. Schumacher has a quiet race. He gets ahead of the McLarens during the

pit stops **(2.)**
> Barrichello spins on lap 2. He climbs back up to 7th. Here he passes Heidfeld **(3.)**
>The two Renaults

spend the race in line astern and retire within the same 2 laps. A disappointment for the crowd come to

cheer its home team **(4.)**
> Panis, here with Webber, will take one point at home **(5.)**
> Jordan's nightmare

continues. Brazil seems a long time ago **(6.)**
> The traditional champagne shower **(7.)**

One-two at the Nurbruging, then one-two in Magny-Cours for the two Williams-BMWs.
∧

A pensive Mark Webber. In Magny-Cours, the Jaguars continued to make progress and the Australian scored points for the third time in a row.
>

After the upheavals of Thursday, the BAR boys had a pretty normal weekend. Jacques Villeneuve finished just outside the points.
>∨

There were plenty of famous faces in the Magny-Cours paddock. To celebrate ten years in Formula 1, Olivier Panis had invited Guy Ligier, the founder of the team which bore his name and with which Panis began his F1 career. The singer Mireille Matthieu came with her mother, while the actor, Jean Reno was invited to watch the race from the Toyota garage.
>

Around ten kilometres from the Magny-Cours circuit is the typically rural French town of Nevers, full of charms typical of the area.
∨

BAR cars seized by French authorities!

17h00, Thursday afternoon. A little man with a dark suit and a stern expression walks into the paddock accompanied by five policemen. He is a bailiff and he is accompanied by Bernie Ecclestone's general factotum, Pascquale Lattunedu, who gave them access passes. The little group immediately heads off in the direction of the BAR garage. Half an hour later, the team's race cars are dismantled and put back in the trucks, before the doors are sealed. The BAR cars had been seized by the French authorities.

The incident revolved around a dark story of advertising commission, which the team apparently owed to PPGI, one of its former sponsors. PPGI had facilitated the signing of a contract between BAR and Teleglobe, worth 50 million dollars to the team. According to PPGI's Canadian director, France Corbeil, his company was owed 3.2 million dollars in commission, which the team was refusing to pay on the grounds that no contract had been signed regarding this commission.

PPGI had therefore brought a court order against the team in a Monaco tribunal, at the end of May. The judge sided with the plaintiff, issuing an order for the cars to be seized. It was only on the Thursday of the Magny-Cours weekend that this was finally done, after BAR had obtained several delaying orders. It was now down to a court in Nevers to rule on the matter.

It was due to convene at 9 o'clock on Friday morning, before the start of that morning's free practice. *"Everything is still possible,"* said the bailiff before leaving the circuit. But there was a more serious problem looming if the team was not allowed to run. *"Bernie (Ecclestone) has told me that if French law seizes the BAR cars, then all the teams will leave Magny-Cours out of solidarity,"* revealed Lattunedu, after a telephone call to the Formula 1 boss.

On Friday, it seemed as though BAR had sorted its problem. In the morning, the Nevers judge found in favour of the English team. The decision was taken at 11h30, which meant that Villeneuve and Button missed morning practice. In the afternoon, despite it being his first run round the track, the Canadian qualified sixth. On Sunday, it seemed that the BAR soap opera was not over yet. After the race, PPGI put out a press release stating that, contrary to general opinion, the Nevers court had found in its favour on Friday morning.

The result was that the bailiff who had turned up on Thursday to lock up the cars was back to seize the team's equipment on Sunday. But it was something of a false alarm and the cars headed back to England. It was another politico-financial tale which did little to improve the image of F1...

Brake problems at McLaren

Fourth past the chequered flag, Kimi Räikkönen had been third for a long time, before giving way to Michael Schumacher after his final pit-stop. *"I lost a huge amount of time in traffic,"* complained the Finn. *"Some drivers seemed to totally ignore the blue flags. On top of that, I had no brakes for the last few laps, because I had lost a rear disc. It's impossible to drive quickly without brakes, so it was not exactly a brilliant day."*

David Coulthard finished fifth. He also lost a place during the pit-stops, when the refuelling nozzle got stuck on his car. *"We had problems with the first nozzle, so we switched to the second one, but that did not want to come off,"* recalled the Scotsman.

results

Practice

All the time trials

N°	Driver	N° Chassis - Engine	Private testing	Pos.	Practice friday	Pos.	Qualifying friday	Pos.	Practice 1 saturday	Pos.	Practice 2 saturday	Pos.	Warm-up	Pos.	Qualifying saturday	Pos.
1.	Michael Schumacher	Ferrari F2003-GA 229			1:28.681	1	1:27.929	11	1:16.495	4	1:15.918	4	1:15.879	5	1:15.480	3
2.	Rubens Barrichello	Ferrari F2003-GA 230			1.29.813	15	1:27.095	10	1:16.190	2	1:16.345	9	1:16.332	8	1:16.166	8
3.	Juan Pablo Montoya	Williams FW25 06 - BMW			1:29.608	13	1:28.988	14	1:16.687	5	1:15.577	2	1:15.697	2	1:15.136	2
4.	Ralf Schumacher	Williams FW25 07 - BMW			1:28.082	2	1:29.327	17	1:16.291	3	1:14.966	1	1:15.092	1	1:15.019	1
5.	David Coulthard	McLaren MP4-17D 08 - Mercedes			1:28.718	7	1:28.937	13	1:16.840	6	1:15.600	3	1:15.823	4	1:15.628	5
6.	Kimi Räikkönen	McLaren MP4-17D 09 - Mercedes			1:28.846	11	1:29.120	16	1:17.050	7	1:16.012	5	1:15.822	3	1:15.533	4
7.	Jarno Trulli	Renault R23-05	1:17.323	3	1:28.296	4	1:29.024	15	1:17.123	9	1:16.376	10	1:19.454	20	1:15.967	6
8.	Fernando Alonso	Renault R23-04	1:16.709	1	1:28.260	3	1:29.455	18	1:16.076	1	1:16.039	6	1:16.262	7	1:16.087	7
9.	Nick Heidfeld	Sauber C22-01 - Petronas			1:29.317	12	1:24.042	3	1:18.455	16	1:18.057	17	1:17.945	15	1:17.445	15
10.	Heinz-Harald Frentzen	Sauber C22-03 - Petronas			1:28.803	10	1:26.151	8	1:18.295	15	1:17.776	14	1:17.378	13	1:17.562	16
11.	Giancarlo Fisichella	Jordan EJ13-03 - Ford	1:18.771	5	1:28.782	9	1:28.502	12	1:18.749	17	1:17.908	16	1:18.427	17	1:18.431	17
12.	Ralph Firman	Jordan EJ13-04 - Ford	1:20.259	9	1:29.640	14	1:23.496	2	1:18.876	18	1:18.670	18	1:18.300	16	1:18.514	18
14.	Mark Webber	Jaguar R4-03	1:17.017	2	1:26.915	1	1:25.178	7	1:17.197	11	1:16.112	7	1:16.801	9	1:16.308	9
15.	Antonio Pizzonia	Jaguar R4-05	1:17.946	4	1:28.442	5	1:24.642	5	1:17.959	14	1:17.036	11	1:17.212	11	1:16.965	11
16.	Jacques Villeneuve	BAR 005-3 - Honda					1:24.651	6	1:17.452	13	1:17.101	12	1:17.304	12	1:16.990	12
17.	Jenson Button	BAR 005-4 - Honda					1:30.731	19	1:17.341	12	1:17.808	15	1:17.091	10	1:17.077	14
18.	Justin Wilson	Minardi PS03/04 - Cosworth	1:19.636	8	1:32.535	18		20	1:19.948	20	1:19.044	20	1:19.454	19	1:19.619	20
19.	Jos Verstappen	Minardi PS03/03 - Cosworth	1:19.289	7	1:32.091	17	1:20.817	1	1:19.089	19	1:18.696	19	1:18.899	18	1:18.709	19
20.	Olivier Panis	Toyota TF103/05			1:28.773	8	1:24.175	4	1:17.186	10	1:16.133	8	1:16.238	6	1:16.345	10
21.	Cristiano da Matta	Toyota TF103/07			1:30.791	16	1:26.975	9	1:17.118	8	1:17.690	13	1:17.382	14	1:17.068	13
44.	Franck Montagny	Renault	1:18.823	6												

Maximum speed

N°	Driver	P1 Qualifs	Pos.	P1 Race	Pos.	P2 Qualifs	Pos.	P2 Race	Pos.	Finish Qualifs	Pos.	Finish Race	Pos.	Trap Qualifs	Pos.	Trap Race	Pos.
1.	M. Schumacher	175,5	2	176,2	10	283,6	4	289,5	2	153,9	17	158,7	5	313,1	1	322,4	2
2.	R. Barrichello	168,1	9	180,8	2	282,2	7	287,6	3	157,8	8	156,3	12	308,6	4	322,4	1
3.	J.P. Montoya	168,1	8	185,4	1	286,6	1	289,5	1	158,7	5	159,1	4	308,9	3	318,4	4
4.	R. Schumacher	170,0	6	178,8	7	286,3	2	287,2	4	157,1	10	158,1	6	310,7	2	319,6	3
5.	D. Coulthard	167,9	11	180,8	3	283,0	6	286,7	6	163,0	1	161,1	2	306,7	7	316,4	5
6.	K. Räikkönen	166,6	12	177,0	9	284,2	3	287,1	5	160,2	3	161,8	1	308,3	5	315,8	7
7.	J. Trulli	174,5	3	172,9	12	278,1	13	280,5	17	157,2	9	157,8	7	305,0	8	308,3	18
8.	F. Alonso	177,7	1	172,4	13	278,4	10	281,2	14	159,0	4	160,4	3	303,9	10	311,8	13
9.	N. Heidfeld	170,1	5	170,0	16	278,9	9	279,6	18	155,8	13	156,3	11	304,3	9	310,7	15
10.	H-H. Frentzen	166,2	13	171,8	14	277,4	16	283,9	9	154,2	16	153,0	17	302,0	13	313,3	10
11.	G. Fisichella	160,8	15	178,3	8	275,8	19	280,8	15	156,7	11	153,4	16	299,2	18	307,6	19
12.	R. Firman	168,3	7	175,2	11	277,1	17	279,5	19	154,9	15	154,0	13	302,0	14	308,5	17
14.	M. Webber	168,0	10	179,1	6	278,2	12	283,4	10	152,1	19	157,3	8	298,6	19	313,2	11
15.	A. Pizzonia	171,9	4	171,2	15	277,9	15	281,9	13	158,1	7	157,0	9	300,3	16	311,0	14
16.	J. Villeneuve	162,3	14	180,5	4	279,1	8	283,0	12	155,7	14	153,6	14	302,3	12	314,1	9
17.	J. Button	160,5	16	180,1	5	278,3	11	284,3	8	161,2	2	156,6	10	302,6	11	315,8	6
18.	J. Wilson	158,6	18	167,6	17	271,5	20	276,8	20	156,0	12	151,3	20	291,5	20	306,5	20
19.	J. Verstappen	154,1	20	166,8	18	278,1	14	280,7	16	153,1	18	152,2	19	302,0	15	309,4	16
20.	O. Panis	157,4	19	165,7	20	283,3	5	285,4	7	158,5	6	153,5	15	307,0	6	314,5	8
21.	C. Da Matta	160,3	17	166,1	19	276,7	18	283,0	11	151,8	20	152,6	18	299,4	17	312,3	12

Race

Classification & Retirements

Pos.	Driver	Team	Lap	Time	Average
1.	R. Schumacher	Williams BMW	70	1:30:49.213	203,866 km/h
2.	J.P. Montoya	Williams BMW	70	+ 13.813	203,350 km/h
3.	M. Schumacher	Ferrari	70	+ 19.568	203,136 km/h
4.	K. Räikkönen	McLaren Mercedes	70	+ 38.047	202,452 km/h
5.	D. Coulthard	McLaren Mercedes	70	+ 40.289	202,369 km/h
6.	M. Webber	Jaguar	70	+ 1:06.380	201,412 km/h
7.	R. Barrichello	Ferrari	69	1 lap	200,917 km/h
8.	O. Panis	Toyota	69	1 lap	200,292 km/h
9.	J. Villeneuve	BAR Honda	69	1 lap	199,367 km/h
10.	A. Pizzonia	Jaguar	69	1 lap	199,335 km/h
11.	C. Da Matta	Toyota	69	1 lap	199,051 km/h
12.	H-H. Frentzen	Sauber Petronas	68	2 laps	197,640 km/h
13.	N. Heidfeld	Sauber Petronas	68	2 laps	196,790 km/h
14.	J. Wilson	Minardi Cosworth	67	3 laps	194,763 km/h
15.	R. Firman	Jordan Ford	67	3 laps	193,628 km/h
16.	J. Verstappen	Minardi Cosworth	66	4 laps	190,566 km/h

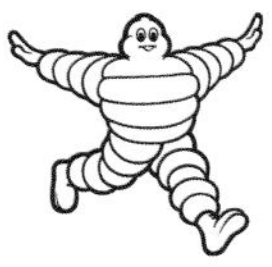

Driver	Team		Reason
J. Trulli	Renault	46	Prob with engine control unit leading to loss of power
F. Alonso	Renault	44	Engine failure
G. Fisichella	Jordan Ford	43	Engine failure
J. Button	BAR Honda	22	Ran out of fuel (prob. with refuelling rig)

Fastest laps

	Driver	Time	Lap	Average
1.	J.P. Montoya	1:15.512	36	210,292 km/h
2.	R. Schumacher	1:15.698	37	209,775 km/h
3.	D. Coulthard	1:15.981	17	208,994 km/h
4.	M. Schumacher	1:16.303	19	208,112 km/h
5.	K. Räikkönen	1:16.609	19	207,281 km/h
6.	J. Trulli	1:17.025	33	206,161 km/h
7.	F. Alonso	1:17.029	11	206,150 km/h
8.	M. Webber	1:17.068	47	206,046 km/h
9.	R. Barrichello	1:17.104	47	205,950 km/h
10.	J. Button	1:17.149	19	205,830 km/h
11.	O. Panis	1:17.398	36	205,168 km/h
12.	A. Pizzonia	1:17.416	67	205,120 km/h
13.	J. Villeneuve	1:17.786	49	204,144 km/h
14.	C. Da Matta	1:17.870	63	203,924 km/h
15.	H-H. Frentzen	1:18.099	18	203,326 km/h
16.	J. Verstappen	1:18.754	66	201,635 km/h
17.	N. Heidfeld	1:18.994	21	201,022 km/h
18.	G. Fisichella	1:19.093	23	200,771 km/h
19.	R. Firman	1:19.345	13	200,133 km/h
20.	J. Wilson	1:19.588	25	199,522 km/h

Pit stops

	Driver	Time	Lap	Stop n°
1.	J. Verstappen	21.735	11	1
2.	A.Pizzonia	22.185	14	1
3.	D. Coulthard	19.953	15	1
4.	R. Firman	23.460	15	1
5.	K. Räikkönen	20.173	16	1
6.	J. Trulli	20.633	16	1
7.	M. Webber	21.470	16	1
8.	O. Panis	21.471	16	1
9.	H-H. Frentzen	21.601	16	1
10.	J.P. Montoya	23.606	17	1
11.	M. Schumacher	20.532	17	1
12.	F. Alonso	21.308	17	1
13.	J. Button	25.710	17	1
14.	R. Schumacher	19.642	18	1
15.	J. Villeneuve	22.313	18	1
16.	C. Da Matta	22.462	19	1
17.	N. Heidfeld	21.930	19	1
18.	R. Barrichello	22.406	20	1
19.	G. Fisichella	22.757	21	1
20.	J. Wilson	25.180	22	1
21.	J. Verstappen	22.251	29	2
22.	A. Pizzonia	23.965	30	2
23.	K. Räikkönen	20.835	31	2
24.	M. Webber	20.855	31	2
25.	D. Coulthard	19.407	32	2
26.	H-H. Frentzen	22.174	32	2
27.	J.P. Montoya	20.968	34	2
28.	J. Trulli	19.539	34	2
29.	O. Panis	20.571	34	2
30.	R. Schumacher	20.536	35	2
31.	M. Schumacher	20.325	35	2
32.	F. Alonso	20.101	36	2
33.	J. Villeneuve	20.961	37	2
34.	R. Firman	24.456	40	2
35.	N. Heidfeld	23.283	42	2
36.	J. Wilson	23.693	42	2
37.	A. Pizzonia	22.809	43	3
38.	R. Barrichello	22.329	45	2
39.	C. Da Matta	21.999	45	2
40.	K. Räikkönen	21.065	47	3
41.	D. Coulthard	33.963	48	3
42.	R. firman	27.579	46	3
43.	M. Webber	23.528	48	3
44.	H-H. Frentzen	25.605	48	3
45.	J.P. Montoya	21.336	50	3
46.	J. Verstappen	22.246	48	3
47.	R. Schumacher	20.878	51	3
48.	M. Schumacher	20.712	52	3
49.	O. Panis	20.151	52	3
50.	J. Villeneuve	21.810	53	3
51.	J. Verstappen	36.302	61	4
52.	J. Verstappen	37.638	64	5

Race leaders

Driver	Laps in the lead	Nber of Laps
R. Schumacher	1 > 70	70

Driver	Nber of Laps	Kilometers
R. Schumacher	70	308,586 km

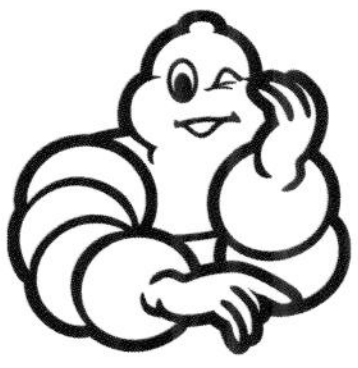

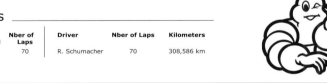

Lap chart

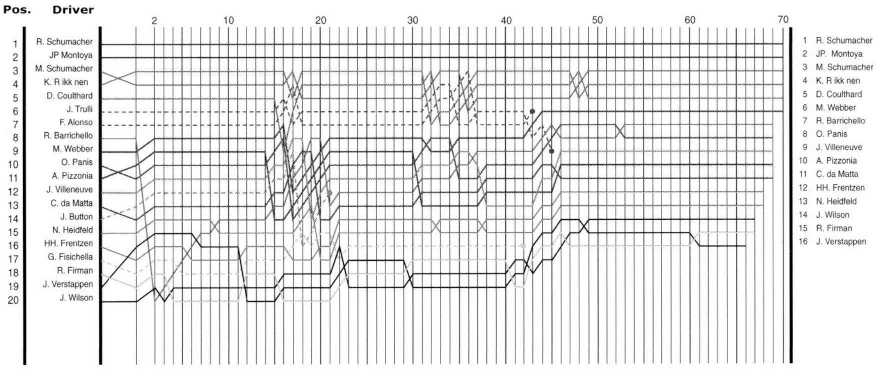

Gaps on the leader board

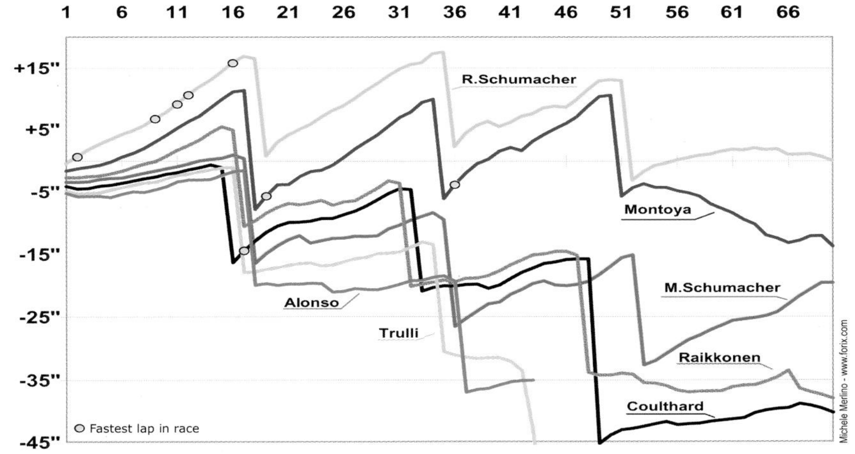

Championship after ten rounds

Drivers

1. M. Schumacher ....(4 wins)................64
2. K. Räikkönen ....(1 win) 56
3. R. Schumacher..........(2 wins)................53
4. J.P. Montoya..............(1 win) 47
5. R. Barrichello...39
6. F. Alonso 39
7. D. Coulthard ....(1 win) 29
8. J. Trulli 13
9. M. Webber..12
10. G. Fisichella ....(1 win) 10
11. J. Button 10
12. H-H. Frentzen...7
13. J. Villeneuve..3
14. C. Da Matta..3
15. O. Panis..2
16. N. Heidfeld...2
17. R. Firman...1
18. A. Pizzonia 0
19. J. Verstappen 0
20. J. Wilson...0

Constructors

1. Scuderia Ferrari Marlboro ......(4 wins) 103
2. BMW Williams F1 Team ....(3 wins) 100
3. West McLaren Mercedes ....(2 wins).........85
4. Mild Seven Renault F1 Team........................52
5. Lucky Strike BAR Honda 13
6. Jaguar Racing...12
7. Jordan Ford.........................(1 win) 11
8. Sauber Petronas..9
9. Panasonic Toyota Racing..............................5
10. European Minardi Cosworth..........................0

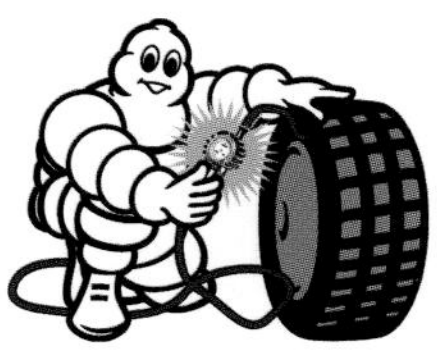

The circuit

Name	Magny-Cours, Nevers
Date	July 6,2003
Length	4411 meters
Distance	70 laps, 308,586 km
Weather	Sunny, 24-25°c
Track temperature	28-31°c

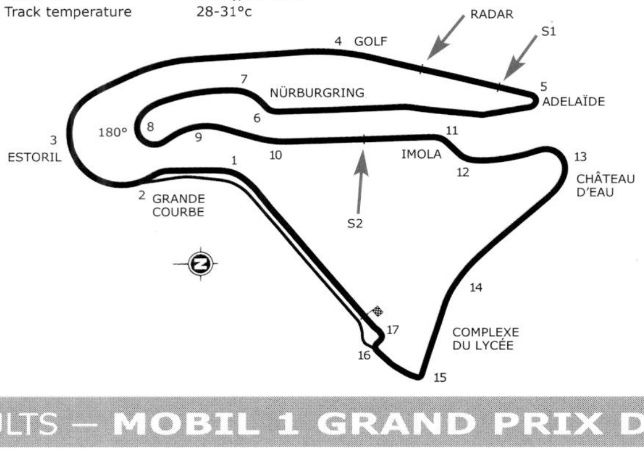

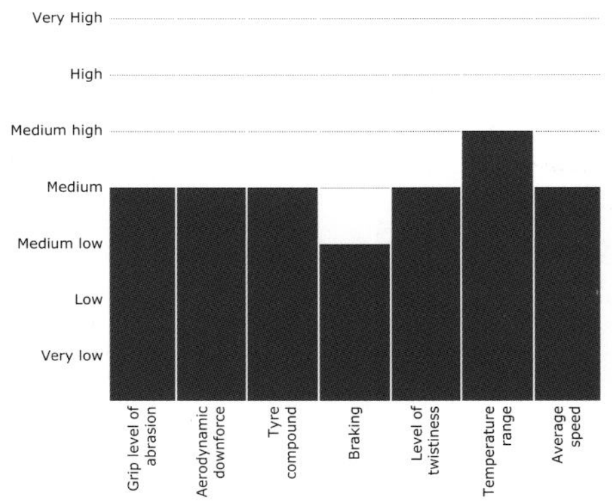

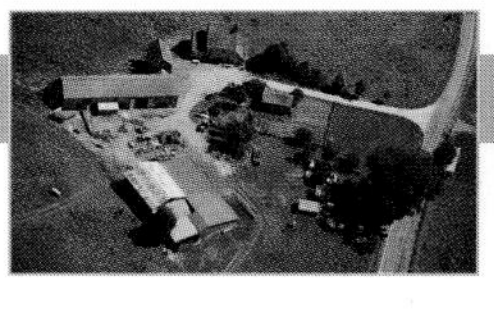

RUBENS AT LAST!

Two appearances for the Safety Car, lots of overtaking and five changes of lead: the British Grand Prix was without a doubt the most exciting race of the season and even featured a lunatic track invasion! In the end, victory went to Brazil's Rubens Barrichello. Michael Schumacher finished fourth at the end of a race which saw him spend most of his time trying to pass the Renaults. The German lost a lot of time during a pit-stop, when he had to wait for the mechanics to finish dealing with Rubens Barrichello. Once refuelled, he rejoined down in 15th place.

Kimi Raikkonen locks a wheel. The Finn qualified third. *"I really did not expect to be in the top three. But I am very happy with my lap. Yesterday, we were really struggling with the balance of the car, but now it is going very well."*

In brief

> The Silverstone circuit had been the target of terrorist threats and apart from the usual security, sniffer dogs were brought in to check the paddock for bombs!

> Budweiser announced a five year sponsorship deal with the Williams team, reckoned to be worth 70 million Euros.

> FIA and some of the teams had been working with the British military to improve the efficiency of refuelling their huge Apache attack helicopters. By borrowing from F1 pit-stop practice, they had managed to reduce fill up time by 50%. A demonstration was staged on Thursday in the presence of Max Mosley and Defence Minister Geoff Hoon. So F1 can have its uses....

> Jenson Button was not to be a prophet in his own land. At Silverstone, the young Englishman went off the track and was last on the grid.

> It was not very hot in England. However, some girls were still dressed for summer...

> Juan Pablo Montoya was only seventh on the British Grand Prix grid. *"I had too much oversteer and poor traction so the car was difficult to drive and very nervous."*

Rubinho takes his second pole

Second out of the pits, having failed to record a time the previous day, Rubens Barrichello set a time which was never beaten during Saturday's qualifying session. The weather at Silverstone was very changeable and the temperature gradually increased throughout the day and the wind was constantly switching direction.

These conditions seemed to favour those running earlier in the session, including Barrichello. *"That's true,"* confirmed the Brazilian. *"Usually the early runners are at a disadvantage because of the track conditions, but today, my only disadvantage was the pressure on my shoulders. Running early, you have to stay calm and do your best. Especially after the problems I had the day before."*

On Friday, Rubinho had tried different settings which had not worked out and had led to him falling off the track.

For his part, Michael Schumacher looked like beating his team-mate's time, until he had a slight off at Abbey corner. *"It was my fault,"* admitted the world champion. *"But at least I am on the grid near Kimi*

(Raikkonen) and Ralf (Schumacher,) my two championship rivals."

Alongside Barrichello on the front row was Jarno Trulli, who had not done that well since the Malaysian Grand Prix in the early part of the season. *"I am really happy,"* rejoiced the Italian. *"But I am also surprised to have done this well. All weekend, I have been struggling with my settings and we only solved the problems just in time for qualifying. I am very confident for the race."*

Starting grid

J. VERSTAPPEN 19 1:25.759	R. FIRMAN 17 1:24.385	G. FISICHELLA 15 1:23.574	O. PANIS 13 1:23.042	M. WEBBER 11 1:22.647	J. VILLENEUVE 9 1:22.591	J.P. MONTOYA 7 1:22.214	M. SCHUMACHER 5 1:21.867	K. RÄIKKÖNEN 3 1:21.695	R. BARRICHELLO 1 1:21.209 (227,900 km/h)
J. BUTTON 20 1:24.468	J. WILSON 18 1:23.844	N. HEIDFELD 16 1:23.187	H-H. FRENTZEN 14 1:22.811	D. COULTHARD 12 1:22.634	A. PIZZONIA 10 1:22.404	F. ALONSO 8 1:22.081	C. DA MATTA 6 1:21.727	R. SCHUMACHER 4 1:21.381	J. TRULLI 2

< Victory for Rubens Barrichello. *"I really had to fight,"* confirmed the Brazilian. *"My car had very good straight line speed, so it was a case of make or break as I had nothing to lose today."* He pulled off no less than six passing moves in the course of the grand prix: two on Kimi Raikkonen, one each on Ralf Schumacher, Ralph Firman, Jarno Trulli and Olivier Panis. Who says you cannot overtake in F1?

A madman runs onto the track and causes chaos

Lap 12 of the race: a madman climbs over the fencing and starts to run along the track, wearing a kilt. After a few moments, he was manhandled to the ground, but it had been a very close call. The lunatic had certainly chosen a good spot, as the Hangar Straight is the quickest section of the Silverstone track. On Sunday, Juan Pablo Montoya was clocked there doing 320.3 km/h!

It was at this point that Neil Horam, a former Irish priest, living in London, decided to spread the word. He got over the spectator fencing and started to run down the middle of the track, towards the oncoming cars. 56 years old, wearing a green kilt, the priest was holding a panel up for the drivers to see, bearing the message: *"Read the Bible, the Bible is always right."*

As it is not that easy to read messages while driving a car, this advice was ignored while the race continued. The man was wrestled to the ground and marched off to a Northampton police station. *"He has been arrested for aggravated trespass, which means he could be given a maximum sentence of 3 months imprisonment and a thousand pound fine,"* explained police spokesman, Andy Roberts.

It could have been much more serious. Olivier Panis was trying to overtake his Toyota team-mate and missed Horam by a mere two metres. In the Jaguar, Mark Webber hesitated a moment before going down his left hand side. *"I was really frightened,"* admitted the Australian. *"To be honest, I was lucky not to kill him!"* Neil Horam's little moment of fame turned the race on its head. Race Control ordered the Safety Car to come out and all the drivers took the opportunity to refuel, creating a dreadful traffic jam in the pit lane. This resulted in Juan Pablo Montoya and Michael Schumacher dropping to 13th and 15th places respectively.

< Jacques Villeneuve goes off the track. He got back on to finish tenth..

Toyota's day

It was almost Toyota's day. For the space of four laps, the two red and white cars were first and second! In fact, Cristiano da Matta led for a total of 17 laps. *"I liked this race a lot. We had a good strategy, the pit-stops worked well and everything went well,"* affirmed the Brazilian. *"I am used to leading races, but this is the first time I have done it in F1 and it was a bit of a special feeling. I knew it would not last, so I made the most of it."* Olivier Panis finished eleventh, having adopted a three stop strategy.

Traffic jam in the pits. As the race was interrupted by a priest, all the drivers headed down pit lane. Several, including Juan Pablo Montoya and Michael Schumacher were forced to wait in line for the fuel pumps.

V<

Finishing third, Kimi Raikkonen closed the gap to Michael Schumacher in the championship by one little point. The Finn lost the lead to Rubens Barrichello on lap 42, before taking a trip across the grass on lap 48, which let Juan Pablo Montoya slip by. *"I don't know what happened,"* he recounted. *"I came into the corner in the normal way and suddenly I lost the back end of the car. I was very lucky to get back on the track."*

Race summary

> Barrichello on pole is caught napping by Trulli and Räikkönen. The Brazilian is about to go on the attack **(1)**.

> Barrichello tackles the leaders. Trulli loses his advantage when the Safety Car appears **(2)**.

> A madman on the track. The Safety Car is called out for a 2nd time **(3)**.

> On lap 12, there's pandemonium in the pits. It would continue for 16 laps. M. Schumacher loses several places and is effectively out of the running **(4)**.

> Da Matta finds himself in the lead. He stays there for 16 laps. Further back, Barrichello is staging an historic comeback **(5)**.

> Villeneuve goes off with 2 laps remaining **(6)**.

> Räikkönen is unable to hold off Barrichello, who is unbeatable today. Montoya takes 2nd place at the end of a thrilling race **(7)**.

As the crow flies

During the last war, Silverstone was a military airfield. Over the years, its runways were transformed into a race track. Today, it is almost impossible to spot which bits of tarmac were used to send the bombers flying off to Germany...

British Grand Prix under threat

Motor sport was practically invented in England. After the last world war, circuits sprang up all over the country, most of them making use of former military airfields.

Silverstone was a notable case in point. Since those far off days, its layout and infrastructure were modified several times. But Bernie Ecclestone and Max Mosley continued to maintain that the circuit did not meet the demands of modern F1, despite the fact that Silverstone had put a lot of effort into modernising its facilities. Since 2002, a four lane road had been built to link it to the M1 motorway coming up from London. The organisers had also limited ticket sales to 90,000 on race day, to avoid the traffic disasters of old. In 2000, the race was held in April and thousands of spectators ended up with their cars bogged down in the grass car parks. 2001 was little better, with huge traffic jams

preventing people getting to the circuit in time to see the race.

The week before this year's race, the British government had agreed an investment of 15 million pounds to help Silverstone revamp the circuit. It might have been too little too late. Max Mosley warned circuit owners the BRDC, (British Racing Drivers Club) that there were no guarantees they would stage the race in 2004. It caused an uproar in England. *"It's a vicious move to destabilise us,"* said triple world champion and BRDC president, Jackie Stewart. *"Bernie (Ecclestone) and Max (Mosley) reckon we should borrow 50 million pounds to improve the infrastructure. It's unrealistic, it is not honest and their criticisms are over the top. Silverstone is definitely better than some venues like Sao Paulo, Budapest or Imola."*

Bernie Ecclestone dismissed this counter-attack. His desk was covered with offers to stage grands prix from China, Bahrain and others, who were prepared to invest hundreds of millions to build new circuits. The old country did not have these means. To make way for these new venues, Ecclestone would have to clear the dead wood and Silverstone looked like a tree about to fall.

Practice

All the time trials

N°	Driver	N° Chassis - Engine	Private testing	Pos.	Practice friday	Pos.	Qualifying friday	Pos.	Practice 1 saturday	Pos.	Practice 2 saturday	Pos.	Warm-up	Pos.	Qualifying saturday	Pos.
1.	Michael Schumacher	Ferrari F2003-GA 231			1:20.992	9	1:19.474	1	1:22:659	3	1:21.608	3	1:22.074	3	1:21.867	5
2.	Rubens Barrichello	Ferrari F2003-GA 230			1:20.604	4		19	1:22.397	2	1:21.587	2	1:21.094	1	1:21.209	1
3.	Juan Pablo Montoya	Williams FW25 06 - BMW			1:21.182	12	1:19.749	2	1:23.141	4	1:21.415	1	1:34.936	18	1:22.214	7
4.	Ralf Schumacher	Williams FW25 07 - BMW			1:21.029	11	1:19.788	3	1:23.596	7	1:21.711	4	1:22.457	5	1:21.727	4
5.	David Coulthard	McLaren MP4-17D 08 - Mercedes			1:20.039	1	1:19.968	7	1:23.888	9	1:22.317	6	1:22.722	8	1:22.811	12
6.	Kimi Räikkönen	McLaren MP4-17D 09 - Mercedes			1:21.407	14	1:21.065	12	1:22.263	1	1:22.400	8	1:21.871	2	1:21.695	3
7.	Jarno Trulli	Renault R23B-05	1:21.721	2	1:20.858	6	1:19.963	6	1:23.609	8	1:22.332	7		20	1:21.381	2
8.	Fernando Alonso	Renault R23B-04	1:21.547	1	1:20.485	3	1:19.907	4	1:23.316	5	1:22.462	9	1:22.498	6	1:22.404	8
9.	Nick Heidfeld	Sauber C22-01 - Petronas			1:23.290	19	1:21.211	14	1:23.939	12	1:23.945	17	1:24.295	14	1:23.844	16
10.	Heinz-Harald Frentzen	Sauber C22-03 - Petronas			1:21.969	15	1:21.363	15	1:24.573	15	1:23.620	14	1:23.376	11	1:23.187	14
11.	Giancarlo Fisichella	Jordan EJ13-04 - Ford	1:22.864	6	1:22.028	16	1:21.500	16	1:25.114	18	1:23.944	16	1:23.792	13	1:23.574	15
12.	Ralph Firman	Jordan EJ13-03 - Ford	1:24.006	7	1:22.135	17	1:22.335	17	1:25.044	17	1:23.981	18	1:24.692	15	1:24.385	17
14.	Mark Webber	Jaguar R4-04	1:22.060	3	1:20.346	2	1:20.171	8	1:23.902	10	1:22.910	11	1:22.429	4	1:22.647	11
15.	Antonio Pizzonia	Jaguar R4-05 & 03	1:22.834	5	1:20.966	8	1:20.877	11	1:24.942	16	1:23.703	15	1:22.630	7	1:22.634	10
16.	Jacques Villeneuve	BAR 005-3 - Honda			1:21.246	13	1:21.084	13	1:23.591	6	1:23.326	12	1:23.073	9	1:22.591	9
17.	Jenson Button	BAR 005-4 - Honda			1:20.933	7	1:20.569	9	1:23.925	11	1:23.455	13	1:23.235	10		20
18.	Justin Wilson	Minardi PS03/04 - Cosworth	1:24.605	9	1:24.086	20		20	1:25.808	19	1:25.906	20	1:25.938	17	1:25.468	18
19.	Jos Verstappen	Minardi PS03/03 - Cosworth	1:24.013	8	1:23.176	18	1:23.418	18	1:26.262	20	1:25.684	19	1:25.731	16	1:25.759	19
20.	Olivier Panis	Toyota TF103/08			1:20.693	5	1:19.959	5	1:24.484	13	1:22.257	5	1:23.462	12	1:23.042	13
21.	Cristiano da Matta	Toyota TF103/07 & 04			1:21.027	10	1:20.765	10	1:24.532	14	1:22.614	10		19	1:22.081	6
34.	Allan McNish	Renault R23B-03	1:22.141	4												

Maximum speed

N°	Driver	P1 Qualifs	Pos.	P1 Race	Pos.	P2 Qualifs	Pos.	P2 Race	Pos.	Finish Qualifs	Pos.	Finish Race	Pos.	Trap Qualifs	Pos.	Trap Race	Pos.
1.	M. Schumacher	307,2	2	318,9	3	257,8	11	256,8	13	298,0	5	303,3	3	254,4	12	260,5	7
2.	R. Barrichello	306,0	4	319,0	2	256,7	13	254,8	15	297,7	6	305,2	2	258,6	8	259,6	9
3.	J.P. Montoya	304,3	6	320,3	1	263,9	3	267,1	2	298,5	3	305,3	1	257,9	9	262,8	3
4.	R. Schumacher	310,6	1	317,3	4	263,6	5	261,1	8	299,8	1	302,6	4	268,9	1	266,4	1
5.	D. Coulthard	305,8	5	317,1	5	257,3	12	261,8	7	298,6	2	301,9	9	253,6	13	262,1	5
6.	K. Räikkönen	307,0	3	316,7	6	259,1	10	258,7	10	298,4	4	302,2	5	267,5	3	263,3	2
7.	J. Trulli	301,4	8	306,3	19	271,2	2	264,5	4	292,3	16	292,8	18	267,8	2	256,5	10
8.	F. Alonso	300,3	11	316,2	8	269,7	3	266,9	3	293,1	14	296,9	11	260,6	7	262,2	4
9.	N. Heidfeld	298,9	13	306,9	18	259,4	9	250,5	19	293,8	9	294,7	15	252,9	15	248,9	15
10.	H-H. Frentzen	300,6	10	316,6	7	250,1	17	255,5	14	293,7	10	301,0	7	263,0	5	245,6	17
11.	G. Fisichella	298,9	12	309,4	16	256,2	14	257,6	12	291,0	17	294,4	17	252,2	16	249,4	14
12.	R. Firman	293,0	19	308,0	17	259,9	8	259,9	9	287,1	19	291,1	20	255,4	10	259,8	8
14.	M. Webber	301,2	9	315,5	9	260,4	7	261,8	6	293,9	8	298,2	8	262,8	6	261,6	6
15.	A. Pizzonia	298,6	15	309,7	15	271,2	1	270,0	1	293,7	11	294,7	16	255,1	11	254,5	12
16.	J. Villeneuve	298,6	14	313,4	11	255,7	15	253,8	16	292,5	15	295,6	13	253,2	14	254,0	13
17.	J. Button	261,4	20	312,2	12	213,9	20	252,3	18	293,5	12	297,5	9	205,9	20	245,4	18
18.	J. Wilson	295,1	18	309,9	14	241,2	19	249,5	20	287,2	18	297,1	10	240,7	19	246,1	16
19.	J. Verstappen	295,5	17	304,9	20	251,9	16	252,4	17	286,0	20	292,6	19	244,5	18	244,8	20
20.	O. Panis	298,2	16	315,1	10	249,1	18	258,4	11	296,0	7	296,7	12	247,1	17	245,0	19
21.	C. Da Matta	302,6	7	310,4	13	262,1	6	264,4	5	293,3	13	295,1	14	263,7	4	254,8	11

Race

Classification & Retirements

Pos.	Driver	Team	Lap	Time	Average
1.	R. Barrichello	Ferrari	60	1:28:37.554	208,757 km/h
2.	J.P. Montoya	Williams BMW	60	+ 5.462	208,543 km/h
3.	K. Räikkönen	McLaren Mercedes	60	+ 10.656	208,339 km/h
4.	M. Schumacher	Ferrari	60	+ 25.648	207,755 km/h
5.	D. Coulthard	McLaren Mercedes	60	+ 36.827	207,321 km/h
6.	J. Trulli	Renault	60	+ 43.067	207,080 km/h
7.	C. Da Matta	Toyota	60	+ 45.085	207,002 km/h
8.	J. Button	BAR Honda	60	+ 45.478	206,986 km/h
9.	R. Schumacher	Williams BMW	60	+ 58.032	206,503 km/h
10.	J. Villeneuve	BAR Honda	60	+ 1:03.569	206,291 km/h
11.	O. Panis	Toyota	60	+ 1:05.207	206,228 km/h
12.	H-H. Frentzen	Sauber Petronas	60	+ 1:05.564	206,214 km/h
13.	R. Firman	Jordan Ford	59	1 lap	205,248 km/h
14.	M. Webber	Jaguar	59	1 lap	205,212 km/h
15.	J. Verstappen	Minardi Cosworth	58	2 laps	201,688 km/h
16.	J. Wilson	Minardi Cosworth	58	2 laps	201,545 km/h
17.	N. Heidfeld	Sauber Petronas	58	2 laps	201,414 km/h

Driver	Team		Reason
F. Alonso	Renault	53	Electrical problem; seized gearbox
G. Fisichella	Jordan Ford	45	Broken right rear suspension, spins
A. Pizzonia	Jaguar	33	Engine

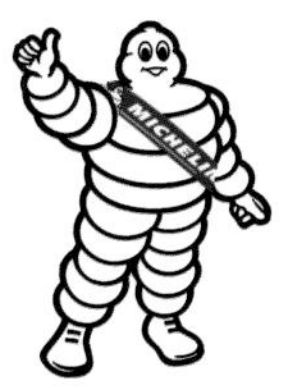

Fastest laps

	Driver	Time	Lap	Average
1.	R. Barrichello	1:22.236	38	225.054 km/h
2.	D. Coulthard	1:22.692	60	223,813 km/h
3.	J. Trulli	1:22.797	9	223,529 km/h
4.	F. Alonso	1:22.819	37	223,470 km/h
5.	K. Räikkönen	1:22.911	9	223,222 km/h
6.	J.P. Montoya	1:22.938	33	223,149 km/h
7.	R. Schumacher	1:22.943	10	223,136 km/h
8.	M. Schumacher	1:23.024	10	222,918 km/h
9.	A. Pizzonia	1:23.158	9	222,559 km/h
10.	O. Panis	1:23.463	47	221,746 km/h
11.	C. Da Matta	1:23.528	32	221,573 km/h
12.	J. Villeneuve	1:23.705	57	221,105 km/h
13.	M. Webber	1:23.833	28	220,767 km/h
14.	J. Button	1:23.912	53	220,559 km/h
15.	H-H. Frentzen	1:23.933	58	220,504 km/h
16.	N. Heidfeld	1:24.537	9	218,928 km/h
17.	G. Fisichella	1:24.823	40	218,190 km/h
18.	R. Firman	1:25.087	33	217,513 km/h
19.	J. Wilson	1:25.859	9	215,558 km/h
20.	J. Verstappen	1:27.021	2	212,679 km/h

Pit stops

	Driver	Time	Lap	Stop n°
1.	C. Da Matta	31.379	6	1
2.	D. Coulthard	52.877	6	1
3.	O. Panis	42.805	6	1
4.	R. Firman	33.784	6	1
5.	A.Pizzonia	36.659	7	1
6.	J. Trulli	32.928	12	1
7.	R. Barrichello	36.529	12	1
8.	K. Räikkönen	33.478	12	1
9.	R. Schumacher	33.110	12	1
10.	M. Schumacher	45.733	12	1
11.	J.P. Montoya	41.882	12	1
12.	F. Alonso	40.626	12	1
13.	J. Villeneuve	35.743	12	1
14.	M. Webber	34.142	12	1
15.	N. Heidfeld	35.371	12	1
16.	J. Button	43.390	12	1
17.	G. Fisichella	34.164	12	1
18.	H-H. Frentzen	46.859	12	1
19.	J. Wilson	35.064	12	1
20.	J. Verstappen	33.453	13	1
21.	R. Schumacher	31.897	19	2
22.	N. Heidfeld	33.623	21	2
23.	A. Pizzonia	33.627	25	2
24.	D. Coulthard	32.725	28	2
25.	J. Wilson	48.197	29	2
26.	C. Da Matta	31.093	30	2
27.	M. Webber	32.571	30	2
28.	O. Panis	31.187	31	2
29.	K. Räikkönen	34.107	35	2
30.	R. Firman	35.424	35	2
31.	N. Heidfeld	31.322	35	2
32.	J. Trulli	33.104	35	2
33.	J. Verstappen	25.265	36	2
34.	J.P. Montoya	33.272	38	2
35.	F. Alonso	49.774	38	2
36.	G. Fisichella	34.276	38	2
37.	R. Barrichello	32.401	39	3
38.	R. Schumacher	33.112	39	2
39.	H-H. Frentzen	32.730	39	2
40.	M. Schumacher	32.689	40	2
41.	J. Villeneuve	32.827	41	2
42.	J. Button	32.099	42	2
43.	C. Da Matta	31.298	44	3
44.	O. Panis	31.212	45	3
45.	D. Coulthard	30.953	47	3
46.	M. Webber	31.540	47	3

Race leaders

Driver	Laps in the lead	Nber of Laps
J. Trulli	1 > 12	12
C. Da Matta	13 > 29	17
K. Räikkönen	30 > 35	6
R. Barrichello	36 > 39	4
K. Räikkönen	40 > 41	2
R. Barrichello	42 > 60	19

Driver	Nber of Laps	Kilometers
R. Barrichello	23	118,243 km
C. Da Matta	17	87,397 km
J. Trulli	12	61,587 km
K. Räikkönen	8	41,128 km

Gaps on the leader board

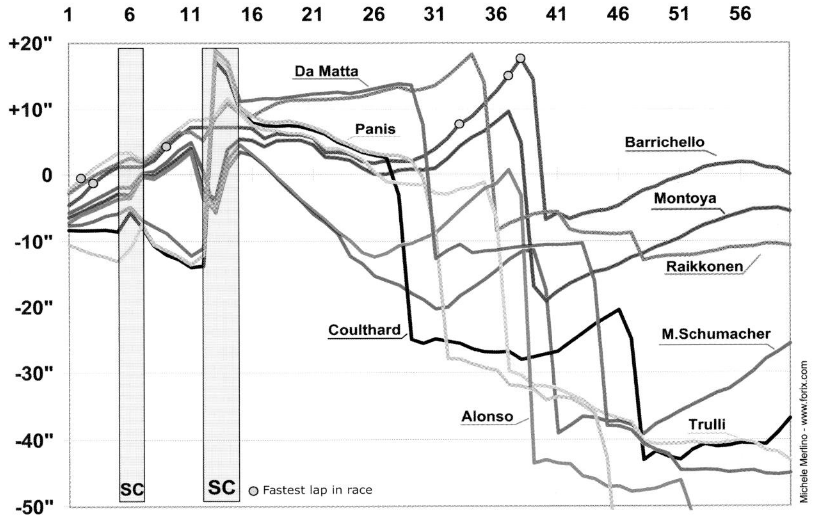
1 6 11 16 21 26 31 36 41 46 51 56
+20"
+10"
0
-10"
-20"
-30"
-40"
-50"
Da Matta
Panis
Barrichello
Montoya
Raikkonen
Coulthard
M.Schumacher
Alonso
Trulli
SC
SC
Fastest lap in race
Michele Merlino - www.forix.com

Lap chart

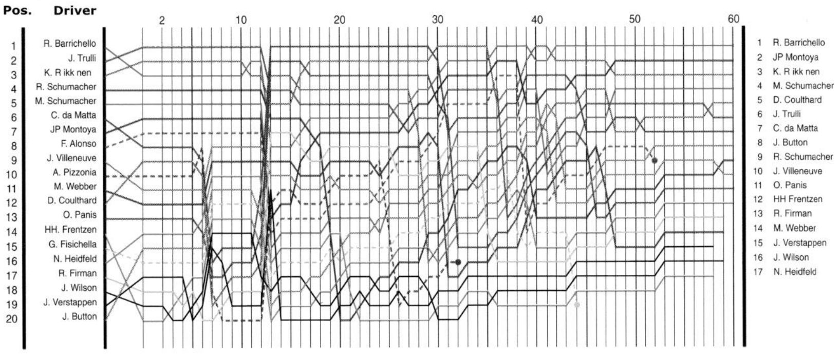
Pos. Driver
2 10 20 30 40 50 60
R. Barrichello
J. Trulli
K. R ikk nen
R. Schumacher
M. Schumacher
C. da Matta
JP Montoya
F. Alonso
J. Villeneuve
A. Pizzonia
M. Webber
D. Coulthard
O. Panis
HH. Frentzen
G. Fisichella
N. Heidfeld
R. Firman
J. Wilson
J. Verstappen
J. Button
1 R. Barrichello
2 JP Montoya
3 K. R ikk nen
4 M. Schumacher
5 D. Coulthard
6 J. Trulli
7 C. da Matta
8 J. Button
9 R. Schumacher
10 J. Villeneuve
11 O. Panis
12 HH Frentzen
13 R. Firman
14 M. Webber
15 J. Verstappen
16 J. Wilson
17 N. Heidfeld

Championship after eleven rounds

Drivers

1. M. Schumacher ....(4 wins)................69
2. K. Räikkönen ....(1 win) 62
3. J.P. Montoya.............(1 win) 55
4. R. Schumacher..........(2 wins)................53
5. R. Barrichello ....(1 win) 49
6. F. Alonso 39
7. D. Coulthard ....(1 win) 33
8. J. Trulli 16
9. M. Webber...12
10. J. Button 11
11. G. Fisichella ....(1 win) 10
12. H-H. Frentzen..7
13. C. Da Matta..5
14. J. Villeneuve..3
15. O. Panis...2
16. N. Heidfeld...2
17. R. Firman...1
18. A. Pizzonia 0
19. J. Verstappen 0
20. J. Wilson..0

Constructors

1. Scuderia Ferrari Marlboro ......(5 wins) 118
2. BMW Williams F1 Team ....(3 wins) 108
3. West McLaren Mercedes ....(2 wins).........95
4. Mild Seven Renault F1 Team.......................55
5. Lucky Strike BAR Honda 14
6. Jaguar Racing...12
7. Jordan Ford..........................(1 win) 11
8. Sauber Petronas..9
9. Panasonic Toyota Racing.............................7
10. European Minardi Cosworth.........................0

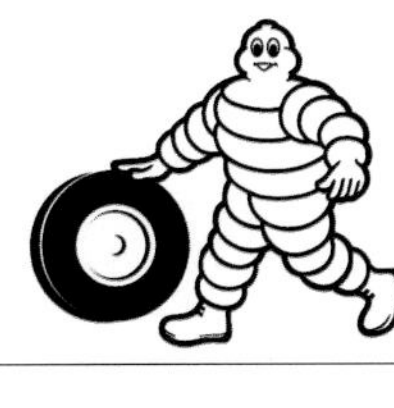

The circuit

Name	Silverstone
Date	July 20, 2003
Length	5141 meters
Distance	60 laps, 308,355 km
Weather	Hot, sunny with some clouds, 20-24°c
Track temperature	29-32°c

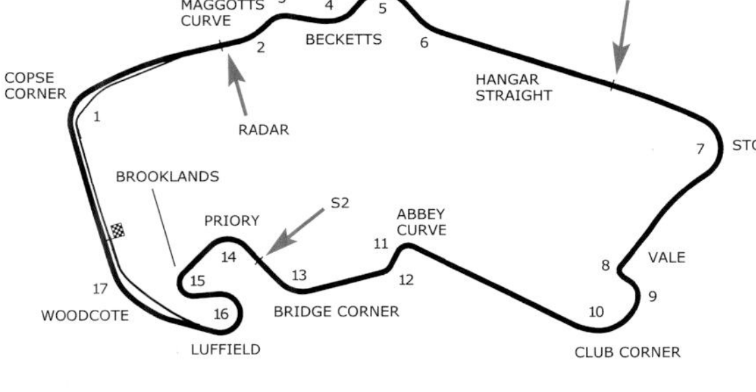
CHAPEL CURVE
MAGGOTTS CURVE
BECKETTS
S1
COPSE CORNER
HANGAR STRAIGHT
RADAR
STOWE
BROOKLANDS
PRIORY
S2
ABBEY CURVE
VALE
WOODCOTE
BRIDGE CORNER
LUFFIELD
CLUB CORNER
1 2 3 4 5 6 7 8 9 10 11 12 13 14 15 16 17

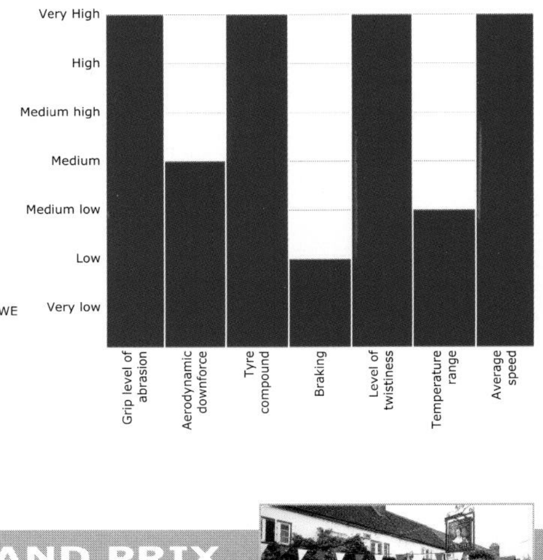
Very High
High
Medium high
Medium
Medium low
Low
Very low
Grip level of abrasion
Aerodynamic downforce
Tyre compound
Braking
Level of twistiness
Temperature range
Average speed

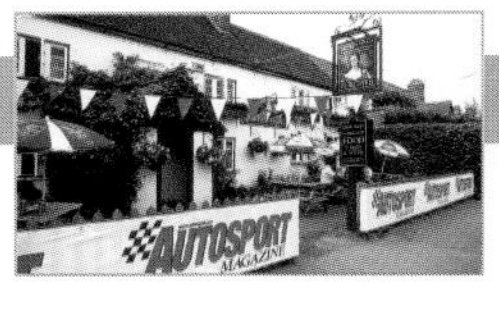
AUTOSPORT

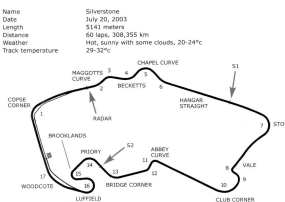

POLE AND VICTORY FOR JUAN PABLO

A spectacular accident eliminated Kimi Raikkonen, Rubens Barrichello, Ralf Schumacher, Heinz-Harald Frentzen, Ralph Firman and Justin Wilson at the start of the German Grand Prix. According to the stewards, it was all Ralf Schumacher's fault.

Way ahead of this drama, having started from pole position, Juan Pablo Montoya was leading the race with ease, never coming under pressure and disconcertingly in control.

The only pole position of the season for Juan Pablo Montoya.

^
Michael Schumacher was sixth on the grid and complaining about his car. *"The handling was not ideal today and things did not go the way I had hoped."*

Changes at Jaguar, who had taken on Justin Wilson to replace Antonio Pizzonia. On Friday, the former Minardi man qualified seventh ahead of Michael Schumacher. On Saturday, he was down to 16th, admitting to have pushed a bit too hard and paying for his lack of experience on Michelin tyres.
>

Bunting with flags from the various Swiss cantons and Alpine horn players could not turn the situation around: the Sauber team celebrated Switzerland's national day without making any progress on the track, with its drivers in 14th and 15th places.
v

The BMW-Williams team was taking no prisoners in Saturday's qualifying session at Hockenheim and the Anglo-German crew put both its cars on the front row. This time, Friday's positions were reversed with Juan Pablo Montoya outpacing Ralf Schumacher.

Just eighteen thousandths of a second separated the two team-mates, which equates to just under 1.1 metres over the 4.5 kilometre lap! *"It is always a bit disappointing to miss out on pole, especially when it's so close,"* admitted Schumacher. *"I had a bit of understeer in the last two corners and that was enough to make the difference. Having said that, second place, only two hundredths down means I*

can have a clear conscience!"

The author of seven pole positions last season, Juan Pablo Montoya was naturally delighted to have taken his first pole position of 2003, although as a result of changes to the regulations, it would also be his last. *"Finally! It took me quite a while to do it,"* sighed the Colombian. *"The car was really good today. We did a lot of work and it paid off."*

Some like it hot

35 degrees ambient and 49 degrees on the track: no way could you walk barefoot on the Hockenheim tarmac. On Saturday, a red hot sun which suffocated the circuit was the hot topic of conversation in the paddock. And with just cause: track temperature was playing a decisive role in terms of tyre performance and that in turn would be a key factor when fighting for the win. *"Such high temperatures are very rare,"* analysed Bridgestone technical director, Hisao Suganuma. *"We have seen temperatures as high as 56 degrees in Malaysia and we are not far off that here."* During qualifying, it seemed that the advantage lay with Michelin, as it often did in hot weather. On Saturday, Michelin therefore managed to get eight drivers into the top ten on the grid. The two Ferraris

In third place one found the Ferrari of Rubens Barrichello, while Michael Schumacher was further back in 6th spot. *"I don't think we could have beaten the Williams,"* lamented Ross Brawn. For his part, Michael Schumacher complained about his car. *"The handling was not ideal today,"* he suggested. *"Things did not go the way I had hoped they would."*

were the only Bridgestone interlopers. *"It is very encouraging to see our teams so well placed,"* rejoiced the French company's motor sport boss, Pierre Dupasquier. *"In this heat, it will be a tough race physically for the drivers, but they will last the distance, as will our tyres. I am not at all worried about them wearing out. Even if a team wanted to only make one pit-stop, our tyres would go the distance."* While the Clermont-Ferrand tyres proved to be the best solution in qualifying, the Bridgestone camp hoped that this would change come the race. *"As we have seen since Friday, our tyres are very consistent over a long run,"* suggested Ferrari technical director Ross Brawn. *"I hope the race will suit us."*

Starting grid

J. VERSTAPPEN 1:19.023 **19**	**J. BUTTON** 1:18.085 **17**	**N. HEIDFELD** 1:17.557 **15**	**J. VILLENEUVE** 1:17.090 **13**	**M. WEBBER** 1:16.775 **11**	**C. DA MATTA** 1:16.550 **9**	**O. PANIS** 1:16.034 **7**	**K. RÄIKKÖNEN** 1:15.874 **5**	**R. BARRICHELLO** 1:15.488 **3**	**J.P. MONTOYA** 1:15.167 (219,064 km/h) **1**
N. KIESA 1:19.174 **20**	**R. FIRMAN** 1:18.341 **18**	**J. WILSON** 1:18.021 **16**	**H-H. FRENTZEN** 1:17.169 **14**	**G. FISICHELLA** 1:16.831 **12**	**D. COULTHARD** 1:16.666 **10**	**F. ALONSO** 1:16.483 **8**	**M. SCHUMACHER** 1:15.898 **6**	**J. TRULLI** 1:15.679 **4**	**R. SCHUMACHER** 1:15.185 **2**

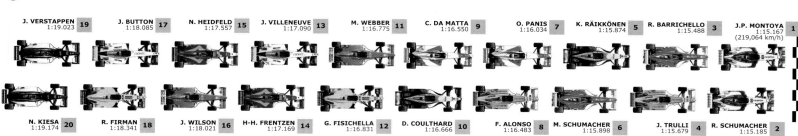

< The first corner accident seen from all angles. Kimi Raikkonen's McLaren came off worst in what would be the crash of the year. Luckily all the drivers involved escaped the spectacular carnage without injury.

Carnage at the first corner. Ralf found guilty.

The German Grand Prix promised to be a race full of surprises and it kept to that promise: at the first corner a major *"carambolage"* wiped out five competitors and important ones at that: Kimi Raikkonen, Ralf Schumacher and Rubens Barrichello all found themselves walking back to the pits after just a few moments of racing.

Ralf Schumacher made a good start from the front row and moved across to the left hand side of the track to get the best line for the first corner, while Kimi Raikkonen was trying to go round the outside of Rubens Barrichello before moving back. The result was that after three hundred metres of racing, the Brazilian found himself the meat in a Williams-McLaren sandwich, touching the former on the right and the latter on the left. The McLaren was immediately sent into a spin, crashing heavily into the left side of Ralf Schumacher's Williams, before making heavy contact with the tyre barrier at the first corner.

Schumacher managed to keep going and returned to his pit at the end of the first lap, but he went no further. *"All the left side, the radiator and the bottom of the chassis were destroyed. There was no way to continue,"* commented the German. He was very disappointed, adding that he had made no sudden movements and had just tried to defend his position. Rubens Barrichello could do nothing about it. *"I think*

that both Ralf and Kimi took big risks," he regretted. *"Especially Kimi who went very wide down the outside, where there is no room. I had made an average start and I braked when I realised there was a chance of a collision, but it was too late."*

A risky move? Naturally, Kimi Raikkonen did not share the Brazilian's views. *"I had made a good start and I had passed Rubens when he touched my rear wheel,"* reckoned the Finn. *"After that there was nothing I could do to control the car. I don't know whose fault it is, but it doesn't matter. What's done is done."*

It was also the end of the race for Ralf Firman and Heinz-Harald Frentzen, who also got tangled up in the accident, while Justin Wilson's Jaguar underwent lengthy repairs in the pits before retiring on lap seven. After the race, a statement from the Hockenheim stewards caught everyone by surprise: they had decided that Ralf Schumacher had caused the accident after the start, because he moved to the left without keeping an eye on the other cars. The German driver was given a penalty of having to start ten places lower on the grid than his qualifying position for the next grand prix in Hungary. The Williams team appealed the decision. The appeal was heard just before the Hungarian Grand Prix, which took place three weeks later. The penalty seemed very severe, especially

taking into account the tortuous and twisty nature of the Hungaroring, which makes overtaking almost impossible. The FIA Appeal Tribunal finally met on the Wednesday before the Hungarian Grand Prix and replaced the penalty with a fine. In Budapest on Thursday, *"new evidence"* but what was it, incited the German GP stewards to reconvene. Rubens Barrichello and Kimi Raikkonen were hauled up before the judges, but after lengthy study of the telemetry off the relevant cars, they decided these two drivers were blameless.

The Toyota team managed to get both its drivers into the points for the first time in its history. Olivier Panis finished 5th and Cristiano da Matta 6th at Hockenheim.
∨

Race summary

> Shortly after the start comes one of the most spectacular accidents of the season. Barrichello, Räikkönen and R. Schumacher all

retire at the first corner **(1)**.

> Räikkönen's McLaren is very badly damaged, illustrating

the force of the impact **(2)**.

> The Renaults make the most of the start accident to mount an

attack on the leaders **(3)**.

> Profiting from the retirement of his main rivals, M. Schumacher

battles with Trulli. A puncture will spoil his race **(4)**.

> Toyota demonstrates exemplary reliability,

with its cars finishing 5th and 6th **(5)**.

> Montoya triumphs and moves up to 2nd place in the Championship

(6).

> Trulli is unwell but is finally rewarded for his efforts **(7)**.

Ralf and Michael at home

The two Schumacher brothers were unable to please their many fans at Hockenheim. The former, having qualified on the front row was eliminated at the first corner. The latter could only qualify sixth and finished seventh. Neither was destined to shine at home.

Juan Pablo Montoya' Sunday stroll

An incredible race from Juan Pablo Montoya in Hockenheim. There were times when the Colombian managed to lap three seconds quicker than his pursuers.

"I don't know how it was possible," said the astonished winner. *"At the start of the race I was going as quickly as I could, but I could not pull out a gap. Then, I settled into a rhythm and the others seemed to go slower. From then on, the gap got bigger. I could not believe it. The team was telling me to take it easy, to slow down and I was still pulling away! I could have gone much quicker. Incredible!"*

The only problem for the Williams driver was the heat. *"It was terribly hot, yes, even more than in Bogota! But I have a new trainer, I trained very hard in the heat and it paid off. In fact, I felt very relaxed in the car. This win is the perfect end to the perfect weekend."*

In the championship, with four races to go, Juan Pablo Montoya was only 6 points down on Michael Schumacher. *"We have come from a long way back. Anything can happen. You only have to look at what happened to Michael today. We really are in a better position than at the start of the season and I think the remaining circuits should suit us. Our car should be very strong, except perhaps in Hungary, a track I do not like that much."*

> And the winner is...Juan Pablo Montoya. Unlike most of his rivals, he had a trouble-free afternoon in Hockenheim.

A triumphal arrival for the two Renaults, which both finished in the points: Jarno Trulli third and Fernando Alonso fourth. The Italian was one of the stars of the race, having been a convincing second for 67 laps, before giving best, first to Michael Schumacher and then to David Coulthard. It was Trulli's first podium with the Renault team. *"For two thirds of the race, I could do nothing about Montoya, but I could keep ahead of those behind me. Then, with fifteen laps to go, my tyres began to blister and there was nothing I could do. All the same, we have had a very good weekend. We were competitive right from the first practice session and a podium is a good reward."*

>

HA great climb up the field from David Coulthard at Hockenheim. Starting from 10th on the grid, the Scotsman finished on the second step of the podium. *"I am very happy with this result, especially after what was a difficult weekend. My car was well balanced and I was able to look after my tyres."*

v

Gremlins hit Scuderia Ferrari

Michael Schumacher would have finished second in the German Grand Prix, but for a puncture four laps from home.

According to the official statement from Bridgestone, the puncture was the result of the Ferrari running over debris as it overtook Jarno Trulli round the outside at the hairpin. *"We will take our revenge in Hungary,"* commented Hisao Suganuma, the Japanese company's technical director. However, rumours in the paddock would have it that the Ferrari's tyre suffered a construction problem, as had already happened the previous day.

"This has been the hardest and most disappointing race of the season," concluded Jean Todt, the Scuderia Ferrari managing director. With Rubens Barrichello having been knocked out at the first corner, the Italian team only scored two points for 7th place at Hockenheim.

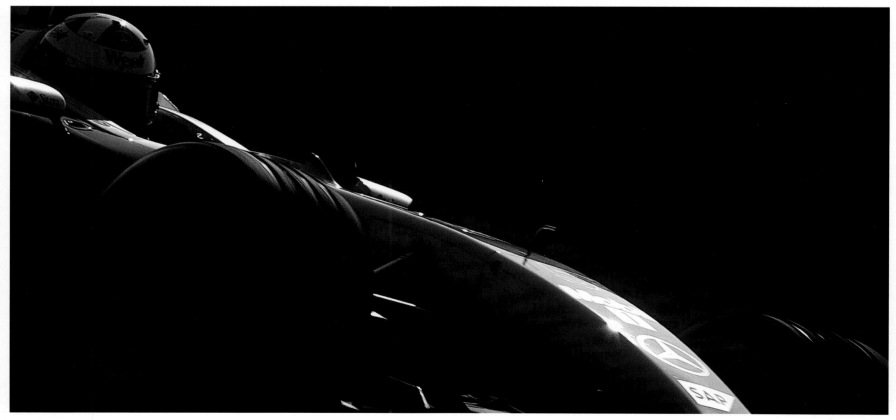

Practice

All the time trials

N°	Driver	N° Chassis - Engine	Private testing	Pos.	Practice friday	Pos.	Qualifying friday	Pos.	Practice 1 saturday	Pos.	Practice 2 saturday	Pos.	Warm-up	Pos.	Qualifying saturday	Pos.
1.	Michael Schumacher	Ferrari F2003-GA 231			1:16.814	11	1:15.456	9	1:16:056	4	1:16.493	8	1:16.532	9	1:15.898	6
2.	Rubens Barrichello	Ferrari F2003-GA 230			1:17.361	16	1:15.399	8	1:15.853	2	1:15.495	2	1:15.924	5	1:15.488	3
3.	Juan Pablo Montoya	Williams FW25 06 - BMW			1:15.890	5	1:14.673	2	1:15.668	1	1:15.716	3	1:15.385	1	1:15.167	1
4.	Ralf Schumacher	Williams FW25 07 - BMW			1:16.401	8	1:14.427	1	1:15.890	3	1:15.387	1	1:15.828	4	1:15.185	2
5.	David Coulthard	McLaren MP4-17D 07 - Mercedes			1:15.523	1	1:15.557	11	1:17.147	11		20	1:16.576	10	1:16.666	10
6.	Kimi Räikkönen	McLaren MP4-17D 09 - Mercedes			1:17.284	15	1:15.276	6	1:16.193	5	1:16.320	6	1:15.964	6	1:15.874	5
7.	Jarno Trulli	Renault R23B-05	1:16.074	1	1:15.617	2	1:15.004	3	1:16.275	6	1:16.305	5	1:16.497	8	1:15.679	4
8.	Fernando Alonso	Renault R23B-04	1:16.190	2	1:15.797	3	1:15.214	5	1:16.371	7	1:16.277	4	1:15.701	2	1:16.483	8
9.	Nick Heidfeld	Sauber C22-01 - Petronas			1:18.121	18	1:15.985	14	1:17.345	13	1:17.647	15	1:17.323	13	1:17.557	15
10.	Heinz-Harald Frentzen	Sauber C22-03 - Petronas			1:17.137	14	1:15.968	13	1:17.180	12	1:17.334	12	1:17.796	16	1:17.169	14
11.	Giancarlo Fisichella	Jordan EJ13-05 - Ford	1:16.983	5	1:17.050	13	1:17.111	17	1:17.419	15	1:17.583	14	1:17.407	14	1:16.831	12
12.	Ralph Firman	Jordan EJ13-03 - Ford	1:17.518	6	1:17.842	17	1:17.044	16	1:18.293	18	1:18.403	17	1:17.840	17	1:18.341	18
14.	Mark Webber	Jaguar R4-04	1:16.887	4	1:15.799	4	1:15.030	4	1:16.953	9	1:16.474	7	1:16.908	11	1:16.775	11
15.	Justin Wilson	Jaguar R4-05	1:17.742	7	1:16.568	9	1:15.373	7	1:18.083	17	1:17.766	16	1:17.903	18	1:18.021	16
16.	Jacques Villeneuve	BAR 005-3 - Honda			1:16.945	12		19	1:17.353	14	1:16.957	10	1:17.421	15	1:17.090	13
17.	Jenson Button	BAR 005-4 - Honda			1:16.187	7	1:15.754	12	1:16.957	10	1:16.954	9	1:17.130	12	1:18.085	17
18.	Nicolas Kiesa	Minardi PS03/01 - Cosworth	1:19.413	10	1:19.030	20			1:19.766	20	1:20.408	19		20	1:19.174	20
19.	Jos Verstappen	Minardi PS03/03 - Cosworth	1:18.518	8	1:18.791	19	1:17.702	18	1:19.433	19	1:19.533	18	1:22.229	19	1:19.023	19
20.	Olivier Panis	Toyota TF103/08			1:16.602	10	1:15.471	10	1:16.560	8	1:17.179	11	1:15.758	3	1:16.034	7
21.	Cristiano da Matta	Toyota TF103/04			1:16.109	6	1:16.450	15	1:17.662	16	1:17.426	13	1:16.341	19	1:16.550	9
34.	Allan McNish	Renault R23B-03	1:16.304	3												
36.	Zsolt Baumgartner	Jordan EJ13-04 - Ford	1:18.912	9												
39.	Gianmaria Bruni	Minardi PS03/02 - Cosworth	1:19.865	11												

Maximum speed

N°	Driver	P1 Qualifs	Pos.	P1 Race	Pos.	P2 Qualifs	Pos.	P2 Race	Pos.	Finish Qualifs	Pos.	Finish Race	Pos.	Trap Qualifs	Pos.	Trap Race	Pos.
1.	M. Schumacher	216,1	9	217,6	5	267,5	3	268,2	3	272,1	5	276,5	2	313,6	12	328,9	6
2.	R. Barrichello	218,4	3			270,0	1			273,6	3			314,6	10		
3.	J.P. Montoya	219,2	1	222,2	1	268,1	2	269,3	1	275,7	1	278,7	1	317,4	4	325,7	8
4.	R. Schumacher	217,4	6	182,9	16	266,6	5	152,6	17	273,9	2			316,3	7	268,6	16
5.	D. Coulthard	217,5	5	218,8	3	261,0	13	265,8	5	270,6	11	275,2	5	316,4	6	330,4	4
6.	K. Räikkönen	216,8	7			263,7	7			271,3	9			315,6	8		
7.	J. Trulli	214,8	11	214,6	12	263,6	8	262,4	11	269,2	15	270,0	11	315,3	9	323,0	12
8.	F. Alonso	213,3	15	216,3	7	259,6	15	264,9	6	270,8	10	271,6	9	308,9	20	324,8	9
9.	N. Heidfeld	214,5	12	215,1	10	259,9	14	263,7	8	269,7	14	269,5	12	311,6	16	324,3	11
10.	H-H. Frentzen	213,1	16	117,6	17	262,9	11	170,4	16	268,9	16			311,6	17	184,0	17
11.	G. Fisichella	213,1	17	215,0	11	263,0	10	261,7	12	270,4	12	271,4	10	313,9	11	324,6	10
12.	R. Firman	211,5	18			258,4	16			266,9	18			309,9	19		
14.	M. Webber	215,4	10	217,0	6	263,6	9	264,2	7	270,2	13	273,8	7	316,9	5	331,0	3
15.	J. Wilson	216,1	8	215,3	9	255,7	20	255,3	13	267,3	17	264,1	14	310,2	18	316,5	15
16.	J. Villeneuve	208,2	20	207,8	15	262,1	12	263,1	10	272,4	4	273,6	8	322,7	1	333,3	1
17.	J. Button	208,8	19	216,0	8	257,9	18	263,3	9	293,5	12	276,2	4	319,3	3	332,4	2
18.	N. Kiesa	213,6	14	213,8	13	257,2	19	253,9	15	265,6	20	263,6	15	313,5	13	318,7	13
19.	J. Verstappen	214,1	13	212,2	14	258,1	17	255,1	14	266,4	19	265,2	13	311,6	15	317,9	14
20.	O. Panis	217,9	4	218,2	4	267,2	4	267,5	4	271,8	7	274,2	6	313,0	14	330,0	5
21.	C. Da Matta	218,8	2	219,1	2	263,7	6	268,7	2	271,9	6	276,5	3	320,3	2	327,0	7

Race

Classification & Retirements

Pos.	Driver	Team	Lap	Time	Average	
1.	J.P. Montoya	Williams BMW	67	1:28:48.769	207,036 km/h	
2.	D. Coulthard	McLaren Mercedes	67	+ 1:05.459	204,523 km/h	
3.	J. Trulli	Renault	67	+ 1:09.060	204,387 km/h	
4.	F. Alonso	Renault	67	+ 1:09.344	204,376 km/h	
5.	O. Panis	Toyota	66	1 lap	203,372 km/h	
6.	C. Da Matta	Toyota	66	1 lap	203,196 km/h	
7.	M. Schumacher	Ferrari	66	1 lap	202,461 km/h	
8.	J. Button	BAR Honda	66	1 lap	201,128 km/h	
9.	J. Villeneuve	BAR Honda	65	2 laps	200,311 km/h	
10.	N. Heidfeld	Sauber Petronas	65	2 laps	200,048 km/h	
11.	M. Webber	Jaguar	64	3 laps	200,923 km/h	Attacks Button, ends up in gravel
12.	N. Kiesa	Minardi Cosworth	62	5 laps	191,143 km/h	
13.	G. Fisichella	Jordan Ford	60	7 laps	189,491 km/h	Engine overheats after losing coolant

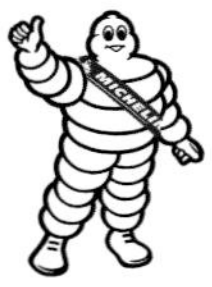

Driver	Team	Lap	Reason
J. Verstappen	Minardi Cosworth	24	Drop in hydraulic pressure
J. Wilson	Jaguar	7	Transmission problem
R. Schumacher	Williams BMW	1	Car damaged after collision with Barrichello
H-H. Frentzen	Sauber Petronas	1	Hit by Firman, rear wing pulled off
R. Barrichello	Ferrari	0	Collision, sandwiched by Raikkonen and R. Schumacher
K. Räikkönen	McLaren Mercedes	0	Collision with Barrichello, crashes into tyre wall
R. Firman	Jordan Ford	0	Hits the back of Frentzen and then Wilson

Fastest laps

	Driver	Time	Lap	Average
1.	J.P. Montoya	1:14.917	14	219,795 km/h
2.	J. Trulli	1:15.740	13	217,406 km/h
3.	O. Panis	1:15.883	34	216,997 km/h
4.	D. Coulthard	1:16.003	14	216,654 km/h
5.	C. Da Matta	1:16.051	35	216,517 km/h
6.	F. Alonso	1:16.074	16	216,492 km/h
7.	M. Schumacher	1:16.081	36	216,432 km/h
8.	J. Button	1:17.430	41	212,661 km/h
9.	M. Webber	1:17.754	46	211,775 km/h
10.	N. Heidfeld	1:18.036	10	211,010 km/h
11.	G. Fisichella	1:18.145	51	210,715 km/h
12.	J. Villeneuve	1:18.235	65	210,473 km/h
13.	J. Wilson	1:19.441	3	207,278 km/h
14.	N. Kiesa	1:20.171	26	205,390 km/h
15.	J. Verstappen	1:20.399	6	204,808 km/h
16.	R. Schumacher		0	
17.	H-H. Frentzen		0	

Pit stops

	Driver	Time	Lap	Stop n°
1.	J. Verstappen	30.271	1	1
2.	J. Villeneuve	33.676	1	1
3.	J. Wilson	5:56.415	1	1
4.	N. Kiesa	34.968	2	1
5.	G. Fisichella	1:01.702	11	1
6.	J. Trulli	29.747	14	1
7.	O. Panis	28.497	15	1
8.	N. Heidfeld	28.230	16	1
9.	J.P. Montoya	28.601	17	1
10.	M. Schumacher	29.034	17	1
11.	C. Da Matta	27.286	17	1
12.	F. Alonso	28.882	18	1
13.	D. Coulthard	30.919	18	1
14.	M. Webber	30.071	20	1
15.	J. Button	29.942	21	1
16.	J. Verstappen	35.088	23	2
17.	N. Kiesa	33.423	24	2
18.	O. Panis	28.359	32	2
19.	J.P. Montoya	27.638	33	2
20.	C. Da Matta	27.794	33	2
21.	J. Villeneuve	34.429	34	2
22.	N. Heidfeld	27.825	34	2
23.	G. Fischella	31.712	32	2
24.	J. Trulli	31.207	38	2
25.	M. Schumacher	31.961	38	2
26.	F. Alonso	32.113	39	2
27.	D. Coulthard	30.241	42	2
28.	J. Button	30.179	43	2
29.	M. Webber	31.296	44	2
30.	N. Kiesa	33.318	43	3
31.	O. Panis	28.438	49	3
32.	J.P. Montoya	28.146	50	3
33.	C. Da Matta	27.350	50	3
34.	N. Heidfeld	27.491	51	3
35.	G. Fischella	30.935	49	3
36.	M. Schumacher	32.746	63	3

Race leaders

Driver	Laps in the lead	Nber of Laps
J.P. Montoya	1 > 17	17
F. Alonso	18	1
J.P. Montoya	19 > 67	49

Driver	Nber of Laps	Kilometers
J.P. Montoya	66	301,884 km
F. Alonso	1	4,574 km

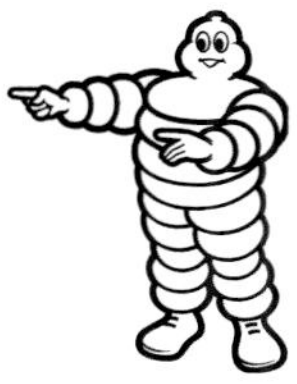

Gaps on the leader board

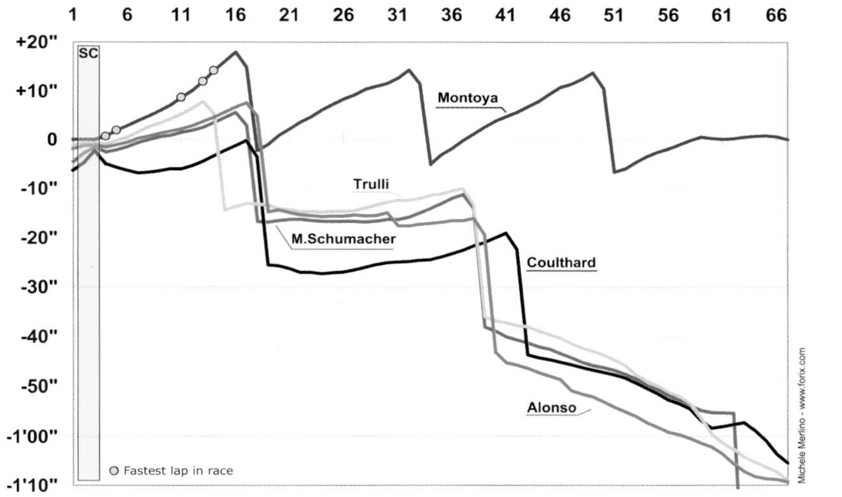

Lap chart

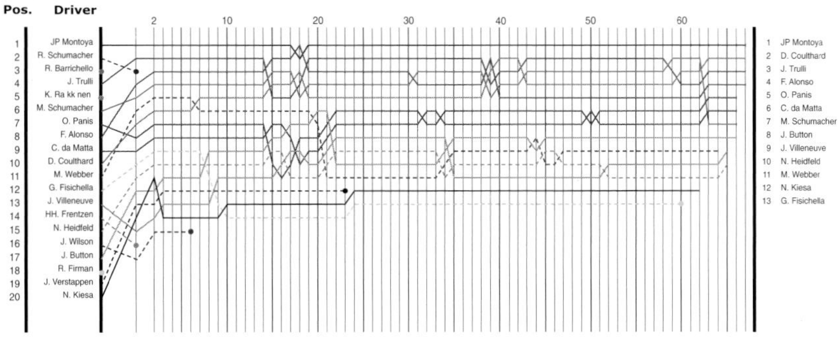

Championship after twelve rounds

Drivers

1. M. Schumacher ....(4 wins)................71
2. J.P. Montoya.............(2 wins)................65
2. K. Räikkönen ....(1 win) 62
3. R. Schumacher..........(2 wins)................53
5. R. Barrichello ....(1 win) 49
6. F. Alonso 44
7. D. Coulthard ....(1 win) 41
8. J. Trulli 22
9. J. Button...12
10. M. Webber..12
11. G. Fisichella ....(1 win) 10
12. C. Da Matta...8
13. H-H. Frentzen 7
14. O. Panis..6
15. J. Villeneuve..3
16. N. Heidfeld..2
17. R. Firman..1
18. A. Pizzonia 0
19. J. Verstappen 0
20. J. Wilson...0
21. N. Kiesa..0

Constructors

1. Scuderia Ferrari Marlboro ......(5 wins).......120
2. BMW Williams F1 Team ....(4 wins).......118
3. West McLaren Mercedes ....(2 wins).......103
4. Mild Seven Renault F1 Team.......................66
5. Lucky Strike BAR Honda 15
6. Panasonic Toyota Racing 14
7. Jaguar Racing..12
8. Jordan Ford...........................(1 win) 11
9. Sauber Petronas 9
10. European Minardi Cosworth..........................0

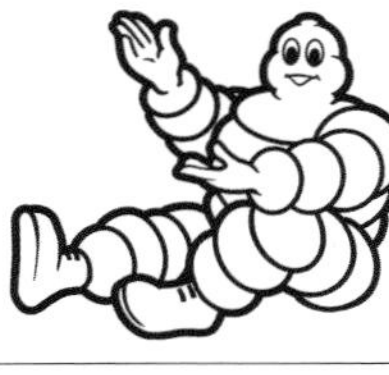

The circuit

Name	Hockenheim
Date	August 3, 2003
Length	4574 meters
Distance	67 laps, 306,458 km
Weather	Sunny and very hot, 34-36°c
Track temperature	46-50°c

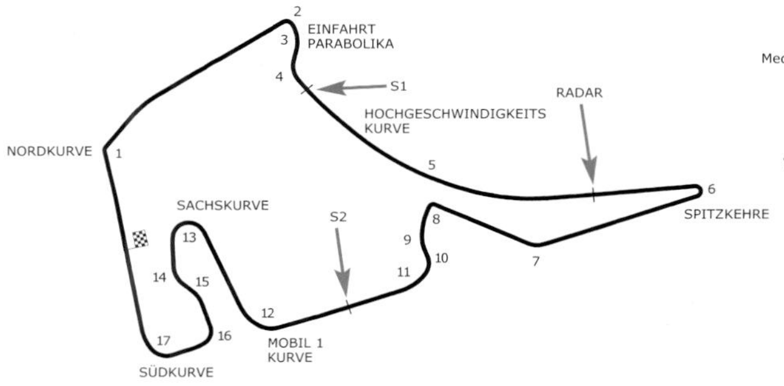

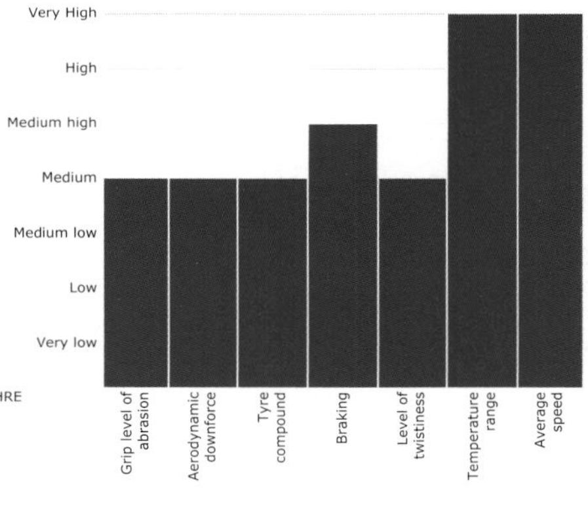

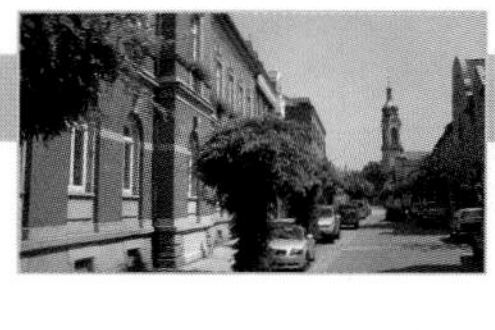

VIVA FERNANDO!

Starting from pole position, Fernando Alonso won the Hungarian Grand Prix as he pleased. He took the chequered flag almost 17 seconds clear of second placed Kimi Räikkönen and Juan Pablo Montoya, third.

It was the Renault driver's maiden F1 win, making him the youngest ever grand prix winner and he also became the first ever Spaniard to win a grand prix. For the Renault team, it was the first win since Austria in 1983, precisely 20 years and 10 days earlier!

Second place for Kimi Räikkönen and third for Juan Pablo Montoya meant that the pair were now very close to Michael Schumacher in the drivers' classification. The Hungarian Grand Prix had been a catastrophe for Ferrari, with Barrichello retiring and Schumacher only eighth.

Michael Schumacher eighth on the grid. Problems at Ferrari.

Will nothing go right in the Ferrari camp? Having qualified eighth on Saturday, Michael Schumacher looked to be in trouble in Budapest, especially at a track where overtaking is almost impossible. Indeed, there were nothing but long faces at Ferrari. *"It is very disappointing and the race will not be easy,"* conceded Jean Todt, who had hoped to see both his cars at least in the top three rows of the grid. Michael Schumacher admitted he was far from happy. *"Of course, I am disappointed, because up until qualifying, I thought we were on the pace. Now we have to work out what happened."*

What had happened seemed perfectly clear. On Saturday, the Bridgestone tyres were not up to the job. Michelin once again had eight cars in the top ten and all the teams running on the French rubber had at least one car in the top half of the grid, while the back end was an all-Bridgestone affair.

For the Japanese manufacturer, the very hot summer had been its downfall as their tyres did not seem to suit the warm conditions and there was no apparent solution in sight. The testing ban which had been in force for a few weeks had not helped Ferrari's cause either, as it coincided with a period when the Scuderia appeared to be treading water.

Fisico to Sauber. No changes at McLaren.

Giancarlo Fisichella, or *"Fisico"* as he is known in the paddock, is not exactly new to the game. Although only 30 years old, the Roman is already in his eighth season of F1. From a total of 119 grands prix starts, he only had one win to his name, in this year's Brazilian Grand Prix, which owed a bit to luck. However, he is regarded as one of the very best Formula 1 drivers, most experts putting him in the top trio alongside Michael Schumacher and Kimi Raikkonen.

In Budapest, he announced he was switching to Sauber for 2004 and 2005, a move which did not seem to offer much in the way of career advancement. The transfer did mean that the Italian would be one step nearer to Ferrari, as the Scuderia supplied its engines to the Swiss team, which it considered as something of a racing laboratory. With that philosophy in mind, Ferrari had also prompted Peter Sauber to take on their current test driver, Felipe Massa for 2004. *"I have been keeping an eye on Giancarlo for several years, as I consider him to be one of the best drivers in F1,"* reckoned the team boss. *"He is quick and never gives up. I am very happy he is joining us."*

On Friday, the McLaren-Mercedes team confirmed its 2004 driver line-up: Kimi Raikkonen, David Coulthard and, in the role of third driver, Alexander Wurz, with Pedro de la Rosa as test driver. No changes there then.

Starting grid

| Z. BAUMGARTNER 19 1:26.678 | H-H. FRENTZEN 17 1:24.569 | C. DA MATTA 15 1:23.982 | G. FISICHELLA 13 1:23.728 | N. HEIDFELD 11 1:23.621 | D. COULTHARD 9 1:23.060 | K. RÄIKKÖNEN 7 1:22.742 | R. BARRICHELLO 5 1:22.180 | M. WEBBER 3 1:22.027 | F. ALONSO 1 1:21.688 (193,071 km/h) |
| N. KIESA 20 1:28.907 | J. VERSTAPPEN 18 1:24.423 | J. VILLENEUVE 16 1:24.100 | J. BUTTON 14 1:23.847 | J. WILSON 12 1:23.660 | O. PANIS 10 1:23.369 | M. SCHUMACHER 8 1:22.755 | J. TRULLI 6 1:22.610 | J.P. MONTOYA 4 1:22.180 | R. SCHUMACHER 2 1:21.944 |

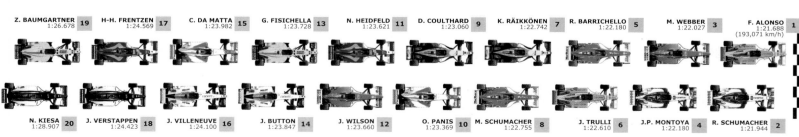

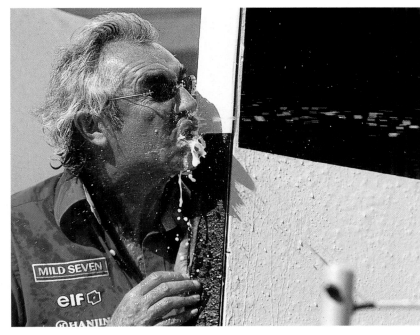

A magnificent first win for Fernando Alonso

Starting from pole position, Fernando Alonso produced a masterly performance to take the first grand prix win of his career in Budapest. He put together a perfect race, leading the Hungarian Grand Prix from start to finish, refuelling three times, losing the lead for just one of the 70 race laps.

The Renault driver had the upper hand at the first corner, ahead of second placed Mark Webber, whose slower pace allowed the Spaniard to escape the pack. After four laps, Alonso already had a 10 second cushion over his pursuers! *"At first, I could see Mark in my mirrors and then, nothing,"* recounted Fernando. *"After eight or nine laps, I asked my team where the others were. They replied, "15 seconds behind you!" I said to myself, "My God, I'm quick!" so I lifted a bit..."*

With nine laps to go, the man who was about to win even offered himself the luxury of lapping Michael Schumacher. A memorable moment. *"It will be a great memory for me. Jarno* (Trulli, his team-mate) *and Michael were ahead of me. I closed on them and then got past. They obviously had more problems than I did. My car was perfect from start to finish."* He crossed the line in triumph. *"I cannot think at the moment. It's too soon and I feel I am dreaming,"* sighed Alonso, as he stepped off the podium. *"It was all quite easy. Except that, with ten laps to go, I could hear noises coming from the engine, the gearbox or maybe they were in my mind. I was very nervous. But the whole weekend has been fantastic. After qualifying, we realised we had a good chance of finishing on the podium, although we were not aiming for the win. It was only in the race, when I realised how big my lead was, that I began to think of it."* In the other Renault, Jarno Trulli finished seventh. In contrast to his team-mate, he found that the car was not holding the road properly. Kimi Raikkonen finished second, after an amazing start, as he went from seventh on the grid to fourth at the first corner. *"The car was definitely better than in qualifying,"* suggested the Finn. *"But I lost a lot of time behind Mark Webber in the early stages, which ruined my chances of catching Fernando later."*

^
"We've won!" The entire Renault team gathered for a family photo after the race.

<
Flavio Briatore seems to be enjoying the champagne on the podium. His joy was all the greater as his driver had lapped Michael Schumacher. *"In the good old days with Benetton, we often found ourselves lapping the Ferraris. Back then, they were less competitive. I have to admit that today, it gave me a special feeling,"* explained the Italian boss. He was getting his revenge for some comments made by Ron Dennis on Saturday. The McLaren man had suggested the Renaults had run light on fuel. *"According to him, we were going to need to refuel on the warm-up lap. He would do better to get on with his work rather than talk rubbish,"* said an amused Briatore.

Race summary

> Starting from pole, Fernando Alonso immediately pulls out a big lead. He would not be seen again that afternoon (**1**).

> Ralf Schumacher spins on the opening lap, ploughs through the pack, narrowly avoiding his team-mate. He gets going to finish 4th, one second behind Montoya (**2**).

> A fright on lap 19. Barrichello suffers a suspension failure braking at the end of the main straight and piles into the barriers (**3**).

> At half distance, local hero, Zsolt Baumgartner retires with a broken engine (**4**).

> Qualified on row 2, Webber drops down the order during the pit stops. He finishes a solid 6th (**5**).

> Overtaken by Alonso, M Schumacher can do no better than 8th (**6**).

> Alonso becomes the youngest winner in history (**7**).

Take it easy Juan Pablo

The Williams team was playing the numbers game in the Hungarian Grand Prix. Thanks to third place, Juan Pablo Montoya had actually closed the gap in the championship to Michael Schumacher by one little point. Kimi Raikkonen was a further point behind the Colombian. It was going to be close come the end of the season.

paddock

Montreal lands in Budapest

In Formula 1, commercial necessity often overrides common sense. With a crowd of 120,000 back in June, the Canadian Grand Prix could claim to be one of the most popular races of the season.

Ever since Jacques Villeneuve arrived on the F1 scene, the number of spectators who flocked to the Notre Dame circuit had grown steadily over the course of the years and the event was a sell-out. Away from the track, the Canadian Grand Prix was a big favourite with the Formula 1 circus, thanks to the attractions of downtown Montreal, including its nightlife and shopping.

Nevertheless, it now looked as though this much loved venue was being scrubbed from the 2004 calendar, which had been published a few days before the Hungarian Grand Prix. The reason for this was that the Canadian parliament had voted through an anti-tobacco law in 1997, with a seven year exemption for the Canadian Grand Prix. Now, that exemption was about to expire and it meant that in 2004, the teams would no longer be able to run their cars in livery that advertised cigarette companies.

F1 commercial rights holder, Bernie Ecclestone had thus contacted the organisers to inform them that their event would no longer feature on the 2004 calendar, as per the contract between the two parties.

The news sent a wave of panic which engulfed Montreal. Bernie Ecclestone's action could have been predicted a long time ago, but the city had only just woken up to the implications. For days, it was the main story in the local papers with the anti-tobacco ayatollahs getting a pasting, while the maths was being done to work out the financial damage to

the hotels, restaurants and shops in the city, reckoned to be around 60 million Canadian dollars. It led to a mass exodus from the banks of the St. Laurence seaway. The mayor of Montreal, Gerald Tremblay, the president of the Chamber of Commerce, Benoit Labonte, the Quebec minister of Sport and Tourism, Jean-Marc Fournier, the Canadian Minister of Justice, Martin Cauchon and Grand Prix organiser, Normand Legault all jumped on a plane to Budapest.

It was an impressive delegation, accompanied by an army of press attaches, wives and secretaries, who overran the Hungarian paddock on Friday. After lunching with Bernie Ecclestone, the missionaries then tackled the team owners to try and convince

them of the importance of their event. Apparently, without too much success. *"Before this trip, I reckoned we had a 5% chance of keeping our grand prix. After today, I would say our chances are about the same. It is a very complex situation,"* reckoned Normand Legault, before heading home for Quebec. Bernie Ecclestone's problem was finding room on the 2004 calendar for two new events, in China and Bahrain. It meant that at least one event would have to go. The fact that Canada counted an on-site audience of 120,000 seemed to count for nothing. However, a few weeks later the Canadian Grand Prix reappeared on the calendar, albeit with a proviso that teams would have to be compensated for running without their lucrative tobacco advertising.

> Start. The cars starting from the left and therefore clean side of the track had a clear advantage. *"It's incredible,"* complained Juan Pablo Montoya, who started from the right. *"I let go of the launch button and nothing happened as everyone went past me. I thought I might lose one place at the start, but I lost four. It's a ridiculous situation."*

Refuelling for third placed Juan Pablo Montoya. *"At the second corner, I tried to pass Michael round the outside, but he just moved right over on me. I was shocked, but that's the way he drives,"* commented the Colombian, who never misses the chance to have a dig at his German rival. The Sauber team was heading home, having failed yet again to pick up a point. Nick Heidfeld finished ninth, while Heinz-Harald Frentzen retired on lap 48, having run out of fuel! *"It was the result of a set of circumstances. My radio wasn't working and I could not hear the team calling me in to refuel. And when they stuck the pitboard out, I was in the middle of overtaking Kiesa's Minardi and I saw nothing. Just rotten luck!"*
>

Michael Schumacher eighth. Crisis at Ferrari

The Minardi team celebrated its 300th grand prix in Budapest. An impressive statistic for a team still chasing its first pole position and first win.
V>

"Say Cheese." The McLaren drivers pose to celebrate renewing their contracts.
V

11h30, Sunday morning. The race is due to start in less than three hours. Behind the Scuderia's transporter, Ross Brawn, the team's technical director is holding an impromptu meeting with Bridgestone's chief engineer, Hisao Suganuma. The tension is clearly etched on their faces. In another part of the paddock, Peter Sauber maintains that the Bridgestone tyres are giving away at least a second per lap to the Michelins here in Hungary. This last minute meeting would change nothing: Michael Schumacher finished the race in eighth place, one lap down on the winner, with Michelin runners taking the top seven places. *"I was never able to run at a decent pace, as I was always stuck behind other cars,"* explained the German. *"Nothing worked the way we wanted. Now, all we can do is roll up our sleeves and work hard!"* For Rubens Barrichello, the afternoon had been even worse. The Brazilian was just starting his twentieth lap when his left rear wheel flew off the car and he crashed heavily. *"We have no idea what happened,"* explained Ross Brawn after the race. *"We have never experienced this sort of problem before and there was no warning from the telemetry. We will*

have to take a close look at the remains of Rubens' car to try and understand the problem."
Fortunately, the Brazilian was uninjured. In the paddock however, he was furious that the medical crews had shown no interest in him! A few days later, Ferrari explained that the failure had been provoked by the Brazilian riding the kerbs. It was a

particularly strange excuse given the inherent strength of the F2003-GA.
The Scuderia would have to work extremely hard to turn the situation around before the next grand prix in three weeks time at Monza. Several test sessions had been planned, with the possible arrival of a new chassis and new tyres.

results

Practice

All the time trials

N°	Driver	N° Chassis - Engine	Private testing	Pos.	Practice friday	Pos.	Qualifying friday	Pos.	Practice 1 saturday	Pos.	Practice 2 saturday	Pos.	Warm-up	Pos.	Qualifying saturday	Pos.
1.	Michael Schumacher	Ferrari F2003-GA 231			1:22.842	9	1:23.430	9	1:23.274	2	1:22.313	2	1:22.210	1	1:22.755	8
2.	Rubens Barrichello	Ferrari F2003-GA 232			1:22.594	4	1:22.892	5	1:23.432	3	1:22.467	3	1:23.457	7	1:22.180	5
3.	Juan Pablo Montoya	Williams FW25 06 - BMW			1:22.592	3	1:23.305	8	1:24.142	6	1:22.494	4	1:22.521	3	1:22.180	4
4.	Ralf Schumacher	Williams FW25 07 - BMW			1:22.757	7	1:22.413	2	1:23.758	4	1:21.939	1	1:22.766	5	1:21.944	4
5.	David Coulthard	McLaren MP4-17D 08 - Mercedes			1:22.797	8	1:22.786	4	1:25.379	13	1:23.293	9	1:23.822	9	1:23.060	9
6.	Kimi Räikkönen	McLaren MP4-17D 09 - Mercedes			1:23.532	11	1:23.695	12	1:24.837	12	1:22.876	6	1:33.177	19	1:22.742	7
7.	Jarno Trulli	Renault R23B-05	1:23.092	3	1:22.464	2	1:22.358	1	1:23.796	5	1:23.074	8	1:23.102	6	1:22.610	6
8.	Fernando Alonso	Renault R23B-04	1:22.230	1	1:23.214	10	1:22.953	6	1:22.950	1	1:22.902	7	1:22.460	2	1:21.688	1
9.	Nick Heidfeld	Sauber C22-01 - Petronas			1:24.535	17	1:23.482	10	1:24.734	10	1:23.838	12	1:24.046	10	1:23.621	11
10.	Heinz-Harald Frentzen	Sauber C22-03 - Petronas			1:23.586	12	1:23.660	11	1:24.617	9	1:24.006	14	1:49.249	20	1:24.569	17
11.	Giancarlo Fisichella	Jordan EJ13-05 - Ford	1:27.399	11	1:24.474	15	1:24.725	16	1:25.566	16	1:24.343	16	1:24.250	11	1:23.726	13
12.	Ralph Firman	Jordan EJ13-03 - Ford	1:26.600	9	1:24.502	16	1:25.223	17	1:26.618	18						
14.	Mark Webber	Jaguar R4-03	1:23.748	4	1:22.741	6	1:22.625	3	1:24.328	8	1:22.848	5	1:22.654	14	1:22.027	3
15.	Justin Wilson	Jaguar R4-05	1:24.209	5	1:24.669	18	1:24.343	15	1:24.800	11	1:23.853	13	1:25.106	15	1:23.660	12
16.	Jacques Villeneuve	BAR 005-6 - Honda			1:23.817	14	1:24.333	14	1:25.815	17	1:24.154	15	1:25.066	14	1:24.100	16
17.	Jenson Button	BAR 005-4 - Honda			1:23.723	13	1:24.313	13	1:25.397	14	1:23.805	11	1:24.268	12	1:23.847	14
18.	Nicolas Kiesa	Minardi PS03/01 - Cosworth	1:26.252	8			1:27.023	19	1:27.188	20	1:27.295	19	1:31.376	18	1:28.907	20
19.	Jos Verstappen	Minardi PS03/02 - Cosworth	1:25.321	6	1:25.579	19	1:26.052	18	1:26.976	19	1:26.498	18	1:26.362	17	1:26.423	18
20.	Olivier Panis	Toyota TF103/08			1:21.770	1	1:22.986	7	1:24.251	7	1:23.789	10	1:23.582	8	1:23.369	10
21.	Cristiano da Matta	Toyota TF103/04			1:22.700	5	1:55.138	20	1:25.545	15	1:24.401	17	1:24.789	13	1:23.982	15
34.	Allan McNish	Renault R23B-03	1:22.855	2												
36/12.	Zsolt Baumgartner	Jordan EJ13-04 - Ford	1:26.006	7									1:26.346	16	1:26.678	19
39.	Gianmaria Bruni	Minardi PS03/03 - Cosworth	1:27.036	10												

Maximum speed

N°	Driver	P1 Qualifs	Pos.	P1 Race	Pos.	P2 Qualifs	Pos.	P2 Race	Pos.	Finish Qualifs	Pos.	Finish Race	Pos.	Trap Qualifs	Pos.	Trap Race	Pos.
1.	M. Schumacher	294,5	3	297,6	3	235,7	13	243,1	6	254,8	4	254,9	7	294,4	6	301,2	6
2.	R. Barrichello	294,2	4	294,5	5	237,1	9	240,0	11	254,4	5	254,7	9	295,1	3	299,5	8
3.	J.P. Montoya	296,5	1	298,1	1	245,0	1	246,9	1	255,5	2	258,0	1	295,0	4	305,8	2
4.	R. Schumacher	294,9	2	298,0	2	244,2	2	245,2	2	257,0	1	257,7	2	298,7	1	307,5	1
5.	D. Coulthard	292,0	5	294,5	6	236,4	11	240,1	10	251,8	8	255,5	6	293,7	7	297,4	11
6.	K. Räikkönen	290,7	8	293,4	7	237,2	8	244,6	3	252,4	6	256,5	4	293,3	8	301,3	5
7.	J. Trulli	285,5	17	285,3	17	228,1	18	235,7	17	248,9	15	249,8	16	285,6	18	292,4	18
8.	F. Alonso	286,7	14	291,1	13	237,5	7	241,3	9	250,6	11	250,5	15	286,3	17	292,5	17
9.	N. Heidfeld	289.3	9	290,7	14	236,1	12	237,1	16	250,4	13	251,8	12	290,4	12	295,7	13
10.	H-H. Frentzen	287,0	13	289,0	15	235,2	14	237,4	15	246,6	17	249,5	18	290,3	14	295,8	12
11.	G. Fisichella	291,2	6	292,8	8	236,7	10	238,4	13	247,5	16	251,3	14	290,4	13	297,8	9
12.	Z. Baumgartner	276,4	20	281,3	20	231,4	15	232,7	18	245,3	20	247,7	20	288,2	16	291,8	19
14.	M. Webber	289,0	10	292,6	9	241,6	3	243,1	5	251,4	9	254,9	8	290,1	15	295,7	14
15.	J. Wilson	286,0	15	291,1	12	238,4	6	239,9	12	251,3	10	253,4	10	291,4	10	297,6	10
16.	J. Villeneuve	287,1	12	287,2	16	226,3	19	238,0	14	250,3	14	251,7	13	291,2	11	294,6	15
17.	J. Button	285,7	16	291,8	10	229,4	17	243,6	4	250,4	12	253,0	11	292,4	9	300,2	7
18.	N. Kiesa	280,5	19	281,4	19	221,9	20	231,1	20	246,0	19	247,8	19	284,3	20	290,2	20
19.	J. Verstappen	282,9	18	283,6	18	229.6	16	231,6	19	246,4	18	249,8	17	284,5	19	292,8	16
20.	O. Panis	287,6	11	291,3	11	239,2	5	241,8	8	254,9	3	256,9	3	295,6	2	303,9	3
21.	C. Da Matta	291,1	7	294,6	4	239,7	4	242,3	7	252,2	7	255,8	5	294,5	5	303,7	4

Race

Classification & Retirements

Pos.	Driver	Team	Lap	Time	Average
1.	F. Alonso	Renault	70	1:39:01.460	185,810 km/h
2.	K. Räikkönen	McLaren Mercedes	70	+ 16.768	185,287 km/h
3.	J.P. Montoya	Williams BMW	70	+ 34.537	184,763 km/h
4.	R. Schumacher	Williams BMW	70	+ 35.620	184,703 km/h
5.	D. Coulthard	McLaren Mercedes	70	+ 56.535	184,059 km/h
6.	M. Webber	Jaguar	70	+ 1:12.643	183,566 km/h
7.	J. Trulli	Renault	69	1 lap	182,981 km/h
8.	M. Schumacher	Ferrari	69	1 lap	182,968 km/h
9.	N. Heidfeld	Sauber Petronas	69	1 lap	182,237 km/h
10.	J. Button	BAR Honda	69	1 lap	181,670 km/h
11.	C. Da Matta	Toyota	68	2 laps	179,497 km/h
12.	J. Verstappen	Minardi Cosworth	67	3 laps	176,594 km/h
13.	N. Kiesa	Minardi Cosworth	66	4 laps	173,635 km/h

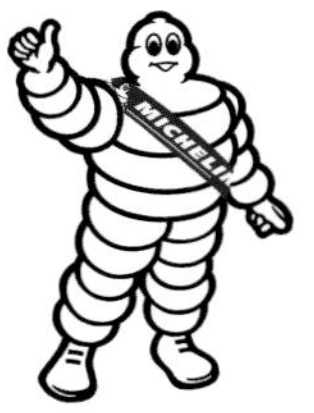

Driver	Team		Reason
H-H. Frentzen	Sauber Petronas	48	Runs out of fuel, radio failure, does not see pit-board
J. Wilson	Jaguar	43	Engine blow up
Z. Baumgartner	Jordan Ford	35	Engine blow up
O Panis	Toyota	34	Broken gearbox
G. Fisichella	Jordan Ford	29	Engine blow up
R. Barrichello	Ferrari	20	Broken top left rear suspension arm, wheel comes off, hits tyre wall
J. Villeneuve	BAR Honda	15	Loss of hydraulic fluid

Fastest laps

	Driver	Time	Lap	Average
1.	J.P. Montoya	1:22.095	37	192,114 km/h
2.	R. Schumacher	1:22.319	55	191,591 km/h
3.	K. Räikkönen	1:22.372	66	191,467 km/h
4.	F. Alonso	1:22.565	47	191,020 km/h
5.	C. Da Matta	1:23.040	35	189,927 km/h
6.	M. Webber	1:23.156	49	189,662 km/h
7.	D. Coulthard	1:23.193	40	189,578 km/h
8.	M. Schumacher	1:23.207	38	189,546 km/h
9.	J. Button	1:23.376	65	189,162 km/h
10.	J. Trulli	1:24.100	34	187,533 km/h
11.	N. Heidfeld	1:24.267	54	187,162 km/h
12.	O. Panis	1:24.414	17	186,836 km/h
13.	H-H. Frentzen	1:24.450	45	186,756 km/h
14.	R. Barrichello	1:24.936	26	186,463 km/h
15.	J. Wilson	1:20.399	26	185,688 km/h
16.	G. Fisichella	1:25.081	13	185,371 Km/h
17.	J. Villeneuve	1:25.278	13	184,943 Km/h
18.	Z. Baumgartner	1:26.464	22	182,406 Km/h
19.	J. Werstappen	1:26.559	60	182,206 Km/h
20.	N. Kiesa	1:27.641	47	179,956 Km/h

Pit stops

	Driver	Time	Lap	Stop n°
1.	J. Wilson	31.841	12	1
2.	J. Verstappen	29.952	12	1
3.	F. Alonso	28.714	13	1
4.	M. Webber	28.980	13	1
5.	N. Kiesa	31.671	13	1
6.	G. Fisichella	33.078	14	1
7.	K. Räikkönen	29.182	15	1
8.	J. Trulli	27.472	15	1
9.	O. Panis	29.823	15	1
10.	R. Barrichello	28.472	16	1
11.	J.P. Montoya	28.589	16	1
12.	C. Da Matta	29.232	15	1
13.	M. Schumacher	28.944	17	1
14.	R. Schumacher	31.232	17	1
15.	N. Heidfeld	29.044	17	1
16.	D. Coulthard	31.536	18	1
17.	J. Button	31.145	18	1
18.	Z. Baumgartner	32.680	19	1
19.	H-H. Frentzen	29.497	22	1
20.	F. Alonso	28.564	30	2
21.	J. Verstappen	30.253	29	2
22.	J. Wilson	29.171	30	2
23.	M. Webber	29.351	31	2
24.	J. Trulli	28.343	32	2
25.	K. Räikkönen	28.913	33	2
26.	N. Kiesa	31.051	32	2
27.	R. Schumacher	27.490	34	2
28.	N. Heidfeld	28.186	34	2
29.	J.P. Montoya	28.187	35	2
30.	C. Da Matta	28.238	34	2
31.	M. Schumacher	34.054	39	2
32.	D. Coulthard	31.537	43	2
33.	J. Button	31.996	43	2
34.	F. Alonso	29.454	49	3
35.	M. Webber	30.306	50	3
36.	M. Schumacher	27.894	50	3
37.	K. Räikkönen	29.725	51	3
38.	J.P. Montoya	28.549	51	3
39.	J. Verstappen	29.332	49	3
40.	J. Trulli	27.855	52	3
41.	N. Heidfeld	28.499	52	3
42.	R. Schumacher	28.706	53	3
43.	N. Kiesa	31.849	50	3
44.	C. Da Matta	28.153	52	3

Race leaders

Driver	Laps in the lead	Nber of Laps
F. Alonso	1 > 13	13
K. Räikkönen	14	1
F. Alonso	15 > 70	56

Driver	Nber of Laps	Kilometers
F. Alonso	69	302,282 km
K. Räikkönen	1	4,381 km

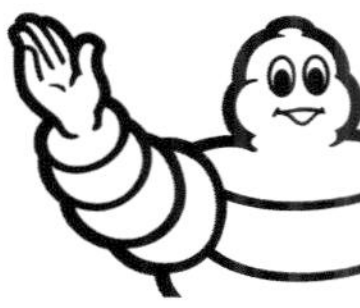

Gaps on the leader board

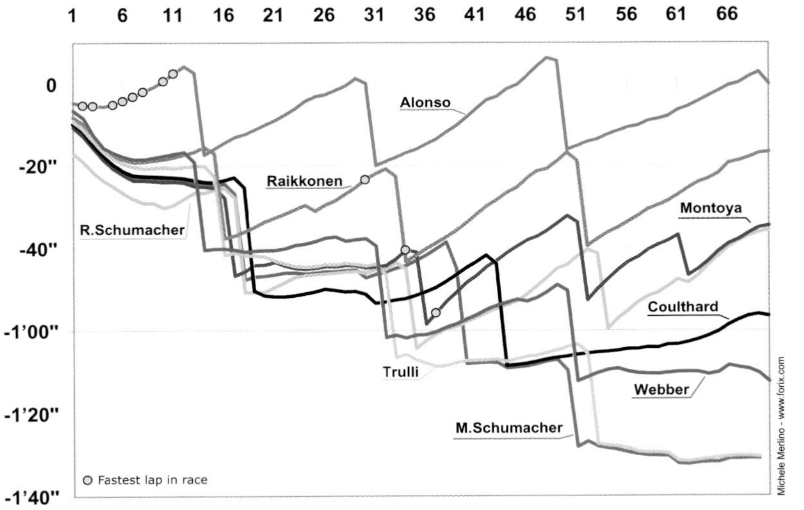

Lap chart

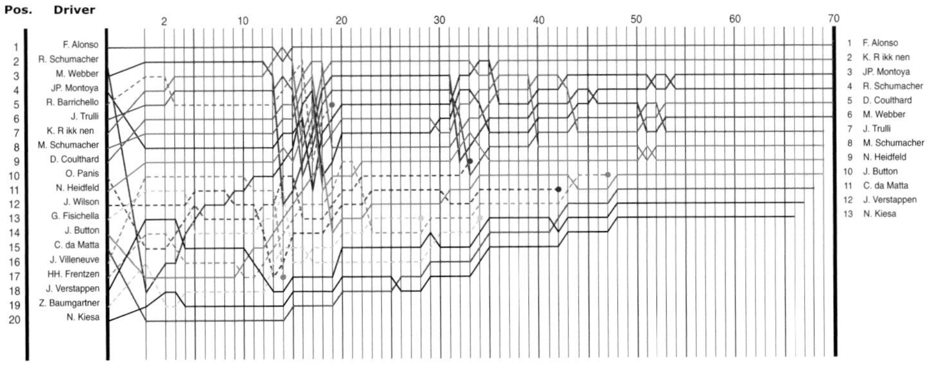

Championship after thirteen rounds

Drivers

1. M. Schumacher ....(4 wins)................72
2. J.P. Montoya.............(2 wins)................71
3. K. Räikkönen ....(1 win) 70
4. R. Schumacher..........(2 wins)................58
5. F. Alonso ....(1 win) 54
6. R. Barrichello ....(1 win) 49
7. D. Coulthard ....(1 win) 45
8. J. Trulli 24
9. M. Webber..15
10. J. Button 12
11. G. Fisichella ....(1 win) 10
12. C. Da Matta...8
13. H-H. Frentzen..7
14. O. Panis 6
15. J. Villeneuve..3
16. N. Heidfeld..2
17. R. Firman..1
18. A. Pizzonia 0
19. J. Verstappen 0
20. J. Wilson..0
21. N. Kiesa...0
22. Z. Baumgartner.....................................-

Constructors

1. BMW Williams F1 Team ....(4 wins) 129
2. Scuderia Ferrari Marlboro ......(5 wins) 121
3. West McLaren Mercedes ....(2 wins) 115
4. Mild Seven Renault F1 Team ..(1 win) 78
5. Lucky Strike BAR Honda 15
6. Jaguar Racing..15
7. Panasonic Toyota Racing 14
8. Jordan Ford..........................(1 win) 11
9. Sauber Petronas..9
10. European Minardi Cosworth..........................0

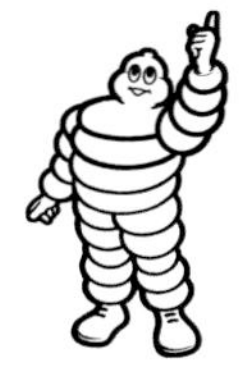

The circuit

Name	Hungaroring, Budapest
Date	August 24, 2003
Length	4381 meters
Distance	70 laps, 306,663 km
Weather	Sunny and hot, 28-31°c
Track temperature	40-47°c

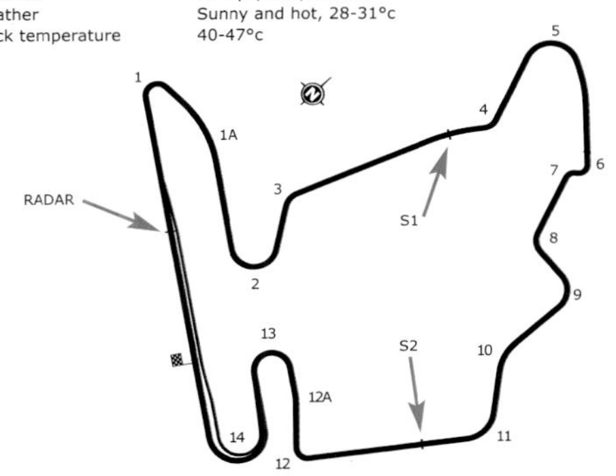

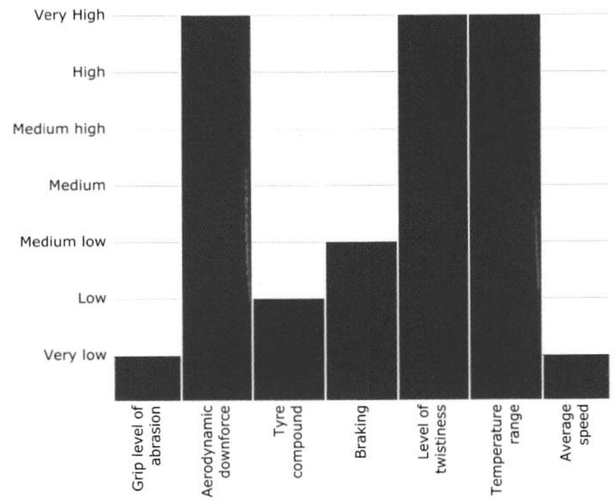

All results : © 2003 Formula One Administration Ltd,
6 Princes Gate, London, SW7 1QJ, England

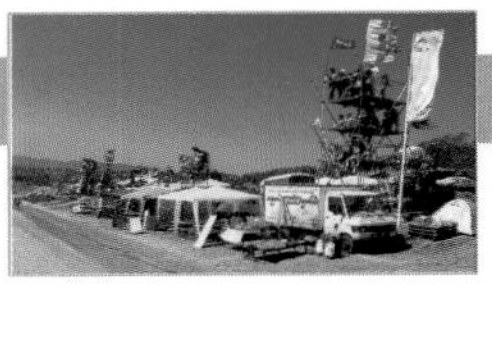

MICHAEL IS BACK!

After the politics of the preceding weeks, notably those concerning tyres, which threatened to wreck the end of the championship, Ferrari got both its drivers onto the podium after the Italian Grand Prix.
After five races without a win – he had not won since Canada, back in June – Michael Schumacher was back on track for the championship with a three point lead over Juan Pablo Montoya.
A triumph in Monza.

> After a very serious accident in testing at this track the previous week, Ralf Schumacher did not feel well after Friday's qualifying and decided to scratch from the rest of the Italian Grand Prix weekend to recuperate. It also meant that he effectively gave up any hopes he had of taking the world championship title. This meant that Williams test and reserve driver, Marc Gene, was brought in to replace him for the event (in photo with comments from Juan Pablo Montoya.) As he had not run on Friday, he was the first man out of pit lane for Saturday's qualifying, in which he finished fifth. An excellent performance, especially as the track was still dirty when he made his run. *"When I got the phone call this morning, to tell me that I was racing, I thought I was still dreaming,"* commented Gene on the subject of his last-minute call up. Luckily for the Spaniard, he had driven at Monza the previous week in testing and already had a good idea about set-up.

Michael Schumacher back on pole

Under the late summer sun at Monza, the crowd was white hot with expectation, hoping to see the Ferraris back on top.

For the past few weeks, the red cars had lacked speed. Michael Schumacher's last pole position dated back to the Austrian Grand Prix in May. Therefore, his pole at Monza, just ahead of Juan Pablo Montoya, was greeted with much enthusiasm. *"I think it was just the right moment to get back on pole,"* reckoned Michael

Schumacher after qualifying. *"Everything went well today."* Just behind him, it was a tiny mistake at the Ascari chicane which robbed Juan Pablo Montoya of the best time, by just 51 thousandths of a second. That is the equivalent of 3.6 metres over the 5.8 kilometre lap! *"I am sure the car will be competitive tomorrow, we have a very good strategy and we should be in good shape in the race,"* the Columbian assured his audience.

Eighth place in qualifying for David Coulthard. He was behind Kimi Räikkönen for the sixth consecutive time and it wasn't over yet.

> v

Second and last grand prix of the season for Zsolt Baumgartner, and 18th spot on the grid.

v

In brief

> The organisers of the first Bahrain Grand Prix, scheduled for 4th April 2004, put on a big show. On Friday evening, they organised a sumptuous party against the backdrop of the Villa Reale palace in Monza. Hundreds of guests got the chance to sample a taste of the country, as the organisers had chartered a Boeing 747 to bring along Bedouin tents, carpets and other props to recreate the atmosphere of the desert in the royal park at Monza.

Major moves behind the scenes

Last European leg of the world championship and the first event after the testing break, the Italian Grand Prix provided the ideal backdrop for a variety of high-level meetings.

The Monza paddock was therefore full of directors and company presidents, be they from the major car manufacturers, suppliers and sponsors, both big and small.

Behind closed doors, a political battle raged in the upper echelons of F1. The major car companies in F1 met yet again with the three banks (Deutsche Bank, Bayerische Landesbank and Morgan Grenfell) who hold 80% of SLEC, the holding company owned by the F1 commercial rights

holder, Bernie Ecclestone.

The banks wanted to unload their shares, which had cost them 1.8 billion dollars. But on Friday, another attempt at reaching agreement collapsed. The constructors were not prepared to pay for SLEC's expensive shares and were still talking about setting up their own championship. As for the banks, they wanted to recoup their investment. *"These banks understand nothing about motor sport,"* said a vociferous Ron Dennis. *"They are asking too much and we are heading for disaster. It is the future of F1 which is at stake here and I am worried that we will not reach an agreement."*

Starting grid

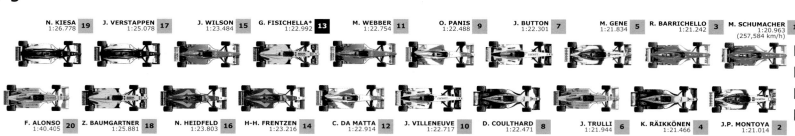

* G. FISICHELLA stalls on the formation lap. He manages to get going, but pits and starts from there.

| N. KIESA 19 | J. VERSTAPPEN 17 | J. WILSON 15 | G. FISICHELLA* 13 | M. WEBBER 11 | O. PANIS 9 | J. BUTTON 7 | M. GENE 5 | R. BARRICHELLO 3 | M. SCHUMACHER 1 |
| 1:26.778 | 1:25.078 | 1:23.484 | 1:22.992 | 1:22.754 | 1:22.488 | 1:22.301 | 1:21.834 | 1:21.242 | 1:20.963 (257,584 km/h) |

| F. ALONSO 20 | Z. BAUMGARTNER 18 | N. HEIDFELD 16 | H-H. FRENTZEN 14 | C. DA MATTA 12 | J. VILLENEUVE 10 | D. COULTHARD 8 | J. TRULLI 6 | K. RÄIKKÖNEN 4 | J.P. MONTOYA 2 |
| 1:40.405 | 1:25.881 | 1:23.803 | 1:23.216 | 1:22.914 | 1:22.717 | 1:22.471 | 1:21.944 | 1:21.466 | 1:21.014 |

^
A good start from pole position for Michael Schumacher. "We have improved our launch control system and it was much better than usual," he explained. "It was very tight at the first corner. I locked my brakes and nearly missed the chicane."

The best ever day in the life of a five times world champion

Scuderia Ferrari had arrived at Monza in a jittery mood. At the previous grand prix in Hungary, Michael Schumacher could only finish eighth, having been lapped by the winner. It seemed that the F2003-GA was going backwards in performance terms and the German had not won since Canada in June. Three weeks had elapsed since then. Three weeks of intensive work during which the Scuderia had reviewed every aspect of the car, from the rear end to the V10 engine. The Bridgestone engineers had also been hard at work, developing their tyres. All this effort resulted in Michael Schumacher taking his fifth win of the season. In fact, once the race was underway, the only moment of doubt came at the second corner. Juan Pablo Montoya tried the impossible in attempting to pass Michael Schumacher at the Roggia chicane. The German managed to keep the Colombian at bay and from then on, the race was transformed into a procession, as Montoya tried but failed to

get on terms with Schumacher. Although he occasionally got very close to the Ferrari, Montoya only managed to lead for a single lap, during the pit stops. *"After my first pit stop, I closed right up to Michael,"* explained the Colombian. *"After the second stop, I was one second behind and was closing by two to three tenths per lap. It was looking good, before I lost a lot of time in traffic. It seemed as though I was stuck behind Frentzen for a year. It was crazy. There were blue flags everywhere and on the straight, it looked like a military parade, but he would not move. I lost four seconds at once and after that, I decided to make sure of second place."* In the championship, the number of contenders had dropped to just three. Having finished second, Montoya was now three points down on the Ferrari driver. *"It's not serious,"* he maintained. *"After all, I knew I could not win all the races and I only gave two points away to Michael. The next grand prix could finish in the reverse

order to this one. All I can do is carry on fighting."*
For Michael Schumacher, after so many barren races, this victory came as a big relief. *"I think this might be the best day of my life. This summer has been terrible because of the testing ban. Everyone worked very hard back at the factory, in an incredible way, giving more than a hundred percent. I thank all of them."* The German was in confident mood for the remaining two races. *"The engine guys have made a huge step forward. It seems that we suffer more on high downforce circuits, which is not the case at Indianapolis or Suzuka."* Ferrari boss, Jean Todt, was naturally in seventh heaven. But he had not forgotten the recent arguments which had raged on the tyre front: *"Until 30th November, I reserve the right to have recourse to article 179.2 of the sporting code, which allows for previous results to be reconsidered,"* he declared on Sunday night.

<
A close call at the second chicane. Juan Pablo Montoya tried everything to pass Michael Schumacher, but to no avail. *"Juan (Pablo Montoya) came up alongside me and nearly got by. It was a tough fight but a fair one and I managed to keep the lead."*

Race summary

> The start is always a tense moment at Monza as the pack funnels down to the first chicane **(1)**.

> Alonso loses his front wing after colliding with Verstappen, but he stages a superb comeback to finish 8th **(2)**.

> Still the opening lap and Montoya tries his luck with M. Schumacher. It was breathtaking, but the German keeps the lead **(3)**.

> Da Matta has a spectacular "off" after a tyre explodes **(4)**.

> Webber fought all race long to pick up the points for 7th place **(5)**.

> Marc Gene replaces Ralf Schumacher at Williams. The reserve driver puts in a solid performance to finish 5th **(6)**.

> M. Schumacher celebrates with Ross Brawn. The Reds regain the upper hand **(7)**.

The mechanics of pleasure

In the 21st century, Formula 1 is getting ever more sophisticated. The big teams' wind tunnels operate 24 hours a day, seven days a week. Electronics rule the roost. Old style mechanical work has not disappeared completely however and is as photogenic as ever.

The tyre war will not take place

The two weeks prior to the Italian Grand Prix had not been straightforward for Pascal Vasselon, the man in charge of Michelin's Formula 1 programme, as his colleagues had to face a drama which burst onto the stage a few days after the Hungarian Grand Prix. After photos of used Michelin tyres were brought to their attention, the FIA decided to modify regulations regarding tyre width. From now on, the tyre's contact patch with the track surface, which could not exceed 27 centimetres, would be checked after the race as well as when new. A tyre's natural tendency under load is to get crushed, thus increasing in width during the race.

This change only affected Michelin as the Bridgestone construction was clearly narrower.

Up until then, the French company's tyres had always met with approval from the FIA. It was impossible to make such a radical change to the tyre construction in just two weeks and there was a risk of disqualification hanging over Williams, McLaren and the other Michelin runners come Sunday night after the race. Why the devil had the Japanese company waited 38 grands prix (since the Michelin tyres were first approved by the FIA) to point this out? It was a mystery. The fact that Michael Schumacher was losing ground in the championship was a coincidence which was too obvious to ignore.

Luckily, in the range of tyres which Michelin had planned to test at Monza in the week prior to the grand prix, a new construction meant that the tyres did not grow in width to the same extent as the older ones.

The FIA checked these new tyres on the Monday and approved them. *"The FIA has declared the matter to be closed, so I do not think we run the risk of disqualification,"* suggested Pascal Vasselon on Thursday evening. *"The new solution we have brought here even brings a slight increase in performance, while at the same time reducing the risk of exceeding the 27 centimetre rule."* All the teams contracted to Michelin thus chose to run on this tyre. The FIA had still not explained how it planned to measure the tyres after the race; a tricky procedure, virtually impossible to carry out with any precision. But it seemed that the risk of disqualification had been buried.

Indeed, there were no problems on this score after the Italian Grand Prix. The 2003 championship was spared a scandal, but it had been a close call.

David Richards to quit the BAR team?

Craig Pollock must have been laughing. Kicked out of the team which he had set up in December 2001, he was no longer a regular visitor to the Formula 1 grands prix. He was still Jacques Villeneuve's manager, but was kept busy running his American ChampCar team and was rumoured to be taking over

ownership of the championship itself in the next few years. Since David Richards had taken over the reins at BAR, there had no great improvement in the team's performance. The Englishman had promised BAT not to over spend on the reduced budget and now news emerged that he had just asked for a 50 million dollar extension to complete the 2003 season. BAT was also not too happy with the fact that Richards was often absent, as he turned his attention to his other projects, including Prodrive and ISC and his involvement in the World Rally Championship.

Richards was therefore under increased pressure. At Monza, BAT boss, Michael Broughton had turned up to see for himself what needed to be done. This immediately prompted rumours in the paddock that Richards was on the way out. It must have amused Craig Pollock no end, as he relaxed in his Alpine chalet.

Practice

All the time trials

N°	Driver	N° Chassis - Engine	Private testing	Pos.	Practice friday	Pos.	Qualifying friday	Pos.	Practice 1 saturday	Pos.	Practice 2 saturday	Pos.	Warm-up	Pos.	Qualifying saturday	Pos.
1.	Michael Schumacher	Ferrari F2003-GA 229			1:21.152	2	1:21.268	3	1:21.623	1	1:21.586	2	1:27.906	19	1:20.963	1
2.	Rubens Barrichello	Ferrari F2003-GA 233			1:21.001	1	1:20.784	2	1:22.146	2	1:22.108	5	1:21.633	1	1:21.242	3
3.	Juan Pablo Montoya	Williams FW25 06 - BMW			1:21.556	4	1:20.656	1	1:22.646	5	1:21.468	1	1:21.819	2	1:21.014	2
4.	Ralf Schumacher	Williams FW25 07 - BMW			1:22.312	9										
5.	David Coulthard	McLaren MP4-17D 08 - Mercedes			1:21.675	5	1:23.154	14	1:22:552	3	1:22.134	6	1:22.480	5	1:22.471	8
6.	Kimi Räikkönen	McLaren MP4-17D 09 - Mercedes			1:21.318	3	1:21.966	5	1:22.718	7	1:22.091	4	1:22.512	6	1:21.466	4
7.	Jarno Trulli	Renault R23B-05	1:22.083	1	1:22.335	10	1:22.034	7	1:22.735	9	1:22.333	8	1:22.581	8	1:21.944	6
8.	Fernando Alonso	Renault R23B-06	1:22.507	2	1:22.100	8	1:22.103	8	1:22.731	8	1:22.399	10	1:22.591	9	1:40.405	20
9.	Nick Heidfeld	Sauber C22-01 - Petronas			1:22.821	13	1:22.547	12	1:24.134	14	1:23.846	15	1:24.157	16	1:23.803	16
10.	Heinz-Harald Frentzen	Sauber C22-02 - Petronas			1:22.929	14	1:22.203	9	1:23.572	12	1:23.461	14	1:23.382	13	1:23.216	14
11.	Giancarlo Fisichella	Jordan EJ13-05 - Ford	1:24.026	7	1:23.794	17	1:24.179	16	1:25.194	16	1:24.627	17	1:23.270	11	1:22.992	13
12.	Zsolt Baumgartner	Jordan EJ13-04 - Ford	1:25.210	9	1:24.891	19	1:24.872	17	1:26.295	19	1:25.916	19	1:26.363	17	1:25.881	18
14.	Mark Webber	Jaguar R4-04 & 03	1:23.191	4	1:22.368	11	1:21.966	6	1:24.454	15	1:23.294	13	1:23.378	12	1:22.754	11
15.	Justin Wilson	Jaguar R4-05	1:23.541	5	1:23.478	16	1:23.609	15	1:23.955	13	1:24.049	16	1:23.601	15	1:23.484	15
16.	Jacques Villeneuve	BAR 005-06 - Honda			1:23.151	15	1:22.858	13	1:23.120	10	1:22.906	11	1:22.472	4	1:22.717	10
17.	Jenson Button	BAR 005-04 - Honda			1:21.913	7	1:22.495	11	1:22.642	4	1:22.378	9	1:22.462	3	1:22.301	7
18.	Nicolas Kiesa	Minardi PS03/01 - Cosworth	1:26.296	10	1:26.903	20	1:26.299	18	1:25.870	17	1:26.160	20	1:27.384	18	1:26.778	19
19.	Jos Verstappen	Minardi PS03/02 - Cosworth	1:23.999	6	1:24.652	18			1:25.934	18	1:24.837	18	1:27.906	20	1:25.078	17
20.	Olivier Panis	Toyota TF103/07			1:22.584	12	1:22.372	10	1:26.295	20	1:22.321	7	1:23.095	10	1:22.488	9
21.	Cristiano da Matta	Toyota TF103/04			1:21.881	6	1:21.829	4	1:23.312	11	1:23.195	12	1:23.467	14	1:22.914	12
34.	Allan McNish	Renault R23B-04	1:22.533	3												
39.	Gianmaria Bruni	Minardi PS03/03 - Cosworth	1:24.318	8												
4.	Marc Gené	Williams FW25 07 - BMW							1:22.685	6	1:21.928	3	1:22.534	7	1:21.834	5

Maximum speed

N°	Driver	P1 Qualifs	Pos.	P1 Race	Pos.	P2 Qualifs	Pos.	P2 Race	Pos.	Finish Qualifs	Pos.	Finish Race	Pos.	Trap Qualifs	Pos.	Trap Race	Pos.
1.	M. Schumacher	348,2	1	349,9	4	346,0	3	352,1	2	330,0	2	332,1	3	362,5	1	368,8	1
2.	R. Barrichello	347,9	2	351,2	3	346,1	1	352,8	2	330,2	1	334,1	1	362,1	2	367,0	3
3.	J.P. Montoya	345,7	4	347,2	8	345,1	4	348,6	9	328,3	4	330,0	7	357,8	6	363,3	7
4.	M. Gené	345,9	3	356,9	1	346,0	2	350,6	4	328,5	3	330,9	4	358,3	4	367,9	2
5.	D. Coulthard	343,7	6	348,9	6	344,3	5	349,5	8	326,4	7	330,4	6	357,9	5	364,6	5
6.	K. Räikkönen	344,8	6	349,8	5	344,1	6	350,3	5	327,9	5	333,4	2	358,4	3	366,3	4
7.	J. Trulli	334,9	15	336,4	19	335,5	15			322,0	11			345,8	17	294,9	20
8.	F. Alonso	327,5	20	342,8	12	332,1	18	342,2	14	321,3	13	321,7	13	347,8	13	357,6	13
9.	N. Heidfeld	337,6	11	345,6	10	337,2	14	344,8	12	320,5	14	324,6	12	347,7	14	360,4	9
10.	H-H. Frentzen	339,1	9	341,7	13	339,3	10	346,7	10	319,7	15	325,0	11	349,4	11	359,2	12
11.	G. Fisichella	335,2	14	338,0	18	337,2	13	340,4	17	321,9	12	320,0	18	345,8	16	354,4	16
12.	Z. Baumgartner	331,1	19	338,1	17	332,1	17	341,1	15	315,8	19	321,3	15	344,2	18	354,3	17
14.	M. Webber	331,8	17	339,0	16	331,5	19	336,3	18	315,9	18	321,1	16	338,7	19	352,0	18
15.	J. Wilson	331,4	18	330,3	20	330,1	20	331,6	19	313,6	20	313,8	19	336,1	20	343,6	19
16.	J. Villeneuve	338,2	10	344,8	11	339,4	9	346,4	11	323,2	10	328,6	9	348,9	12	359,6	11
17.	J. Button	336,7	12	347,3	7	339,1	11	349,5	7	324,3	9	329,2	8	352,3	9	362,5	8
18.	N. Kiesa	332,0	16	340,3	14	333,7	16	342,6	13	317,2	17	321,3	14	346,1	15	355,1	15
19.	J. Verstappen	336,0	13	339,1	15	337,9	12	340,9	16	319,6	16	320,2	17	351,2	10	355,8	14
20.	O. Panis	342,7	7	346,9	9	343,2	7	349,6	6	327,2	6	330,5	5	355,6	7	360,0	10
21.	C. Da Matta	342,7	8	351,9	2	340,0	8	351,4	3	325,1	8	328,5	10	353,6	8	363,5	6

Race

Classification & Retirements

Pos.	Driver	Team	Lap	Time	Average
1.	M. Schumacher	Ferrari	53	1:14:19.838	247,585 km/h
2.	J.P. Montoya	Williams BMW	53	+ 5.294	247,292 km/h
3.	R. Barrichello	Ferrari	53	+ 11.835	246,930 km/h
4.	K. Räikkönen	McLaren Mercedes	53	+ 12.834	246,875 km/h
5.	M. Gené	Williams BMW	53	+ 27.891	246,046 km/h
6.	J. Villeneuve	BAR Honda	52	1 lap	242,351 km/h
7.	M. Webber	Jaguar	52	1 lap	241,475 km/h
8.	F. Alonso	Renault	52	1 lap	241,316 km/h
9.	N. Heidfeld	Sauber Petronas	52	1 lap	241,208 km/h
10.	G. Fisichella	Jordan Ford	52	1 lap	238,725 km/h
11.	Z. Baumgartner	Jordan Ford	51	2 laps	236,323 km/h
12.	N. Kiesa	Minardi Cosworth	51	2 laps	234,772 km/h
13.	H-H. Frentzen	Sauber Petronas	50	3 laps	241,611 km/h

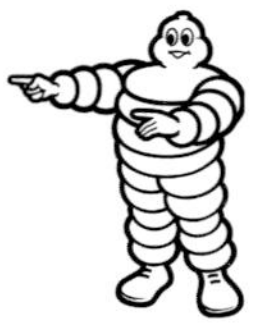

Driver	Team		Reason
D. Coulthard	McLaren Mercedes	46	Engine cuts out because of low fuel pressure
O. Panis	Toyota	36	Brake problem
J. Verstappen	Minardi Cosworth	28	Oil leak after radiator holed
J. Button	BAR Honda	25	Loss of 2nd gear, then 1st, 6th and 7th
C. Da Matta	Toyota	4	Left rear tyre fails, spins
J. Wilson	Jaguar	3	Gearbox then transmission problem
J. Trulli	Renault	1	Hydraulic problem

Fastest laps

	Driver	Time	Lap	Average
1.	M. Schumacher	1:21.832	14	254,848 km/h
2.	K. Räikkönen	1:22.032	32	254,227 km/h
3.	J.P. Montoya	1:22.126	31	253,936 km/h
4.	FR. Barrichello	1:22.171	13	253,797 km/h
5.	M. Gené	1:22.413	12	253,052 km/h
6.	D. Coulthard	1:22.427	10	253,009 km/h
7.	J. Villeneuve	1:23.039	13	251,144 km/h
8.	F. Alonso	1:23.195	47	250,673 km/h
9.	J. Button	1:23.225	13	250,583 km/h
10.	O. Panis	1:23.303	10	250,348 km/h
11.	H-H. Frentzen	1:23.518	14	249,704 km/h
12.	M. Webber	1:23.778	10	248,929 km/h
13.	N. Heidfeld	1:24.225	9	247,608 km/h
14.	G. Fisichella	1:24.936	52	244,967 km/h
15.	Z. Baumgartner	1:25.549	38	243,776 km/h
16.	J. Verstappen	1:25.816	22	243,017 Km/h
17.	N. Kiesa	1:26.127	49	242,140 Km/h
18.	C. Da Matta	1:26.148	3	242,081 Km/h
19.	J. Wilson	1:59.265	2	174,861 Km/h

Pit stops

	Driver	Time	Lap	Stop n°
1.	F. Alonso	45.153	1	1
2.	J. Verstappen	39.636	1	1
3.	D. Coulthard	31.145	11	1
4.	O. Panis	31.058	11	1
5.	K. Räikkönen	30.863	13	1
6.	M. Gené	30.633	13	1
7.	M. Webber	31.177	13	1
8.	N. Heidfeld	31.739	13	1
9.	N. Kiesa	31.855	13	1
10.	R. Barrichello	29.735	14	1
11.	M. Schumacher	30.032	15	1
12.	J. Button	31.383	15	1
13.	H-H. Frentzen	32.081	15	1
14.	J.P. Montoya	29.599	16	1
15.	J. Verstappen	44.353	16	2
16.	Z. Baumgartner	32.069	19	1
17.	G. Fisichella	33.551	27	1
18.	J. Verstappen	33.812	26	3
19.	F. Alonso	32.480	29	2
20.	R. Barrichello	31.342	31	2
21.	O. Panis	31.585	31	2
22.	J.P. Montoya	30.136	32	2
23.	D. Coulthard	29.967	32	2
24.	M. Webber	31.173	33	2
25.	N. Kiesa	32.566	32	2
26.	M. Schumacher	30.679	34	2
27.	K. Raikkonen	30.900	34	2
28.	H-H. Frentzen	30.873	34	2
29.	M. Gené	31.255	35	2
30.	N. Heidfeld	29.333	35	2
31.	Z. Baumgrtner	30.961	35	2

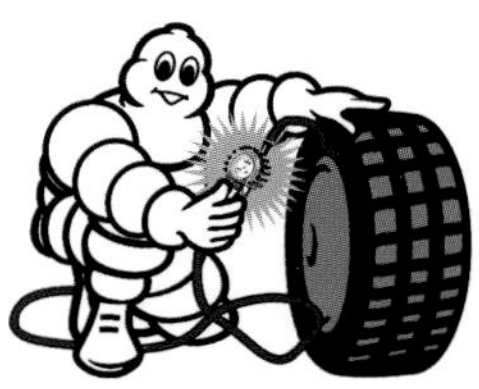

Race leaders

Driver	Laps in the lead	Nber of Laps
M. Schumacher	1 > 15	15
J.P. Montoya	16	1
M. Schumacher	17 > 53	37

Driver	Nber of Laps	Kilometers
M. Schumacher	52	300,927 km
J.P. Montoya	1	5,793 km

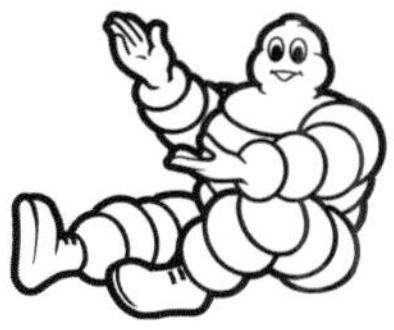

Lap chart

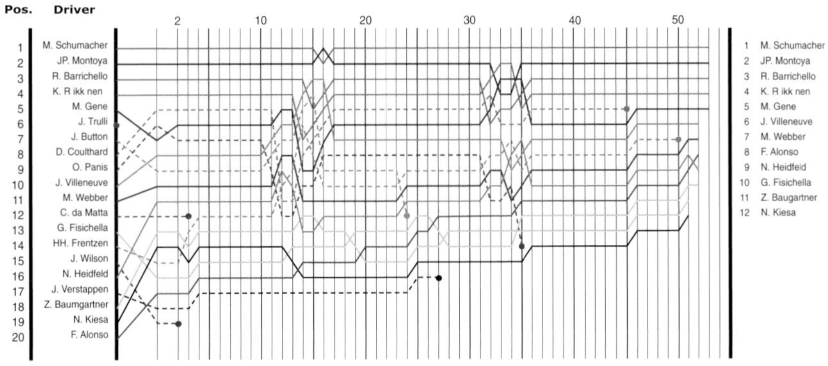

Gaps on the leader board

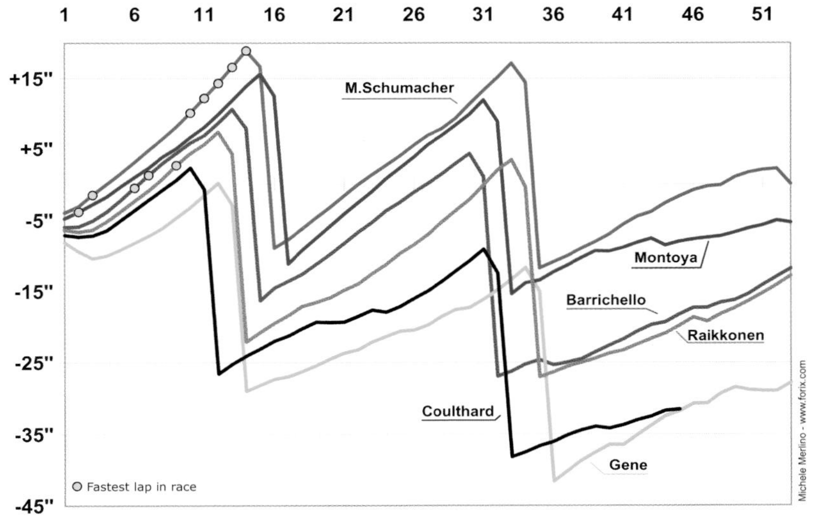

Championship after fourteen rounds

Drivers

1. M. Schumacher ....(5 wins)................82
2. J.P. Montoya.............(2 wins)................79
3. K. Räikkönen ....(1 win) 75
4. R. Schumacher..........(2 wins)................58
5. R. Barrichello ....(1 win) 55
6. F. Alonso ....(1 win) 55
7. D. Coulthard ....(1 win) 45
8. J. Trulli 24
9. M. Webber...17
10. J. Button 12
11. G. Fisichella ....(1 win) 10
12. C. Da Matta..8
13. H-H. Frentzen...7
14. O. Panis 6
15. J. Villeneuve...6
16. M. Gené..4
17. N. Heidfeld 2
18. R. Firman..1
19. A. Pizzonia 0
20. J. Verstappen 0
21. J. Wilson...0
22. Z. Baumgartner 0
23. N. Kiesa..0

Constructors

1. BMW Williams F1 Team ....(4 wins) 141
2. Scuderia Ferrari Marlboro ......(6 wins) 137
3. West McLaren Mercedes........(2 wins) 120
4. Mild Seven Renault F1 Team ..(1 win) 79
5. Lucky Strike BAR Honda 18
6. Jaguar Racing..17
7. Panasonic Toyota Racing 14
8. Jordan Ford........................(1 win) 11
9. Sauber Petronas...9
10. European Minardi Cosworth.........................0

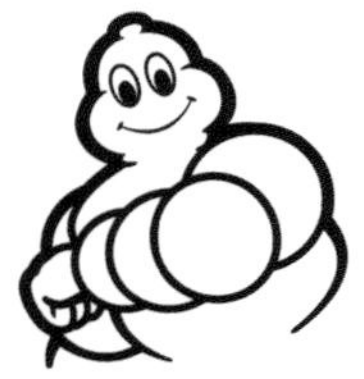

The circuit

Name	Autodromo nazionale Monza
Date	September 14, 2003
Length	5793 meters
Distance	53 laps, 306,720 km
Weather	Sunny and hot, 23-24°c
Track temperature	41-43°c

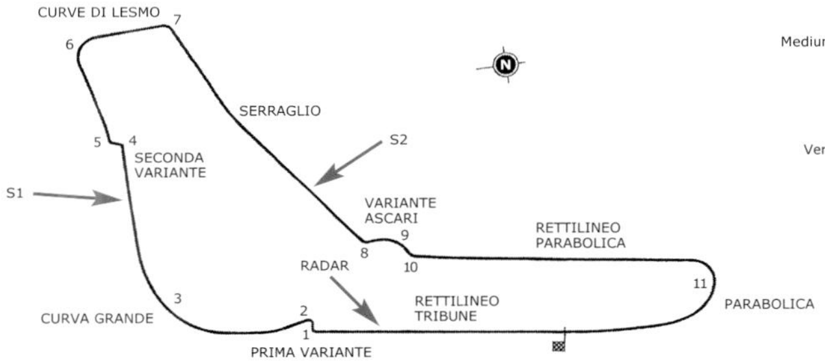

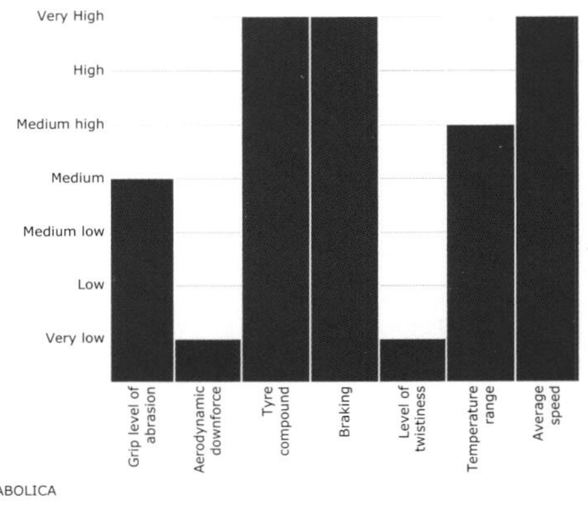

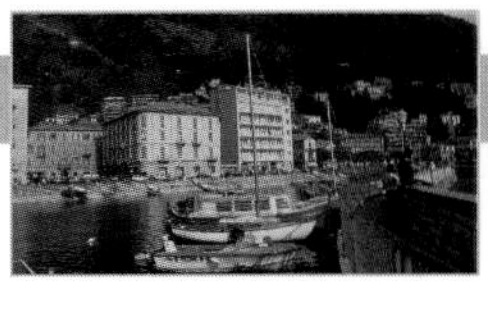

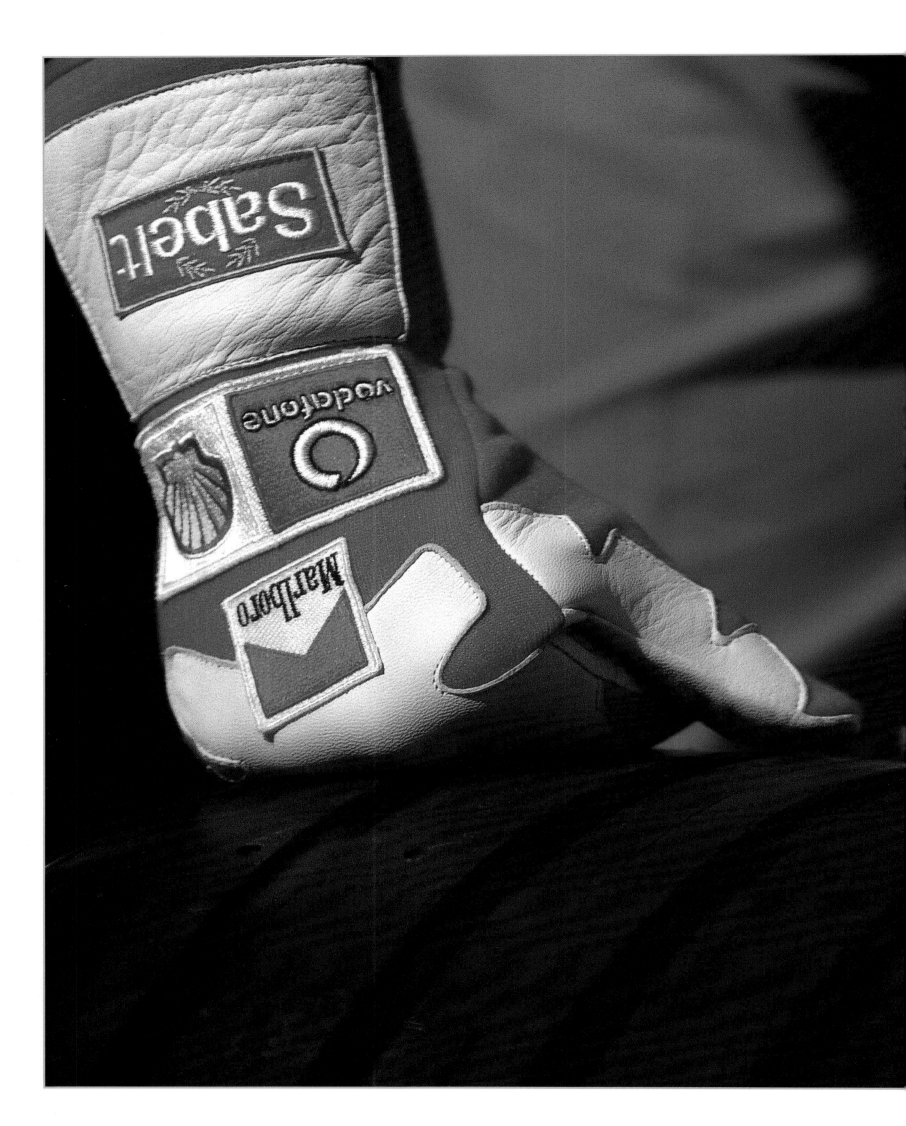

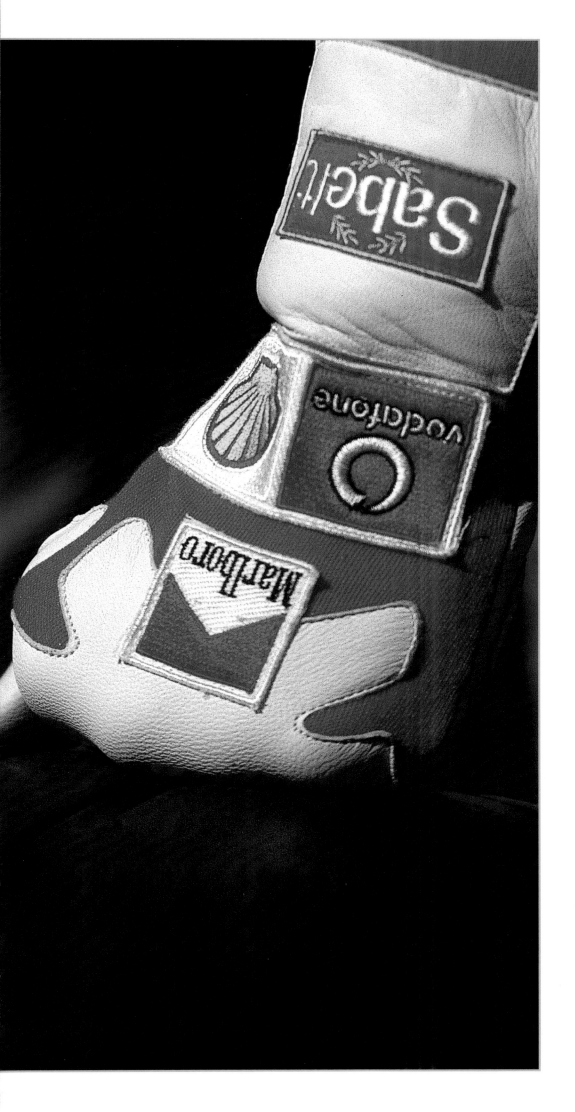

THE SCUDERIA STRIKES A DECISIVE BLOW

Having won at Indianapolis, Michael Schumacher now only needed one little point to take his sixth world championship title. Having finished second, Kimi Raikkonen still had a mathematical chance of becoming world champion at the final round in Suzuka. But the triumphal march of the red cars, partly helped by the rain which fell on the Brickyard, had pretty much put the title out of anyone else's reach. It had certainly wiped out any chance Juan Pablo Montoya might have been clinging onto and he was now out of the hunt for the title.

> Second pole of the season for Kimi Räikkönen. It came just in time for the Finn, as the world championship entered its decisive stage.

> Indianapolis town centre, with its restaurants and shopping malls was where you could find all the Formula 1 folk when they were off-duty.

Kimi Räikkönen on pole

With his faraway look and his inbred timidity, Kimi Räikkönen was very much regarded as the anti-hero, whose chances of taking the title could not be taken very seriously. But the score sheet delivered another message. Quietly and systematically racking up the points, the Finn was only giving away seven to Michael Schumacher and four to Juan Pablo Montoya on the eve of the penultimate round of the season.

On Saturday, having taken pole position, his second of the season, the Finn clung firmly to his usual phlegmatic approach. *"I was not very happy with the car on Friday, but we managed to sort it in time for qualifying and there we are. I think we have found a good strategy for the race, but it will be a long one. We will see what happens. In any case I have more to win than to lose. I am not too bothered about the championship, but I will try and do my best."* Michael Schumacher's most dangerous adversary, Juan Pablo Montoya was fourth on the grid, on the dirty side of the track.

No love lost at Indianapolis

Formula 1 and Uncle Sam seem to mix as well as oil and water. The five year contract which tied the Indianapolis Speedway and Bernie Ecclestone's SLEC company was due to come to an end in 2004. The event was a flop. In order to avoid the embarrassment of empty grandstands, this year, the organisers had been forced to offer thousands of seats to schools, institutions and local clubs. In 2000, the hotels were all packed and charging way over the odds, but this time there were plenty of free rooms. As if the event did not look sick enough as it was, the 2004 race has been scheduled for June, just three weeks after the famous 500 Miles race, which is the main event of the year at Indy. It looked as though the 2004 Grand Prix would have even less spectators which would entail a bigger financial loss. It was as good as signing a death warrant for the United States Grand Prix.

On Thursday, the three drivers still in the running for the world title, posed with Bernie Ecclestone.
∨

Starting grid

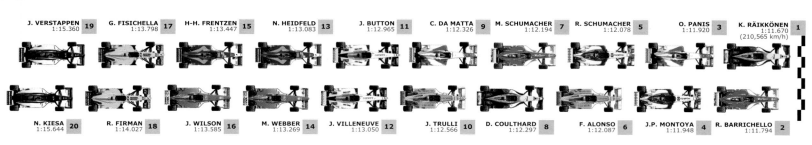

Row 1 (odd)		Row 2 (even)	
J. VERSTAPPEN 1:15.360 — 19		N. KIESA 1:15.644 — 20	
G. FISICHELLA 1:13.798 — 17		R. FIRMAN 1:14.027 — 18	
H-H. FRENTZEN 1:13.447 — 15		J. WILSON 1:13.585 — 16	
N. HEIDFELD 1:13.083 — 13		M. WEBBER 1:13.269 — 14	
J. BUTTON 1:12.965 — 11		J. VILLENEUVE 1:13.050 — 12	
C. DA MATTA 1:12.326 — 9		J. TRULLI 1:12.566 — 10	
M. SCHUMACHER 1:12.194 — 7		D. COULTHARD 1:12.297 — 8	
R. SCHUMACHER 1:12.078 — 5		F. ALONSO 1:12.087 — 6	
O. PANIS 1:11.920 — 3		J.P. MONTOYA 1:11.948 — 4	
K. RÄIKKÖNEN 1:11.670 (210,565 km/h) — 1		R. BARRICHELLO 1:11.794 — 2	

the race

< Start: the drivers on the left side of the track get away better than their colleagues on the right side. Out in front, Rubens Barrichello makes a very bad start and slows Juan Pablo Montoya.

Michael Schumacher a point away from glory

The Indianapolis Speedway hosted a race which turned out to be truly chaotic. The excitement came right at the start with plenty of overtaking all the way down the order. Olivier Panis for example, found himself running second in the early stages, but was passed first by Ralf Schumacher, then by brother Michael, before making his first pit-stop. Back on track, the Frenchman stopped a further three times before retiring on lap 27.

Michael Schumacher was leading on lap 7, when the rain arrived to spoil his plans as he was passed, first by David Coulthard's McLaren and then by Juan Pablo Montoya's Williams. The Colombian had come from a long way back, after surviving a collision with Rubens Barrichello. It was around lap 18 that the light rain turned into a real shower. When the skies cleared again ten laps later, Jenson Button found himself leading

from Heinz-Harald Frentzen, as both men had chosen just the right moment to come in to fit rain tyres.

From then on and after Button retired, for Michael Schumacher it was just a case of bringing his car home. *"This was a very important day and a great result as far as the championship is concerned,"* he claimed in the post race press conference. *"I am very happy, it is so fantastic. In Monza, I experienced the best day of my life, but today is also very important. It is a crucial moment for the championship."*

His only mistake on the day was to refit *"dry"* tyres at his first pit-stop at the moment the rain intensified. *"We had already seen this situation before here, when the rain comes and goes,"* he continued. *"It was a gamble and my rivals made the same mistake. But afterwards, in the wet, the car was fantastic. We knew our rain tyres would*

work better than those of our rivals, but so far this season, we had not been able to use them." Behind the winner came Kimi Räikkönen, who managed to claw his way back up the order to finish second in his McLaren. The Finn had led most of the first part of the race and could no doubt have won, but for the weather. *"We were very unlucky with the weather,"* he confirmed. *"But what could I do about that? I fought hard and did my best. The situation is not so good now, because Michael has a big lead in the championship. It will be difficult. But having said that, anything can happen at Suzuka."* With a nine point lead over the Finn, Michael Schumacher now only needed to score a single point to become world champion. *"It is a very comfortable position for me of course, but you never know,"* he commented. *"First we will have to finish the race. Luckily, we have a very reliable car and I am very optimistic. I would go so far as to say that my aim at Suzuka will be to win, not just to score one little point."*

All is lost for Juan Pablo

All was now lost for Juan Pablo Montoya, as he was no longer in the running for the world championship title. After an average start, the Colombian was given a penalty for having nudged Rubens Barrichello. It was a shame for the thousands of South Americans who had made the trip to Indianapolis to support him.

Two Ferraris on the podium: a triumph for the Scuderia <

Magnificent result for the Sauber team, which got both its cars home in the points, with one driver on the podium. v

Race summary

> Despite a poor grid position, M. Schumacher is fourth at the first corner. He sets off in pursuit of the leaders (1).

> Montoya's championship hopes are dashed at this precise moment. He hits Barrichello in a dubious passing move

and will be penalised. His race is effectively over (2).

> The rain starts to fall and M. Schumacher is

struggling up against the Michelin runners. He bides his time and picks them off one by one, as the track dries (3).

> Button makes the most of the weather to lead, ahead of the Saubers (4).

> Trulli is brilliant in the

rain and finishes 4th (5).

> Frentzen celebrates 3rd place in parc ferme: an unexpected

result (6).

> A winning smile, as M. Schumacher knows the title is getting closer (7).

The Saubers emerge from the shadows

What a day for the Sauber team. Its cars had barely scored any points since the early part of the season, apart from a single point for eighth place at the Nurburgring. But in Indy, a handy strategy and a whiff of luck when the rain arrived, saw both drivers finish in the points.

> A backlit shot of David Coulthard. He qualified eighth, while his team-mate was on pole position. The Scotsman retired from the race with gearbox problems.

(right) Retirement for Jenson Button, who waves to the crowd at Indianapolis. The Englishman had led the race between laps 23 and 37!
(below) Kimi Räikkönen duels with a Jaguar. This grand prix featured several overtaking moves.
∨

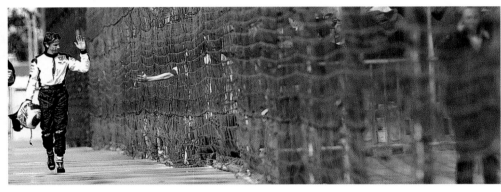

The Sauber team pulled from the sea

> It's in the bag. Michael Schumacher's sixth win of the season was also one of his most important victories, as it virtually assured him of the world championship title.

A Sauber on the podium! No one could quite believe it had happened, not even the members of the Swiss team. With a third place for Heinz-Harald Frentzen and a fifth for Nick Heidfeld, the squad picked up no less than ten points at once. It was enough to propel them from the penultimate and ninth place in the Constructors' championship straight up to fifth, ahead of BAR, Jaguar, Toyota and Jordan. It was a crazy and unexpected result for the team and Peter Sauber himself.

The team boss could hardly remember his own name in the Indianapolis paddock on Sunday night. *"This is really fantastic,"* he said with a smile as big as his eternal cigar. *"And it was all down to Heinz-Harald's savvy in deciding to fit rain tyres straight away."*

Indeed, it was the German driver who had come on the radio and asked his team to get the rain tyres ready when he pitted for fuel. Most of the other drivers had to make two pit-stops; the first for fuel and the second for rain tyres.

At the finish, Heinz-Harald could not find the words to describe his feelings. *"We have had a really difficult season,"* he began. *"This year, a podium finish never figured as one of our realistic targets. But the conditions were perfect today. I like the rain and we always seem more competitive in the wet. I had fun out there, but I was concentrating very hard to make sure I finished. We have already had a lot of mechanical failures this season when I was in the points, like at Monza, before being forced to retire. I tried not to think about it, not to think about the gearbox problems which have occurred so often. And it worked!"*

Nick Heidfeld's fifth place only added to the joy of the Swiss team. They will not forget lap 48 in a hurry; the lap when Frentzen found himself in the lead. *"We will party tonight,"* confirmed the German. *"We had not planned anything, so I am happy to accept any sort of invitation!"*

> Difficult moments for Michael Schumacher: the rain has begun to fall, but everyone is still running on "dry" tyres. The Ferrari did not shine in these conditions.
∨

results

Practice

All the time trials

N°	Driver	N° Chassis - Engine	Private testing	Pos.	Practice friday	Pos.	Qualifying friday	Pos.	Practice 1 saturday	Pos.	Practice 2 saturday	Pos.	Warm-up	Pos.	Qualifying saturday	Pos.
1.	Michael Schumacher	Ferrari F2003-GA 229			1:11.656	5	1:10.736	8		17	1:11.139	3	1:12.688	6	1:12.194	7
2.	Rubens Barrichello	Ferrari F2003-GA 233			1:11.499	4	1:09.835	2	1:12.510	4	1:11.112	1	1:12.537	5	1:11.794	2
3.	Juan Pablo Montoya	Williams FW25 06 - BMW			1:11.842	8	1:10.372	5	1:12.495	3	1:11.232	4	1:12.083	2	1:11.948	4
4.	Ralf Schumacher	Williams FW25 07 - BMW			1:11.339	2	1:10.222	4	1:12.468	2	1:12.060	9	1:12.958	9	1:12.078	5
5.	David Coulthard	McLaren MP4-17D 08 - Mercedes			1:11.967	10	1:10.450	6		20	1:11.355	5	1:12.951	8	1:12.297	8
6.	Kimi Räikkönen	McLaren MP4-17D 09 - Mercedes			1:11.876	9	1:10.756	9		19	1:11.493	6	1:12.177	4	1:11.670	1
7.	Jarno Trulli	Renault R23B-05	1:10.986	1	1:11.153	1	1:09.566	1	1:12.408	1	1:11.124	2		20	1:12.566	10
8.	Fernando Alonso	Renault R23B-06	1:10.987	2	1:11:692	6	1:10.556	7	1:12.741	5	1:12.135	10	1:12.079	1	1:12.087	6
9.	Nick Heidfeld	Sauber C22-01 - Petronas			1:13.601	18	1:17.768	15	1:14.439	13	1:12.380	12	1:13.612	13	1:13.083	13
10.	Heinz-Harald Frentzen	Sauber C22-03 - Petronas			1:13.881	19	1:13.541	13	1:13.363	8	1:12.680	14	1:13.925	14	1:13.447	15
11.	Giancarlo Fisichella	Jordan EJ13-05 - Ford	1:12.263	6	1:12.849	15	1:12.227	12	1:18.267	16	1:13.458	17	1:14.347	16	1:13.798	17
12.	Ralph Firman	Jordan EJ13-04 - Ford	1:12.762	7	1:13.167	16	1:19.383	17		18	1:13.749	18	1:14.508	17	1:14.027	18
14.	Mark Webber	Jaguar R4-03	1:11.586	4	1:11.794	7	1:10.081	3	1:13.573	9	1:11.800	8	1:13.019	10	1:13.269	14
15.	Justin Wilson	Jaguar R4-05	1:12.142	5	1:12.387	13	1:19.491	18	1:13.781	10	1:13.275	16	1:13.982	15	1:13.585	16
16.	Jacques Villeneuve	BAR 005-6 - Honda			1:12.656	14	1:18.547	16	1:13.960	11	1:12.931	15	1:13.600	12	1:13.050	12
17.	Jenson Button	BAR 005-4 - Honda			1:12.331	12	1:11.847	10	1:14.911	15	1:12.186	11	1:13.203	11	1:12.695	11
18.	Nicolas Kiesa	Minardi PS03/01 - Cosworth	1:13.655	10	1:13.537	17	1:21.973	19	1:14.493	14	1:14.781	20	1:15.258	19	1:15.644	20
19.	Jos Verstappen	Minardi PS03/02 - Cosworth	1:13.196	9	1:18.255	20		20	1:14.411	12	1:14.335	19	1:14.985	18	1:15.360	19
20.	Olivier Panis	Toyota TF103/08			1:11.388	3	1:17.666	14	1:13.306	7	1:11.758	7	1:12.127	3	1:11.920	3
21.	Cristiano da Matta	Toyota TF103/02			1:12.084	11	1:11.949	11	1:13.098	6	1:12.671	13	1:12.699	7	1:12.326	9
34.	Allan McNish	Renault R23B-04	1:11:253	3												
36.	Bjorn Wirdheim	Jordan EJ13-02 - Ford	1:13.678	11												
39.	Gianmaria Bruni	Minardi PS03/03 - Cosworth	1:13.129	8												

Maximum speed

N°	Driver	P1 Qualifs	Pos.	P1 Race	Pos.	P2 Qualifs	Pos.	P2 Race	Pos.	Finish Qualifs	Pos.	Finish Race	Pos.	Trap Qualifs	Pos.	Trap Race	Pos.
1.	M. Schumacher	262,7	6	267,3	4	163,0	20	174,1	5	337,5	4	347,1	3	344,8	4	355,7	2
2.	R. Barrichello	262,9	5	247,8	20	167,4	12	172,1	14	338,4	3	341,5	8	345,7	3	349,9	5
3.	J.P. Montoya	268,5	1	269,1	1	164,0	18	172,4	13	341,8	2	352,0	1	350,3	1	358,9	1
4.	R. Schumacher	263,2	4	268,7	2	163,3	19	170,0	17	342,7	1	347,1	2	350,1	2	352,8	3
5.	D. Coulthard	261,3	9	267,7	3	167,3	13	178,8	2	334,6	6	343,1	5	339,5	7	349,5	6
6.	K. Räikkönen	264,4	3	265,6	7	171,1	5	174,3	4	334,6	5	343,6	4	340,3	5	346,7	10
7.	J. Trulli	261,3	10	265,2	9	169,8	7	175,9	3	330,7	7	341,7	7	339,8	6	351,2	4
8.	F. Alonso	262,2	7	266,8	5	176,2	1	179,6	1	330,4	8	339,9	10	336,7	8	347,1	8
9.	N. Heidfeld	254,7	18	259,9	12	166,1	14	173,8	8	329,5	10	335,7	14	331,2	16	342,0	14
10.	H-H. Frentzen	253,8	19	253,4	19	172,3	4	173,3	10	328,6	12	335,1	16	331,2	17	342,2	13
11.	G. Fisichella	256,4	17	262,3	11	167,7	10	172,8	12	324,2	19	329,7	20	328,5	20	335,8	20
12.	R. Firman	257,5	14	256,7	16	164,3	17	168,2	19	315,8	18	333,9	17	331,0	18	337,6	19
14.	M. Webber	260,4	11	265,2	8	168,4	9	172,9	11	315,9	15	338,8	11	332,2	14	345,9	11
15.	J. Wilson	260,1	12	263,6	10	174,1	3	171,0	16	326,0	17	338,3	12	331,4	15	346,7	9
16.	J. Villeneuve	257,5	15	256,2	17	168,7	8	169,6	18	329,8	9	337,9	13	336,5	9	344,1	12
17.	J. Button	258,9	13	258,8	15	165,8	15	166,2	20	329,3	11	342,4	6	334,5	11	349,1	7
18.	N. Kiesa	248,2	20	259,1	14	167,7	11	172,0	15	323,8	20	331,1	19	329,3	19	338,5	18
19.	J. Verstappen	256,8	16	256,0	18	165,5	16	173,5	9	327,9	16	332,9	18	333,0	12	339,9	16
20.	O. Panis	261,9	8	259,4	13	176,0	2	173,8	7	328,4	13	335,4	15	334,6	10	339,0	17
21.	C. Da Matta	264,4	2	266,7	6	170,4	6	174,0	6	328,2	14	340,6	9	332,9	13	341,7	15

Race

Classification & Retirements

Pos.	Driver	Team	Lap	Time	Average
1.	M. Schumacher	Ferrari	73	1:33:35.997	196,164 km/h
2.	K. Räikkönen	McLaren Mercedes	73	+ 18.258	195,528 km/h
3.	H-H. Frentzen	Sauber Petronas	73	+ 37.964	194,847 km/h
4.	J. Trulli	Renault	73	+ 48.329	194,490 km/h
5.	N. Heidfeld	Sauber Petronas	73	+ 56.403	194,213 km/h
6.	J.P. Montoya	Williams BMW	72	1 lap	191,159 km/h
7.	G. Fisichella	Jordan Ford	72	1 lap	191,114 km/h
8.	J. Wilson	Jaguar	71	2 laps	189,631 km/h
9.	C. Da Matta	Toyota	71	2 laps	188,372 km/h
10.	J. Verstappen	Minardi Cosworth	69	4 laps	185,384 km/h
11.	N. Kiesa	Minardi Cosworth	69	4 laps	183,863 km/h

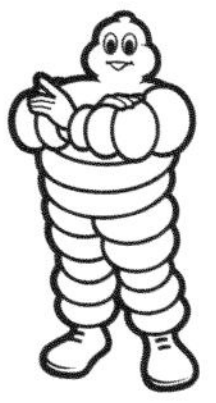

Driver	Team		Reason
J. Villeneuve	BAR Honda	64	Engine blow up
R. Firman	Jordan	49	Spin
D. Coulthard	McLaren Mercedes	46	Gearbox problem
F. Alonso	Renault	45	Engine failure
J. Button	BAR honda	42	Engine blow up
O. Panis	Toyota	28	Spin
M. Webber	Jaguar	22	Crashes into tyre wall
R. Schumacher	Williams BMW	22	Broken left rear suspension and rear wing following spin and collision
R. Barrichello	Ferrari	3	Collision with Montoya, car stuck in gravel trap

Fastest laps

	Driver	Time	Lap	Average
1.	M. Schumacher	1:11:473	13	211,145 km/h
2.	F. Alonso	1:11.525	9	210,991 km/h
3.	J.P. Montoya	1:11.595	9	210,785 km/h
4.	K. Räikkönen	1:11.617	9	210,720 km/h
5.	R. Schumacher	1:11.655	13	210,609 km/h
6.	D. Coulthard	1:12:009	12	209,573 km/h
7.	J. Trulli	1:12.015	14	209,556 km/h
8.	J. Button	1:13.038	10	206,621 km/h
9.	N. Heidfeld	1:13.085	13	206,488 km/h
10.	M. Webber	1:13.099	12	206,448 km/h
11.	C. DA Matta	1:13.231	13	206,076 km/h
12.	J. Wilson	1:13.324	12	205,815 km/h
13.	H-H. Frentzen	1:13.338	71	205,775 km/h
14.	O. Panis	1:13.340	12	205,770 km/h
15.	J. Villeneuve	1:13.538	62	205,216 km/h
16.	G. Fisichella	1:13.630	13	204,959 Km/h
17.	R. Barrichello	1:13.905	2	204,197 Km/h
18.	R. Firman	1:14.687	11	202,059 Km/h
19.	N. Kiesa	1:14.737	67	201,924 Km/h
20.	J. Verstappen	1:15.257	68	200,528 Km/h

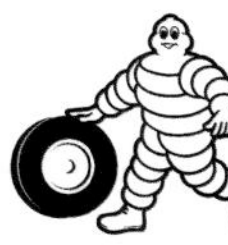

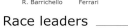

Pit stops

	Driver	Time	Lap	Stop n°
1.	R. Firman	34.500	1	1
2.	J. Verstappen	31.839	2	1
3.	R. Firman	29.128	5	2
4.	O. Panis	37.576	6	1
5.	J. Villeneuve	30.564	6	1
6.	N. Kiesa	32.332	6	1
7.	C. Da Matta	28.990	7	1
8.	J. Villeneuve	28.513	9	2
9.	R. Firman	27.823	9	3
10.	O. Panis	31.067	10	2
11.	N. Kiesa	32.123	10	2
12.	C. Da Matta	27.282	11	2
13.	R. Schumacher	29.792	15	1
14.	J.P. Montoya	36.522	17	1
15.	D. Coulthard	30.949	17	1
16.	N. Heidfeld	29.648	17	1
17.	F. Alonso	29.107	18	1
18.	O. Panis	37.304	17	3
19.	K. Räikkönen	31.477	19	1
20.	H-H. Frentzen	32.400	19	1
21.	M. Schumacher	31.126	20	1
22.	J. Trulli	29.274	20	1
23.	J. Verstappen	30.861	19	2
24.	J. Wilson	32.807	21	1
25.	J. Button	31.455	21	1
26.	M. Schumacher	29.106	21	2
27.	R. Firman	18.230	19	4
28.	C. Da Matta	26.682	20	3
29.	G. Fisichella	38.382	21	1
30.	N. Heidfeld	29.213	21	2
31.	K. Räikkönen	26.871	22	2
32.	F. Alonso	29.077	22	2
33.	J. Villeneuve	31.535	20	3
34.	N. Kiesa	36.955	20	3
35.	J.P. Montoya	18.086	22	2
36.	J. Trulli	28.682	22	2
37.	R. Firman	30.666	20	5
38.	J.P. Montoya	30.088	23	3
39.	O. Panis	32.031	25	4
40.	D. Coulthard	30.345	30	2
41.	J. Wilson	37.005	32	2
42.	C. Da Matta	36.234	32	4
43.	F. Alonso	29.281	36	3
44.	D. Coulthard	18.441	35	3
45.	J.P. Montoya	29.023	38	4
46.	K. Räikkönen	27.879	41	3
47.	C. Da Matta	27.174	40	5
48.	J. Trulli	28.170	42	3
49.	G. Fisichella	42.710	44	2
50.	R. Firman	29.651	42	6
51.	J. Verstappen	42.418	43	3
52.	M. Schumacher	31.332	48	3
53.	J. Villeneuve	30.057	46	4
54.	C. Da Matta	17.981	46	6
55.	H-H. Frentzen	29.359	49	2
56.	N. Kiesa	36.589	47	4
57.	N. Heidfeld	28.409	51	3
58.	N. Kiesa	31.187	48	5

Race leaders

Driver	Laps in the lead	Nber of Laps
K. Räikkönen	1 > 18	18
M. Schumacher	19	1
M. Webber	20 > 21	2
D. Coulthard	22	1
J. Button	23 > 37	15
M. Schumacher	38 > 47	10
H-H. Frentzen	48	1
M. Schumacher	49 > 73	25

Driver	Nber of Laps	Kilometers
M. Schumacher	36	150,912 km
K. Räikkönen	18	75,456 km
J. Button	15	62,880 km
M. Webber	2	8,384 km
D. Coulthard	1	4,192 km
H-H. Frentzen	1	4,192 km

Gaps on the leader board

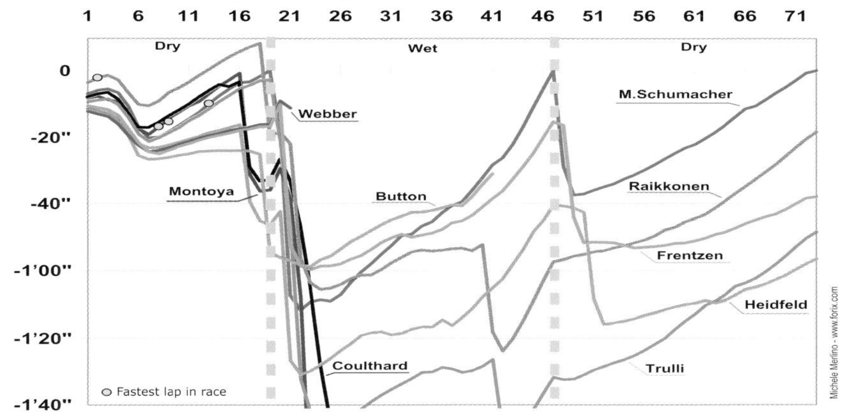
1 6 11 16 21 26 31 36 41 46 51 56 61 66 71
Dry
Wet
Dry
0
-20"
-40"
-1'00"
-1'20"
-1'40"
M.Schumacher
Webber
Montoya
Button
Raikkonen
Frentzen
Heidfeld
Coulthard
Trulli
Fastest lap in race
Michele Merlino - www.forix.com

Lap chart

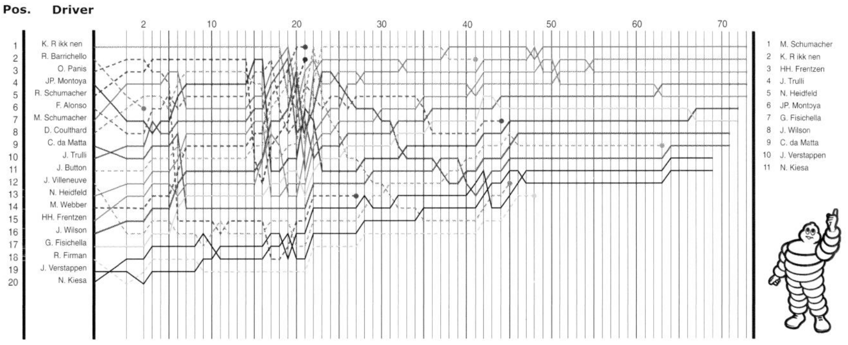
Pos. Driver
2
10
20
30
40
50
60
70
K. R ikk nen
R. Barrichello
O. Panis
JP. Montoya
R. Schumacher
F. Alonso
M. Schumacher
D. Coulthard
C. da Matta
J. Trulli
J. Button
J. Villeneuve
N. Heidfeld
M. Webber
HH. Frentzen
J. Wilson
G. Fisichella
R. Firman
J. Verstappen
N. Kiesa
1 M. Schumacher
2 K. R ikk nen
3 HH. Frentzen
4 J. Trulli
5 N. Heidfeld
6 JP. Montoya
7 G. Fisichella
8 J. Wilson
9 C. da Matta
10 J. Verstappen
11 N. Kiesa

Championship after fifteen rounds

Drivers

1. M. Schumacher ....(6 wins)................92
2. K. Räikkönen ....(1 win) 83
3. J.P. Montoya..............(2 wins)................82
4. R. Schumacher...........(2 wins)................58
5. R. Barrichello ....(1 win) 55
6. F. Alonso ....(1 win) 55
7. D. Coulthard ....(1 win) 45
8. J. Trulli 29
9. M. Webber...17
10. H-H. Frentzen...13
11. G. Fisichella ....(1 win) 12
12. J. Button 12
13. C. Da Matta..8
14. N. Heidfeld...6
15. O. Panis...6
16. J. Villeneuve...6
17. M. Gené...4
18. R. Firman...1
19. J. Wilson..1
20. A. Pizzonia 0
21. J. Verstappen 0
22. N. Kiesa...0
23. Z. Baumgartner 0

Constructors

1. Scuderia Ferrari Marlboro ......(7 wins) 147
2. BMW Williams F1 Team ....(4 wins) 144
3. West McLaren Mercedes ....(2 wins) 128
4. Mild Seven Renault F1 Team ..(1 win) 84
5. Sauber Petronas 19
6. Lucky Strike BAR Honda 18
7. Jaguar Racing..18
8. Panasonic Toyota Racing 14
9. Jordan Ford.........................(1 win) 13
10. European Minardi Cosworth...........................0

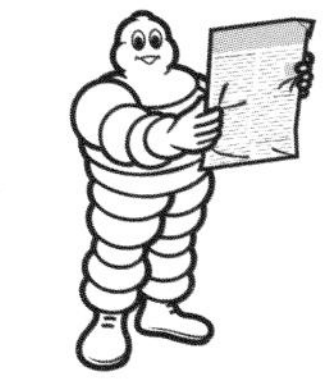

The circuit

Name	Indianapolis
Date	September 28, 2003
Length	4192 meters
Distance	73 laps, 306,016 km
Weather	changeable, overcast with intermittent rain, 10-13°c
Track temperature	16-20°c

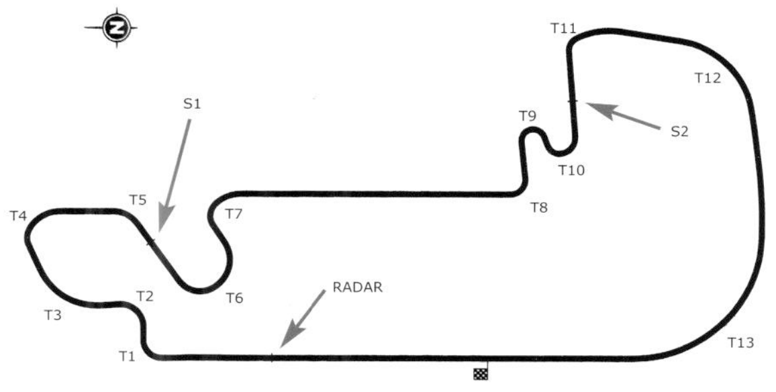
T1
T2
T3
T4
T5
T6
T7
T8
T9
T10
T11
T12
T13
S1
S2
RADAR

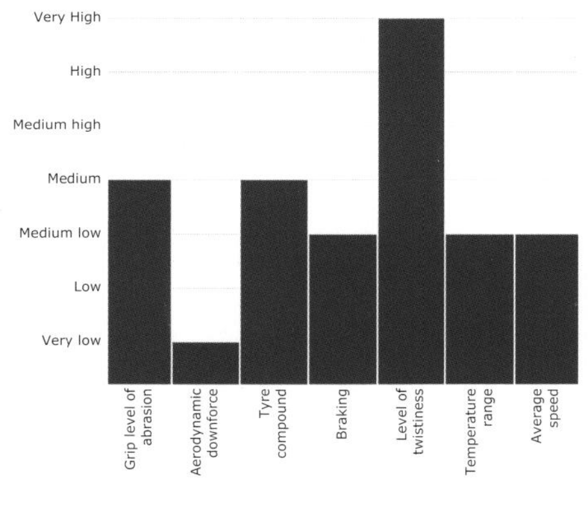
Very High
High
Medium high
Medium
Medium low
Low
Very low
Grip level of abrasion
Aerodynamic downforce
Tyre compound
Braking
Level of twistiness
Temperature range
Average speed

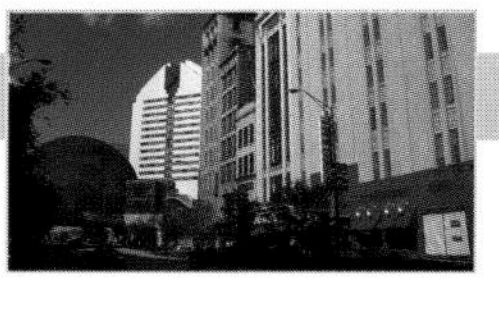

SCHUMACHER JOINS THE PANTHEON OF SPORT

At Suzuka, the Ferrari driver notched up his sixth world championship title, setting a new outright record.

He has thus definitely become a legend in motor sport terms. He also holds the record for the most number of wins and fastest race laps.

However, the German nearly lost it all in this Japanese Grand Prix. He finished eighth, picking up a solitary point, to end up the season just two points ahead of Kimi Raikkonen.

For Ferrari, it was a total triumph, as the team picked up the Constructors' title for a fifth consecutive year. Williams, which had been in the running for this award, made a hash of things, failing to score any points for the first time this season.

> Kimi Räikkönen attacks the Suzuka circuit. He would qualify eighth.

Rain turns up for Suzuka qualifying

After a sunny morning, the skies clouded over at Suzuka before rain turned up to play its part just twelve minutes before the end of Saturday's qualifying session.

The difficult conditions relegated Michael Schumacher to 14th spot, while the last two men to take to the track, Ralf Schumacher and Jarno Trulli never even managed to complete a timed lap.

Pole position thus went to Rubens Barrichello in the Ferrari, with the Williams-BMW of Juan Pablo Montoya alongside him on the front row.

Behind them came the big surprise of the weekend, as the second row of the grid belonged to Toyota, with Cristiano da Matta third and Olivier Panis fourth. It was by far their best qualifying performance of the season.

> No signs of stress for the two Ferrari drivers who tried their hand at slot-car racing before qualifying.

In brief

> The BAR team approached Michelin regarding a supply of tyres for 2004. The French marque could not refuse (to be paid for the service!) by BAR, as according to article 76b of the Formula 1 sporting regulations, a tyre manufacturer must be prepared to supply up to 60% of the field. BAR's current supplier, Bridgestone, was not too impressed with the idea. In Suzuka, the Japanese company put out a press release, explaining that it had the team under contract until the end of 2004. A legal battle was on the cards.

> The 2004 season would be made up of 18 grands prix. A quick amendment to the Quebec anti-tobacco laws seemed to indicate that the Canadian Grand Prix could go ahead. On the other hand, the French Grand Prix was apparently under threat, as the organisers had yet to pay the bill for 9.5 million dollars from SLEC.

> The Suzuka circuit had welcomed 5 million spectators since it opened its gates in 1987. The organisers had added up the crowd figures from each day to reach a total of 5,049,000 spectators, which included the figure of 54,000 from this year's Friday gate.

> Takuma Sato under the rising sun at Suzuka. Following Jacques Villeneuve's departure (see page 212,) and following a request from Honda, the Japanese driver replaced the Canadian in the BAR team.

Starting grid

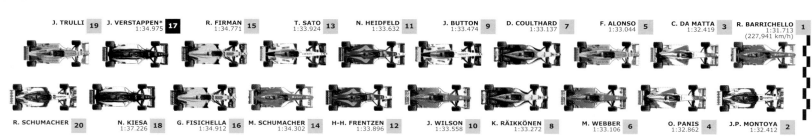

* J. VERSTAPPEN
Comes into the pits after the formation lap to refuel. So he starts from the pit lane.

Position	Driver	Time
19	J. TRULLI	
17	J. VERSTAPPEN*	1:34.975
15	R. FIRMAN	1:34.771
13	T. SATO	1:33.924
11	N. HEIDFELD	1:33.632
9	J. BUTTON	1:33.474
7	D. COULTHARD	1:33.137
5	F. ALONSO	1:33.044
3	C. DA MATTA	1:32.419
1	R. BARRICHELLO	1:31.713 (227,941 km/h)
20	R. SCHUMACHER	1:37.226
18	N. KIESA	1:37.226
16	G. FISICHELLA	1:34.912
14	M. SCHUMACHER	1:34.302
12	H-H. FRENTZEN	1:33.896
10	J. WILSON	1:33.558
8	K. RÄIKKÖNEN	1:33.272
6	M. WEBBER	1:33.106
4	O. PANIS	1:32.862
2	J.P. MONTOYA	1:32.412

Michael Schumacher, the best ever?

Heaven and hell. Michael Schumacher went through the full range of racing emotions in a nail-biting 2003 Japanese Grand Prix. He had to finish eighth to be sure of taking the world title. Having qualified fourteenth, because of the rain which arrived towards the end of qualifying, the German completed the opening lap in twelfth place. On lap six, he broke the nose of his Ferrari as he tried to pass Takuma Sato in the BAR and was forced to pit for repairs.

He set off again plum last. Hell and panic in the Ferrari camp and also in the mind of the man who could see that sixth title come under threat. *"I do not blame Takuma, it was just a racing accident,"* explained Michael Schumacher. *"But after that it was all a bit of a mess. I had to fight to climb through the field and I had a long duel with Da Matta. Ralf hit me from behind... a very strange race. I knew that Montoya had retired and the McLarens were just behind Rubens. In this situation, your brain starts to spin. You think about*

<
Almost a night time podium. The race start had been delayed to 14h30 local time so that European TV spectators did not have to get up too early in the morning on a Sunday...and the skies get dark early in Japan.

Ferrari takes the Constructors' title

The standings in the Constructors' Championship on the eve of this Japanese Grand Prix were very close between Ferrari and Williams.

But, come the end of the season finale, thanks to problems for the Williams duo and a win for Rubens Barrichello, the balance shifted to a 14 point lead in favour of the Italians. This meant that the Scuderia had taken its fifth consecutive title, another outright record in the history of F1. *"In my view, what the team has achieved is even more of an achievement than my six world titles,"* stressed Michael Schumacher. *"Ferrari has just won the constructors' title for the fifth consecutive time and that is really extraordinary. After races like those in Hockenheim and Budapest this year, some people said we were finished and beaten. And then, we are in front again. We never give up and without a doubt, that is one of the great strengths of the Ferrari team."*

the worst situation; Rubens might retire, the rain could come and change everything, race strategy...I had to finish in the points to be sure of the title, just in case. This eighth place looked a long way off and seemed inaccessible. It was a very strange race and very tiring."*

But in the end, he took that eighth place and the title was in the bag. Paradise! In any case, out in front, Rubens Barrichello had won, which meant that he had handed his team-mate the title by keeping Kimi Räikkönen off the top step of the podium.

No matter, the job was done and the newly crowned champion seemed very moved after the race: *"the season has been very difficult, especially the last part. I was very nervous today and the race was*

really difficult. Without any doubt, it was one of the toughest of my career. I feel empty, completely exhausted and I don't really feel anything. I cannot express what I feel. I took my other titles with wins, but today I have got it with an eighth place and that is a strange feeling. I am simply proud of what all of us in the team have accomplished."* From now on, it was holiday time for the six-times world champion. *"Michael is heading back to Switzerland on Monday and will stay in Vufflens-le-Chateau until Friday,"* explained his press attaché, Sabine Kehm. *"It will be a total rest. He needs it. Next weekend, he will go to the Mugello circuit for Ferrari's annual finals day, but nothing else is planned."*

Michael Schumacher spent most of his grand prix attacking Takuma Sato. He even left him his front wing in the early stages of the race.
v<

The little ceremony to celebrate the title took place at night. Which cannot be seen in the photo at the front of this Grand Prix report on pages 206-207!
v

Kimi Räikkönen, just one lap of happiness

Kimi Raikkonen will remember lap 13 of this Japanese Grand Prix for a long time. For one lap, he led the race while Michael Schumacher was only in 16th place, having pitted to change his front wing. For those few seconds, the Finn was the *"virtual"* world champion. Unfortunately for him, the race did not stop there and he finished second, thanks to a two stop strategy. *"Of course, I am second again!"* he said and indeed he was for the seventh time this season. *"I would have preferred to have won, but our car was not really*

capable of winning the title this year. We improved it a lot compared with 2002 and if we continue to make progress at this rate next year, then we can fight for the title. I tried everything here, but the rain in qualifying did not help. We were a bit unlucky from that point of view..."*

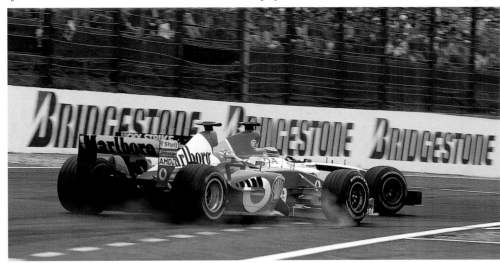

Race summary

> Barrichello starts from pole and leads into the first corner. Michael Schumacher can be seen at the back on the left. He is attacking

from 14th place on the grid **(1)**.
> On the opening lap, Montoya takes the lead and pulls away. He was

later let down by his hydraulic system **(2)**.
> In traffic, Michael Schumacher hits Sato and pits for a new nose

(3).
> Da Matta fights with Button. The Brazilian finishes 7th after a superb qualifying

performance **(4)**.
> Räikkönen finishes 2nd with Coulthard right behind. McLaren takes 3rd place in the

Constructors' championship **(5)**.
> Button 4th and Sato 6th. A rare joyful moment for the BAR

team **(6)**.
> Barrichello victorious, Schumacher triumphal: a great end to the season for Ferrari **(7)**.

Looking to the future

So Kimi Räikkönen will have to wait before becoming world champion. No matter, as the Finn has a long future ahead of him.

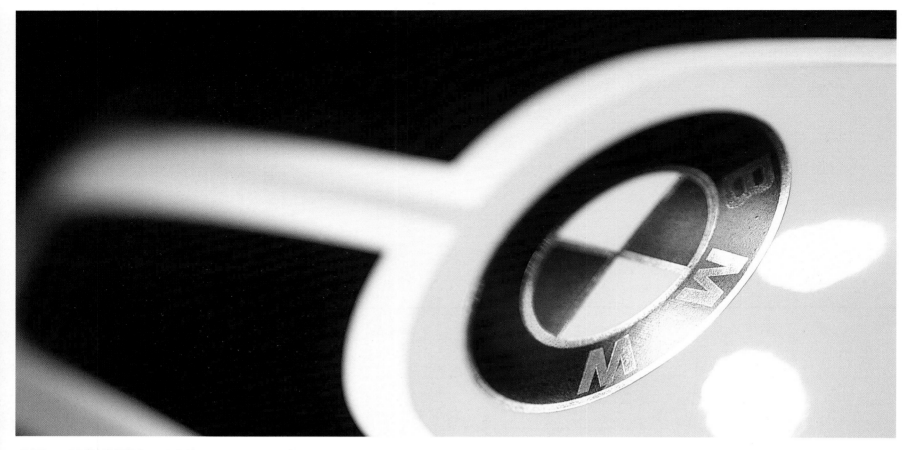

(top)
The Williams team had a magnificent 2003 season, but it ended in chaos at Suzuka. The title fight will have to wait, which is a shame for Michelin, who failed to take the title, despite technically dominating its rival.

(above)
Jarno Trulli scores points again with a fifth place finish.

Long faces at Williams

There were plenty of long faces in the Williams camp: On Sunday night, around seven o'clock, chief engineer, Frank Dernie, confided that he was off to his bed! He found time to grumble about the team's poor start to the season, which in the end cost them the world championship crown. On the eve of the Monaco Grand Prix, Juan Pablo Montoya was 23 points down on Michael Schumacher, a chasm which the Colombian never managed to close. The team actually came quite close to taking the constructors' title, as it was trailing Ferrari by just three points coming into Suzuka. At the start of the race, Juan Pablo Montoya was soon in the lead and it looked as though Williams was going to be the dominant force, but it was an illusion quickly shattered. The Colombian had hydraulic problems and team-mate Ralf Schumacher had a chaotic race. Williams failed to pick up a single point in Suzuka, the first time that had happened this season. They certainly picked the wrong moment.

>
Mission accomplished for Rubens Barrichello: he effectively kept Kimi Räikkönen out of the title chase by winning the Japanese Grand Prix.

>>
In Japan, many of the spectators use photographic equipment which makes European professional photographers green with envy.

Jacques Villeneuve absent from Suzuka: gone or sacked?

Jacques Villeneuve absent from Suzuka: gone or sacked?
Stephanie Morin, reporter for the *"La Presse"* Montreal newspaper, was clearly upset in the Suzuka paddock. Having travelled from Montreal, as she does for every grand prix, with the sole aim of reporting on Jacques Villeneuve's weekend, there was not much for her to do. Because the Canadian driver never showed his face at Suzuka and gave no explanation as to his absence. Jock Clear, his race engineer since 1996 and also a close friend had no news and appeared very disappointed with the driver's attitude.
Because Villeneuve was actually in Japan earlier in the week. He spent three days in Tokyo during which time his manager, Craig Pollock, was working on his appearance at Suzuka, as well as trying to find him a drive for 2004. In the end, discussions with the BAR team as to this Japanese Grand Prix ended with a flight back to Europe for the Canadian, without stopping off at the track. Left or sacked? The driver's press attaché, Jules Kulpinski was in Suzuka and informed the media that he had simply decided not to bother taking part in the final race of the season. *"I learnt of the decision from Jacques while I was on the train coming to Suzuka,"* explained Geoff Willis, the BAR team technical director. *"We hardly had time to turn around and ask Takuma Sato to replace him."*
With no clear statement from Villeneuve himself, the paddock rumour mill was soon in full swing. Apparently, Honda wanted Takuma Sato to race in front of his home crowd at Suzuka circuit. It certainly did the trick as the spectators arrived in their thousands. There had never been such a big crowd at Suzuka on a Saturday!
Of course, Jacques Villeneuve would have been compensated for his enforced absence and the sum involved was reckoned to be two million dollars. However, it seemed strange that the Canadian would accept this, as his bank account was not exactly in need of a top-up and his reputation would be seriously damaged by his no-show. His career was thus coming to an end with no farewell or fanfare and certainly without any real plausible explanation.
David Richards did not hold back when it came to criticising his former driver. *"It's a shame to finish an F1 career like this. It's a bit tawdry,"* he declared on Friday.
Would Jacques Villeneuve find a drive for 2004? It was looking far from likely. It seemed as though his career had come to an end at Indianapolis, two weeks earlier, after five seasons struggling at BAR and with no wins to his name since 1997. A real waste.

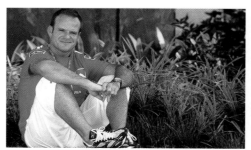

Practice

All the time trials

N°	Driver	N° Chassis - Engine	Private testing	Pos.	Practice friday	Pos.	Qualifying friday	Pos.	Practice 1 saturday	Pos.	Practice 2 saturday	Pos.	Warm-up	Pos.	Qualifying saturday	Pos.
1.	Michael Schumacher	Ferrari F2003-GA 229			1:31.009	2	1:30.464	3	1:32.989	2	1:31.705	3		19	1:34.302	14
2.	Rubens Barrichello	Ferrari F2003-GA 233			1:31.217	4	1:30.758	7	1:33.350	3	1:32.796	5	1:33.963	3	1:31.713	1
3.	Juan Pablo Montoya	Williams FW25 06 - BMW			1:31.654	7	1:31.201	8	1:33.405	4	1:31.422	2	1:33.211	1	1:32.412	2
4.	Ralf Schumacher	Williams FW25 07 - BMW			1:32.208	11	1:30.343	2	1:32.931	1	1:31.149	1	1:34.750	7		19
5.	David Coulthard	McLaren MP4-17D 07 - Mercedes			1:31.019	3	1:30.482	4	1:34.309	9			1:34.790	9	1:33.137	7
6.	Kimi Räikkönen	McLaren MP4-07D 06 - Mercedes			1:31.303	6	1:30.558	5	1:34.523	12	1:32.930	6		20	1:33.272	8
7.	Jarno Trulli	Renault R23B-05	1:32.891	3	1:30.727	1	1:30.281	1	1:34.349	10	1:32.343	4		18		20
8.	Fernando Alonso	Renault R23B-06	1:32.367	2	1:31.276	5	1:30.624	6	1:34.398	11	1:33.107	8	1:33.972	4	1:33.044	5
9.	Nick Heidfeld	Sauber C22-01 - Petronas			1:32.694	14	1:31.783	10	1:33.749	5	1:34.558	15	1:35.450	11	1:33.632	11
10.	Heinz-Harald Frentzen	Sauber C22-03 - Petronas			1:32.422	13	1:31.892	12	1:34.718	16	1:33.694	12	1:47.062	16	1:33.896	12
11.	Giancarlo Fisichella	Jordan EJ13-05 - Ford	1:33.497	4	1:33.956	17	1:33.313	18	1:36.705	18	1:35.476	16	1:34.869	10	1:34.912	16
12.	Ralph Firman	Jordan EJ13-04 - Ford	1:34.054	6	1:33.306	16	1:33.057	17	1:36.368	17	1:35.620	17	1:36.515	14	1:34.771	15
14.	Mark Webber	Jaguar R4-03	1:33.897	5	1:31.977	8	1:31.305	9	1:34.599	15	1:33.807	13	1:34.504	6	1:33.106	6
15.	Justin Wilson	Jaguar R4-05	1:34.297	7	1:32.735	15	1:32.291	15	1:34.119	7	1:33.952	14	1:35.778	12	1:33.558	10
16.	Takuma Sato	BAR 005-06 - Honda			1:32.295	12	1:31.832	11	1:34.554	14	1:33.662	11	1:34.138	5	1:33.924	13
17.	Jenson Button	BAR 005-04 - Honda			1:34.445	18	1:32.374	16	1:34.171	8	1:33.411	10	1:34.757	8	1:33.474	9
18.	Nicolas Kiesa	Minardi PS03/01 - Cosworth	1:36.558	11	1:35.900	20	1:36.181	20	1:38.075	20	1:37.884	19	1:38.929	15	1:37.226	18
19.	Jos Verstappen	Minardi PS03/02 - Cosworth	1:35.579	9	1:35.180	19	1:34.836	19	1:36.928	19	1:37.379	18	1:35.853	13	1:34.975	17
20.	Olivier Panis	Toyota TF103/08			1:32.011	9	1:31.908	13	1:34.541	13	1:33.082	7		17	1:32.862	4
21.	Cristiano da Matta	Toyota TF103/07			1:32.133	10	1:32.256	14	1:33.963	6	1:33.133	9	1:33.481	2	1:32.419	3
34.	Allan McNish	Renault R23B-04	1:32.170	1												
36.	Satoshi Motoyama	Jordan EJ13-02 - Ford	1:35.044	8												
39.	Gianmaria Bruni	Minardi PS03/03 - Cosworth	1:35.695	10												

Maximum speed

N°	Driver	P1 Qualifs	Pos.	P1 Race	Pos.	P2 Qualifs	Pos.	P2 Race	Pos.	Finish Qualifs	Pos.	Finish Race	Pos.	Trap Qualifs	Pos.	Trap Race	Pos.
1.	M. Schumacher	290,4	4	292,4	4	311,5	7	322,7	2	291,7	7	296,7	2	289,6	17	315,0	1
2.	R. Barrichello	291,1	3	291,8	5	313,7	1	317,1	5	292,6	5	293,4	6	305,9	5	299,7	13
3.	J.P. Montoya	288,6	7	290,6	8	312,3	2	308,5	16	293,4	3	292,2	9	306,2	4	301,7	10
4.	R. Schumacher	290,2	6	295,1	1	311,6	6	323,7	1	293,8	2	296,3	4	288,6	18	306,4	5
5.	D. Coulthard	292,7	1	295,0	2	311,9	4	318,3	4	294,1	1	299,1	1	309,2	1	309,9	2
6.	K. Räikkönen	291,4	2	294,8	3	311,6	5	318,9	6	292,7	4	296,7	3	303,3	9	304,2	7
7.	J. Trulli	241,6	20	287,0	14	297,9	20	313,7	10			289,6	14	175,3	20	297,6	15
8.	F. Alonso	286,1	11	286,8	15	303,9	15	309,4	13	287,4	13	289,6	15	302,3	11	306,9	3
9.	N. Heidfeld	284,6	14	288,3	11	307,0	12	311,5	11	286,7	16	289,6	13	304,9	9	301,5	11
10.	H-H. Frentzen	286,0	12	286,0	16	308,7	11	310,2	12	287,0	14	288,9	16	306,3	3	293,2	17
11.	G. Fisichella	280,8	19	283,9	19	303,7	17	306,6	19	283,4	19	286,4	19	296,3	15	298,8	14
12.	R. Firman	281,2	18	284,9	17	303,8	16	305,9	20	283,6	18	286,1	20	301,0	12	291,7	18
14.	M. Webber	285,5	13	289,0	9	301,6	19	309,1	15	286,8	15	295,2	5	298,9	14	297,6	16
15.	J. Wilson	286,1	10	287,8	12	302,8	18	309,1	14	289,0	11	290,0	12	300,3	13	303,2	8
16.	T. Sato	284,1	15	287,3	13	309,4	9	316,6	6	288,0	12	291,1	11	304,1	7	304,7	6
17.	J. Button	286,6	9	288,5	10	309,1	10	316,5	7	289,6	9	292,2	8	307,4	2	302,3	9
18.	N. Kiesa	281,8	17	283,9	18	304,1	14	307,8	17	285,8	17	287,5	17	282,2	19	287,5	20
19.	J. Verstappen	283,2	16	283,5	20	306,1	13	307,7	18	289,4	10	286,7	18	293,8	16	288,7	19
20.	O. Panis	288,3	8	291,5	6	309,8	8	315,2	9	290,3	8	292,0	10	303,8	8	301,1	12
21.	C. Da Matta	290,3	5	291,5	7	312,1	3	316,4	8	292,2	6	292,4	7	302,6	10	306,7	4

Race

Classification & Retirements

Pos.	Driver	Team	Lap	Time	Average
1.	R. Barrichello	Ferrari	53	1:25:11.743	216,611 km/h
2.	K. Räikkönen	McLaren Mercedes	53	+ 11.085	216,142 km/h
3.	D. Coulthard	McLaren Mercedes	53	+ 11.614	216,120 km/h
4.	J. Button	BAR Honda	53	+ 33.106	215,217 km/h
5.	J. Trulli	Renault	53	+ 34.269	215,169 km/h
6.	T. Sato	BAR Honda	53	+ 51.692	214,443 km/h
7.	C. Da Matta	Toyota	53	+ 56.794	214,231 km/h
8.	M. Schumacher	Ferrari	53	+ 59.487	214,119 km/h
9.	N. Heidfeld	Sauber Petronas	53	+ 1:00.159	214,091 km/h
10.	O. Panis	Toyota	53	+ 1:01.844	214,022 km/h
11.	M. Webber	Jaguar	53	+ 1:11.005	213,643 km/h
12.	R. Schumacher	Williams BMW	52	1 lap	212,496 km/h
13.	J. Wilson	Jaguar	52	1 lap	211,230 km/h
14.	R. Firman	Jordan Ford	51	2 laps	208,064 km/h
15.	J. Verstappen	Minardi Cosworth	51	2 laps	206,477 km/h
16.	N. Kiesa	Minardi Cosworth	50	3 laps	203,960 km/h

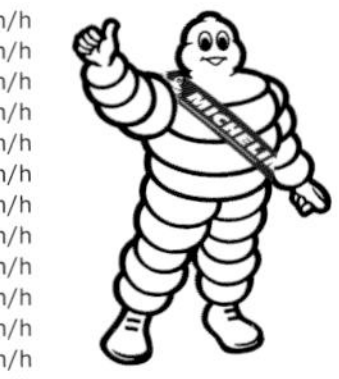

Driver	Team	Lap	Reason
G. Fisichella	Jordan Ford	34	Runs out of fuel after insufficient amount taken on at 1st refuelling
F. Alonso	Renault	18	Engine problem
H-H. Frentzen	Sauber Petronas	10	Engine blows up after an oil leak caused by collision with R. Schumacher
J.P. Montoya	Williams BMW	10	Drop of hydraulic pressure caused by faulty joint

Fastest laps

	Driver	Time	Lap	Average
1.	R. Schumacher	1:33.408	43	223,805 km/h
2.	D. Coulthard	1:33.416	14	223,786 km/h
3.	M. Schumacher	1:33.553	14	223,458 km/h
4.	R. Barrichello	1:33.703	18	223,100 km/h
5.	J. Montoya	1:33.830	2	222,798 km/h
6.	F. Alonso	1:34.255	8	221,794 km/h
7.	K. Räikkönen	1:34.488	12	221,247 km/h
8.	J. Trulli	1:34.546	26	221,111 km/h
9.	J. Button	1:34.605	14	220,973 km/h
10.	M. Webber	1:34.635	24	220,903 km/h
11.	N. Heidfeld	1:34.991	31	220,075 km/h
12.	J. Wilson	1:35.014	11	220,022 km/h
13.	O. Panis	1:35.023	53	220,001 km/h
14.	C. Da Matta	1:35.192	16	219,610 km/h
15.	T. Sato	1:35.290	28	219,385 km/h
16.	G. Fisichella	1:35.824	33	218,162 Km/h
17.	H-H. Frentzen	1:36.601	7	216,407 Km/h
18.	R. Firman	1:36.662	15	216,271 Km/h
19.	J. Verstappen	1:37.869	51	213,603 Km/h
20.	N. Kiesa	1:38.754	6	211,689 Km/h

Pit stops

	Driver	Time	Lap	Stop n°
1.	M. Schumacher	41.400	6	1
2.	J. Wilson	29.081	9	1
3.	H-H. Frentzen	36.905	9	1
4.	C. Da Matta	27.991	10	1
5.	M. Webber	28.377	10	1
6.	O. Panis	28.836	11	1
7.	J. Trulli	29.224	11	1
8.	N. Kiesa	38.377	11	1
9.	R. Barrichello	28.552	12	1
10.	F. Alonso	28.640	12	1
11.	D. Coulthard	28.157	12	1
12.	K. Räikkönen	30.416	13	1
13.	R. Firman	40.333	13	1
14.	R. Schumacher	28.666	14	1
15.	G. Fisichella	31.141	14	1
16.	T. Sato	30.197	15	1
17.	N. Heidfeld	29.560	15	1
18.	J. Button	30.374	16	1
19.	J. Verstappen	30.858	19	1
20.	J. Wilson	28.366	21	2
21.	M. Webber	28.998	22	2
22.	C. Da Matta	28.294	24	2
23.	R. Schumacher	27.517	24	2
24.	M. Schumacher	28.286	24	2
25.	O. Panis	28.613	25	2
26.	R. Barrichello	28.590	26	2
27.	R. Firman	35.895	25	2
28.	D. Coulthard	28.537	26	2
29.	J. Trulli	30.476	32	2
30.	T. Sato	31.563	32	2
31.	N. Kiesa	36.367	31	2
32.	K. Räikkönen	30.230	33	2
33.	J. Button	31.624	33	2
34.	N. Heidfeld	30.119	33	2
35.	J. Wilson	30.688	34	3
36.	M. Webber	29.867	35	3
37.	M. Schumacher	28.786	37	3
38.	C. Da Matta	27.874	38	3
39.	R. Schumacher	28.522	38	3
40.	J. Verstappen	29.803	37	2
41.	O. Panis	28.125	39	3
42.	R. Barrichello	28.425	40	3
43.	D. Coulthard	27.104	41	3
44.	R. Schumacher	38.255	41	4

Race leaders

Driver	Laps in the lead	Nber of Laps
J.P. Montoya	1 > 8	8
R. Barrichello	9 > 12	4
K. Räikkönen	13	1
J. Button	14 > 16	3
R. Barrichello	17 > 40	24
D. Coulthard	41	1
R. Barrichello	42 > 53	12

Driver	Nber of Laps	Kilometers
R. Barrichello	40	232,280 km
J.P. Montoya	8	46,258 km
J. Button	3	17,421 km
K. Räikkönen	1	5,807 km
D. Coulthard	1	5,807 km

Lap chart

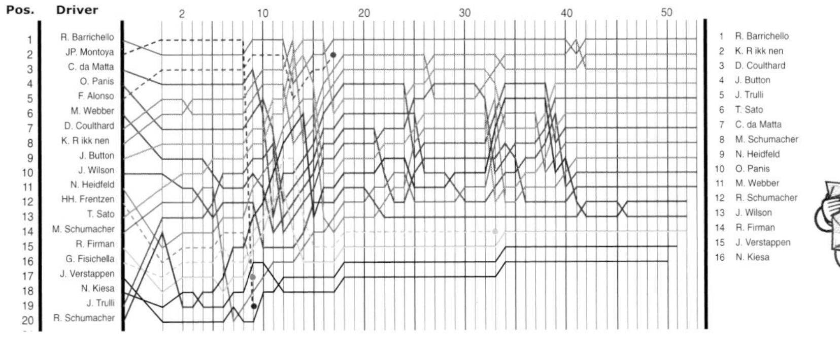
Pos.
Driver
2
10
20
30
40
50
R. Barrichello
JP. Montoya
C. da Matta
O. Panis
F. Alonso
M. Webber
D. Coulthard
K. R ikk nen
J. Button
J. Wilson
N. Heidfeld
HH. Frentzen
T. Sato
M. Schumacher
R. Firman
G. Fisichella
J. Verstappen
N. Kiesa
J. Trulli
R. Schumacher
1 R. Barrichello
2 K. R ikk nen
3 D. Coulthard
4 J. Button
5 J. Trulli
6 T. Sato
7 C. da Matta
8 M. Schumacher
9 N. Heidfeld
10 O. Panis
11 M. Webber
12 R. Schumacher
13 J. Wilson
14 R. Firman
15 J. Verstappen
16 N. Kiesa

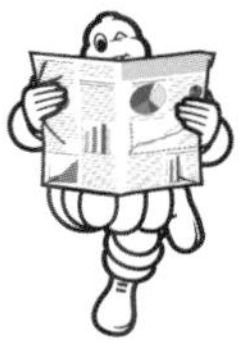

Gaps on the leader board

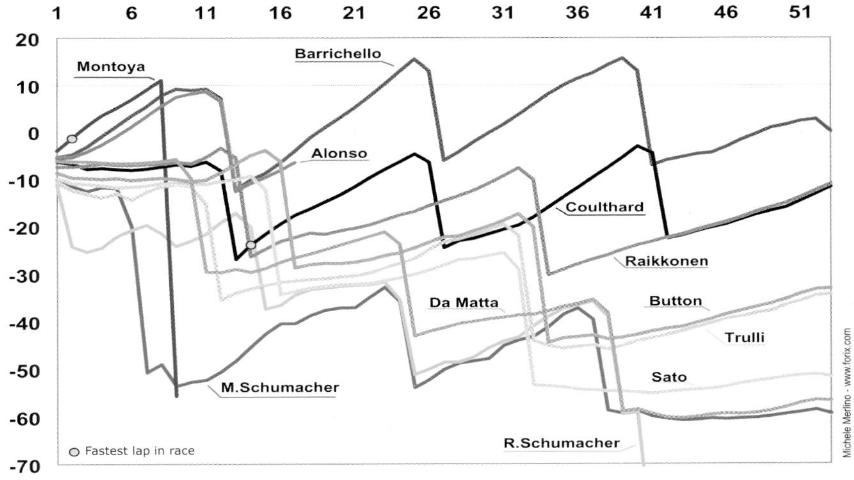
1
6
11
16
21
26
31
36
41
46
51
20
10
0
-10
-20
-30
-40
-50
-60
-70
Montoya
Barrichello
Alonso
Coulthard
Raikkonen
Da Matta
Button
Trulli
Sato
M.Schumacher
R.Schumacher
Fastest lap in race
Michele Merlino - www.fonix.com

Championship after sixteen round

Drivers

1. **M. Schumacher** ....(6 wins)................93
2. K. Räikkönen ....(1 win) 91
3. J.P. Montoya.............(2 wins)................82
4. R. Barrichello ....(2 wins)................65
5. R. Schumacher..........(2 wins)................58
6. F. Alonso ....(1 win) 55
7. D. Coulthard ....(1 win) 51
8. J. Trulli 33
9. J. Button 17
10. M. Webber..17
11. H-H. Frentzen 13
12. G. Fisichella ....(1 win) 12
13. C. Da Matta 10
14. N. Heidfeld 6
15. O. Panis...6
16. J. Villeneuve 6
17. M. Gené...4
18. T. Sato..3
19. R. Firman...1
20. J. Wilson 1
21. A. Pizzonia 0
22. J. Verstappen 0
23. N. Kiesa...0
24. Z. Baumgartner 0

Constructors

1. **Scuderia Ferrari Marlboro** .(8 wins) 158
2. BMW Williams F1 Team ....(4 wins) 144
3. West McLaren Mercedes ....(2 wins) 142
4. Mild Seven Renault F1 Team ..(1 win) 88
5. Lucky Strike BAR Honda 26
6. Sauber Petronas 19
7. Jaguar Racing...18
8. Panasonic Toyota Racing 16
9. Jordan Ford.........................(1 win) 13
10. European Minardi Cosworth..........................0

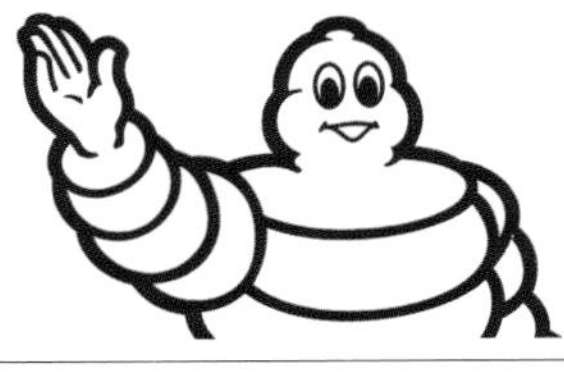

The circuit

Name	Suzuka circuit
Date	October 12, 2003
Length	5807 meters
Distance	53 laps, 307,573 km
Weather	Overcast, quite humid, 21-22°c
Track temperature	22-25°c

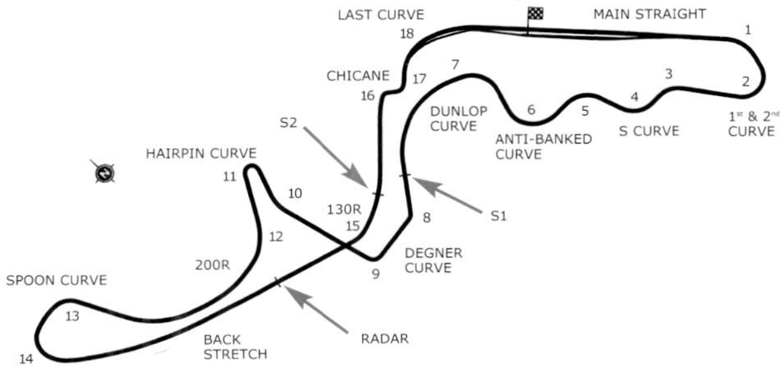
LAST CURVE
MAIN STRAIGHT
18
1
CHICANE
17
7
3
2
16
DUNLOP CURVE
6
5
4
S2
ANTI-BANKED CURVE
S CURVE
1st & 2nd CURVE
HAIRPIN CURVE
11
10
130R
15
8
S1
12
DEGNER CURVE
9
200R
SPOON CURVE
13
BACK STRETCH
RADAR
14

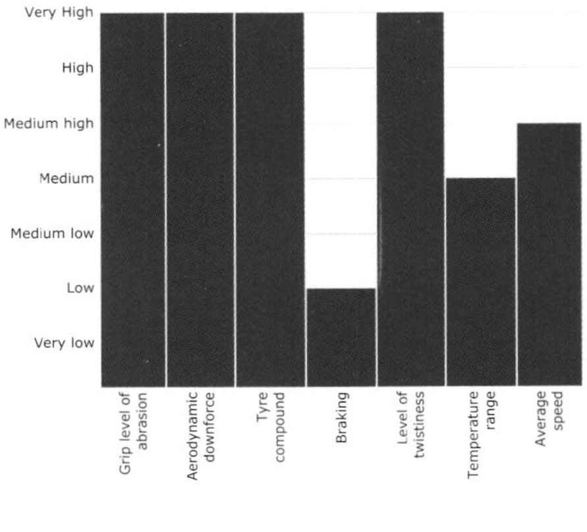
Very High
High
Medium high
Medium
Medium low
Low
Very low
Grip level of abrasion
Aerodynamic downforce
Tyre compound
Braking
Level of twistiness
Temperature range
Average speed

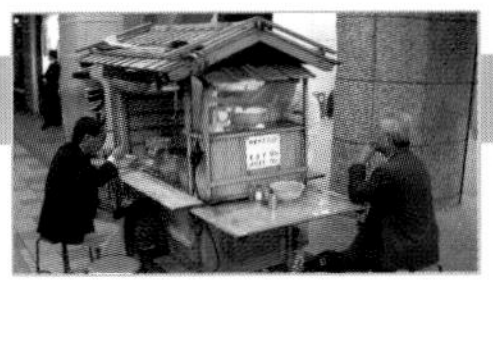

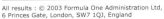

by Didier Braillon, «L'Equipe»

Go Alonso go!

Two youthful records have now been broken. On 22nd March in Sepang, Fernando Alonso took the first pole position of his short career at the age of 21 years and 248 days. He thus did better than Rubens Barrichello who, until then, had been the youngest ever driver to start from the number one slot on the grid. When he did it at the wheel of a Jordan-Hart at Spa in 1994, the Brazilian was 22 years and 96 days old. Fernando obviously had the talent to give his all over a single lap. On 24th August in Budapest, he took his first grand prix win, the first for a Renault car for two decades, Alonso had not aged much since his last record breaking achievement, as he was now 22 years and 26 days old. In the big record book of the F1 World Championship which dates back to 1950, the record had stood for forty four years, when New-Zealander Bruce McLaren won at Sebring in 1959, at the wheel of a Cooper-Climax. McLaren, who went on to create his own team, was 22 years and 104 days old at the time. The young Spaniard from Oviedo couldn't quite believe it in Hungary. *"I feel as though I am somewhere else,"* he admitted. *"The last part of the race was incredible. I started to*

take in what was happening and when I crossed the line, my first thought was for my team." Spain was not exactly a major player in F1 with only five of Alonso's fellow countrymen having scored points in the past: Alfonso de Portago, Francesco Godia, Luis Perez-Sala, Marc Gene and Pedro de la Rosa. Alonso reckoned that the massive media coverage generated at home by his achievements was *"very nice,"* but he has a wise head on his shoulders and said he was keeping his feet firmly on the ground. Unlike some other baby superstars, there was no sudden change of attitude or different paint jobs on his helmet. He comes from a family of modest means, much like Michael Schumacher and was taken in hand by his father who worked in an explosives factory, while his mother worked in a commercial centre. They say that once, in the middle of an F1 test session, Alonso senior gave his son a slap. *"I don't remember, but it's entirely possible,"* reckoned the talented young lad. *"No doubt I had done something he did not approve of. My parents never judge me in terms of my job, but only in terms of my behaviour and I expect that from them. I have everything to*

learn from them and I know their judgement is pretty good." He lives in England, in the university city of Oxford, in order to be near the Renault factory. He has been there since he was taken on as test driver in 2002, immediately after his first season in F1 with the Minardi team. Alonso had to learn to cope on his own from an early age. He was karting from the age of 13 to 17, which involved a move to Italy. *"I did not go to school there. A boy in my class in Spain, photocopied the work and sent it to me, then when I was back in Oviedo I would go to school again."* He seems to be overburdened with nicknames, as his school mates used to call him Karras. *"We saw a film where the main character was a baddy called Karras, who killed everyone."* The Renault team refer to him as Ciccio Toro, the nice little bull, but Alonso himself prefers Fernando, or Fer, or maybe Fernie, *"because it's shorter. I am not an idol,"* he maintains. *"My win in Hungary has not changed me and I am the same as always. Of course it was a big moment for me, but I have a long career ahead of me and I hope this win is just the first step."* All the evidence points to that being the case.

The undoubted revelation of the season, there is little doubt that all eyes will be on Fernando Alonso next year.

>

Villeneuve at the end of the road

"There's nothing left to break," he admitted during the summer, commenting on the fact his reputation as a champion had reached rock bottom. Seven years after taking the title with Williams-Renault, beating off Michael Schumacher's Ferrari in the much talked about final race at Jerez, Jacques Villeneuve reached the end of his difficult road when, prior to the Japanese Grand Prix, BAR-Honda announced on 7th October, that he would be replaced by Takuma Sato in 2004. His pride hurt, he cried off from competing in Japan, even though the news could hardly have come as a surprise. When he started his F1 career, he felt he was there to *"have some fun,"* now at the age of thirty two, he was desperately trying to hang onto his drive and to rebuild his reputation within a

team which, in the early days, had been his and now looked like a pile of ruins. *"It could not be worse,"* he said with a tired sigh, adding that *"all the damage has been done and my reputation has suffered so now I must pay the price. That's life."* All these remarks seemed completely out of character. He claimed that in 2003, he had never worked so hard or derived so little pleasure from racing. He had also discarded his panoply of images: his roller blades, his grunge clothes, his hair dyed all the colours of the rainbow. All the signs of the free spirit which had been seen as a marketing tool had disappeared. It seemed that this fifth year with British American Racing, the team put together in 1993 by his friend and manager Craig Pollock, had made him think about tucking his shirt in his trousers. *"It would be nice to have one good day,"* he admitted. *"But when things go wrong, it is hard to get out of the downward spiral"*. The BAR-Honda engineers reckoned their driver was frustrated. *"Because of all the mechanical problems he has had to put up with, he is so keen to get a good result that he tends to over drive."* Qualifying laps would often end in the gravel traps and he was often out-qualified by team-mate Jenson Button, who was not always running the same fuel load. Between the 2001 and 2002 seasons, Villeneuve struggled to deal with the eviction of Craig Pollock and the arrival of David Richards to head the BAR team. The new boss tried to get rid of Villeneuve before the start of the 2003 season, mainly because of his vast salary, reckoned to be in the region of 15 million dollars per season over a five year deal! What now? He admitted to fancying having a crack at the Le Mans 24 Hours, once again for *"fun"* but rejected the idea of racing single seaters anywhere else but in F1. But, barring miracles, his absence means that in 2004, his enemy Michael Schumacher will be the only world champion on the grid.

^
Despite getting to the podium in Indianapolis, Heinz-Harald Frentzen and indeed his Sauber team had a quiet year.

A pensive Jacques Villeneuve wonders what the future holds.
<

McLaren, the upper hand in 2004?

Can a failure presage an advantage? When the 2003 season came to a close, the car McLaren should have run, the MP4-18, never made an appearance, even though it was supposed to take over from the 17 in the early stages of the season. In the end, the team competed in most grands prix with an evolution of the MP4-17, the D version, while the 18 first turned a wheel at the Paul Ricard circuit on 21st May.

"There is always a strong sense of expectation in these circumstances," declared McLaren managing director Martin Whitmarsh. *"This time, those feelings are even stronger, as we believe this car represents a significant step forward,"* while Ron Dennis added, *"we are on time, not late. Having won the first two races of the season in Melbourne and Sepang with the MP4-17D, we have recalculated our programme. The initial aim in not having the MP4-18 ready for the start of the season was to give us more research time before defining its final design. In mid-March we decided to delay its arrival and we are sticking to that. The more we can concentrate on key elements of its performance the more the car will, we hope, gain a march on the competition."* Designed by former Arrows man Mike Coughlan, who comes from the John Barnard school, under the direction of Adrian Newey, a first glance seemed to indicate the team was taking plenty of risks. With its curved nose and a fin running the length of its engine cover, it was immediately nicknamed, *"the dolphin,"* but it proved somewhat fragile. In testing, it often broke down and twice it suffered serious crashes, one with Kimi Raikkonen, the other with Alexander Wurz and it also had problems passing the FIA crash tests, taking several attempts to get through. First, it was due to appear in Monaco, then Montreal, the Nurburgring, Magny-Cours and Silverstone. Then in August, it was decided to shelve its racing career completely, even though, behind closed doors, it had apparently set some stunning lap times, because the 2004 car will be known as the MP4-19. *"Our next car will be the result of data acquired in private testing with 18 and we will have derived great benefit from it,"* concluded Ron Dennis at the end of the season. With the corners knocked off the mythical 18, the new car might feature a few steps backwards in some areas and combined with a revolutionary gearbox, the 19 might prove to be a serious contender when it appears in Melbourne in 2004.

David Coulthard managed a win in the opening round in Australia, but he was largely out-paced by his young team-mate.

Once again the Ferrari-Michael Schumacher tandem triumphed over adversity and won at the last.

Renault returns to the fold

Renault has always adopted an innovative attitude to the sport since its first foray into Formula 1 with a turbo engine. Its second period, as a simple engine supplier this time, saw it pioneer the V10 configuration. For its return as a complete team in 2002, it had banked on an engine with a very wide 111 degree V angle, much wider than the 90 or 72 degrees used by the competition. However, before the halfway point of the season, the team announced that this very unusual RS23 engine, powering the Renault RE23 car would be abandoned in favour of a more

conventional smaller angle to its V10. The news came after Alonso's surprising pole in Sepang and before his convincing win in Budapest. The 111 degree engine had been designed by Jean Jacques His on his return to Renault. It caused all sorts of reliability problems, which required various compromises in other areas of the package. It was also down on power compared with the opposition. Nevertheless, it did have some advantages. His defended it without question, but when it was canned, he moved to Ferrari-Maserati. The advantages of the wide angle were that it had a very

low centre of gravity, even though the engine block had to be made heavier. It integrated well with the chassis, helping to optimise aerodynamics around the rear of the car. The RE23 seemed well suited to most tracks, after disastrous winter testing and was one of the big surprises of the season. Given its performance through the year, a return to a more conventional engine seems almost daring! Because tackling Ferrari, BMW, Mercedes and Toyota with the same style of narrow V10 in 2004 might not be as easy as trying something new.

^
One of the major players throughout the season was Mark Webber, who managed to make his presence felt despite a car that was a long way off those of the top three teams.

The Toyota team made real progress in its second season of Formula 1.
<

Recap of the 2003 season

Position in the Championship	Driver	Team	1. Australian Grand Prix	2. Malaysian Grand Prix	3. Brazilian Grand Prix	4. San Marino Grand Prix	5. Spanish Grand Prix	6. Austrian Grand Prix	7. Monaco Grand Prix	8. Canadian Grand Prix	9. European Grand Prix	10. French Grand Prix	11. British Grand Prix	12. German Grand Prix	13. Hungarian Grand Prix	14. Italian Grand Prix	15. United States Grand Prix	16. Japanese Grand Prix	Number of pole positions	Number of victories	Number of fastest laps	Number of laps in the lead	Number of kilometers in the lead	Number of points
1	Michael SCHUMACHER	Ferrari	4	6	A	**1**	**1**	**1**	3	**1**	5	3	4	7	8	**1**	**1**	8	5	6	5	303	1432,847	93
2	Kimi RÄIKKÖNEN	McLaren Mercedes	3	**1**	2	2	A	2	2	6	A	4	3	A	2	4	2	2	2	1	3	138	679,590	91
3	Juan Pablo MONTOYA	Williams BMW	2	12	A	7	4	A	**1**	3	2	2	2	**1**	3	2	6	A	1	2	3	144	633,506	82
4	Rubens BARRICHELLO	Ferrari	A	2	A	3	3	3	8	5	3	7	**1**	A	A	3	A	**1**	3	2	3	80	428,961	65
5	Ralf SCHUMACHER	Williams BMW	8	4	7	4	5	6	4	2	**1**	**1**	9	A	4	-	A	12	3	2	1	164	737,923	58
6	Fernando ALONSO	Renault	7	3	3	6	2	A	5	4	4	A	A	4	**1**	8	A	A	2	1	1	97	441,076	55
7	David COULTHARD	McLaren Mercedes	**1**	A	4	5	A	5	7	A	(15)	5	5	2	5	A	A	3	-	1	-	39	180,366	51
8	Jarno TRULLI	Renault	5	5	8	13	A	8	6	A	A	A	6	3	7	A	4	5	-	-	-	14	68,267	33
9	Jenson BUTTON	BAR Honda	10	7	A	8	9	4	-	A	7	A	8	8	10	A	A	4	-	-	-	18	80,301	17
10	Mark WEBBER	Jaguar	A	A	(9)	A	7	7	A	7	6	6	14	(11)	6	7	A	11	-	-	-	2	8,364	17
11	Heinz-Harald FRENTZEN	Sauber Petronas	6	9	5	11	A	A	A	A	9	12	12	A	A	(13)	3	A	-	-	-	1	4,192	13
12	Giancarlo FISICHELLA	Jordan Ford	(12)	A	**1**	(15)	A	A	10	A	12	A	A	(13)	A	10	7	A	-	1	-	1	4,279	12
13	Cristiano DA MATTA	Toyota	A	11	10	12	6	10	9	(11)	A	11	7	6	11	A	9	7	-	-	-	17	87,397	10
14	Nick HEIDFELD	Sauber Petronas	A	8	A	10	10	A	11	A	8	13	17	10	9	9	5	9	-	-	-	-	-	6
15	Olivier PANIS	Toyota	A	A	A	9	A	A	13	8	A	8	11	5	A	A	A	10	-	-	-	-	-	6
16	Jacques VILLENEUVE	BAR Honda	9	A	6	A	A	12	A	A	A	9	10	9	A	6	A	-	-	-	-	-	-	6
17	Marc GENE	Williams BMW	-	-	-	-	-	-	-	-	-	-	-	-	-	5	-	-	-	-	-	-	-	4
18	Takuma SATO	BAR Honda	-	-	-	-	-	-	-	-	-	-	-	-	-	-	-	6	-	-	-	-	-	3
19	Ralph FIRMAN	Jordan Ford	A	10	A	A	8	11	12	A	11	15	13	A	-	-	A	14	-	-	-	-	-	1
20	Justin WILSON	Minardi Cosworth / Jaguar	A	A	A	A	11	13	A	A	13	14	16	A	A	A	8	13	-	-	-	-	-	1
	Then:																							
21	Antonio PIZZONIA	Jaguar	(13)	A	A	14	A	9	A	(10)	10	10	A	-	-	-	-	-	-	-	-	-	-	0
22	Jos VERSTAPPEN	Minardi Cosworth	11	13	A	A	12	A	A	9	14	16	15	A	12	A	10	15	-	-	-	-	-	0
23	Nicolas KIESA	Minardi Cosworth	-	-	-	-	-	-	-	-	-	-	-	12	13	12	11	16	-	-	-	-	-	0
24	Zsolt BAUMGARTNER	Jordan Ford	-	-	-	-	-	-	-	-	-	-	-	-	A	11	-	-	-	-	-	-	-	0

Number of laps and kms completed in 2003

Driver	Maximum 1090 laps	Maximum 5175,022 kms	GP finished / GP contested
1. M. Schumacher	987	4651,939	15/16
2. Montoya	903	4221,428	13/16
3. Alonso	892	4182,301	11/16
4. Da Matta	892	4111,472	12/16
5. Heidfeld	873	4117,370	12/16
6. Coulthard	853	3976,112	10/16
7. Räikkönen	851	3993,127	13/16
8. R.Schumacher	842	3945,638	13/15
9. Webber	822	3930,599	9/16
10. Trulli	800	3715,855	11/16
11. Button	782	3796,593	11/15
12. Barrichello	767	3639,626	11/16
13. Verstappen	753	3612,631	10/16
14. Fisichella	752	3503,416	5/16
15. Panis	691	3245,279	7/16
16. Wilson	670	3150,271	7/16
17. Villeneuve	662	3054,717	7/15
18. Frentzen	639	3121,281	8/16
19. Firman	639	2995,653	8/14
20. Pizzonia	482	2295,382	4/11
21. Kiesa	297	1442,880	5/5
22. Baumgartner	85	444,081	1/2
23. Gene	53	306,720	1/1
24. Sato	53	307,573	1/1

Number of victories

M. Schumacher	70	J. Herbert	3
A. Prost	51	P. Hill	3
A. Senna	41	M. Hawthorn	3
N. Mansell	31	J.P. Montoya	3
J. Stewart	27	D. Pironi	3
J. Clark	25	E. De Angelis	2
N. Lauda	25	P. Depailler	2
J.M. Fangio	24	J-F Gonzales	2
N. Piquet	23	J-P. Jabouille	2
D. Hill	22	P. Revson	2
M. Häkkinen	20	P. Rodriguez	2
S. Moss	16	J. Siffert	2
J. Brabham	14	P. Tambay	2
E. Fittipaldi	14	M. Trintignant	2
G. Hill	14	W. Von Trips	2
A. Ascari	13	B. Vukovich	2
D. Coulthard	13	J. Alesi	1
Ma. Andretti	12	F. Alonso	1
A. Jones	12	G. Baghetti	1
C. Reutemann	12	L. Bandini	1
J. Villeneuve	11	J-P. Beltoise	1
G. Berger	10	J. Bonnier	1
J. Hunt	10	V. Brambilla	1
R. Peterson	10	J. Bryan	1
J. Scheckter	10	F. Cevert	1
D. Hulme	8	L. Fagioli	1
J. Ickx	8	G. Fisichella	1
R. Arnoux	7	P. Flaherty	1
R. Barrichello	7	P. Gethin	1
T. Brooks	6	R. Ginther	1
J. Laffite	6	S. Hanks	1
R. Patrese	6	I. Ireland	1
J. Rindt	6	J. Mass	1
R. Schumacher	6	L. Musso	1
J. Surtees	6	A. Nannini	1
G. Villeneuve	6	G. Nilson	1
M. Alboreto	5	C. Pace	1
G. Farina	5	O. Panis	1
C. Regazzoni	5	J. Parsons	1
K. Rosberg	5	K. Räikkönen	1
J. Watson	5	L. Scarfiotti	1
D. Gurney	4	B. Sweikert	1
E. Irvine	4	J. Rathman	1
B. McLaren	4	T. Ruttman	1
T. Boutsen	3	P. Taruffi	1
P. Collins	3	L. Wallard	1
H-H. Frentzen	3	R. Ward	1

Total number of points scored

M. Schumacher	1038	D. Pironi	101
A. Prost	798.5	M. Brundle	98
A. Senna	614	J. Herbert	98
N. Piquet	485.5	P. Hill	98
N. Mansell	482	G. Fisichella	94
D. Coulthard	451	F. Cevert	89
N. Lauda	420.1	S. Johanson	88
M. Häkkinen	420	C. Amon	83
G. Berger	386	J-F Gonzales	77,64
J. Stewart	360	J-P. Beltoise	77
D. Hill	360	T. Brooks	75
R. Barrichello	337	M. Trintignant	72,33
C. Reutemann	310	J. Mass	71
G. Hill	289	P. Rodriguez	71
E. Fittipaldi	281	D. Warwick	71
R. Patrese	281	E. Cheever	70
J.M. Fangio	277.5	O. Panis	70
J. Clark	274	J. Trulli	70
J. Brabham	255	J. Siffert	68
J. Scheckter	259	A. Nannini	65
D. Hulme	248	P. Revson	61
J. Alesi	241	A. De Cesaris	59
R. Schumacher	235	C. Pace	58
J. Laffite	228	L. Bandini	58
J. Villeneuve	219	W. Von Trips	56
C. Regazzoni	212	F. Alonso	55
A. Jones	206	J. Behra	53,14
R. Peterson	206	L. Villoresi	49
B. McLaren	196.5	P. Collins	47
E. Irvine	191	I. Ireland	47
M. Alboreto	186.6	J. Button	45
S. Moss	186.5	L. Musso	44
R. Arnoux	181	P. Taruffi	41
J. Ickx	181	J. Bonnier	39
Ma. Andretti	180	M. Salo	33
J. Surtees	180	M. Blundell	32
J. Hunt	179	L. Fagioli	32
J. Watson	169	J-P. Jarier	31,5
J.P. Montoya	163	I. Capelli	31
H-H. Frentzen	161	G. Nilson	31
K. Rosberg	159,5	**Then:**	
K. Räikkönen	124	N. Heidfeld	25
E. De Angelis	122	C. Da Matta	10
J. Rindt	109	T. Sato	5
R. Ginther	107	M. Gene	4
G. Villeneuve	107	R. Firman	1
P. Tambay	103	J. Wilson	1

Number of Grand Prix contested

Riccardo Patrese	256	Jochen Mass	112	Mark Blundell	63	Eliseo Salazar	37
Michele Alboreto	215	Mika Salo	111	Erik Comas	63	Alberto Ascari	36
Andrea de Cesaris	213	Elio de Angelis	109	Olivier Grouillard	62	Tim Schenken	36
Gerhard Berger	210	Piercarlo Ghinzani	108	Pedro de la Rosa	62	Andrea de Adamich	35
Nelson Piquet	207	Jo Bonnier	107	Jochen Rindt	61	Rupert Keegan	35
Jean Alesi	201	Jos Verstappen	107	Rolf Stommelen	60	Bernd Schneider	34
Alain Prost	200	Stefan Johansson	103	Henri Pescarolo	59	Luigi Villoresi	33
Michael Schumacher	195	Bruce McLaren	101	Hector Rebaque	58	Ricardo Rosset	33
Nigel Mansell	190	Chris Amon	100	Jean Behra	57	Shinji Nakano	33
Rubens Barrichello	180	Jackie Stewart	100	Pedro Rodriguez	55	Fernando Alonso	33
Jacques Laffite	178	Jo Siffert	99	Jean-Pierre Jabouille	55	Marc Gene	32
Graham Hill	177	Pedro Paulo Diniz	99	Luca Badoer	55	Chico Serra	32
Niki Lauda	171	Ukyo Katayama	97	Manfred Winkelhock	54	Luis Perez-Sala	32
Martin Brundle	165	Ivan Capelli	96	Philippe Streiff	54	Pedro Lamy	32
Thierry Boutsen	164	Patrick Depailler	95	Richie Ginther	53	Toranosuke Takagi	32
Johnny Herbert	163	James Hunt	92	Alexander Wurz	52	Ricardo Zonta	32
Rene Arnoux	162	Marc Surer	88	Juan-Manuel Fangio	51	Mark Webber	32
Ayrton Senna	162	Jean-Pierre Beltoise	87	Innes Ireland	50	Carel-Godin de Beaufort	31
Mika Hakkinen	162	Jonathan Palmer	87	Mike Hailwood	50	Peter Revson	31
Derek Warwick	161	Aguri Suzuki	87	Kimi Räikkönen	50	Gunnar Nilsson	31
Heinz-Harald Frentzen	157	Dan Gurney	86	Juan-Pablo Montoya	50	Jose-Froilan Gonzalez	30
David Coulthard	157	Maurice Trintignant	85	Phill Hill	49	Peter Gethin	30
John Watson	155	Bertrand Gachot	84	Jackie Oliver	49	Raul Boesel	30
Emerson Fittipaldi	147	Arturo Merzario	83	Yannick Dalmas	49	David Brabham	30
Eddie Irvine	147	Bruno Giacomelli	82	Mike Hawthorn	48	Robert Manzon	29
Carlos Reutemann	146	Stefano Modena	81	Roy Salvadori	48	Trevor Taylor	29
Eddie Cheever	143	Mauricio Gugelmin	80	Eric Bernard	47	Mike Beuttler	29
Olivier Panis	141	Satoru Nakajima	79	Francois Cevert	46	Huub Rothengatter	29
Clay Regazzoni	139	Vittorio Brambilla	78	Christian Danner	46	Eric van de Poele	29
Jean-Pierre Jarier	139	Alessandro Nannini	78	Alex Zanardi	44	Enrique Bernoldi	28
Jacques Villeneuve	131	Gabriele Tarquini	78	Christian Fittipaldi	43	Wolfgang von Trips	27
Mario Andretti	130	Hans-Joachim Stuck	77	Masten Gregory	42	Piers Courage	27
Keke Rosberg	128	Roberto Moreno	75	Lorenzo Bandini	42	Roberto Guerrero	27
Jack Brabham	127	Alex Caffi	75	Tom Pryce	42	Paul Belmondo	27
Pierluigi Martini	124	Nicola Larini	75	Karl Wendlinger	42	Bob Anderson	26
Ronnie Peterson	123	Stirling Moss	73	Brett Lunger	41	Harald Ertl	26
Giancarlo Fisichella	123	Jim Clark	73	Jan Lammers	41	Andrea Montermini	26
Damon Hill	122	Jos Carlos Pace	73	Mauro Baldi	41	Luigi Musso	25
Patrick Tambay	120	Teo Fabi	71	Tony Brooks	40	Tony Maggs	25
Jacky Ickx	119	Didier Pironi	70	Emanuele Pirro	40	**Then:**	
Alan Jones	116	Jyrki Jarvi Lehto	70	Louis Rosier	39	Takuma Sato	18
Philippe Alliot	115	Gianni Morbidelli	70	Howden Ganley	38	Cristiano Da Matta	16
Ralf Schumacher	115	Gilles Villeneuve	67	Giuseppe Farina	37	Justin Wilson	16
Jody Scheckter	113	Nick Heidfeld	66	Peter Collins	37	Ralpf Firman	14
Jarno Trulli	112	Jenson Button	66	Mike Spence	37	Antonio Pizzonia	11
John Surtees	112	Derek Daly	64	Wilson Fittipaldi	37	Nicolas Kiesa	5
Denny Hulme	112	Harry Schell	63	Brian Henton	37	Szolt Baumgartner	2

Number of pole positions

A. Senna	65	R. Patrese	8
M. Schumacher	55	J. Laffite	7
J. Clark	33	E. Fittipaldi	6
A. Prost	33	P. Hill	6
N. Mansell	32	J.P. Jabouille	6
J.M. Fangio	29	A. Jones	6
M. Häkkinen	26	C. Reutemann	6
N. Lauda	24	C. Amon	5
N. Piquet	24	G. Farina	5
D. Hill	20	C. Regazzoni	5
Ma. Andretti	18	K. Rosberg	5
R. Arnoux	18	P. Tambay	5
J. Stewart	17	M. Hawthorn	4
S. Moss	16	D. Pironi	4
A. Ascari	14	R. Schumacher	4
J. Hunt	14	T. Brooks	3
R. Peterson	14	E. De Angelis	3
J. Brabham	13	T. Fabi	3
G. Hill	13	J-F. Gonzales	3
J. Ickx	13	D. Gurney	3
J. Villeneuve	13	J-P. Jarier	3
G. Berger	12	J. Scheckter	3
D. Coulthard	12	**Then:**	
J.P. Montoya	11	F. Alonso	2
J. Rindt	10	H-H. Frentzen	2
R. Barrichello	9	K. Räikkönen	2
J. Surtees	8	G. Fisichella	1

Number of fastest laps

M. Schumacher	56	J. Villeneuve	9
A. Prost	41	J. Hunt	8
N. Mansell	30	G. Villeneuve	8
J. Clark	28	R. Schumacher	7
M. Häkkinen	25	E. Fittipaldi	6
N. Lauda	24	H-H. Frentzen	6
J.M. Fangio	23	J-F. Gonzalez	6
N. Piquet	23	D. Gurney	6
G. Berger	21	M. Hawthorn	6
D. Hill	19	P. Hill	6
S. Moss	19	J. Laffite	6
A. Senna	19	C. Reutemann	6
D. Coulthard	18	M. Alboreto	5
C. Regazzoni	15	G. Farina	5
J. Stewart	15	C. Pace	5
J. Ickx	14	D. Pironi	5
A. Jones	13	J. Scheckter	5
R. Patrese	13	J. Watson	5
R. Arnoux	12	J. Alesi	4
J. Brabham	12	J.P. Beltoise	4
A. Ascari	11	P. Depailler	4
R. Barrichello	11	K. Räikkönen	4
J. Surtees	11	J. Siffert	4
Ma. Andretti	10		
G. Hill	10	**Then:**	
D. Hulme	9	F. Alonso	1
J.P. Montoya	9	G. Fisichella	1
R. Peterson	9	E. Irvine	1

Number of laps in the lead

M. Schumacher	3'959	R. Arnoux	507
A. Senna	2'931	K. Rosberg	512
A. Prost	2'683	E. Fittipaldi	478
N. Mansell	2'058	D. Hulme	449
J. Clark	1'940	J. Rindt	387
J. Stewart	1'918	C. Regazzoni	360
N. Piquet	1'633	R. Schumacher	356
N. Lauda	1'590	J.P. Montoya	331
M. Häkkinen	1'490	J. Surtees	307
D. Hill	1'363	D. Pironi	295
J.M. Fangio	1'347	J. Watson	287
S. Moss	1'164	J. Laffite	283
G. Hill	1'106	J-F. Gonzalez	272
A. Ascari	927	J. Alesi	265
D. Coulthard	894	M. Hawthorn	225
J. Brabham	825	M. Alboreto	218
Ma. Andretti	799	D. Gurney	204
G. Berger	754	P. Tambay	197
R. Peterson	694	**Then:**	
J. Scheckter	674	K. Räikkönen	159
J. Hunt	666	H-H. Frentzen	150
C. Reutemann	650	F. Alonso	97
J. Villeneuve	634	J. Trulli	52
R. Barrichello	597	G. Fisichella	36
A. Jones	589	J. Button	18
R. Patrese	565	C. Da Matta	17
G. Villeneuve	534	O. Panis	16
J. Ickx	528	M. Webber	2

Number of kilometers in the lead

M. Schumacher	18'523	E. Fittipaldi	2'235
A. Senna	13'430	K. Rosberg	2'165
A. Prost	12'474	J. Surtees	2'117
J. Clark	10'110	D. Hulme	1'971
N. Mansell	9'503	J. Rindt	1'898
J.M. Fangio	9'316	C. Regazzoni	1'851
J. Stewart	9'160	R. Schumacher	1'722
N. Piquet	7'756	M. Hawthorn	1'635
M. Häkkinen	7'201	D. Gurney	1'612
N. Lauda	7'058	J.P. Montoya	1'565
D. Hill	6'339	P. Hill	1'528
G. Hill	4'767	J. Laffite	1'519
J. Brabham	4'540	J. Alesi	1'285
D. Coulthard	4'195	T. Brooks	1'268
G. Berger	3'718	D. Pironi	1'240
Ma. Andretti	3'577	J. Watson	1'238
J. Hunt	3'363	P. Tambay	974
R. Peterson	3'262	P. Collins	946
C. Reutemann	3'255	**Then:**	
J. Ickx	3'119	K. Räikkönen	769
J. Villeneuve	2'970	H-H. Frentzen	750
J. Scheckter	2'851	F. Alonso	441
A. Jones	2'847	J. Trulli	233
G. Farina	2'651	G. Fisichella	176
R. Arnoux	2'571	C. Da Matta	87
R. Patrese	2'553	J. Button	80
R. Barrichello	2'853	O. Panis	53
G. Villeneuve	2'251	M. Webber	8

The 54 World Champions

Year	Driver	Country	Team	Number of races	Number of poles	Number of victories	Number of fastest laps
1950	Giuseppe Farina	ITA	Alfa Roméo	7	2	3	3
1951	Juan Manuel Fangio	ARG	Alfa Roméo	8	4	3	5
1952	Alberto Ascari	ITA	Ferrari	8	5	6	5
1953	Alberto Ascari	ITA	Ferrari	9	6	5	4
1954	Juan Manuel Fangio	ARG	Mercedes/Maserati	9	5	6	3
1955	Juan Manuel Fangio	ARG	Mercedes	7	3	4	3
1956	Juan Manuel Fangio	ARG	Lancia/Ferrari	8	5	3	3
1957	Juan Manuel Fangio	ARG	Maserati	8	4	4	2
1958	Mike Hawthorn	GB	Ferrari	11	4	1	5
1959	Jack Brabham	AUS	Cooper Climax	9	1	2	1
1960	Jack Brabham	AUS	Cooper Climax	10	3	5	3
1961	Phil Hill	USA	Ferrari	8	5	2	2
1962	Graham Hill	GB	BRM	9	1	4	3
1963	Jim Clark	GB	Lotus Climax	10	7	7	6
1964	John Surtees	GB	Ferrari	10	2	2	2
1965	Jim Clark	GB	Lotus Climax	10	6	6	6
1966	Jack Brabham	AUS	Brabham Repco	9	3	4	1
1967	Denny Hulme	NZ	Brabham Repco	11	0	2	2
1968	Graham Hill	GB	Lotus Ford	12	2	3	0
1969	Jackie Stewart	GB	Matra Ford	11	2	6	5
1970	Jochen Rindt	AUT	Lotus Ford	13	3	5	1
1971	Jackie Stewart	GB	Tyrrell Ford	11	6	6	3
1972	Emerson Fittipaldi	BRE	Lotus Ford	12	3	5	0
1973	Jackie Stewart	GB	Tyrrell Ford	15	3	5	1
1974	Emerson Fittipaldi	BRE	McLaren Ford	15	2	3	0
1975	Niki Lauda	AUT	Ferrari	14	9	5	2
1976	James Hunt	GB	McLaren Ford	16	8	6	2
1977	Niki Lauda	AUT	Ferrari	17	2	3	3
1978	Mario Andretti	USA	Lotus Ford	16	8	6	3
1979	Jody Scheckter	SA	Ferrari	15	1	3	1
1980	Alan Jones	AUS	Williams Ford	14	3	5	5
1981	Nelson Piquet	BRE	Brabham Ford	15	4	3	1
1982	Keke Rosberg	FIN	Williams Ford	16	1	1	0
1983	Nelson Piquet	BRE	Brabham BMW Turbo	15	1	3	4
1984	Niki Lauda	AUT	McLaren TAG Porsche Turbo	16	0	5	5
1985	Alain Prost	FRA	McLaren TAG Porsche Turbo	16	2	5	5
1986	Alain Prost	FRA	McLaren TAG Porsche Turbo	16	1	4	2
1987	Nelson Piquet	BRE	Williams Honda Turbo	16	4	3	4
1988	Ayrton Senna	BRE	McLaren Honda Turbo	16	13	8	3
1989	Alain Prost	FRA	McLaren Honda	16	2	4	5
1990	Ayrton Senna	BRE	McLaren Honda	16	10	6	2
1991	Ayrton Senna	BRE	McLaren Honda	16	8	7	2
1992	Nigel Mansell	GB	Williams Renault	16	14	9	8
1993	Alain Prost	FRA	Williams Renault	16	13	7	6
1994	Michael Schumacher	GER	Benetton Ford	14	6	8	9
1995	Michael Schumacher	GER	Benetton Renault	17	4	9	7
1996	Damon Hill	GB	Williams Renault	16	9	8	5
1997	Jacques Villeneuve	CAN	Williams Renault	17	10	7	3
1998	Mika Häkkinen	FIN	McLaren Mercedes	16	9	8	6
1999	Mika Häkkinen	FIN	McLaren Mercedes	16	11	5	6
2000	Michael Schumacher	GER	Ferrari	17	9	9	2
2001	Michael Schumacher	GER	Ferrari	17	11	9	3
2002	Michael Schumacher	GER	Ferrari	17	7	11	7
2003	Michael Schumacher	GER	Ferrari	16	5	6	5

Constructors Championship 2003

Position	Team	Number of points	Number of poles	Number of victories	Number of fastest laps	Number of laps in the lead	Number of kms in the lead
1.	Ferrari	158	8	8	8	383	1,861,808
2.	McLaren Mercedes	142	2	2	3	177	859,956
3.	Williams BMW	140	4	4	4	308	1,371,429
4.	Renault	88	2	1	1	111	509,343
5.	BAR Honda	23	-	-	-	-	-
6.	Sauber Petronas	19	-	-	-	-	-
7.	Jaguar	17	-	-	-	-	-
8.	Toyota	16	-	-	-	-	-
9.	Jordan Ford	13	-	1	-	-	-
10.	Minardi Cosworth	0	-	-	-	-	-

Number of Constructors Championship (existing since 1958)

13: Ferrari
1961 - 64 - 75 - 76 - 77 - 79 - 82 - 83 - 99 - 2000 - 2001 - 2002 - 2003

9: Williams
1980 - 81 - 86 - 87 - 92 - 93 - 94 - 96 - 97

8: McLaren
1974 - 84 - 85 - 88 - 89 - 90 - 91- 98

7: Lotus
1963 - 65 - 68 - 70 -72 - 73 - 78

2: Cooper 1959 - 60
Brabham 1966 - 67

1: Vanwall 1958
BRM 1962
Matra 1969
Tyrrell 1971
Benetton 1995

Number of pole positions per make

Ferrari	166
Williams	123
McLaren	114
Lotus	107
Brabham	39
Renault	33
Benetton	15
Tyrrell	14
Alfa Roméo	12
BRM	11
Cooper	11
Maserati	10
Ligier	9
Mercedes	8
Vanwall	7
March	5
Matra	4
Shadow	3
Lancia	2
Jordan	2
Arrows	1
Honda	1
Lola	1
Porsche	1
Stewart	1
Toleman	1
Wolf	1

Number of victories per make

Ferrari	167
McLaren	137
Williams	112
Lotus	79
Brabham	35
Benetton	26
Tyrrell	23
BRM	17
Cooper	16
Renault	16
Alfa Roméo	10
Ligier	9
Maserati	9
Matra	9
Mercedes	9
Vanwall	9
Jordan	4
March	3
Wolf	3
Honda	2
Eagle	1
Hesketh	1
Penske	1
Porsche	1
Shadow	1
Stewart	1

Number of fastest laps per make

Ferrari	167
Williams	125
McLaren	112
Lotus	70
Brabham	41
Benetton	36
Tyrrell	20
Renault	19
BRM	15
Maserati	15
Alfa Roméo	14
Cooper	13
Matra	12
Ligier	11
Mercedes	9
March	7
Vanwall	6
Surtees	4
Eagle	2
Honda	2
Jordan	2
Shadow	2
Wolf	2
Ensign	1
Gordini	1
Hesketh	1
Lancia	1
Parnelli	1

Number of Grand Prix per make

Ferrari	686
McLaren	559
Lotus	491
Williams	440
Tyrrell	430
Brabham	394
Ligier	326
Minardi	303
Arrows	291
Benetton	260
Jordan	213
BRM	197
March	197
Sauber	179
Renault	156
Lola	149
Osella	132
Cooper	129
Surtees	118
Alfa Romeo	110
Shadow	104
Ensign	99
Footwork	91
ATS	89
Prost	83
BAR	83
Dallara	78
Toyota	33

Family picture of the 2003 World Championship. From left to right, back row: Jacques Villeneuve, Jenson Button, Giancarlo Fisichella, Ralph Firman, Jarno Trulli and Fernando Alonso. Second row: Ralf Schumacher, Juan Pablo Montoya, Nick Heidfeld, Heinz-Harald Frentzen, David Coulthard, Kimi Räikkönen, Cristiano da Matta and Olivier Panis. Front row: Mark Webber, Antonio Pizzonia, Michael Schumacher, Rubens Barrichello, Jos Verstappen and Justin Wilson.

Sporting regulations

The FIA will organise the FIA Formula One World Championship (the Championship) which is the property of the FIA and comprises two titles of World Champion, one for drivers and one for constructors. It consists of the Formula One Grand Prix races which are included in the Formula One calendar and in respect of which the ASNs and organisers have signed the organisation agreement provided for in the 1998 Concorde Agreement (Events). All the participating parties (FIA, ASNs, organisers, competitors and circuits) undertake to apply as well as observe the rules governing the Championship and must hold FIA Super Licences which are issued to drivers, competitors, officials, organisers and circuits.

REGULATIONS
1. The final text of these Sporting Regulations shall be the English version which will be used should any dispute arise as to their interpretation. Headings in this document are for ease of reference only and do not form part of these Sporting Regulations.
2. These Sporting Regulations were published on 30 October 2002 and come into force on 1 January 2003 and replace all previous FIA Formula One World Championship Sporting Regulations.

LICENCES
10. All drivers, competitors and officials participating in the Championship must hold a FIA Super Licence. Applications for Super Licences must be made to the FIA through the applicant's ASN. The driver's name will remain on the list for Super Licences for one year.

CHAMPIONSHIP EVENTS
11. Events are reserved for Formula One cars as defined in the Technical Regulations.
12. Each Event will have the status of an international restricted competition.
13. The distance of all races, from the start signal referred to in Article 138 to the chequered flag, shall be equal to the least number of complete laps which exceed a distance of 305 km. However, should two hours elapse before the scheduled race distance is completed, the leader will be shown the chequered flag when he crosses the control line (the Line) at the end of the lap during which the two hour period ended. The Line is a single line which crosses both the track and the pit lane.
14. The maximum number of Events in the Championship is 17, the minimum is 8.
15. The final list of Events is published by the FIA before 1 January each year.
16. An Event which is cancelled with less than three months written notice to the FIA will not be considered for inclusion in the following year's Championship unless the FIA judges the cancellation to have been due to force majeure.
17. An Event may be cancelled if fewer than 12 cars are available for it.

WORLD CHAMPIONSHIP
18. The Formula One World Championship driver's title will be awarded to the driver who has scored the highest number of points, taking into consideration all the results obtained during the Events which have actually taken place.
19. Points will not be awarded for the Championship unless the driver has driven the same car throughout the race in the Event in question.
20. The title of Formula One World Champion Constructor will be awarded to the make which has scored the highest number of points, results from both cars being taken into account.
21. The constructor of an engine or rolling chassis is the person (including any corporate or unincorporated body) which owns the intellectual property rights to such engine or chassis. The make of an engine or chassis is the name attributed to it by its constructor. If the make of the chassis is not the same as that of the engine, the title will be awarded to the former which shall always precede the latter in the name of the car.
22. Points for both titles will be awarded at each Event according to the following scale: 1st: 10 points, 2nd: 8 points, 3rd: 6 points, 4th: 5 points, 5th: 4 points, 6th: 3 points, 7th: 2 points, 8th: 1 point
23. If a race is stopped under Articles 153 and 154, and cannot be restarted, no points will be awarded in case A, half points will be awarded in case B and full points will be awarded in case C.
24. The drivers finishing first, second and third in the Championship must be present at the annual FIA Prize Giving ceremony.

DEAD HEAT
25. Prizes and points awarded for all the positions of competitors who tie, will be added together and shared equally.
26. If two or more constructors or drivers finish the season with the same number of points, the higher place in the Championship (in either case) shall be awarded to:
a) the holder of the greatest number of first places,
b) if the number of first places is the same, the holder of the greatest number of second places,
c) if the number of second places is the same, the holder of the greatest number of third places and so on until a winner emerges.
d) if this procedure fails to produce a result, the FIA will nominate the winner according to such criteria as it thinks fit.

COMPETITORS APPLICATIONS
42. Applications to compete in the Championship may be submitted to the FIA at any time between 1 March two years prior to the Championship in which the applicant wishes to compete and 15 November immediately preceding such Championship, on an entry form as set out in Appendix 2 hereto accompanied by the entry fee provided for in the Agreement, together with the deposit provided for in Article 45 where applicable. Applications from Teams not already competing in the Championship will only be considered where a place is available, taking into account all the Teams who are entitled to compete under the Agreement. Entry forms will be made available by FIA who will notify the applicant of the result of the application within thirty days of its receipt. Successful applicants are automatically entered in all Events of the Championship and will be the only competitors at Events.
43. Applications shall include:
a) confirmation that the applicant has read and understood the Agreement (including its schedules), the Code, the Technical Regulations and the Sporting Regulations and agrees, on its own behalf and on behalf of everyone associated with its participation in the Championship, to observe them,

b) the name of the team (which must include the name of the chassis),
c) the make of the competing car,
d) the make of the engine,
e) the names of the drivers. A driver may be nominated subsequent to the application upon payment of a fee fixed by the FIA,
f) an undertaking by the applicant to participate in every Event with the number of cars and drivers entered.
g) an undertaking that the car does not make use of any component, system, software or device which has been (or might reasonably be suspected to have been) designed, supplied or constructed by or with the help of anyone who has been involved on behalf of the FIA with checking Formula One electronic systems during the 24 months immediately preceding the application.
44. A competitor may change the make and/or type of engine at any time during the Championship. All points scored with an engine of different make to that which was first entered in the Championship will count (and will be aggregated) for the assessment of Benefits, however such points will not count towards (nor be aggregated for) the FIA Formula One Constructors Championship.
45. With the exception of those whose cars have scored points in the Championship of the previous year, applicants must supply information about the size of their company, their financial position and their ability to meet their prescribed obligations. Any applicant which did not take part in the Championship for the previous year must also deposit US$48,000,000 (forty-eight million United States dollars) with the FIA when submitting its application. This sum will be returned to it forthwith if its application is refused or in twelve equal monthly instalments (including interest) commencing immediately after the first Event in which it competes, provided it has met and continues to meet all the requirements of the Agreement and its schedules. If the applicant fails to appear for the Championship for which it has entered, its deposit will be forfeit save only that the applicant may delay its participation by one year, in which case US$12,000,000 (twelve million United States dollars) will be forfeit and the balance repaid as set out above.
46. All applications will be studied by the FIA which will publish the list of cars and drivers accepted together with their race numbers on 1 December (or the following Monday if 1 December falls on a week-end), having first notified unsuccessful applicants as set out in Article 42.
47. No more than 24 cars will be admitted to the Championship, two being entered by each competitor.
48. If in the opinion of the Formula One Commission a competitor fails to operate his team in a manner compatible with the standards of the Championship or in any way brings the Championship into disrepute, the FIA may exclude such competitor from the Championship forthwith.

INCIDENTS
53. Incident means any occurrence or series of occurrences involving one or more drivers, or any action by any driver, which is reported to the stewards by the race director (or noted by the stewards and referred to the race director for investigation) which:
- necessitated the stopping of a race under Article 153;
- constituted a breach of these Sporting Regulations or the Code;
- caused a false start by one or more cars;
- caused a collision;
- forced a driver off the track;
- illegitimately prevented a legitimate overtaking manoeuvre by a driver;
- illegitimately impeded another driver during overtaking.
54. (a) It shall be at the discretion of the stewards to decide, upon a report or a request by the race director, if
a) driver or drivers involved in an incident shall be penalised.
b) If an incident is under investigation by the stewards, a message informing all Teams of this will be displayed on the timing monitors.
c) If a driver is involved in a collision or Incident (see Article 53), and has been informed of this by the stewards no later than 30 minutes after the race has finished, he must not leave the circuit without their consent.
55. The stewards may impose any one of three penalties on any driver involved in an Incident:
a) A drive-through penalty. The driver must enter the pit lane and re-join the race without stopping at his pit;
b) A ten second time penalty. The driver must enter the pit lane, stop at his pit for at least ten seconds and then re-join the race.
c) a drop of ten grid positions at the following Event. However, should either of the time penalties be imposed during the last five laps, or after the end of a race, Article 56 b) below will not apply and 25 seconds will be added to the elapsed race time of the driver concerned.
56. Should the stewards decide to impose a time penalty, the following procedure will be followed:
a) The stewards will give written notification of the time penalty which has been imposed to an official of the team concerned and will ensure that this information is also displayed on the timing monitors.
b) From the time the steward's decision is notified on the timing monitors the relevant driver may cover no more than three complete laps before entering the pits and proceeding to his pit where he shall remain for the period of the time penalty. Whilst a car is stationary in the pits as a result of incurring a time penalty it may not be worked on. However, if the engine stops it may be started after the time penalty period has elapsed.
c) When the time penalty period has elapsed the driver may rejoin the race.
d) Any breach or failure to comply with Articles 56 b) or 56 c) may result in the car being excluded.
57. Any determination made or any penalty imposed pursuant to Articles 55 shall be without prejudice to the operation of Articles 160 or 161 of the Code.

PROTESTS
58. Protests shall be made in accordance with the Code and accompanied by a fee of 2000 US Dollars.

SANCTIONS
59. The stewards may inflict the penalties specifically set out in these Sporting Regulations in addition to or instead of any other penalties available to them under the Code.

CHANGES OF DRIVER
60. During a season, each team will be permitted one driver change for their first car and will be permitted to have three drivers for their second car who may be changed at any time provided that any driver change is

made in accordance with the Code and before the start of the second qualifying practice session. After 16.00 on the day of scrutineering, a driver change may only take place with the consent of the stewards. In all other circumstances, competitors will be obliged to use the drivers they nominated at the time of entering the Championship except in cases of force majeure which will be considered separately. Any new driver may score points in the Championship.

PIT LANE
66. (a) For the avoidance of doubt and for description purposes, the pit lane shall be divided into two lanes The lane closest to the pit wall is designated the "fast lane", and the lane closest to the garages is designated the "inner lane". Other than when cars are at the pit exit under Articles 134 or 157, the inner lane is the only area where any tyre rubber left when cars leave their pit stop position, Competitors may not attempt to enhance the grip of the surface in the pit lane unless a problem has been clearly identified and a solution agreed by the FIA Safety Delegate.
c) Competitors must not paint lines on any part of the pit lane.
d) No equipment may be left in the fast lane. A car may enter or remain in the fast lane only with the driver sitting in the car behind the steering wheel in his normal position, even when the car is being pushed.
e) Team personnel are only allowed in the pit lane immediately before they are required to work on a car and must withdraw as soon as the work is complete.
f) It is the responsibility of the Competitor to release his car after a pit stop only when it is safe to do so.

SPORTING CHECKS
67. At the first Event of each Championship, the FIA will check all licences.

SCRUTINEERING
68. Initial scrutineering of the car will take place three days (Monaco: four days) before the race between 10.00 and 16.00 in the garage assigned to each team.
69. Unless a waiver is granted by the stewards, competitors who do not keep to these time limits will not be allowed to take part in the Event.
70. No car may take part in the Event until it has been passed by the scrutineers.
71. The scrutineers may:
a) check the eligibility of a car or of a competitor at any time during an Event,
b) require a car to be dismantled by the competitor to make sure that the conditions of eligibility or conformity are fully satisfied,
c) require a competitor to pay the reasonable expenses which exercise of the powers mentioned in this Article may entail,
d) require a competitor to supply them with such parts or samples as they may deem necessary.
72. Any car which, after being passed by the scrutineers, is dismantled or modified in a way which might affect its safety or call into question its eligibility, or which is involved in an accident with similar consequences, must be re-presented for scrutineering approval.
73. The race director or the clerk of the course may require that any car involved in an accident be stopped and checked.
74. Checks and scrutineering shall be carried out by duly appointed officials who shall also be responsible for the operation of the parc fermé and who alone are authorised to give instructions to the competitors.
75. The stewards will publish the findings of the scrutineers each time cars are checked during the Event. These results will not include any specific figure except when a car is found to be in breach of the Technical Regulations.

SUPPLY OF TYRES IN THE CHAMPIONSHIP AND TYRE LIMITATION DURING THE EVENT
76. Supply of tyres:
a) Any tyre company wishing to supply tyres to Formula One Teams must notify the FIA of its intention to do so no later than 1 January preceding the year during which such tyres will be supplied. Any tyre company wishing to cease the supply of tyres to Formula One Teams must notify the FIA of its intention to do so no later than 1 January of the year preceding that in which such tyres were to be supplied.
b) No tyre may be used in the Championship unless the company supplying such tyres accepts and adheres to the following conditions:
- one tyre supplier present in the Championship: this company must equip 100% of the entered teams on ordinary commercial terms;
- two tyre suppliers present: each of them must, if called upon to do so, be prepared to equip up to 60% of the entered teams on ordinary commercial terms;
- three or more tyre suppliers present: each of them must, if called upon to do so, be prepared to equip up to 40% of the entered teams on ordinary commercial terms;
- each tyre supplier must undertake to provide no more than two specifications of dry-weather tyre to each Team at each Event, each of which must be of one homogeneous compound;
- each tyre supplier must undertake to provide no more than one specification of wet-weather tyre at each Event which must be of one homogenous compound;
- if, in the interests of maintaining current levels of circuit safety, the FIA deems it necessary to reduce tyre grip, it shall introduce such rules as the tyre suppliers may advise or, in the absence of advice which achieves the FIA's objectives, specify the maximum permissible contact areas for front and rear tyres.
77. Quantity and type of tyres:
a) During the Event no driver may use more than forty dry-weather tyres and twenty eight wet-weather tyres. From the forty dry-weather tyres each driver will be allocated twelve (six front and six rear) for use on the first day of practice, these tyres may not be used at any other time during the Event. No more than eight (four front and four rear) of the twelve tyres allocated for the first day of practice may be of one specification. Before the second qualifying practice begins each driver must nominate which specification of tyre he will use for the remainder of the Event.
b) All dry-weather tyres must incorporate circumferential grooves square to the wheel axis and around the entire circumference of the contact surface of each tyre.
c) Each front dry-weather tyre, when new, must incorporate 4 grooves which are:
- arranged symmetrically about the centre of the tyre tread;
- at least 14mm wide at the contact surface and which taper uniformly to a minimum of 10mm at the lower surface;

- at least 2.5mm deep across the whole lower surface;
- 50mm (+/- 1.0mm) between centres. Furthermore, the tread width of the front tyres must not exceed 270mm.
d) Each rear dry-weather tyre, when new, must incorporate 4 grooves which are:
- arranged symmetrically about the centre of the tyre tread;
- at least 14mm wide at the contact surface and which taper uniformly to a minimum of ?
surface;
- at least 2.5mm deep ~~~
- 50mm (+/- 1.0mm) ~~~
referred to in c) and d) above
is fitted to a wheel and inflated to ~~~
e) A wet-weather tyre is one which has been designed for use on a wet or damp track. All wet-weather tyres must, when new, have a contact area which does not exceed 280cm_ when fitted to the front of the car and 440cm_ when fitted to the rear. Contact areas will be measured over any square section of the tyre which is normal to and symmetrical about the tyre centre line and which measures 200mm x 200mm when fitted to the front of the car and 250mm x 250mm when fitted to the rear. For the purposes of establishing conformity, only void areas which are greater than 2.5mm in depth will be considered. Prior to use at an Event, each tyre manufacturer must provide the technical delegate with a full scale drawing of each type of wet-weather tyre intended for use. With the exception of race day, wet-weather tyres may only be used after the track has been declared wet by the race director and, during the remainder of the relevant session, the choice of tyres is free.
f) Tyre specifications will be determined by the FIA no later than 1 September of the previous season. Once determined in this way, the specification of the tyres will not be changed during the Championship season without the agreement of the Formula One Commission.
78. Control of tyres:
a) All tyres which are to be used at an Event will be marked with a unique identification.
b) From among the twenty-eight dry-weather tyres available to each driver following the first day of practice, the FIA technical delegate will choose at random sixteen tyres (eight front and eight rear) which are the only dry-weather tyres which such car may use in qualifying practice.
c) At any time during an Event, and at his absolute discretion, the FIA technical delegate may select the dry-weather tyres to be used by any Team from among the total stock of tyres which such Team's designated supplier has present at the Event.
d) A competitor wishing to replace one unused tyre by another unused one must present both tyres to the FIA technical delegate.
e) The use of tyres without appropriate identification is strictly forbidden.
79. Wear of tyres:
The Championship will be contested on grooved tyres. The FIA reserve the right to introduce at any time a method of measuring remaining groove depth if performance appears to be enhanced by high wear or by the use of tyres which are worn so that the grooves are no longer visible.

WEIGHING
80. (a) During each qualifying practice session cars will be weighed as follows:
1) the FIA will install weighing equipment in an area as close to the first pit as possible, this area will be used for the weighing procedure;
2) cars will be selected at random to undergo the weighing procedure. The FIA technical delegate will inform the driver by means of a red light at the pit entrance that his car has been selected for weighing;
3) having been signalled (by means of a red light), that his car has been selected for weighing, the driver will proceed directly to the weighing area and stop his engine;
4) the car will then be weighed and the result given to the driver in writing;
5) if the car is unable to reach the weighing area under its own power it will be placed under the exclusive control of the marshals who will take the car to be weighed;
6) a car or driver may not leave the weighing area without the consent of the FIA technical delegate;
7) if a car stops on the circuit and the driver leaves the car, he must go to the weighing area immediately on his return to the pits in order for his weight to be established.
b) After the race each car crossing the Line will be weighed. If a driver wishes to leave his car before it is weighed he must ask the technical delegate to weigh him in order that his weight may be added to that of the car.
c) The relevant car may be excluded should its weight be less than that specified in Article 4.1 of the Technical Regulations when weighed under a) or b) above, save where the deficiency in weight results from the accidental loss of a component of the car.
d) No solid, liquid, gas or other substance or matter of whatsoever nature may be added to, placed on, or removed from a car after it has been selected for weighing or has finished the race or during the weighing procedure. (Except by a scrutineer when acting in his official capacity).
e) Only scrutineers and officials may enter the weighing area. No intervention of any kind is allowed there unless authorised by such officials.
81. Any breach of these provisions for the weighing of cars may result in the exclusion of the relevant car.

SPARE CAR
84. A competitor may use several cars for practice and the race provided that:
a) he has no more than four cars available for use at any one time:
b) he uses no more than two cars for free practice sessions on each of the two practice days held under Article 113 a) and b);
c) he uses no more than three cars during each qualifying practice;
d) they are all of the same make and were entered in the Championship by the same competitor;
e) they have been scrutineered in accordance with these Sporting Regulations;
f) each car carries its driver's race number.
85. No change of car is permitted after the start of the race. Any driver wishing to change car must have got out of his original car and left the grid before the 15 second signal which immediately precedes the start.
86. A change of car will be deemed to have taken place once a driver is seated in his new car and such changes may only take place in the pit lane.

GENERAL SAFETY
87. Official instructions will be given to drivers by means of the signals laid out in the Code. Competitors must not use flags similar in any way whatsoever to these.
88. Drivers are strictly forbidden to drive their car in the opposite direction to the race unless this is absolutely necessary in order to move the car from a dangerous position. A car may only be pushed to remove it from a ~~~~ by the marshals.
~~~~ to go to
~~~~ ntion to
~~~ is
~~~~~ practice and the race, drivers may use only the track and must at all times observe the provisions of the Code relating to driving behaviour on circuits.
91. A driver who abandons a car must leave it in neutral or with the clutch disengaged and with the steering wheel in place.
92. Repairs to a car may be carried out only in the paddock, pits and on the grid.
93. The organiser must make at least two fire extinguishers of 5 kg capacity available at each such pit and ensure that they work properly.
94. Save as provided in Article 135, refuelling is allowed only in the pits. However, with the exception of cars forced to abort their qualifying run due to red flags being displayed on the circuit, fuel may not be added to or removed from a car during a qualifying practice session.
95. The driver may remain in his car throughout refuelling but, unless an FIA approved race refuelling system is used, the engine must be stopped. Race refuelling systems may not be used during, or immediately after, any practice session. Whilst being used in the race all team personnel working on the car must wear clothing which will protect all parts of their body from fire. The competitor must ensure that an assistant with an extinguisher (minimum capacity, 25kg,) ready to work is beside the car throughout all refuelling operations.
96. Oil replenishment is forbidden during the race. All orifices for oil filling must be designed in such a way that the scrutineers can seal them.
97. Save as specifically authorised by the Code or these Sporting Regulations, no one except the driver may touch a stopped car unless it is in the pits or on the starting grid.
98. At no time may a car be reversed in the pit lane under its own power.
99. During the periods commencing 15 minutes prior to and ending 5 minutes after every practice session and the period between the commencement of the formation lap which immediately precedes the race and the time when the last car enters the parc fermé, no one is allowed on the track, the pit entry or the pit exit with the exception of:
a) marshals or other authorised personnel in the execution of their duty;
b) drivers when driving or on foot, having first received permission to do so from a marshal;
c) team personnel clearing equipment from the grid after all cars have left the grid on the formation lap;
d) mechanics under Article 137 only. Other than by driving on the track, Competitors are not permitted to attempt to alter the grip of any part of the track surface.
100. During a race, the engine may only be started with the starter except:
a) in the pit lane where the use of an external starting device is allowed, or;
b) under Article 142c) or d).
101. Drivers taking part in practice and the race must always wear the clothes, helmets and head and neck supports specified in the Code.
102. A speed limit of 60 km/h in practice and 80km/h during the race (60km/h in Monaco), or such other speed limits as the Permanent Bureau of the Formula One Commission may decide, will be enforced in the pit lane. Except in the race, any driver who exceeds the limit will be fined US$250 for each km/h above the limit (this may be increased in the case of a second offence in the same Championship season). During the race, the stewards may impose a time penalty on any driver who exceeds the limit.
103. If a driver has serious mechanical difficulties during practice or the race he must leave the track as soon as it is safe to do so.
104. The car's rear light must be illuminated at all times when it is running on wet-weather tyres. It shall be at the discretion of the race director to decide if a driver should be stopped because his rear light is not working. Should a car be stopped in this way it may re-join when the fault has been remedied.
105. Only six team members participating may (all of whom shall have been issued with and wearing special identification) are allowed in the signalling area during practice and the race. People under 16 years of age are not allowed in the pit lane.
106. Animals, except those which may have been expressly authorised by the FIA for use by security services, are forbidden in the pit area and on the track and in any spectator area.
107. The race director, the clerk of the course or the FIA medical delegate can require a driver to have a medical examination at any time during an Event.
108. Failure to comply with the general safety requirements of the Code or these Sporting Regulations may result in the exclusion of the car and driver concerned from the Event.

FREE PRACTICE, QUALIFYING PRACTICE AND WARM UP
109. Save where these Sporting Regulations require otherwise, pit and track discipline and safety measures will be the same for all practice sessions as for the race.
110. No driver may start in the race without taking part in a qualifying practice session.
111. During all practice sessions there will be a green and a red light at the pit exit. Cars may only leave the pit lane when the green light is on. Additionally, a blue flag and/or a flashing blue light will be shown at the pit exit to warn drivers leaving the pits if cars are approaching on the track.
112. Unless written permission has been given by the FIA to do otherwise, the circuit may only be used for purposes other than the Event after qualifying has finished on each day of practice and on the day of the race no less than one hour before the pit lane is opened.
113. Free practice sessions will take place:
a) Two days (Monaco: three days) before the race from 11.00 to 12.00.
b) The day before the race from 09.00 to 09.45 and from 10.15 to 11.00.

114. Qualifying practice sessions will take place:
a) Two days (Monaco: three days) before the race from 14.00 to 15.00. During this session each driver will be permitted to complete only one timed lap and will leave the pit lane to complete this lap in the order of the current driver's World Championship standings (at the first Event of the 2003 World Championship this order will be determined by the finishing order of the 2002 Championship with new d[illegible] in numeric[illegible] order [illegible] permi[illegible] arr[illegible] si[illegible]
b) The day before the race from 14.[illegible] this session each driver will be permitted to complete only one timed lap and will leave the pit lane to complete this lap in the reverse order of times achieved during the first qualifying session (the slowest driver going first). The times at which cars will be permitted to leave the pits during this session will again be arranged in order that each driver is able to complete his single timed lap whilst no other car is on the track.
115. Warm Up: a free practice session will take place the day before the race from 13.30 to 13.45.
116. The interval between the free and second qualifying practice session may never be less than 1 hour and 30 minutes. Only in the most exceptional circumstances can a delay in free practice or other difficulty on race morning result in a change to the starting time of the race.
117. If a car stops during practice it must be removed from the track as quickly as possible so that its presence does not constitute a danger or hinder other competitors. If the driver is unable to drive the car from a dangerous position, it shall be the duty of the marshals to assist him. In the event of a driving infringement during practice, the Stewards may delete any qualifying times from the driver concerned. In this case, a Team will not be able to appeal against the steward's decision.
118. The clerk of the course may interrupt practice as often and for as long as he thinks necessary to clear the track or to allow the recovery of a car. In the case of free practice only, the clerk of the course with the agreement of the stewards may decline to prolong the practice period after an interruption of this kind. Furthermore if, in the opinion of the stewards, a stoppage is caused deliberately, the driver concerned may have his times from that session cancelled and may not be permitted to take part in any other practice session that day.
119. On the second day of practice, all cars abandoned on the circuit during the first free practice session will be brought back to the pits prior to the start of the second and may be used in that session. No part of a car abandoned in the parc fermé or on the track may be used until the car is returned to the garage of the relevant Team.
120. Should one or more sessions be thus interrupted, no protest can be accepted as to the possible effects of the interruption on the qualification of drivers admitted to start.
121. All laps covered during the second qualifying practice will be timed to determine the driver's position at the start in accordance with Article 127. With the exception of a lap on which a red flag is shown each time a car leaves the pit lane or crosses the Line it will be deemed to have completed one lap.

STOPPING THE PRACTICE

122. Should it become necessary to stop the practice because the circuit is blocked by an accident or because weather or other conditions make it dangerous to continue, the clerk of the course shall order a red flag and the abort lights to be shown at the Line. Simultaneously, red flags will be shown at all marshal posts. When the signal is given to stop, all cars shall immediately reduce speed and proceed slowly back to their respective pits, and all cars abandoned on the track will be removed to a safe place. At the end of each practice session all drivers may cross the Line only once.

PRESS CONFERENCES AND DRIVERS PARADE

123. The FIA press delegate will choose a maximum of five drivers who must attend a press conference in the media centre for a period of one hour at 15.00 on the day before first practice. At Events taking place in North or South America this press conference will take place at 11.00. These drivers' Teams will be notified no less than 48 hours before the conference. In addition, a maximum of two Team personalities may be chosen by the FIA press delegate to attend this press conference. On the first day of practice, a minimum of three and a maximum of six drivers and/or team personalities, (other than those who attended the press conference on the previous day and subject to the consent of the team principal) will be chosen by ballot or rota by the FIA press delegate during the Event and must make themselves available to the media for a press conference in the media centre for a period of one hour at 15.00. No driver may enter into a contract which restricts his right to talk to any representative of the media during an Event. It shall be the duty of each Team to ensure that their drivers do not unreasonably refuse to speak to any representative of the media during the Event.
124. Immediately after the second qualifying practice the first three drivers in qualifying will be required to make themselves available for television interviews in the unilateral room and then attend a press conference in the media centre for a maximum period of 30 minutes.
125. Two hours and forty five minutes before the race all drivers must attend a drivers parade, Competitors will be given details of the parade by the Press Delegate.

THE GRID

126. At the end of the second qualifying practice, the fastest time achieved by each driver during that session will be officially published (see Article 51).
127. The grid will be drawn up in the order of the fastest time achieved by each driver in the second qualifying practice session. Should two or more drivers have set identical times, priority will be given to the one who set it first.
128. The fastest driver will start the race from the position on the grid which was the pole position in the previous year or, on a new circuit, has been designated as such by the FIA safety delegate.
129. The starting grid will be published four hours before the race. Any competitor whose car(s) is (are) unable to start for any reason whatsoever (or who has good reason to believe that their car(s) will not be ready to start) must inform the clerk of the course accordingly at the earliest opportunity and, in any event, no later than 45 minutes before the start of the race. If one or more cars are withdrawn the grid will be closed up accordingly. The final starting grid will be published 45 minutes before the start of the race.
130. The grid will be in a staggered 1 x 1 formation and the rows on the grid will be separated by 16 metres.
131. Any car which has not taken up its position on the grid by the time the ten minute signal is shown will not be permitted to do so and must start from the pits in accordance with Article 134.

MEETINGS

13[illegible] Meetings, chaired by the race director, will take [illegible] the da[illegible] before first practice and 17.00 [illegible] first must be attended [illegible] second by all drivers. [illegible] consider another meeting [illegible] three hours before the race, Competitors will be informed no later than three hours after the end of the second qualifying practice. All drivers and Team Managers must attend.

STARTING PROCEDURE

133. 30 minutes before the time for the start of the race, the cars will leave the pits to cover a reconnaissance lap. At the end of this lap they will stop on the grid in starting order with their engines stopped. Should they wish to cover more than one reconnaissance lap, this must be done by driving down the pit lane at greatly reduced speed between each of the laps.
134. 17 minutes before the starting time, a warning signal announcing the closing of the pit exit in 2 minutes will be given. 15 minutes before the starting time, the pit exit will be closed and a second warning signal will be given. Any car which is still in the pits can start from the pits provided it reached the pit exit under its own power. If more than one car is affected they must line up in the order in which they reached the pit exit. Where the pit exit is immediately after the Line, cars will join the race when the whole field has passed the pit exit on its first racing lap. Where the pit exit is immediately before the Line, cars will join the race as soon as the whole field has crossed the Line after the start.
135. Refuelling on the starting grid may only be carried out prior to the 5 minute signal and by using an un-pressurised container, with a maximum capacity of 12 litres, which has been fitted with one or more dry break couplings connecting it to the car. Any such container may only be used once during each starting procedure.
136. The approach of the start will be announced by signals shown ten minutes, five minutes, three minutes, one minute and fifteen seconds before the start of the formation lap, each of which will be accompanied by an audible warning. When the ten minute signal is shown, everybody except drivers, officials and team technical staff must leave the grid.
When the five minute signal is shown all cars must have their wheels fitted. After this signal wheels may only be removed in the pits. Any car which does not have all its wheels fitted at the five minute signal must start the race from the back of the grid or the pit lane. When the one minute signal is shown, engines should be started and all team personnel must leave the grid by the time the 15 second signal is given. If any driver needs assistance after the 15 second signal he must raise his arm and, when the remainder of the cars able to do so have left the grid, his team may attempt to rectify the problem. In this case, marshals with yellow flags will stand beside any car (or cars) concerned to warn drivers behind.
When the green lights are illuminated, the cars will begin the formation lap with the pole position driver leading. When leaving the grid, all drivers must proceed at a greatly reduced speed until clear of any Team personnel standing beside the track. Marshals will be instructed to push any car (or cars) which remain on the grid into the pit lane after 30 seconds.
During the formation lap practice starts are forbidden and the formation must be kept as tight as possible.
Overtaking during the formation lap is only permitted if a car is delayed when leaving its grid position and cars behind cannot avoid passing it without unduly delaying the remainder of the field. In this case, drivers may only overtake to re-establish the original starting order. Any driver who is delayed leaving the grid may not overtake another moving car if he was stationary after the remainder of the cars had crossed the Line, and must start the race from the back of the grid. If more than one driver is affected, they must form up at the back of the grid in the order they left to complete the formation lap. If the Line is not situated in front of pole position, for the purposes of this Article only, it will be deemed to be a white line one metre in front of pole position.
A time penalty will be imposed on any driver who, in the opinion of the Stewards, unnecessarily overtook another car during the formation lap.
137. Any driver who is unable to start the formation lap must raise his arm and, after the remainder of the cars have crossed the Line, his mechanics may attempt to rectify the problem under the supervision of the marshals. If the car is still unable to start the formation lap it will be pushed into the pit lane by the shortest route and the mechanics may work on the car again.
138. When the cars come back to the grid at the end of the formation lap, they will stop on their respective grid positions, keeping their engines running. There will be a standing start, the signal being given by means of lights activated by the permanent starter. Once all the cars have come to a halt the five second light will appear followed by the four, three, two and one second lights. At any time after the one second light appears, the race will be started by extinguishing all red lights.
139. During the start of a race, the pit wall must be kept free of all persons with the exception of properly authorised officials and fire marshals all of whom shall have been issued with and shall be wearing the appropriate pass.
140. Any car which is unable to maintain starting order during the entire formation lap or is moving when the one second light comes on must enter the pit lane and start from the pits as specified in Article 134. This will not apply to any car which is temporarily delayed during the lap and which is able to regain its position, without endangering itself or any other car, before the leading car has taken up its position on the grid.
141. If, after returning to the starting grid at the end of the formation lap, a car develops a problem that could endanger the start, the driver must immediately raise his hands above his head and the marshal responsible for that row must immediately wave a yellow flag. If the start is delayed as a result, a marshal with a yellow flag will stand in front of the car concerned to prevent it from moving until the whole field has left the grid on the new formation lap. The driver concerned may then start the race from the back of the grid and any vacant positions will not be filled. Should there be more than one car involved, their new positions at the back of the grid will be determined in accordance with their respective final grid positions. If a problem cannot be rectified before the commencement of the new formation lap the car must be pushed into the pit lane by the shortest route. The Team may then attempt to rectify the problem and, if successful, the car may then start from the pit lane. Should there be more than one car involved their starting order from the pit lane will be determined by the order in which they reached the pit exit under their own power.
142. If a problem arises when the cars reach the starting grid at the end of the formation lap the following procedure shall apply:
a) If the race has not been started, the abort lights will be switched on, all engines will be stopped and the new formation lap will start 5 minutes later with the race distance reduced by one lap. The next signal will be the three minute signal.
b) If the race has been started the marshals alongside the grid will wave their yellow flags to inform the drivers that a car is stationary on the grid.
c) If, after the start, a car is immobilised on the starting grid, it shall be the duty of the marshals to push it into the pit lane by the fastest route. If the driver is able to re-start the car whilst it is being pushed he may rejoin the race.
d) If the driver is unable to start the car whilst it is being pushed his mechanics may attempt to start it in the pit lane. If the car then starts it may rejoin the race. The driver and mechanics must follow the instructions of the track marshals at all times during such a procedure.
143. Should Article 142 apply, the race will nevertheless count for the Championship no matter how often the procedure is repeated, or how much the race is shortened as a result.
144. No refuelling will be allowed on the grid if more than one start procedure proves necessary under Article 142.
145. A time penalty will be imposed for a false start judged using an FIA supplied transponder which must be fitted to the car as specified.
146. Only in the following cases will any variation in the start procedure be allowed:
a) If it starts to rain after the five minute signal but before the race is started and, in the opinion of the race director Teams should be given the opportunity to change tyres, the abort lights will be shown on the Line and the starting procedure will begin again at the 15 minute point. If necessary the procedure set out in Article 142 will be followed.
b) If the start of the race is imminent and, in the opinion of the race director, the volume of water on the track is such that it cannot be negotiated safely even on wet-weather tyres, the abort lights will be shown on the Line simultaneously with a "10" board with a red background. This "10" board with a red background will mean that there is to be a delay of ten minutes before the starting procedure can be resumed. If weather conditions have improved at the end of that ten minute period, a "10" board with a green background will be shown. The "10" board with a green background will mean that the green light will be shown in ten minutes. Five minutes after the "10" board with the green background is shown, the starting procedure will begin and the normal starting procedure signals (i.e. 5, 3, 1 min., 15 second) will be shown. If however, the weather conditions have not improved within ten minutes after the "10" board with the red background was shown, the abort lights will be shown on the Line and the "10" board with the red background will be shown again which will mean a further delay of ten minutes before the starting procedure can be resumed. This procedure may be repeated several times. At any time when a "10" board (with either a red or green background) is shown, it will be accompanied by an audible warning.
c) If the race is started behind the safety car, Article 152(o) will apply.
147. The stewards may use any video or electronic means to assist them in reaching a decision. The stewards may overrule judges of fact. A breach of the provisions of the Code or these Sporting Regulations relating to starting procedure, may result in the exclusion of the car and driver concerned from the Event.

THE RACE

148. Team orders which interfere with a race result are prohibited.
149. A race will not be stopped in the event of rain unless the circuit is blocked or it is dangerous to continue (see Article 153).
150. If a car stops during the race (except under Article 142c and d), it must be removed from the track as quickly as possible so that its presence does not constitute a danger or hinder other competitors. If the driver is unable to drive the car from a dangerous position, it shall be the duty of the marshals to assist him. If any such assistance results in the engine starting and the driver rejoining the race, the car will be excluded from the results of the race.
151. During the race, drivers leaving the pit lane may only do so when the pit exit light is green and on their own responsibility, a marshal with a blue flag, or a flashing blue light, will also warn the driver if cars are approaching on the track.

SAFETY CAR

152. a) The FIA safety car will be driven by an experienced circuit driver. It will carry an FIA observer capable of recognising all the competing cars, who is in permanent radio contact with race control.
b) 30 minutes before the race start time the safety car will take up position at the front of the grid and remain there until the five minute signal is given. At this point (except under o) below) it will cover a whole lap of the circuit and enter the pit lane.
c) The safety car may be brought into operation to neutralise a race upon the decision of the clerk of the course. It will be used only if competitors or officials are in immediate physical danger but the circumstances are not such as to necessitate stopping the race.
d) When the order is given to deploy the safety car, all observer's posts will display waved yellow flags and a board "SC" which shall be maintained until the intervention is over.
e) During the race, the safety car with its orange lights on, will start from the pit lane and will join the track regardless of where the race leader is.
f) All the competing cars will form up in line behind the safety car no more than 5 car lengths apart. All overtaking on the track is forbidden (except under o) below), unless a car is signalled to do so from the safety car.
g) When ordered to do so by the clerk of the course the observer in the car will use a green light to signal to any cars between it and the race leader that they should pass. These cars will continue at reduced speed and without overtaking until they reach the line of cars behind the safety car.
h) The safety car shall be used at least until the leader is behind it and all remaining cars are lined up behind him. Once behind the safety car, the race leader must keep within 5 car lengths of it (except under j) below) and all remaining cars must keep the formation as tight as possible.
i) While the safety car is in operation, competing cars may stop at their pit, but may only rejoin the track when the green light at the pit exit is on. It will be on at all times except when the safety car and the line of cars following it are about to pass or are passing the pit exit. A car rejoining the track must proceed at reduced speed until it reaches the end of the line of cars behind the safety car.
j) When the clerk of the course calls in the safety car, it must extinguish its orange lights, this will be the signal to the drivers that it will be entering the pit lane at the end of that lap. At this point the first car in line behind the safety car may dictate the pace and, if necessary, fall more than five car lengths behind it. As the safety car is approaching the pit entrance the yellow flags and SC boards at the observer's posts will be withdrawn and waved green flags will be displayed for no more than one lap.
k) When the safety car has pulled off the circuit and the cars are approaching the Line, green lights will be shown. Overtaking remains strictly forbidden until the cars pass the green light at the Line unless a car slows with an obvious problem.
l) Each lap completed while the safety car is deployed will be counted as a race lap.
m) If the race is stopped under Article 154 Case C, the safety car will take the chequered flag and all cars able to do so must follow it into the pit lane and into the parc fermé.
n) If the race ends whilst the safety car is deployed it will enter the pits at the end of the last lap and the cars will take the chequered flag as normal without overtaking.
o) In exceptional circumstances the race may be started behind the safety car. In this case, at any time before the one minute signal its orange lights will be turned on. This is the signal to the drivers that the race will be started behind the safety car. When the green lights are illuminated the safety car will leave the grid with all cars following in grid order no more than 5 car lengths apart. There will be no formation lap and race will start when the leading car crosses the Line for the first time.
Overtaking, during the first lap only, is permitted if a car is delayed when leaving its grid position and cars behind cannot avoid passing it without unduly delaying the remainder of the field. In this case, drivers may only overtake to re-establish the original starting order. Any driver who is delayed leaving the grid may not overtake another moving car if he was stationary after the remainder of the cars had crossed the Line, and must form up at the back of the line of cars behind the safety car. If more than one driver is affected, they must form up at the back of the field in the order they left the grid.
A time penalty will be imposed on any driver who, in the opinion of the Stewards, unnecessarily overtook another car during the first lap.

STOPPING A RACE

153. Should it become necessary to stop the race because the circuit is blocked by an accident or because weather or other conditions make it dangerous to continue, the clerk of the course shall order a red flag and the abort lights to be shown at the Line. Simultaneously, red flags will be shown at all marshal posts. When the signal is given to stop all cars shall immediately reduce speed in the knowledge that:
- the race classification will be that at the end of the lap two laps prior to that during which the signal to stop the race was given,
- race and service vehicles may be on the track,
- the circuit may be totally blocked because of an accident,
- weather conditions may have made the circuit undriveable at racing speed,
- the pit lane will be open.
154. The procedure to be followed varies according to the number of laps completed by the race leader before the signal to stop the race was given:
Case A. Less than two full laps. If the race can be restarted, Article 155 will apply.
Case B. Two or more full laps but less than 75% of the race distance (rounded up to the nearest whole number of laps). If the race can be restarted, Article 156 will apply.
Case C. 75% or more of the race distance (rounded up to the nearest whole number of laps). The cars will be sent directly to the parc fermé and the race will be deemed to have finished when the leading car crossed the Line at the end of the lap two laps prior to that during which the signal to stop was given.

RESTARTING A RACE

155. Case A.
a) The original start shall be deemed null and void.
b) The length of the restarted race will be the full original race distance.
c) The drivers who are eligible to take part in the race shall be eligible for the restart either in their original car or in a spare car.
d) Any driver who was forced to start from the back of the grid or the pit lane during the original start may start from his original grid position;
e) After the signal to stop the race has been given, all cars able to do so will proceed directly but slowly to either:
- the pit lane or;
- if the grid is clear, to their original grid position or;
- if the grid is not clear, to a position behind the last grid position as directed by the marshals.
f) Cars may be worked on in the pits or on the grid. If work is carried out on the grid, this must be done in the car's correct grid position and must in no way impede the re-start.
g) Refuelling will be allowed until the five minute signal is shown.
156. Case B.
a) Other than the race order at the end of the lap two laps prior to that during which the signal to stop was given and the number of laps covered by each driver, the original race will be deemed null and void.
b) The length of the re-started race will be three laps less than the original race distance less the number of classified laps completed by the leader before the signal to stop was given.
c) The grid for the re-started race will be arranged in the race order at the end of the lap two laps prior to that during which the signal to stop was given.
d) Only cars which took part in the original start will be eligible for the re-start and then only if they returned under their own power by an authorised route to either:
- the pit lane or;
- to a position behind the last grid position as directed by the marshals.
e) No spare car will be eligible.
f) Cars may be worked on in the pits or on the grid. If work is carried out on the grid, this must be done in the car's correct grid position and must in no way impede the re-start.
g) Refuelling is only permitted in the pits. If a car is refuelled it must take the re-start from the back of the grid and, if more than one car is involved, their positions will be determined by their race order at the end of the lap two laps prior to that during which the signal to stop was given. In this case their original grid positions will be left vacant.
157. In both Case A and Case B:
a) 10 minutes after the stop signal, the pit exit will close.
b) 15 minutes after the stop signal, the five minute signal will be shown, the grid will close and the normal start procedure will recommence.
c) Any car which is unable to take up its position on the grid before the five minute signal will be directed to the pits. It may then start from the pits as specified in Article 134. The Organiser must have sufficient personnel and equipment available to enable the foregoing timetable to be adhered to even in the most difficult circumstances.

FINISH

158. The end-of-race signal will be given at the Line as soon as the leading car has covered the full race distance in accordance with Article 13. Should two hours elapse before the full distance has been covered, the end-of-race signal will be given to the leading car the first time it crosses the Line after such time has elapsed.

159. Should for any reason (other than under Article 153) the end-of-race signal be given before the leading car completes the scheduled number of laps, or the prescribed time has been completed, the race will be deemed to have finished when the leading car last crossed the Line before the signal was given. Should the end-of- race signal be delayed for any reason, the race will be deemed to have finished when it should have finished.
160. After receiving the end-of-race signal all cars must proceed on the circuit directly to the parc fermé without stopping, without receiving any object whatsoever and without any assistance (except that of the marshals if necessary). Any classified car which cannot reach the parc fermé under its own power will be placed under the exclusive control of the marshals who will take the car to the parc fermé.

PARC FERME

161. Only those officials charged with supervision may enter the parc fermé. No intervention of any kind is allowed there unless authorised by such officials.
162. When the parc fermé is in use, parc fermé regulations will apply in the area between the Line and the parc fermé entrance.
163. The parc fermé shall be sufficiently large and secure that no unauthorised persons can gain access to it.

CLASSIFICATION

164. The car placed first will be the one having covered the scheduled distance in the shortest time, or, where appropriate, passed the Line in the lead at the end of two hours. All cars will be classified taking into account the number of complete laps they have covered, and for those which have completed the same number of laps, the order in which they crossed the Line.
165. If a car takes more than twice the time of the winner's fastest lap to cover its last lap this last lap will not be taken into account when calculating the total distance covered by such car.
166. Cars having covered less than 90% of the number of laps covered by the winner (rounded down to the nearest whole number of laps), will not be classified.
167. The official classification will be published after the race. It will be the only valid result subject to any amendments which may be made under the Code and these Sporting Regulations.

PODIUM CEREMONY

168. The drivers finishing the race in 1st, 2nd and 3rd positions and a representative of the winning constructor must attend the prize-giving ceremony on the podium and abide by the podium procedure set out in Appendix 3 (except Monaco); and immediately thereafter make themselves available for a period of 90 minutes for the purpose of television unilateral interviews and the press conference in the media centre.

Meaning of the flags

- White flag: service vehicle on track
- Blue flag: (immobile): a car is close behind you
  (waving): a car is about to overtake you
- Yellow flag: (immobile): overtaking is prohibited, danger
  (waving) immediate danger, slow down
- Red flag: (by marshals and the Clerk of the race): stopping of the race on the Line
- Green flag: end of danger, free track
- Yellow with red stripes flag: danger, slippery surface
- Black flag: (with car number): stop on the next lap
- Black with yellow circle flag: your car is in danger
- Black and white flag: non-sporting behaviour, warning
- Chequered flag: end of the race or of the practice

SHARE THE PASSION

Michelin has been back in Formula One for just three years.
Our tyres have improved, our victories have multiplied.
The tenacity of our partner teams and our people challenged
the balance of power this season. We race for tyre perfection.
For the track or for you, every Michelin tyre shares this passion
for performance. Now you know why Michelin races ahead.

Share the Spirit

www.michelinf1.com